Geographic Areas

To commemorate its 75th anniversary,
Seattle Trust & Savings Bank assisted
in the publication of this book.

A Guide to Architecture in Washington State

A Guide to Architecture in Washington State

An Environmental Perspective

Sally B. Woodbridge and Roger Montgomery

Essay on Landscape Design, by David C. Streatfield

University of Washington Press
Seattle and London

Library of Congress Cataloging in Publication Data
Woodbridge, Sally Byrne.
  A guide to architecture in Washington State.

  Bibliography: p.
  Includes index.
  1. Architecture—Washington (State)—Guide-books.
I. Montgomery, Roger, joint author. II.   Streatfield,
David C. III.   Title.
NA730.W2W66   917.97'0443   80-51076
ISBN 0-295-95761-1
ISBN 0-295-95779-4 (pbk.)

Maps by the Morgan Fairchild Group,
based on information provided by the authors.

To Victor Steinbrueck

Contents

Preface

A general enthusiasm for exploring the man-made environment in Washington and communicating its riches prompted this guide. The authors, carpetbaggers from California, have periodically traveled around the state for the past six years or so, viewing, mapping, and photographing Washington's architecture and landscape design. During this time we have witnessed significant changes, not only in the new forms and buildings that the landscape has acquired, but in the rejuvenation of the past. We began writing for other birds of passage like ourselves who, because of their unfamiliarity with the state, would be certain to miss outstanding pieces of it. In the interim we have sensed in the state a great surge of interest in the built environment, in its preservation, its history, and its interpretation. For this reason we have ended by being more interested in writing for the resident population as an increasingly interested audience and, necessarily, the caretakers of our subject matter.

Guidebooks in this field reflect the nature and distribution of their subject matter. Just as most book and building users, viewers, designers, and commentators inhabit the more urban areas, so architecture and environmental design are concentrated in these areas. This largely explains why Seattle, its environs, and the densely settled part of the Puget Sound area bulk so large in this book. In covering these metropolitan areas we have had the help of many knowledgeable people and institutions as acknowledged in the following section. We also have spent more time here

than in other parts of the state, one of us becoming a temporary resident of Seattle on several occasions.

Although the larger urban areas dominate these pages we have been more selective in choosing what is included from them. In the major metropolitan areas we have limited our coverage to generally acknowledged major works, important historical monuments, and representative examples, given the local context, of styles, building types, and the like. In smaller cities, towns, and nonurban areas we have been relatively more inclusive where we have been able to do the necessary fieldwork and where we have been able to build on the work of others. But we cannot pretend to have traveled every highway, visited every town, and searched out every rural and back country structure.

Another type of question about the selection of entries concerns the matter of taste. In terms both of coverage and of our interpretive comments, many decisions have been made that depend largely on the tastes of the authors. We have tried to be catholic, open to all stylistic persuasions, sensitive to the differences and the fact that there may be many equally valid approaches to environmental design. Our experience with this kind of work suggests the problem is far larger in the abstract than in practice. Given equally careful attention, disagreement on such matters seems to be surprisingly rare. Still, ultimately, taste operates. Our tastes, eclectic and universalistic though we believe them to be, tend to value most strongly that which is seriously done, with loving attention to detail and context, and with a spark that illuminates the traditional themes of architecture and design. We have valued serious art, even if sometimes inaccessible, over pop and flash; and, above all, we have valued craftsmanship over quick job and formula work.

Because of continuing research into the components of the man-made environment, guidebooks are never definitive. Rather they reflect the current state of knowledge as well as present attitudes and taste about the accumulated cultural heritage they attempt to encompass. Our guide is no exception to this generalization. We are aware of lacunae in the text, particularly in respect to parts of central and eastern Washington where much primary research on the built environment remains to be done. It is our fervent hope that enough material will be discovered in coming years to cause the present volume to burst its binding. In the meantime we beg the reader's indulgence for those errors and omissions that are always painful to the knowledgeable few. We welcome additions and corrections in the confident expectation that the boundaries of knowledge will continue to expand.

Acknowledgments

Dennis Andersen, Special Collections, University of Washington Library

Claire Bishop, City/County Historic Preservation Officer, Spokane

Al Bumgardner, F.A.I.A.

Kenneth Brooks, F.A.I.A.

Shirley Courtois

Steven Dotterrer

Dave Fukui

Phil Jacobson, F.A.I.A.

Katheryn H. Krafft

Tom Kubota

Moritz Kundig

Earl Layman, Historic Preservation Officer, Office of
    Urban Conservation, Seattle

Peter Montgomery

J. M. Neil, City Conservator, Office of Urban Conservation, Seattle

Patricia Sias, Historic Preservation Officer, Tacoma

James Vandermeer, Historian, Washington State Office of Archaeology
    and Historic Preservation, Olympia

Ruth Whitehouse, Clare Gilbert, and Helen Hamblin

A Guide to the Guide

This is a guide to the most notable man-made structures, gardens, parks, environmental design, and engineering works that compose the physical structure of the towns, cities, and countryside of Washington. The time span begins with what remains of the early settlement of the state by fur traders, miners, and lumbermen in the mid-nineteenth century and ends with projects substantially completed in 1979.

In the interests of producing a portable guide, we have had to devise ways of being selective yet catholic in our presentation of the material. As explained above in the Preface, we have to this end been more selective in the dense, metropolitan areas than in smaller cities, towns, and rural communities. The sheer mass of buildings in the former along with the repetition of building types and neighborhood forms encouraged us to concentrate our coverage on major works in the better known, most representative and accessible areas and to spotlight a few interesting examples from the rest. In the less metropolitan places we have tried to present a more complete inventory, since such places are physically easier to tour and to comprehend as a whole.

Geographic Organization

The guide is organized geographically on the assumption that most users, both residents and visitors, will begin viewing and traveling in Seattle and its surrounding metropolitan area. For this reason it opens with coverage of Seattle, starting downtown with the Pioneer Square district. From here the sections follow in a geographic spiral out from downtown, through the neighborhoods into the suburban communities. The spiral continues around Puget Sound moving from Tacoma to Olympia, then up the Sound to Port Townsend and across to Everett. Along the way smaller places are covered in appropriate order either in separate sections or as parts of the major areas. From Everett the guide continues up the coast to Bellingham, across to the San Juans and the Olympic Peninsula, then down to the Columbia River through places like Aberdeen and Hoquiam. Going upstream to Vancouver the sections that follow cover the crossings of the Cascades, the principal towns and cities of the east slope, and the Columbia Plateau. At Spokane a second geographic spiral begins downtown and moves out through the residential areas. The guide ends with a section on Walla Walla. As the user becomes familiar with this sequence, the running heads at the tops of the pages will help him locate things. An abbreviated table of contents on the inside front cover, and the index, which includes place names, should clarify remaining questions about the guide's geographic organization.

Maps

Locations of individual buildings, gardens, and other works are mapped in each locality in which more than a very few entries occur. These maps follow a simple graphic formula which represents main streets, main bodies of water including rivers and streams, and principal public open spaces. These features are named. Numbered circles indicate the entry locations. Maps are drawn to three common scales (except for Seattle's Pioneer Square, which requires a different scale because of its dense concentration of entries). Most maps represent areas one mile wide—a reasonable area to cover on foot. For some areas, particularly in suburban districts, maps represent a three-mile-wide swath. Obviously a car is necessary in touring these areas. Finally, for several of the larger metropolitan areas overall maps are provided which show the general locations of outlying entries and provide a key to the areas covered by the more detailed maps. In all cases north lies at the top of the page. Since errors and omissions are inescapable, we advise the guide user to also consult road maps and street maps of the various localities. Incidentally, in the smaller cities tourists may often obtain very good local maps.

Entries

Each separately listed entry gives the name of the building, the date, the name of the architect, landscape architect, or designer if available, and the address. A number preceding an entry refers to the accompanying map. The date given indicates when construction was substantially complete. More or less additional descriptive or interpretive material is provided under each entry depending on the importance and intrinsic interest of the work, and on the availability of data. Entries are collected into text sections according to the geographic organization discussed in the paragraphs above. Within each section the order of entries is derived again from geographic location, so as to achieve a coherent sequence that can be easily followed by a touring observer.

Admission to Buildings

In a very few cases, buildings are listed that are not visible from a public thoroughfare. This is only done in places where the importance of the building demands its inclusion, and should not be taken as permission to trespass. In fact, in no way does the listing of any private building in this guide give the user permission to enter the grounds or building. In general, those who wish to see the grounds or interiors of private buildings should apply to the office of the architect, not the owner.

Federal, state, county, and city public buildings are generally open between the hours of 10:00 A.M. and 5:00 P.M. on weekdays. A number of historic buildings open to the public are included in the guide. Information about these buildings is included in the introduction to the section or in the individual entry.

Photographs

Many of the buildings listed in the guide are illustrated in photographs—some accompanying the text, and others in the Photo History or Glossary. Photographs accompanying the text are keyed to the numbered entries through the captions.

Photo History

A Photo History showing in chronological sequence buildings representative of each period follows the introductory essays. Architects are identified, when known, and each photograph is keyed to the text by means of a cross-reference to the section and entry in which the work appears.

Glossary of Architectural Styles

The major architectural styles found in the guide are identified and illustrated in the Glossary. It is arranged in chronological order and includes a description of each style and a list of its chief characteristics.

Selected Bibliography

A list of published readings is provided for the benefit of those who wish to delve further into the subject matter of the text.

Index

Significant places—towns, neighborhoods, parks, etc.—as well as individual buildings and architects are indexed at the back of the guide.

A Guide to Architecture in Washington State

Introduction

Evidence of major human impact is recent in the Northwest. About a hundred years ago people of European descent began energetically cutting forests, plowing fields, and building towns across the territory that would become the state of Washington. For centuries before that, Native Americans lived in gentle symbiosis with this land and its resources, hardly marking it save for modest coastal agricultural clearing. By comparison the white man's impact has been enormous. In but a hundred years he has turned North America's wildest big river into a series of still water pools. He has largely demolished the densest timber stand on earth. He has turned the pristine landscape of Puget Sound into the site of an emergent megalopolis with all that means in smog, dirty water, and mangled land; and occasionally in clean cities, worthy architecture, and delightful gardens. Yet for all he has done, the natural environment, especially in the eyes of the newcomer, still dominates the works of man. The recent eruptions of Mount St. Helens are awesome reminders of the power of the landscape and the effects it can have on human settlements.

Geographically Washington State consists of two sharply distinct regions divided by the Cascade Mountain Range. Certainly this division has distinguished human life since long before Europeans dominated the area. Climate defines the regions. On the west slope annual rainfall ranges as high as two hundred inches and skies tend to be leaden-looking year round. Across the divide, on the east slope of the Cascades and on the Columbia Plateau, skies are blue, the sun strong, and rain rare. Soils are different as, of course, are vegetation, fauna, and the whole look of everything.

Because of these influences, even the first European settlements served very different purposes in the two regions. On the east side transportation dominated, first as access to riches in furs and gold, later as the last link to be closed in the transcontinental rail system. The land these paths crossed proved productive for dryland grain and irrigated crops. Today the east side is a great agricultural region dotted with market towns and railroad junction points, presided over by Spokane, the regional capital. The settlement pattern of eastern Washington follows the ordered hierarchies of classical human geography.

The other side of the mountains grew timber easily exploited for export by virtue of the deeply penetrating saltwater bays and sounds. With coal and commerce, lumber provided the base for an often booming local economy. Now urban, diversified, and thoroughly tied to the world economy, the wet side of the mountains has become in little more than a hundred years one of North America's major metropolitan centers. Its chain of cities and suburbs, and its logged over or still timbered hinterlands, have begun to flow together in one regional economy, awkwardly labeled Pugetopolis.

Architecture and environmental design during the hundred years of development and the previous pioneer years intimately relate to the economic, social, political, and general cultural history of the territory. People built mainly what they needed to build, or thought they needed, and what their resources in money, materials, labor, and understanding permitted them to build. They built usually in close conformance to socially established norms they brought with them. The idea of the homestead with its complex of barns, sheds, cabins, and houses, all designed to evolve into a proper farmstead centered on a fashionable house, came across the prairie with the settlers.

The economics of resource exploitation and transportation provided the rationale for the towns. As they became cities, speculation, land exploitation, and the business of town life took charge. Where there was a surplus in personal or communal wealth, self-conscious professional architecture emerged. Later it diversified and expanded to encompass town planning, landscape and urban design, civic art, and all the branches of environmental design.

The history of the buildings, landscapes, and towns produced by this design work falls into five main chronological phases, each connected to distinct periods in the evolution of the culture, social economy, and political economy. The first half of the nineteenth century was a period of primitive exploration and exploitation mainly by fur traders. From 1850 to 1880 a pioneer settlement era brought to Washington the first significant number of white immigrants, and set the stage for the third chapter, the great boom between 1880 and 1910. After that a quiescent period lasted until about 1940. Since then rapid population growth and economic boom times have returned.

Most of the architecture and allied environmental arts date from the two boom periods. From the long centuries before white settlement little record remains. What we know of these times comes mainly from the reports and journals of European and U.S. travelers, fur traders, missionaries, and some few early settlers. They reported the existence along the coast of great wooden longhouses, though perhaps more modest than those farther north in modern British Columbia. Other than the few that have been restored in exhibition areas like the Makah Museum at Neah Bay, these are gone from Washington State. In the interior the Native Americans of the Columbia Plateau developed an ingenious pithouse architecture. But because little remains to be seen, this guide perforce begins with the period of the white peoples' exploration.

Exploration, 1800–50

Lewis and Clark came down the gorge of the Columbia River in the fall of 1805 to winter at its mouth. This symbolic possession by the United States of the Oregon Territory including the land that was to become Washington began the first stage of its transformation. During the next generation and a half, fur trappers and traders, missionaries, and the U.S. Army occupied the vast territorial landscape covering present-day Oregon, Washington, and Idaho as well as parts of Montana, Wyoming, and British Columbia. Almost nothing remains of their slight physical impact. This first phase in the imperial expansion of U.S.

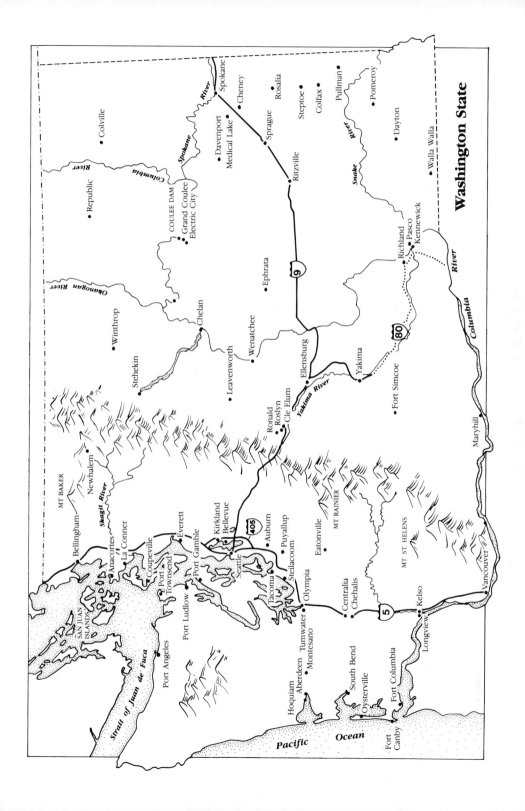

Washington State

authority through the Northwest involved but a few hundred people; the principal constructions were temporary at best. Materials at hand satisfied basic shelter needs. Small garden clearings were planted to feed their makers, and perhaps to provision passing pioneers on their way to California gold, Willamette Valley homesteads, or the later gold rush on western Oregon's Rogue River.

In the aftermath of Lewis and Clark, the future state of Washington was systematically exploited of beaver pelts for the China trade first by the English North West Company that bought out the American Astor Company in 1811, then by its successor, the Hudson's Bay Company. Nothing but archaeological evidence remains of the network of posts, variously called forts or houses, established by the London merchants, their Scots managers, and their French-Canadian work force. Names, historic markers, and interpretive centers mark posts at Fort Colville, Fort Okanogan, Fort Nez Perce, and Fort Spokane or Spokane House. At Fort Nisqually, now moved to Tacoma's Point Defiance Park, only one building, the Granary (1833), is completely original. The ambitious, recent restoration of Fort Vancouver by the U.S. Park Service re-creates the image of the Hudson's Bay Company's headquarters for Oregon Territory. Chief Factor McLoughlin's house there is architecturally pretentious compared to the other buildings that make up the post. But McLoughlin was a colorful and finally insubordinate company man who certainly sensed the importance of architecture.

Gold in California, the lesser lure of rich Oregon farmland, and the spiritual drive behind the Protestant missionary movement ended the Native Americans' reign in the Northwest and their relatively peaceful coexistence with the white fur traders. By the late 1840s settlers in increasing numbers successfully negotiated the arduous Oregon

Fort Nisqually (courtesy of City of Tacoma)

Trail following roughly the footsteps of Lewis and Clark as they crossed the Bitterroot Mountains and came down into the Snake and Columbia valleys in present-day Washington. Few stopped; most continued on down the Columbia River Gorge to destinations in the Willamette Valley, and after 1849 to California and El Dorado. Already the missions had arrived. In 1832 the Methodists set up shop at Salem, Oregon, and four years later the American Board of Missions sponsored posts at Lapwai in Idaho and Waiilatpu in eastern Washington. The last choice was fateful. After ten years of earnest work with the Native Americans and more successful ministering to Oregon Trail travelers from the United States, the missionaries were killed in the famous Whitman Massacre of 1847. The ensuing long military campaign, in the by then well-established genocidal mode, "freed" Washington Territory by pacifying and largely doing away with the native population.

The Whitman Massacre brought the U.S. Army to Washington Territory. The military, in contrast to the fur traders, explorers, and missionaries, brought pattern-book designs and engineers with them to the Northwest. Fort Simcoe, one of the last of the Indian Wars posts, established in 1856 on the eastern slopes of the Cascades near Yakima, is the state's most notable example from the presettlement period. Its principal structure adheres to the picturesque "Gothicky" style popularized by A. D. Downing in the East. This architectural sensibility can be definitely ascribed to Captain Jerome, the Dallas-based quartermaster for Colonel Wright's Indian campaigns through the 1850s, and to Jerome's German immigrant architect, Louis Scholl, for the principal buildings of his various posts.

Remaining also from this period are a few of the civil forts or blockhouses such as those on Whidbey Island near Coupeville and on San Juan Island. While in literal terms the dates for the most sophisticated military work come after the beginning of the pioneer period, their political and economic origin is earlier. They are indeed the closing passage of the exploration period, and the conclusion of this episode cleared the way for pioneer settlement.

Pioneer Period, 1850–80

In Washington permanent settlement began gradually in the years just prior to 1850. Pushing northward from the longtime outpost at Fort Vancouver, some few farmers and loggers found their way to focal points of development in the Cowlitz Valley like Marys Corner, where the first U.S. district court north of the Columbia convened. Domestic structures consisted of log cabins such as the John R. Jackson house (1845) in Marys Corner and Richard Covington's hewn log house (1846) moved in 1926 to Vancouver's Leverich Park. In 1850 the imposing Judge Lancaster house was completed; except for this remarkable mansion, no major architectural works remain from this period.

The settlements of Tumwater and Olympia attracted others who came over the Cowlitz Trail all the way north to its terminus at Budd Inlet on Puget Sound. Just north of here, Steilacoom prospered because of its port and nearby fort from which Byrd's Mill Road, established by the Oregon Territorial Legislature as a

Judge Lancaster house, Vancouver (courtesy of State Office of Archaeology and Historic Preservation)

military road in 1852, ran east into the Puyallup Valley and across the mountains to the Yakima Valley.

Timber was the force behind the network of small settlements that extended in the early 1850s up the shores of Puget Sound to the Fairhaven-Whatcom cluster of towns, now Bellingham. The small band of pioneers who abandoned Alki to found Seattle in 1852 welcomed Henry Yesler's interest in building his sawmill there and provided him with land. But it was not for their use that he milled lumber. Instead it was to build and rebuild San Francisco, gold capital of the West, which had a stimulating predilection for burning itself down regularly. When local California timber supplies diminished, Puget Sound with its virtually limitless forests and easy water access provided the most feasible alternative source.

In 1850 the whole state contained but a thousand people, in contrast to the twelve thousand or so that had settled by then in the Willamette Valley of Oregon. (A table of populations appears on page 11.) Olympia, which was designated territorial capital in 1853, existed; so did the beginnings of most of the chain of settled places around Puget Sound and connecting south along the stage route from Budd Inlet to Vancouver.

The end of the Indian Wars and the official opening of eastern Washington for settlement in 1858 brought pioneers from the east who homesteaded vast livestock ranches, except where crop farming took hold around Walla Walla. The 1860 gold discoveries along the Clearwater River in present-day Idaho made Walla Walla an outfitting base. The boom accelerated when gold was found elsewhere in Idaho, in the Blue and Wallowa mountains of Oregon, as far east as Helena and Virginia City, Montana, and north across the Canadian border at Kootenay. All of these fields were best reached through Walla Walla after traveling up the Columbia from Portland and the Pacific. While nothing really remains of the 1860s city—the mining camps lie outside the state—Walla Walla's substantial cultural and architectural character derives from its early importance as a regional economic center. Though the gold rush encouraged cattle ranching by generating a demand for beef, the truly spectacular crop was wheat. The deep, volcanic soils of the plateaus around Walla Walla were compared to those of Sicily, called the breadbasket of Rome. From mining supply post, Walla Walla evolved rapidly into a center for marketing, flour milling, and agricultural implement manufacturing. Perhaps the most interesting fragments of building from these prerailroad days are the hewn log farmhouses collected in a park at the county's Pioneer Museum on the west side of old Fort Walla Walla.

Transportation made important strides between 1850 and 1880. Starting in 1861, the Oregon Steam Navigation Company, a monopoly by virtue of its absolute control of the necessary portage routes around the fierce Columbia rapids, offered daily steamboat service on the river from Portland to the Dalles, and twice weekly service from there to Wallula at the mouth of the Walla Walla River. When the water was high enough, freight and passengers could move up the Snake River as far as Lewiston, Idaho. A stage and wagon freight line tied Wallula to Walla Walla. For a

generation the Columbia River system, despite its many portages, changes of mode or vehicle, and sensitivity to the elements, provided the main transportation corridor in the Northwest.

By the mid-1870s, transportation innovation presaged the explosive boom of the next decade. Steamboating was limited by annually recurring low water and impossibly hazardous rapids. Scarce resources and primitive technology made overland wagon travel slow, undependable, and expensive. Obviously railroads were the answer. In 1853 the federal government commissioned Territorial Governor Isaac Stevens to reconnoiter the region for feasible transcontinental railroad routes. Though thirty years passed before rails connected Washington to the East, incremental efforts were made. First the Oregon Steam Navigation Company laid down tracks for horse cars to portage people and goods around the cascades of the Columbia. In 1862 tracks ran around the Dalles and Celilo Rapids farther upstream, and steam powered the trains. By 1873 the steamship company had purchased the right of way for a rail line that would extend from Portland to Wallula. When developed this line would be part of the Northwest's first transcontinental railroad.

In 1868 the Northern Pacific railroad was chartered and received an enormous federal land grant as a bounty for constructing the connection across the Rockies and Cascades to Puget Sound. Initially little happened beyond a slow extension of tracks westward from Duluth, Minnesota. As with many early railroad enterprises, land development profits were as interesting to speculators as railroad revenues. Knowing the enormous land value effects of the Pacific terminus designation, Jay Cooke, capitalist promoter of the Northern Pacific, and his associates chose an empty site on Commencement Bay which they then platted as Tacoma. Their first tracks, completed in 1873, connected Tacoma with the Columbia River at Kalama replacing a particularly unpleasant overland stage route and promoting the predictable boom. In an effort to compete in this race to become Puget Sound's chief city, Seattle started two locally based railroads of its own. Though the ultimate goal was to link with eastern centers, the rails never got more than a score of miles out of town. Still, by making it possible to transport coal from the King County fields to Seattle's port where it fueled ocean vessels and supplied San Francisco factories, these tracks helped make the diversified local economy that would one day dominate the Northwest.

As the 1870s closed, another bit of railroad, totally local in inspiration and financing, gave further intimations of the future. Under the entrepreneurial leadership of Dr. Dorsey Baker, the Walla Walla and Columbia Railroad was incorporated in 1868 and had by 1875 completed a narrow gauge line connecting that inland center and its burgeoning wheatlands with the regular steamship service at Wallula. The new railroad symbolized the growth of an agriculture-based economy in eastern Washington. Already in the 1870s settlement had moved north of the Snake River into the equally rich Palouse country. Here too as in the western part of the territory, the stage was set for the long

economic boom that would populate and create the state of Washington.

Boom, 1880–1910

In 1883 a transcontinental railroad finally arrived in Washington Territory opening it to eastern markets and easy migration. In thirty short years the state's population grew a phenomenal 1400 percent. Cities like Spokane happened almost overnight; the best situated and equipped older settlements almost instantly became important cities. For example, in 1880 Seattle had about 4,000 inhabitants. Thirty years later there were a quarter of a million. In fact, the whole Puget Sound area increased at a rate only slightly less spectacular, going from 30,000 in 1880 to nearly 700,000 by 1910. The accompanying table shows population growth during this period in the context of later and earlier stages of growth.

Three factors, transportation changes among them, generated this frantic expansion in Washington. Firstly, population growth in Europe and on the U.S. east coast and the economic forces that generated it created the migration pressure to occupy and develop what remained of the American frontier. Secondly, of the few regions still open after 1880, the Northwest with its immense timber resources and rich wheatlands was for many the most appealing frontier. Only lastly, the engineering technique, management and entrepreneurial capacity, and capital resources now existed to quickly complete multiple railroad connections to this previously unserved territory. Though they were a long time coming, the process of building the railroads created a boom

Population Growth in Washington State
(Numbers rounded to nearest thousand)

Year	State	Puget Sound Metro*	Seattle	Tacoma	Olympia	Spokane	Walla Walla
1850	1	0.5	. . .	. . .	0.4†	. . .	. . .
1880	75	25	4	1	1	. . .	2
1910	1,142	583	237	84	7	104	19
1940	1,736	962	368	109	13	122	18
1970	3,409	1,760	531	155	23	171	24

SOURCE: U.S. Census, author's estimates

* Comprised of the following counties: Island, King, Kitsap, Pierce, Skagit, Snohomish, Thurston, and Whatcom. This includes the following present-day Standard Metropolitan Statistical Areas: Seattle-Everett and Tacoma.

† Includes environs such as Steilacoom.

psychology. In fact, the fortunes of the Northwest were slavishly tied to the insatiable hunger for profits and power manifested by the robber baron builders of the railroads, Jay Cooke, Ben Holliday, Henry Villard, James J. Hill, and Edward H. Harriman. For years their corporations dominated commerce and culture in the state.

The railroads brought their architecture with them straight from the East via the midwestern centers of Chicago, St. Paul, and Minneapolis. Even before trains started running, speculators and railroad land companies ignited building booms, concentrating on developing central business districts. Thus the first such districts in Port Townsend, Tacoma, Seattle, Spokane, and Fairhaven, all towns touched by the railroad fever, have blocky commercial buildings of stone and brick with principal facades styled in variations on the Romanesque Revival theme that was fashionable in the East and Midwest.

In some cases the railroad entrepreneurs and land developers imported their own architects. In Everett, A. F. Heide, and in Fairhaven the firm of Longstaff & Black, had their way paid and their practices subsidized by railroad interests. These architects stayed on to become the first resident practitioners; they were joined by other designers who moved out west on their own drawn by the opportunities produced by the railroad boom. The railroad's first company buildings, beginning with the 1888 Northern Pacific Headquarters Building in Tacoma, were designed by eastern architects. The most opulent example is the 1909–11 Union Station in Tacoma designed by the Philadelphia firm of Reed & Stem. At the other end of the spectrum is the 1881 Dayton Depot with a rustic, residential cast, doubtless designed by in-house staff from stock plans.

Union Station, Tacoma

Whether designers came because of the railroads or because of the market for their services caused by the 1889 fires in Seattle and Spokane, they brought with them an eclectic vocabulary of Romanesque and Italian Renaissance forms and motifs. These were used to give authority to governmental as well as commercial blocks. Important examples of the latter remain, such as the county courthouses at Port Townsend, Olympia, and Spokane built by architect W. A. Ritchie. Equipped only with a correspondence course in architecture from the U.S. Treasury Department, Richie designed some of the state's most imposing early buildings. Such informal preparation for practice was characteristic of this first wave of architects in Washington Territory. Eclecticism also dignified the first buildings for higher education, another important early field

of practice: the Old Main buildings of the state normal schools, such as Barge Hall at Ellensburg; and similar structures at the private colleges, Memorial Hall at Whitman College in Walla Walla, for instance, and the first building on the present campus of the University of Washington, Denny Hall.

Previous to the westward movement of architects beginning in the late eighties, pattern-book design and plan services out of eastern centers sufficed to fill the needs of commercial and residential building. A notable exception to this rule was the semi-professional service provided by a member of the Order of the Sisters of Charity of Providence, Mother Joseph. Daughter of a Canadian builder-architect, Mother Joseph had some solid training in building before she came to Vancouver as Mother Superior. There she took charge of the

Denny Hall, University of Washington. Photo: James O. Sneddon (courtesy of UW)

design and construction of what is one of the state's most sophisticated early buildings, the 1873 Providence Academy. Mother Joseph was allegedly well known in the Northwest territory and built other structures connected with her order's missionary activities. She climbed ladders, wielded tools, and generally served as architect, carpenter, and contractor.

Clearly there were competent builders using the pattern books. Early photographs of Seattle, for example, show clusters of Gothic and Greek Revival houses, long since replaced by sub-sequent buildings. Now the only examples of these styles are in smaller towns: the 1868 Rothschild house in Port Townsend and the 1869 Tom Crellin house in Oysterville. The fact that fashion had left these styles behind in other parts of the country attests to the provincial character of much of the Washington Territory. It is also clear that the first wave of architects tended both to settle in and devote their energies to the large city markets. In outlying places even quite imposing houses such as Hoquiam's Castle (1897) were apparently pattern-book designs.

The immigrant designers of the late eighties brought with them a variety of training and cultural baggage. Elmer Fisher, who at seventeen migrated from Edinburgh to Worcester, Massachusetts, opened an office in Vancouver, B.C., in 1886, in Victoria in 1887, and in Seattle in 1888. He allegedly built about one hundred of the buildings of post-fire Seattle before migrating south to Los Angeles, probably for the boom there, where he died. In Seattle he shared the field with firms like Saunders & Houghton, A. Wickersham, and John Parkinson. Parkinson too abandoned Seattle for Los Angeles where he had a most influential office in which Fisher ended up working.

Likewise in post-fire Spokane there were architects such as C. B. Seaton, C. Ferris White, and Herman Preusse who demonstrated a firm command of the stylish eclectic Romanesque/Renaissance modes.

The other prolific Spokane architect of the period, Kirtland Kelsey Cutter, attended the New York Art Student's League; but like many others he was largely self-trained, having spent some years touring Europe where he studied in Dresden and Florence. He came to Spokane to look around and work some for his banker uncle. Like Fisher he profited from calamity and after the 1889 fire built scores of buildings in both

Downtown Seattle, shortly after the 1889 fire (courtesy of Photo Collection, UW Library)

downtown and the new affluent suburbs. Clients with a million in cash and only the vaguest notion of what constituted style sent Cutter off buying in the East and in Europe to make sure that they got whatever the latest and best might be. To judge from what remains of his work and what is known though destroyed, Cutter was for a time the state's leading architect. As fate would have it, his own house in Spokane burned along with his records so we do not have all the facts in hand. Still, a selection of his work from Spokane and Seattle shows not only a formidable range of building types but also consistent high quality.

After the turn of the century as the rough edges of communities began to smooth and the demand for architects' services continued, more people with academic and professional training appeared. C. Alfred Breitung, Austrian born and European trained, came to Seattle around 1900 to produce buildings of considerable authority such as the Holy Names Academy and the Home of the Good Shepherd. Charles Bebb, English born and educated at King's College, began private practice with Leonard L. Mendel and later formed a firm with Carl Gould, a New Yorker who graduated from Harvard and attended the Ecole des Beaux Arts from 1899 to 1903. Gould came to Seattle in 1908 after working for such prominent eastern architects as McKim, Mead & White, George C. Post, and Daniel Burnham. Perhaps the most prolific firm of this generation was headed by John Graham, Sr., born in Liverpool in 1872, educated on the Isle of Man and then apprenticed to an English architect. He came to Seattle about 1900 and, after a brief practice with David Myers, opened his own office in

1911. Most of the buildings erected downtown during the 1920s and 1930s came from the drawing boards of his office. This practice continues today as John Graham and Co. David Myers and Joseph Schack were two other up and coming architects of 1910. Their firm was also very long lived: Myers and Schack joined A. M. Young in 1920, became Young & Richardson in 1941, and, after other mutations, remain alive and well today as TRA (The Richardson Associates). Joseph C. Cote, W. Marbury Somervell, Stephen & Stephen, Harlan Thomas, Daniel Huntington, and A. Warren Gould were also among the principal architects of the peak year 1910. This new cohort of designers was generally connected to a nationwide professional educational network. Their clientele was relatively stable and their firms had a greater life expectancy than did those at the beginning of the boom. With increasing stability and academic influence came a broader based eclecticism that drew on the whole medieval period from Romanesque to Tudor including varieties of Gothic. New motives included the Roman, Renaissance, and Baroque combinations that stamped the products of those trained either at the Beaux Arts in Paris or the American architecture schools directed by Beaux Arts graduates. Another source of new design ideas drew on the American past transmuted to produce the parade of Colonial styles, including the California Mission Revival.

Just after the turn of the century, two architects, Andrew Willatsen and Ellsworth Storey, arrived from the Midwest imbued with the new architectural ideas not in the standard academic eclectic mode. In the years to come they would strongly influence the architectural scene around Seattle. Willatsen, a Dane, was in the Oak Park office of Frank Lloyd Wright from 1904 to 1906 and worked on such important projects as the Larkin Building in Buffalo. He came to Seattle in 1907 in a brief partnership with Barry Byrne, also of Wright's office.

Byrne later moved on, but Willatsen remained in Seattle. Not long after they began practice, Willatsen & Byrne designed two houses, the Clarke house (1909) and the Kerry-Trimble house (1910–11) that represent the Prairie School's finest Northwest flowering. Much of Willatsen's other Puget Sound work also faithfully reflects his master's.

Ellsworth Storey, a native of Chicago and graduate of the University of Illinois, arrived in 1903 accompanied by his wife and parents. In 1904 and 1905 he built for their use two adjacent houses in one of the newly developing suburban areas, Madrona Park, on Lake Washington. These and other houses, some of which Storey built on speculation, established his reputation. Reserved by nature and never interested in large-scale practice, Storey maintained a small but influential office. His work has been compared to the California architects of the First San Francisco Bay tradition, Maybeck, Morgan, Howard, and Thomas, but there is no evidence that he knew these practitioners. It is clear that he was thoroughly imbued with the principles of the Craftsman or Arts & Crafts Style, which was well entrenched in Canada and British Columbia and available in America through such publications as Gustav Stickley's *Craftsman* magazine. Craftsman

Charles Clarke house, Seattle (courtesy of Photo Collection, UW Library)

influence was ubiquitous in the Northwest region and is exemplified by the work of contemporaries such as Samuel Maclure in Victoria and Vancouver and Cutter in Washington. Storey's talent and inspiration are best seen in the series of modest dwellings he did in Seattle and in the park structures in the Moran State Park on Orcas Island. It is perhaps true that limitations of budget, which were rarely if ever a factor in Cutter's work, produced the touches that make Storey's buildings stand out as personal creations.

A lack of individuality, but for Storey, characterizes Northwest architecture at this time. This reflects the absence of a demand for local identity. On the contrary, the typical architect's client whether for houses or commercial buildings wanted a product that would give prestige to his home and place of business by virtue of using the accepted symbols and fashions. The more recent the locality, the greater the desire to age it through appearances. Perhaps the most dramatic example of this approach is Sam Hill's Maryhill of 1914, designed about the time of his Seattle mansion of 1908–9 by Hornblower & Marshall of Washington, D.C. Rising mirage-like from the barren slopes above the Columbia River Gorge, this stuccoed concrete mansion asserts through its stylistic packaging that it is an eighteenth century chateau on the Loire. To learn that Hill built it for the purpose of entertaining friends among European royalty is only to compound the improbability of it all at the same time that it verifies the conservative need to use well-known stylistic conventions. In general the use of period revival styles,

Maryhill (courtesy of State Office of Archaeology and Historic Preservation)

common throughout the country, represented a nostalgia for the past. In the Northwest the ubiquity of Colonial and Tudor Revival styles testifies also to the frontier longing for instant permanence, and to a frontier reliance on visual historicism to replace real history.

Returning to the general effects of the boom and the railroads, we find that in less than forty years they had created the main features of the human landscape we know: not only cities like Tacoma and Spokane, but most of the small towns and cities across the state, and the general patterns of the agricultural economy. The railroads promoted the great agricultural regions, chiefly the Palouse wheatlands and the irrigated orchardlands of the Yakima and Wenatchee valleys. Between 1883 and 1909 five distinct rail connections tied eastern Washington to Puget Sound. They crisscrossed the state with trunk lines and spurs. In contrast, only one line to the east and one south to California served the larger territory of Oregon. Intense efforts to build markets for these lines led to the advertising of eastern Washington homesteads in the Midwest and East as well as Europe. With four railroads Spokane became "Capital of the Inland Empire." Westward across the Columbia Plateau the railroad-built towns survive, and present-day development echoes their early hierarchies of importance. Cheney, for instance, was briefly a railroad terminus and later a section town. Given this relative prominence it competed for a few years with Spokane and it qualified as the site for a state normal school. Now, with higher education a major urban growth industry, the normal school has metamorphosed into Eastern Washington University and helped transform Cheney into a minor growth pole in the postrailroad era. Lesser towns unblessed by the railroad remain lesser and in some cases have disappeared.

Major changes occurred in western Washington and Puget Sound too. Together, Tacoma and Seattle surpassed Portland as the principal Pacific grain port. The sale of vast Northern Pacific landgrant forests to Weyerhaeuser laid foundations for the move of large-scale timber products manufacturers from the Midwest. The Great Northern boomed Everett into a center of this enlarged industry. The industrial and commercial growth of the cities created jobs and migration. These, in turn, produced a surge in town building that expanded central business and industrial districts and constructed most of the in-town residential districts in these places.

In comparison with architecture, the other environmental design professions had yet to get a foothold in Washington. In part this was a reflection of the larger world to the east. At the turn of the century, city planning as a distinct design field had only just got started—the Chicago Columbian Exhibit of 1893 is usually given as the starting point. Landscape architecture, though defined in mid-century in America as field of practice by the senior Olmsted, had few practitioners until well into the twentieth century. Engineers, architects, horticulturists, surveyors, and amateurs did most city, garden, and park design. Nowhere in the country was this more true than in the Northwest.

Town design, whether directly the work of the railroads as in the case of Cheney and Everett or not as in Walla Walla and

Capitol Group, Olympia. Photo: A. Curtis, c. 1935 (courtesy of Photo Collection, UW Library)

Vancouver, fell to surveyors and company engineers. The only significant exceptions occurred when some small pieces of larger cities were laid out according to the designs of the Olmsted Brothers, a Boston-based firm of landscape architects and planners. The Rockwood area of Spokane and the parkway developments strung along Lake Washington Boulevard in Seattle are examples. The latter were part of a citywide park and boulevard plan which stands as the first major work of civic design in the Northwest. The Olmsted firm's work brought Virgil Bogue to Seattle from Brooklyn, New York, where he had done engineering for major parks. In both Seattle and Tacoma, Bogue did waterfront development and railroad planning. He also authored the ill-fated Seattle Plan (1911), an ambi-

tious work in the then fashionable City Beautiful or Beaux Arts mode.

Though the boom years were marked by some ups and downs in the economy, most notably the sharp depression of 1893, the period overall was one of continuing optimism and growth. It quickly set the urban patterns for the region, and in doing so set the hierarchies of place that would register so clearly in the designed environments constructed over future years. It was a time of heroic and intense activity. The quiet period that followed was perhaps necessary simply to revive spent energies after such exhausting years.

Interwar, 1910–40

The great Northwest boom died in the teens. The lumber market fizzled in

1912. Poor harvests plagued the wheat-lands, and homesteads were abandoned in the driest areas. In 1915 the nation's business cycle slumped. World War I stimulated a frenzied but short boom, marked by labor strife, notably the Everett Massacre, the Seattle General Strike, and the Centralia Riot. Behind these events lay more fundamental factors: the good farmland had all been settled, the railroads built, perhaps overbuilt, but a solid basis for an independent, mixed regional and urban economy had yet to develop.

Growth during the generation after 1910 slowed to a trickle compared to the previous generation. Between 1910 and 1940 state population grew but 52 percent in contrast to 1400 percent in the earlier thirty-year period. Some of the major urban areas were hit even harder. Spokane, for example, which hardly existed in 1880, exploded between then and 1910, but grew not at all in the following decade. Some important places actually shrunk, Walla Walla, for instance. After the fantastic population expansion of the earlier period, this era of slow growth and stagnation must have seemed traumatically discouraging to the boosters and the land developers, and painful even to the plain working people looking for better jobs ahead.

For others, though, the teens and twenties, even the Great Depression, were viewed happily indeed. Roger Sale in his fine biography of Seattle points out, "I have spoken to many people born in Seattle between about 1910 and 1930 and I have yet to meet one who does not say that Seattle in the twenties and thirties was a wonderful place in which to grow up." It must have been harder, though, in the small towns, farms, and lumber camps than it was in the Puget Sound metropolis where the wealth accumulated in the previous years capitalized a great deal of building in downtown and hence the illusion of continuing development.

Architecture and the other environmental design arts matured considerably during this period. In 1914 Carl Gould founded the Department of Architecture at the University of Washington, an act that signaled the growing maturity and strengthening local base of the profession. The number of firms whose principal partners were well grounded in academic traditions, chiefly Beaux Arts, increased. A. H. Albertson, who came to Seattle in 1907 with a professional degree from Columbia, formed a firm with Paul Richardson and Joseph Wilson that produced, among other outstanding works, the Northern Life Tower (1928), the Northwest's finest example of the Moderne skyscraper. John Graham, Sr., designed most of the late teens and twenties commercial buildings in Seattle, as well as some in Tacoma, in the urbane, eclectic Classic modes propagated from eastern centers. Other similar practices competed in the field: Schack, Young & Myers, and Thomas, Grainger & Thomas, for example.

Though firms did not really specialize some dominated in certain fields. Somervell & Cote designed many of Seattle's most characterful small libraries while James Stephen turned out the city's stock of monumental wooden school buildings. B. Marcus Priteca was *the* Northwest theater designer before he temporarily left for Los Angeles in 1922. Though Seattle was the logical

Lakeland Village Administration Building, Medical Lake

place for the architectural profession to solidify, Spokane, the eastern capital, continued to be a fertile ground. Harold Whitehouse, a New Englander who came to Spokane about 1905 and returned later to Cornell for professional training, established the firm of Whitehouse & Price. Their work dominated architectural practice in the Inland Empire into the post-World War II period.

Smaller firms and individual practitioners that contributed importantly during the late twenties and thirties are exemplified by Arthur Loveless, Loveless & Fey, R. C. Reamer, J. Lister Holmes, John Stoddard, William Bain, Floyd Naramore, and Perry Johanson. The joint practice of the last three architects grew into one of the most important post-World War II firms, Naramore, Bain, Brady & Johanson. A major educator and member of the University of Washington architecture faculty for many years was Lionel Pries, who

studied at the University of Pennsylvania and came up to Seattle from California about 1928. His influence on the generation of architects who dominated the postwar period was profound.

The architect who best qualifies as the progenitor of Modern architecture in the Northwest is Paul Thiry. Graduated from the University of Washington in 1928, Thiry spent the thirties doldrums alternately designing houses and traveling. His small but influential residential designs in Seattle brought the European International Style to Washington. He journeyed widely across the United States, to France, and to Japan where he visited his classmate, the woodworker George Nakashima, and did some work with Antonin Raymond in Tokyo. Always outspoken and frequently involved in civic affairs, Thiry's professional influence was most significant in a crucial period when architectural ideas were beginning to focus on the technology-dominated world of the future, but, because of the depression and world war, there were few opportunities to express them in actual building.

Locally based practices in the allied fields of landscape architecture, town planning, and civic design remained limited, though thinking among landscape people had matured significantly as David Streatfield points out in his following essay. City planning was chiefly caught up in the highway and street problems raised by the growing use of the automobile. Toward the end of the period, federal agencies sponsored pioneering demonstrations in city planning methods in Spokane and Tacoma. Though neither would affect the layout of its city, both influenced the nature of planning practice in the postwar years.

Perhaps the most important accomplishment of the interwar period was the creation of the infrastructure necessary to knit the state and its cities together by automobile. Washingtonians turned early to cars. From the beginning people in towns and cities tended to be too spread out to walk yet not packed closely enough to support rail transit. Almost as soon as it became a practical, widely marketed product, the car took over as the dominant mode of personal transportation. The pioneer American sociologist Roderick McKenzie spent his most productive years in Seattle during the 1920s. While there he studied the early ascendancy of the automobile. Writing of the Puget Sound area in 1929, he found:

Rearrangement of Centers. The influence of the motor car and the new system of highways is reflected in the decline of so many of the old communal centers and the development of new ones. Up to 1910, settlement was confined almost entirely to the salt-water rim and along the river

valleys. Towns and villages were spaced from five to ten miles apart depending upon land utilization and topography. The settlements in one valley were quite largely isolated from those in a neighboring valley, frequently but a few miles distant. Towns along the Sound were united by boat or train, both of which followed circuitous routes. The coming of the motor car and highways immediately effected a new spatial pattern for the entire region. The motor highway, unlike the railroad, is not confined to the valleys nor does it slavishly follow the jagged coastline and meandering mountain streams. Every year the work of straightening and leveling the motor route progresses so that at present the Pacific Highway, which unites all the larger towns of the region has become a comparatively straight line between centers.

Although the effect of motor transportation has been most pronounced during the last five years, its influence is discernible in the settlement changes that occurred in the decade 1910–1920. During that ten year period, twenty-six incorporated places lost in population. Nor were these logging camps that declined with the cutting of the timber. Many were agricultural villages located in valleys where production had steadily increased. A study of the map shows that many of the declining places are located within a ten-mile radius of a larger center of population. Most of the villages along the Pacific Highway decreased in population between 1910 and 1920. Likewise practically all the Cascade-rim villages declined. Branch highways serving as outlets to the larger towns along the Sound are responsible, undoubtedly for a considerable portion of this decline.

But aside from changing old towns and villages the motorization of the region is effecting a new pattern of population distribution and communal centers. The highways, of which there are at present 972 miles of cement pavement outside city corporations, are assuming the characteristics of city streets. This is especially true of the Pacific Highway, along which homes and places of business have grouped with amazing rapidity. . . . The Pacific Highway . . . traverses the logged-off upland and therefore fails to touch many of the intermediary valley centers. On the other hand it has occasioned the rise of a series of new minor centers located at cross roads and other strategic points.

The cities of this region are rapidly growing together. Topographic peculiarities—the Sound on one side and lakes and valleys on the other—are hastening the process by preventing lateral spread. The zones between cities are devoted largely to various forms of leisure-time enterprises. Tourist camps, golf courses, dance halls, road houses intermixed with a variety of supplementary types of business, such as service stations, garages, fruit and 'hot-dog' stands, form a series of successive zones leading out from each of the larger centers. [*On Human Ecology*, pp. 238–40]

There it is! Already in the 1920s strip commercial development and urban-suburban sprawl, combined with rural depopulation, had begun in a pattern that would become dominant forty years later in the second boom.

In 1915 the good roads movement was successful in lobbying for a state highway department and establishing public priorities for paved road access to every county seat and all major scenic resources such as the circuit of the Olympic Peninsula. Federal highway aid commenced soon afterward. Routes 5, 10, and 15 were constructed across the Cascades. Later the federal public works projects designed to combat the depression further improved and extended the network of all-weather roads. Accomplishments included the Murrow Bridge across Lake Washington and the ill-fated Tacoma Narrows Bridge. In all major components but the freeways, the state road network was complete by 1940.

Related to the highway movement was the parallel development of natural landscape for recreational purposes. Particularly in the 1930s, cars brought the masses to the scenic landscape and created the market demand for expanding and developing public holdings as scenic recreation areas. With the help of federal aid such as the Civilian Conservation Corps, state and federal parks were developed and improved. Moran State Park on Orcas Island and the Sunrise district on Mt. Rainier offer fine examples of park design and architecture.

If the Washington highway system was the most ubiquitous environmental residue of these quiet years, other works even bolder in concept triggered changes of similar magnitude. Nowhere in North America, perhaps nowhere in the world, has a great natural waterway been more completely transformed than the Columbia. Once the wildest of major North American rivers, it was tamed by the Rock Island and Bonneville dams and the even more heroic Grand Coulee reclamation and power project. Through the Bonneville Power Administration, electricity from these installations flowed into a regional distribution network destined eventually to serve areas as far away as California. These works set the stage for the final subjugation of the river by a complete chain of dams that would be built at the beginning of the next period.

The Columbia River Project had many antecedents. Certainly the successful beginning of the Tennessee Valley Authority in the early New Deal years provided a favorable national political climate. Seattle Light's Skagit River development acted as an important local progenitor. Though tiny in comparative size and limited to hydropower, it proved local folk could harness a wild river to do their work. Politically more important, it proved the value of socially produced power as a catalyst for regional development.

Grand Coulee Dam (courtesy of Historical Society of Seattle and King County)

The Columbia River Project far overshadows all other New Deal vintage public enterprises in the Northwest. Some programs hardly touched the area. None of the Resettlement Administration's carefully planned migrant worker camps or suburban greenbelt towns are to be found in Washington. The dam site towns at Bonneville and Grand Coulee, and some exemplary public housing in Seattle—Yesler Terrace (1940) and Holly Park (1942)—represent the major achievements in New Deal vintage social housing.

The whole panoply of depression era, federally aided development programs led to a new perspective on large-scale planning. This was reinforced by special purpose New Deal agencies such as the National Resources Planning Board with its state and regional affiliates, which were especially active in the Northwest. Statewide planning for highways, parks and recreation, power, dryland irrigation, and economic development as well as public housing and demonstration city planning projects infused environmental design with a new global perspective.

One interesting experiment in idealized settlement actually preceded the depression years and came instead from the private sector: Longview, begun in 1922. R. A. Long, head of the southern-based Long-Bell Lumber Company, assembled a team of notable

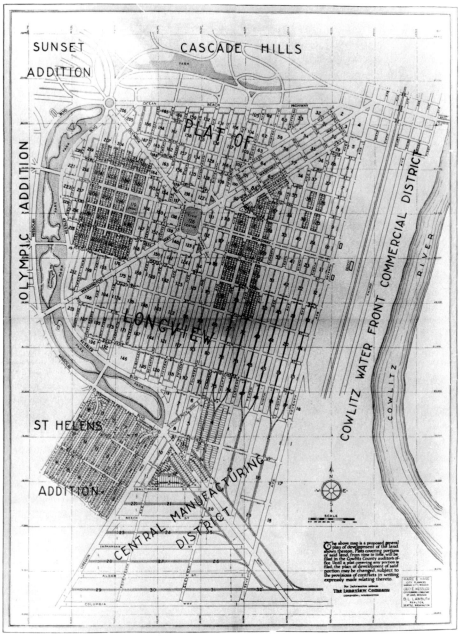

Plan of Longview, 1922 (courtesy of Oregon Historical Society)

planners, developers, and designers to produce the Northwest's only textbook New Town. Overdesigned and underdeveloped, Longview remains an anomaly in the second Northwest boom.

While Long-Bell was constructing its new regional empire, the Simpson Lumber Company under the leadership of Mark Reed learned how to manage sustained-yield forests in the more productive parts of the Olympic Peninsula. Public intervention in timber management increased sharply during the depression with the rapid expansion of the U.S. Forest Service and the Bureau of Land Management. These actions laid the basis for the accelerated and in some ways less destructive exploitation of the forests in the future.

During the interwar period important changes took place in the local corporate enterprise. The somewhat colonial private economy, totally dominated by the railroads and eastern capital, that had managed affairs during the preceding boom period gradually gave way to a more locally autonomous one. In a way this was the larger process of which the growing architectural autonomy of the Northwest was a specific symptom. Major national lumber companies moved their headquarters and operations to the Northwest. New industries successfully incubated. One of the smaller firms, The Boeing Company, weathered the birth pangs of the aircraft industry and the trauma of the depression by energetic pursuit of government and military work and by diversification. Boeing joined with the immense power resources of the Columbia to symbolize

and in fact generate much of the second boom as the oncoming war finally ended the Great Depression.

Second Boom, 1940–Present

The outbreak of World War II in Europe refueled the regional economy. America's entry into the conflict poured millions into shipyards, the aircraft industry, and Puget Sound military bases. Then, in the postwar years, as the relative wealth and power of Washington increased, and its attractiveness as human habitat became more evident, it developed new independence economically, culturally, and in terms of the environmental arts.

The period began with a revival of the historic economic base of the state. The war stimulated the demand for Washington's wheat and timber. Two generations of infrastructure investment began to pay off. The Columbia River Project provided the power for aluminum, chemicals, and later plutonium refining. This rapidly expanded and diversified the industrial base. The irrigation projects opened new land to cultivation as demand soared. Railroads, highways, and in-place urban infrastructure such as housing, water and power supplies, schools, and commercial enterprise, supported a great surge in population. Puget Sound ports boomed; the naval base expanded at Bremerton; the handy mudflats in Tacoma and Seattle became temporary shipways, and helped supply armed forces in the Pacific. Most crucial, certainly to the Seattleites, was Boeing. War had transformed the corporation into a rich human resource of engineering and management talent. From

Puget Sound basin (courtesy of Earth Rotating Orbital Satellite)

this base evolved a world center of aerospace technology and production.

In the early war years, emergency construction programs for new plants and workers' housing dominated the urban development scene. After a hiatus in the mid-1940s a new thrust emerged: the urbanization, or perhaps more accurately suburbanization, of the Puget Sound region. The second boom was on.

The population of the state has doubled in the last thirty years. Most of that growth is urban-suburban and concentrated in Pugetopolis. From the standpoint of environmental design the increase can be divided into a succession of population cohorts requiring in turn housing, education, and jobs. In the 1950s new suburban houses, elementary and high schools, shopping centers, suburban medical facilities, and the like provided a living environment for the bulging population. While these needs continued into the next decade, the sixties saw new requirements too. From an architectural standpoint, perhaps the most important of these new needs was the necessity of multiplying many times the capacity of the state's colleges and universities. With the seventies this population entered the job market, office buildings and downtown development came to the fore architecturally, and major medical and governmental institutions expanded to keep pace with demand.

Behind the second boom lie economic forces that differ importantly from those that stimulated the first expansion sixty years earlier. In contrast to the situation in 1910 when prices for wheat and lumber, Washington's chief exports, were set far away in a world market,

today the prices of Boeing 747s are established at home in Seattle. Instead of being at the mercy of others, the local economy today wields substantial monopoly power in world markets. The region has, in a sense, come of age from a provincial and colonial past.

The reordering of corporate power is not the only economic force behind the environmental changes of recent years. The initiatives of the thirties with respect to infrastructure have been vigorously pursued. Today, in addition to the much improved older road network, two interstate freeways cross the state intersecting in Seattle. The fact that Ellensburg is on west-east Interstate 90 but neither Wenatchee nor Yakima is may have almost as powerful effects as railroad decisions a hundred years earlier. In Puget Sound, north-south Interstate 5 is further knitting patterns into a single conurbation.

Development of the Columbia River has almost exceeded its potential. Seven new mainstream hydro dams on the Columbia and three on the Snake generate power and provide constant-level navigational pools. Palouse wheat once again moves by boat, and now does not have to wait on the high water season to do so. Grand Coulee has been expanded to serve peaking power demand in an extension that breaks new ground for environmental design by adding the internationally noted architect Marcel Breuer to the design team. Closely tied to Columbia electrical energy has been the expansion and development of the U.S. Energy Department's vast Hanford Works. It is a world center for nuclear power research as well as a bomb fuel plant. The population center it spawned, known as Tri-Cities, has become the newest urban center of the Northwest.

A strong economy, population growth, and suburbanization combine today to produce a very favorable climate for the design professions. Fields such as landscape architecture, urban design, and town planning that hardly existed prior to World War II have drawn many people to set up practice. Names like Richard Haag, Grant and Ilze Jones, Dirk Jongejan, Terry Gerrard, and Robert Chittock in Seattle have come to the fore in landscape design, some with statewide practices that extend into innovative areas such as environmental planning. Several national city-planning firms have branches in the state, and several of the major local architectural firms have entered this growing field. Interesting new forms of practice have

emerged such as the urban design work of Folke Nyberg in Seattle and the multidisciplinary planning and design practice of the Environmental Concern, Inc., of Spokane. However, these branches of practice still remain somewhat underdeveloped. It is architecture that has really burgeoned here.

Following the war, a generation of young architects, most of them educated at the University of Washington under Lionel Pries and others, returned home to practice. The building boom that was to expand architectural practice in all dimensions in the next two decades was slow to get under way. In the beginning the needs of suburbanization consumed everyone's talents and energies. The leading practitioner of the postwar period was Paul Hayden Kirk, whose beautifully scaled post-and-beam houses were widely published. Kirk also used

House by Paul Hayden Kirk (see Bellevue, 24). Photo: Vern and Elizabeth Green

this structural style in a series of highly influential, residentially scaled medical and dental clinics. But the steadiest demand was for houses. As the major metropolis, Seattle attracted the largest number of architects. Architects such as Roland Terry, Bert Tucker, Robert Shields, Victor Steinbrueck, John T. Jacobsen, John R. Sproule, Robert Dietz, Wendell Lovett, Gene Zema, Fred Bassetti, and Ralph Anderson, all graduates of the University of Washington, were joined by important newcomers, John Morse, Ibsen Nelsen, Al Bumgardner, and Omer Mithun.

Not only the houses but also the related suburban building types—schools, churches, small shopping centers—built in the 1950s and 1960s around Puget Sound reveal the degree of assimilation of Modern movement ideas by this generation. In smaller cities too, the postwar boom produced enough demand for architectural services to enable influential practices to get started. In Tacoma, Robert Billsborough Price was perhaps the best known among a group that included Lea, Pearson & Richards; Harris, Reed & Litzenberger; James McGranahan; and Alan Liddle. In Spokane the leaders included Bruce Walker, Kenneth Brooks, John McGough, Thomas Adkison, and William Trogdon. As time advanced most of these firms had opportunities to branch out widely into new fields such as college and university building. Recently such larger commissions have provided a showcase for the creative energies of architects and other environmental designers.

In addition to the small and middle-sized offices that have given the profession a rich diversity in recent decades, large firms—The Richardson Associates; Naramore, Bain, Brady & Johanson; and John Graham and Co.—heirs to the corporate and commercial building practices that began in the teens and twenties, have transformed city skylines with their work.

In the 1970s another generation, also mostly University of Washington graduates, have come to the fore. Young firms such as Hobbs/Fukui, Olson/Walker, Calvin/Gorasht, and Barnett Schorr have established reputations, largely in the residential field to this point but with a growing emphasis on other building types and design for adaptive reuse of older structures.

To sum up, architecture is alive and well in the state of Washington. The largely self-taught, pioneering profession has matured. The increasingly complex demands of the future will be met, one trusts, with increasingly sophisticated and sensitive solutions.

Characteristic Patterns

The architecture and man-made landscapes of the Northwest can be understood as a set of variations on a few characteristic themes or patterns. Relatively little of the architecture and landscape design aims at high art status and equivalently little achieves it. This means that, using a narrow art-historical approach to architecture in the region, there is relatively little to say. But to look at design in the state of Washington from such a point of view is to misinterpret it. A more productive view sees design within a broader cultural context. Seen in this way, architecture and environmental design reveal a set of coherent patterns and take on greater meaning.

In the pages that follow, both professionally designed and vernacular, or nonprofessionally designed, patterns are examined. First, four professionally constructed characteristic types are presented in chronological order: the nineteenth century business district, the turn-of-the-century zone of better residence, the post-World War II custom house suburban subdivision, and the higher education campus. The Introduction concludes with a short discussion of several of the most interesting vernacular patterns. While other characteristic patterns exist besides those covered here, the authors have found these the most

important. Seeing the architecture and landscape and civic design of the region in terms of these patterns enhances both the pleasure and the understanding of the onlooker.

Late Nineteenth Century Business Districts

Among the most memorable passages in Washington's historic architecture are the late nineteenth century business districts. The Pioneer Square area in Seattle, the old center of Port Townsend and Bellingham's Fairhaven district, lonely shards of equivalent areas in Tacoma and Spokane, bits in the smaller cities, and an occasional ensemble in a rural county seat such as Pomeroy or Colfax confront

Port Townsend in the early 1890s (courtesy of Photo Collection, UW Library)

the onlooker and remain fixed in the mind.

In common with other aspects of architecture, the stylistic inspiration of the Romanesque Revival used in these districts came west with the new settlers. The range of the style's expression is evident in a comparison between Seattle's Pioneer Building (1889–90) by one of the period's most prolific designers, Elmer Fisher, and the nearby Maynard Building (1892) by A. Wickersham. The former is rugged and bombastic; the latter, smooth and refined. The reason the style is found so pervasively from east to west wherever central business districts were built is undoubtedly its adaptability and susceptibility to standardization. Exteriors were brick, often with cut stone trim, sometimes with whole basement stories of stone. Interior and floor framing were timber often combined with cast-iron columns. Ornamental detail could be turned out in terra cotta, wood or pressed sheet metal for cornices, bracketed entablatures, and window and door trim.

Significantly, these business blocks now appear anonymous, like background music, providing a rhythmic beat on the main streets of old downtowns. But certainly many were professionally designed, their designers attracted, like everyone else, by the burgeoning development and the work opportunities. Typically the buildings were financed, built, and owned by important local businessmen. One of their ingratiating features is the construction date and the name of the builder-owner chiseled boldly on the pediment or entablature.

Less commonly, corporate interests, the railroads chiefly, and eastern-backed land companies financed development.

Gardens, parks, and public open spaces were for the most part conspicuously absent from the late nineteenth century business districts in Washington. The triangular patch that is Pioneer Square is unique in this regard. Civic design concerned with the conscious harmonizing of individual buildings did not exist. Business districts grew up on lots platted by surveyors bent on establishing the easiest, most litigation-free system of parceling marketable land: hence the typical small square blocks about 250 feet on a side, the storefront-width 25-foot lots, and the ubiquitous gridiron street plan. Olmsted's 1873 effort to deviate from this in Tacoma met with dismay and derision; it was abandoned before a lot was sold or a street laid out. Remaining ensembles representing the characteristic central business district pattern exhibit varying degrees of arrested development. Although the buildings themselves were designed to sit wall to wall, creating a solid front on the street, the booster spirit always outran available capital leaving the gap-toothed effect of Port Townsend or Bellingham's Fairhaven. In this regard Seattle's Pioneer Square district, totally built up except for modern demolitions, is the exceptional rather than the typical development. Time has ill-used these districts, adding its ravages to their originally imperfect realization. What the viewer sees today represents but a fragment of their one-time splendid appearance. Fire, of course, was the most destructive of these agents. Every nineteenth century business district experienced repeated fires. The 1889 fires in Seattle and Spokane were simply the most dramatic.

In the twentieth century, the power of entrepreneurial profit-making and the drive for ever higher use intensities have been the most destructive forces. Important, presently existing commercial monuments such as the Larson Building (1931) in Yakima have replaced significant earlier structures, in this case a bank. This trend continues. Seattle's 1974 Federal Office Building and the 1977 Rainier Tower both replaced lower density structures of architectural and historical importance.

Fortunately this process of destruction has abated. With the awakening of public consciousness of the irreplaceable nineteenth century business districts, preservation and recycling are now well entrenched in most places. While the quality varies from the painstaking rehabilitations characteristic of Seattle's Pioneer Square district and the Pike Place Market to the more modest efforts in less populous communities like Port Townsend and Fairhaven, the future looks good for what remains. Washington has come to cherish its early commercial blocks as key components of the regional environment.

Turn-of-the-Century Zone of Better Residence

A district of fine houses near the business district emerged in every urban center in Washington around the turn of the century, though the distance from downtown varied depending on the site of the city. The term "zone of better residence" refers to the fact that more well-to-do social classes built their better—that is, costlier and bigger—

residences in these areas. While explosive population growth had begun twenty years earlier, an upper or middle class architectural clientele only accompanied the attainment of a certain critical urban size, age, and amassed personal wealth. Professional design services reached the necessary stage of maturity at the same time, making local talent available in a field that rarely justified the expense of imported talent. For this reason many of the best works of major Washington architects like Cutter, Graham, and Bebb & Mendel appear in these zones, as well as most of the work of lesser-known local designers.

The kinds of architectural ideas embodied in these residential zones varied somewhat from one locality to another within an overall vocabulary of turn-of-the-century design ideas. In Walla Walla, for instance, taste favored the Colonial Revival Style in white-painted wood, with formal central hall plans, columned porticoes, and the rest. In nearby Spokane, Colonial Revival mansions existed cheek by jowl with other styles, particularly the eclectic mix of Tudor and Elizabethan called Jacobean by many historians. This style was the hallmark of work by the internationally known English architect Richard Norman Shaw, who along with Eden Nesfield cast a long shadow over North American residential design from the turn of the century into the twenties. Another, interrelated influence from England was that of the Arts & Crafts movement identified with William Morris and architect Phillip Webb. Both of these influences permeated the Northwest in the work of designers like Samuel Maclure in British Columbia. The work of Maclure was paralleled

Amasa B. Campbell house, Spokane (courtesy of Eastern Washington State Historical Society)

by that of Kirtland K. Cutter in Spokane, and in Seattle by John Graham, Sr.; Joseph Cote; Schack, Young & Myers; and Bebb & Mendel, who were building in the first exclusive suburbs on First Hill, Queen Anne Hill, and Capitol Hill.

Another instructive architectural contrast exists between the Grand Avenue district in Everett and the Stadium-Seminary area of Tacoma. The stately homes of the former district have the stamp of the fashionable plan-book designs employed by the contractor-builder. Naturally enough in a lumber milling town they are mainly ample

wood structures with simple, two-story, central hall plans. This relative regularity and modesty contrasts with the more adventuresome variety in Tacoma as well as the more imposing scale of mansions there such as the Rust House. Because of its more cosmopolitan character, Tacoma had more practicing architects and access to a broader range of architectural ideas. Materials varied across the whole palette; plans were as varied as lot sizes allowed. Proceeding up the scale, the comparable zones in Seattle—First Hill, Capitol Hill, Queen Anne Hill—are richer still. Here, there is both a layering of ideas produced by progressive development and a full range of employable talents. Still another pattern, at the other end of the scale, is visible in the Nob Hill section of Yakima. Largely because the city was more isolated, personal fortunes newer, and development spread over a longer time span, the houses are more modest, more varied, and more interspersed with working class dwellings. The result, while hardly prime architecture, is a rich catalogue of popular styles dating from the last years of the nineteenth century to the mid-twentieth.

In terms of civic design, these districts initially followed the grid plan with perhaps the single embellishment of a grandly named, sometimes more grandly proportioned main street. Occasionally a block or two would be dedicated as a park as in Coeur d'Alene Park in Spokane, Pioneer Park in Walla Walla, or Elizabeth Park in Bellingham. Only gradually did ambitious and innovative ideas take root. In some places a new pattern of site design using curved streets, larger, often odd-shaped lots, lower densities, and more scenic open space appeared. The culmination of this development occurs in Seattle's Highlands. Here were built the ultimate turn-of-the-century mansions in a landscape that transcended the limitations of growing cities to achieve that northwestern ideal of the villa in the forest, a theme David Streatfield explores in the following essay. The Olmsted Brothers' plan for The Highlands made it possible to achieve this ideal by using the contour hugging, curved street layout pioneered earlier in the East by the senior Olmsted. This theme appears rarely in the Northwest compared with other parts of the country. Spokane's Rockwood district, Tacoma's Gravelly Lake area, and Seattle's Denny Blaine Addition, all the work of the Olmsted Brothers, almost complete the list of such planned neighborhoods.

Small cities and towns could not muster the affluence to support a whole district of fine houses. Even so, inevitably some imposing homes were built. Usually they would naturally cluster near downtown on the better side of the tracks. The Meeker house (1890) in Puyallup, the North Broadway area in Aberdeen, and the McInnis house (1899) in Davenport exemplify such relatively grand dwellings isolated in smaller localities.

In the years between 1920 and 1970 all of these better residence areas suffered some erosion. Fires and other disasters took out some houses, changed land uses took others. Now after a half century of limbo most are coming back in terms of peoples' preferences and associated real estate values. The zones of better residence, but for the rare exceptions such as The Highlands, are no longer the exclusive preserves of the most elite, and seem now destined to be well cared for and preserved by a new, more heterogeneous group of inhabitants.

Post-World War II Custom House Suburb

Not until after the Second World War did sufficient economic and development energy accumulate to produce another important and characteristic architecture-landscape ensemble. In the postwar years, the suburban, low-density, custom house subdivision often on heavily wooded land emerged to join the earlier archetypes. In contrast to the previous boom's zone of better residence, these districts were located on the far-out rural fringe and were even more anti-urban. To begin with they denied the urban street tradition entirely. Even the old Olmsted curved street districts had houses that fronted on the streets and produced collectively an urban streetscape. Not so in the new districts. These houses tended to disappear into their setting, opening no more than the carport to the street and turning their lively side to the privacy of the back garden. If the site was large enough or irregular, it was possible to hide the house altogether or so shroud it with vegetation that it would disappear. Very low density development—that is, few dwellings per unit area—was a necessity for these exclusive preserves of contemporary houses.

The difference in their collective expression from that of the prewar garden suburb which still retained an orientation to the street, is most striking in one of the Northwest's most perfectly realized examples of this development, the Hilltop Community south of Bellevue. Here the unfamiliar visitor can almost believe that he has come to an undeveloped piece of land, so hidden in natural landscaping are the houses, mostly designed by famous local architects. One of the rare examples of a successful cooperative development, Hilltop is, in effect, so good that it does not show at all. Nearby, nearly all of Mercer Island conforms to this pattern. It is the largest and most architecturally rich such area in the state. Elsewhere on the shores of Lake Washington, in Medina for instance, or in the western part of Seattle on Magnolia Bluff or south at Three Tree Point,

good examples of such development occur, as they do in secluded suburbs of Tacoma and the southern reaches of Spokane. In fact, every urban agglomeration with an outer fringe of interesting or previously untouched topography has been developed to some degree in this way.

On a landscape and urban design level, these suburban areas ideally should use streets that are aligned with the contours and that wind through the trees in loops and cul-de-sacs. However, given the state's predilection for numbered gridiron layouts, the actual result is a compromise between the two. Ideally too the layouts of these districts have centrally located public or community facilities, especially public schools. This ideal was often achieved. Norwood Village on the southeastern outskirts of Bellevue probably typifies best the street plan and school arrangement.

Another aspect of these postwar subdivisions is the individuality of their houses. While all tended to be designed within the stylistic bounds of contemporary architecture, each was custom tailored to its own view of the woods, its orientation, and the outdoor living potentials of its particular site. A critical principle in designing these districts was to achieve a minimum disturbance to natural earthforms and vegatation. This meant bulldozers were not always called in to make standardized lots for standardized designs. Instead, as in Omer Mithun's Bellevue tract, Surrey Downs, all the trees were saved and the houses were fitted among them on sites left alone as much as possible. Though many of the actual designs were prepared by builders and talented amateurs, these districts

House by Wendell Lovett (see Mercer Island, 14)

provided an exquisite opportunity for the just emerging native-born-and-raised generation of architects.

Though local in realization, the custom house design drew inspiration from a variety of sources. Perhaps the most important was the International Style with its anti-historical stance. This made architects free from bondage to past images of the house and advocated in their place a direct construction-based aesthetic. Seattle's Paul Thiry comes to mind in connection with introducing these ideas in the 1930s. Contemporaneously in nearby Portland, architects Pietro Belluschi and John Yeon produced a few landmark designs that demonstrated how the International Style might be domesticated into a less purist, more expressively timber-built architecture admirably suited to the Northwest. In California similar adaptive experiments succeeded. Oriental, particularly traditional Japanese, architecture powerfully affected Northwest designers. Vernacular influences came in too from barns, pioneer houses, and the like. As important as any of the other motives, a design approach to the landscape contributed perhaps the most important new starting point. House and site were seen inextricably tied together so that house design started by literally asking how to use the site most sensibly, at the same time making the least negative impact on it.

Houses of the 1950s and 1960s by many architects explored these general themes in multiple variations. Paul Thiry, Paul Hayden Kirk, Victor Steinbrueck, Gene Zema, Ralph Anderson, Wendell Lovett, Fred Bassetti, John Morse, Ibsen Nelsen, Omer Mithun, and Al Bumgardner all worked in the Seattle area;

Robert Billsborough Price and Alan Liddle in Tacoma's environs; and Bruce Walker, Kenneth Brooks, Royal McClure, and Tom Adkison worked in Spokane.

The houses of these designers were typically wooden post-and-beam structures with a dominant roof form, flat, gabled, or monopitched, and generous overhanging eaves sheltering nonbearing screen walls of glass and wood. Their interior plan combined the living and dining areas into one space adjacent to a more or less open kitchen, thus creating a clear view from one side of the house to the other and, consequently, an illusion of greater space. Popularized by *Sunset* magazine and other consumer periodicals, and repeatedly featured in the professional architectural and landscape journals, the custom-designed house has become a nationally recog-

Lockwood Townhouses, Bellevue

nized symbol of the Washington life style, and perhaps its most attractive design accomplishment.

What does the future hold for these postwar custom house subdivisions? In general they show signs of robust good health. The verdure embowers them more with each passing year, contributing to an increasingly dominant woodland look—and to the increasing invisibility of the dwellings themselves. Where opportunities exist new dwellings are built on passed-over lots in the old subdivisions. But economics and a more anti-growth development ethic suggest new districts of this type will be rare indeed in years to come.

Higher Education Campuses

College and university campuses provide the last of the characteristic designed environments to be discussed. The campus has a less uniquely regional identity than the two characteristic types of residential district. It represents a local manifestation of national motives somewhat analogous to the late nineteenth century business district but different in that the accretion of buildings over many years has produced a multi-layered quality in the architecture and site planning.

From Pullman to Seattle, campuses concentrate in one small area a wealth of serious architecture. Almost always a parallel richness exists in landscape design, site planning, and urban design. The main academic institutions, with the dates of founding, are: University of Washington, Seattle, 1861; Eastern Washington University, Cheney, 1890; Central Washington University, Ellensburg, 1890; Washington State University, Pullman, 1892; Western Washington University, Bellingham, 1893; Whitman College, Walla Walla, 1859; Pacific Lutheran University, Tacoma, 1890; University of Puget Sound, Tacoma, 1888; Seattle Pacific University, Seattle, 1891; Seattle University, Seattle, 1892; the new community college campuses at Walla Walla, 1974, and Seattle, 1974; and Evergreen College, Olympia, 1967.

The pattern of all but the newest campuses is predictable—an Old Main building from the late nineteenth century, a first quad composed of rather unspecialized facilities, then later the beginnings of expansion and architectural differentiation often in the 1920s though earlier at the University of Washington and Washington State. The latter stage usually exhibits a consistent imported style, such as Washington's Collegiate Gothic, and conforms to a master plan as typified by the Bebb & Gould plan on the same campus. In the second boom period of 1950 through the 1970s, economic growth, burgeoning population, and social changes causing longer school attendance powered an enormous expansion of the state's campuses. This happened simultaneously with the emergence of a large and local architectural and landscape design community. The result was a flowering of seriously designed collegiate structures and campus expansion plans.

From an architectural standpoint the fifties, sixties, and seventies can be roughly characterized as stylistic subperiods. Though physical expansion on the campuses had barely begun by the end of the 1950s, a small legacy of this period remains on most campuses. A good representative is the collection of buildings completed about 1960 at Central Washington including the Library by Bassetti & Morse, Nicholson Pavilion by Ralph Burkhard, and the halls by Maloney. With respect to single structures, the architectural motives of the period which were primarily purist visions of the International Style are beautifully embodied in the Faculty Center (1960) by Steinbrueck and Kirk on the University of Washington campus. At Whitman College the Harper Joy Theater (1958) offers a different but equally winning version of fifties consciousness. Campus planning and associated landscape and urban design considerations figured rather minimally during this period. Energies went directly into building and the results were often destructive from an overall campus planning perspective.

During the mid and late 1960s enormous development activity took place on all campuses, planning ideas matured, and styles changed. Bold development plans and heroic building budgets led most institutions to an expansion that dwarfed the older campuses. Architecture matured but lost its purist vision. Academic formalism and various Brutalist-Structuralist tendencies became dominant. Buildings in this set of styles spread everywhere. One of the best in terms of scale, detailing, and concept is the Richardson Associates' design for the Aerospace and Engineering Research Laboratory (1969) at Washington. On the Pullman campus, the Naramore, Bain, Brady & Johanson Fine Arts Center (1960) embodies a more expressionistic, less refined academicism. Among the high points of architecture

in this period is Bassetti's sequence of designs for student housing at Washington (1960), Western Washington (1961–65), and Central Washington (1965–70).

As the sixties ended and the seventies began, a last spurt of building occurred which seems now to have ended. Architecture became more expressionistic, brute concrete became the favored material, and designs took on an aggressive life of their own. Nelsen's buildings at Western Washington (1973–74), and the work of Adkison et al. at Whitman (1968) and Eastern Washington (1977), illustrate the direction. Brooks' Performing Arts Complex (1977) at Pasco Community College provides a particularly sophisticated version of the late Brutalist Style.

The most recent period also witnessed the phenomenon of the instant new campus. Among the better of them are Evergreen College in Olympia (1971), Seattle Community College (1973), and Walla Walla Community College (1976). North Seattle Community College (1974), designed by Mahlum & Mahlum, provides the Northwest with an example of a current international ideal, the Brutalist megastructure, a single rectangular concrete monolith housing all the campus facilities. Evergreen, built during the seventies by a variety of designers, the most ambitious instant campus in the state, displays the growing maturity of campus planning as the boom advanced, and the parallel importance of landscape and urban design ideas.

Such larger planning and design concepts were in turn applied to some of the older campuses with great success. At

Fine Arts Center, Washington State University. Photo: Morley Baer

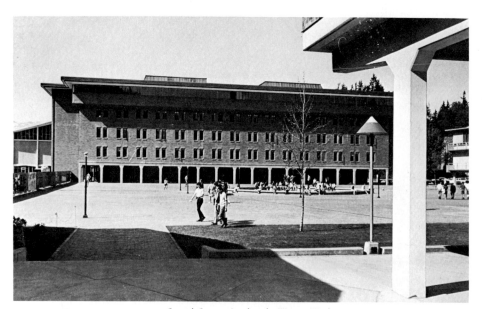

Central Campus Quadrangle, Western Washington University (courtesy of WWU)

Pacific Lutheran University, for instance, Richard Haag Associates' landscape design transformed a pedestrian group of buildings into a felicitous campus. In what is one of the most successful and certainly one of the rarest accomplishments anywhere, George Bartholick's urban design–oriented planning at Western Washington has made a miscellany of buildings into a memorable and integrated whole, chiefly by thoughtful placing of each new facility and sensitive handling of interstitial spaces.

The higher education campuses of Washington contain a disproportionate share of the state's best architecture.

This has been true since the beginning of professional practice in the region. The long-gone, white, wooden Colonial palace built for the University of Washington in the 1860s was prophetic. As the first highly self-conscious work of architecture in the state it established the place of higher education as a patron for design and the campus as the locus of much of the region's best work. The recent cycle of campus expansion and new campus development had added enormously to these riches especially in the larger-scale dimensions of environmental design.

Characteristic Vernacular Landscapes

Most of the human impact on the landscape, including most building design, takes place without the aid of ordained design professionals. Surprisingly often this produces preponderantly vernacular landscapes which exhibit great coherence, economy, and social utility, not to mention charm and a sure sense of design. Missing is the touch of the professional designer who works in a highly self-conscious way that places the work of the moment in the context of the formal history and culture of design. In contrast, to the extent the vernacular designers refer to design history, it occurs in an unsophisticated way.

This guide and this introductory essay deal primarily with the self-conscious products of professional designers. Only in the earliest periods of the pioneers and before the railroad era does vernacular architecture outweigh professional design in the works selected for inclusion. Prior to 1880, most entries are the work of unidentified amateurs, trappers, missionaries, soldiers, gold prospectors,

Steptoe barn

ranchers, and farmers. After 1880, and especially after 1920 when the wealth of extant work requires the exercise of more strict selection criteria, less and less vernacular work is included. In part this is appropriate since the greater professional specialization of recent times has militated against serious design by the hand of amateurs. Today a Dr. John McLoughlin, Chief Factor of the Hudson's Bay Company post in Vancouver who successfully combined the roles of physician, corporate manager, community leader, and architect, would be impossible.

The earliest vernacular works accompanied the exploitation of natural resources. Although the mill town is illustrated by the carefully preserved setting in Port Gamble, no examples could be found of the prototypical mill itself with its accretive growth of working buildings, machines, log ponds, and other site development patterns. Good examples of mining camps exist in Roslyn and Liberty up river from Ellensburg where continuous occupancy has preserved two outstanding vernacular environments.

Pioneer farmsteads as such have not been as carefully documented in Washington as in neighboring Oregon. Many, however, remain. The Olmstead Place near Ellensburg provides a fairly complete picture of the pioneer farm with its later mutations. However, the real riches of vernacular farm design are in the wheatlands of eastern Washington. The land itself, the pattern of crops and fields, is in large part a result of a vernacular design process. Until modern times, each farmstead was dominated by the great horse and mule barns built to house enormous teams of work animals

required before the coming of the diesel caterpiller tractor and self-propelled combine. Many of these barns remain. A proper study of Washington barns remains to be done and time is short— each year takes its toll. A whole district that demands attention before urbanization destroys its vernacular riches is the Skagit River delta, punctuated with some of the finest large dairy and feed barns in the West.

Most older towns, especially ones like Pomeroy that have not boomed a second time, retain their nineteenth century vernacular business blocks, variants of the more self-consciously professional designs in larger centers. All older towns and cities contain areas more or less parallel to the better residence zone. In middle to working class residential districts, Washington communities developed a neighborhood environment that is one of the region's strengths. Wherever such districts appeared during the first two decades of the twentieth century, the permutations on the Classic Box house type with machine-made ornament give great character. One of the finest of these areas, and one that comes

Classic Box, 1155 17th Avenue East, Seattle

close to being a zone of better residence but for the swankier areas nearby, is the Capitol Hill Addition in Seattle. Here and elsewhere such districts are characterized by closely spaced basic boxlike houses, with minimal front yards on relentlessly gridironed city streets. Occasional schools, churches, and strips of commercial storefronts on streetcar lines punctuate the grid. When the wealthier inhabitants abandoned the cities for the suburbs during the twenties and thirties, these areas continued a slow, accretive development. Styles changed. Most typical of the twenties and thirties development was a steep-roofed builder's Tudor cottage exemplified by several streetscapes in the Montlake area of Seattle. Today, the shift in real estate markets has given these districts new life. Modest in-town housing today seems to have a bright future in many Washington localities.

Another ubiquitous vernacular landscape was the automobile-oriented, arterial street, commercial strip. The early evolution of such strips in the Puget Sound region has been discussed earlier in this Introduction. The strip reached its apogee in the forties and fifties before the freeways were built. Pacific Highway, Route 99, from Vancouver north to the Canadian border was both the first and the most intensively developed. The Federal Way section between Tacoma and Sea-Tac Airport perhaps best typifies the strip. In eastern Washington, Sprague Avenue East outside of Spokane is the premier strip. Nowadays afficionados of pop have begun to cherish strip commercial building design. There are riches awaiting pop historians in the state.

Since the 1950s an enormous amount of vernacular development has sprawled over the landscape, converting much of western Washington to Pugetopolis and invading the countryside near all population centers. Inland, whole valleys are being transformed; for instance, the Yakima area is changing from horticulture to sprawl development and will continue to do so unless the energy crunch intervenes. No doubt intriguing, even attractive, vernacular design exists in this matrix. Certainly eye-catching are the miniaturized but muscle-bound little branch banks that have sprouted throughout suburbia. But it is too early to sort out the vernacular of the second boom, let alone testify to its worth.

Conclusion

In little more than a century the European-derived culture and economy of the United States have transformed the Washington landscape. The Northwest now takes its place among the major settled regions of the country and the world. The recent history of the region and Washington is recorded and symbolized in the buildings and gardens and towns that people have designed and built. Always these designs have been tied to the larger economy and culture of the nation and the world beyond. At the same time, and increasingly as Washington has matured, a local character has evolved as counterpoint to the universalistic qualities. Though the built environment still does not compete with nature in terms of regional identity, the new consciousness about architecture and design promises an interesting and hopeful future.

Landscape Design in Washington

by David C. Streatfield

The state of Washington has become well known for its rich and diverse natural landscapes. Yet the settlement of the state went through the usual process of cultural colonialism associated with frontier societies, and adaptation to the different characters of the natural landscapes was a late development. There were no local traditions to guide development other than those of the Indians, and they were completely ignored. By the turn of the century attitudes toward the landscape had become polarized, as they are still, between exploitation and conservation. While John Muir retreated to Mount Rainier for contemplation and mystical union with nature, entrepreneurs and developers celebrated the fact that "the subjugation of the wilderness has been made easy because the settler has needed to lose neither time nor energy in reaching the scene of his future labors." As a result of this attitude, the cities created in Washington State did not differ in any major way from those in other regions.

The most significant developments in landscape design have occurred in western Washington, and this is reflected in the choice of the following examples. This does not, however, suggest any diminution in the quality of designs in the eastern part of the state, but it does reflect a slower rate of growth and a smaller number of landscape designers.

In the earliest years of development, cities and towns tended to follow the ubiquitous gridiron plan. The first serious attempt at a different approach was Frederick Law Olmsted's plan for Tacoma (1873), in which long gently curving blocks followed the contours of the land with a chain of parks sweeping down the bluffs to the waterfront. A local newspaper captured the incredulity with which the proposal was received when it reported that "the blocks were shaped like melons, pears and sweet potatoes. . . . It was a pretty fair park plan but condemned itself for a town."

Wright Park (1888) in Tacoma, designed by the eastern landscape architect E. O. Schwagerl, typifies the accepted adherence to gardenesque taste with its sentimental statues, lake, conservatory, and groves of exotic trees imported from Europe. The smaller Chetzemoka Park (c. 1905) in Port Townsend exemplifies the parallel and related delight in the rustic with its elaborate entrance, band shelter, and boulder-lined stream courses.

City developers surpassed landscape designers in their disregard of regional character. In Seattle, the forests were completely felled with the exception of two small parks, Schmitz and Ravenna, and the steep hills were developed with streets on a grid plan. The steepness of the hills did, however, produce an accommodation in that the lots were smaller and streets narrower than any to be found in comparable cities in California. Denny Hill was sluiced into Elliott Bay leaving a legacy of large rocks which were used in garden walls well into the twenties. Spokane fared better in the development of Rockwood, where the

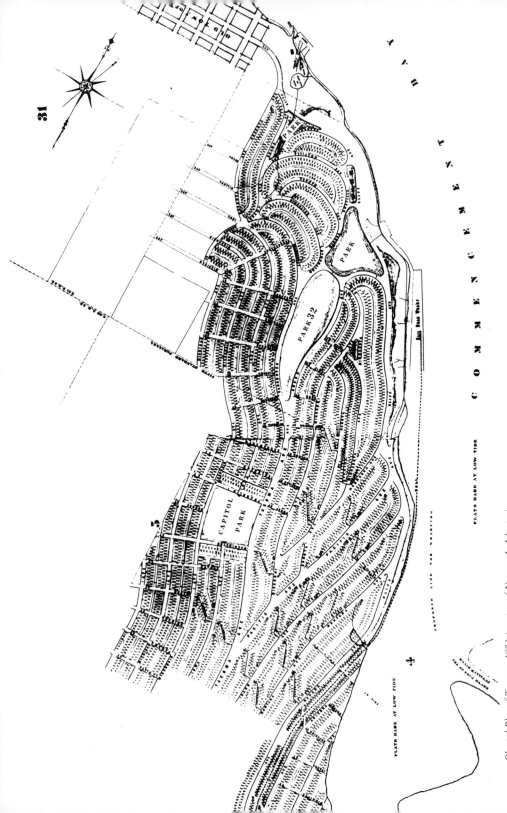

Olmsted Plan of Tacoma, 1873 (courtesy of Norman J. Johnston)

large volcanic boulder outcrops were retained and the winding streets followed the natural contours.

By 1903, when the Olmsted Brothers of Brookline, Massachusetts, prepared a park plan for Seattle, the only areas left for park development were the sites of former private amusement parks and land unsuitable for development because of unstable soil and steepness. The Olmsted plan sought to bring order to the disjointed city. It was similar in principle to the Boston park plan by the elder Olmsted and Charles Eliot. It comprised a chain of parks linked by parkways and boulevards, the most dramatic feature being the twenty-five-mile drive from the Bailey Peninsula, now Seward Park, to Fort Lawton, now Discovery Park, which afforded views over Lake Washington toward the Cascade Mountains and over Puget Sound to the Olympic Mountains. The plan also incorporated a sort of early mini-park provision of playgrounds within 1½ miles of every house.

Each park was designed to have its own identity. The central parks were to be "neat and smooth" as in Volunteer Park and Leschi Park, and the outlying parks

Lake Washington Boulevard South. Photo: A. Curtis, c. 1920 (courtesy of Photo Collection, UW Library)

Volunteer Park. Photo: A. Curtis, c. 1913 (courtesy of Washington State Historical Society)

were to be more "wild" as at Colman Park and Seward Park. The Olmsted Brothers had a marked antipathy toward the native plants. Firs looked well from a distance but were "mean and crowded at close quarters." Since they believed that these trees were susceptible to factory smoke they recommended that "fir trees, in fact all conifers, and evergreens would better be removed at once." The native undergrowth was replaced as can be seen in Volunteer Park where "exotic shrubbery" was used as a facer planting to the fir trees.

The park plan for Spokane (1906) was similar to the Seattle system, with large parks linked by boulevards, but the parks were actually developed much later. Despite the Olmsted Brothers' positive attitude toward the drama of the Spokane River they did not recommend a river park, probably because of the cost or for reasons of political expediency. After 1900 the elder Olmsted's tran-

scendentalist vision of the park as a place for spiritual rejuvenation was challenged by the increasing public interest in active recreation. The Olmsted Brothers continued to provide a broad landscape treatment where possible, and although they were often forced to incorporate more formal features such as bandstands, they fiercely resisted the placing of large structures such as art museums within the parks. Larger parks were easier to design. The scheme of Hare & Hare of Kansas City for Point Defiance Park (1906) in Tacoma had a "wildwood" section with one of the most monumental log bridges ever erected in the West, separate areas for athletics, and a zoo. But there was clearly cultural confusion in their choice of the Japanese style for the park building.

The Highlands subdivision (1909) north of Seattle, designed by the Olmsted Brothers, established the ideal landscape image of the house in the forest which

Point Defiance Park. Photo: E. A. Lynn, c. 1906 (courtesy of Washington State Historical Society)

has been adopted by the upper classes ever since and has continued to dominate the imagery of residential and commercial development in the suburbs. It was laid out with two-lane roads, utility lines buried among the lush second growth fir forest, and houses and gardens placed in clearings. The C. D. Stimson house (1914), with its oval lawn and elaborate planting of shrubs and flowering trees creating a separate space inside the forest, is a typical example. At "Thornewood" on American Lake in Tacoma the gardens were treated as walled or hedged enclosures within the forest with vistas aligned on the lake or Mount Rainier.

By 1910 there was a consensus among landscape designers that a natural approach was most appropriate for the design of gardens and suburbs in this region. Classical landscapes were rarely attempted, probably because they require such high levels of maintenance in the damper western part of the state. A notable exception is Charles Adams Platt's exquisite Merrill house (1909) in Seattle. By placing the house close to the road and the carriage house on the next street Platt created a generous level area for the formal garden where the beds were changed with the seasons. The adjoining lot was treated as a small park which set off the elegant house by folding it into the broader landscape.

City Beautiful improvements were proposed but few materialized. However, the Rainier Vista on the University of Washington campus, the only surviving feature of the Alaska-Yukon-Pacific Exposition (1909), is a reminder of the grandiloquent gesture of which the City Beautiful movement was capable. Indeed, when Mount Rainier is visible this boulevard is still one of the most memorable man-made landscapes in the state.

Merrill house, c. 1914 (courtesy of Washington State Historical Society)

The Olmsted Brothers had been consultants to the campus for several years. But their loosely organized scheme of courtyards was rejected in 1915 in favor of one by Bebb & Gould which was more closely modeled on the quadrangles of Oxford and Cambridge. Bebb & Gould established a pattern of landscape development in which one moved from a series of axially organized formal quadrangles to progressively wilder landscapes at the edges, a pattern which began to be eroded in the fifties when the university started to expand on a previously unanticipated scale.

By the twenties, landscape design in Washington had achieved a degree of regional identity which surpassed that of architecture. Elmer Grey, a member of the architectural establishment of Southern California, felt that the region had not yet found itself architecturally but marveled at its parks and suburbs. This regional identity was almost entirely due to the lush stands of second growth fir which Grey, mistakenly, believed to be virgin timber. There were local designers who consciously strove to fashion an appropriate idiom for the region such as Otto Holmdahl, a Swedish naval architect who had an extensive residential practice in the western part of the state. At Madera (1925), on Gravelly Lake, he created an eclectic arrangement of spaces carved out of the forest with Japanese, Spanish, and Italian gardens. But the beautifully graded lawns near the house emphasized the edge of the forest where dogwoods and other understory trees were brought forward. At "Kewn" (c. 1923) F. J. Cole created a series of long glades among the firs in which exotic flowers and shrubs were naturalized.

Kewn. Photo: Lawrence Lindsley, c. 1925 (courtesy of Photo Collection, UW Library)

Causland Park (1920) in Anacortes by Louis LePage, although outside the mainstream of landscape design, is one of the finest landscapes of the decade. Built to honor the dead of World War I, its superbly crafted and highly plastic retaining walls and band shelter establish a fusion of built form and landscape which is quite remarkable.

Longview (1922) by Hare & Hare, with George Kessler as consultant, was one of the most ambitious planned towns built in the region. Yet the plan with its central square, radial streets, and crescent shaped park separating the segregated residential districts is old fashioned. Its success depended on reaching the anticipated ultimate population and it did not attempt to deal with the issue of regional character. This criticism could also be leveled at the Olmsted Brothers' partially completed scheme for the state capitol in Olympia (1928). Its Beaux Arts planning is a typical product of the City Beautiful era.

The thirties were dominated by the public works program of the Works Progress Administration, and Civilian Conservation Corps. The Arboretum of the University of Washington in Washington Park (1939–41) has a series of beautifully crafted structures such as the lodges and the belvedere overlooking the principal feature, Azalea Way, a former speed track converted into a glade designed to provide a succession of spring flowering displays. Butler Sturtevant was the landscape designer for several housing schemes such as Holly Park in Seattle, the naval housing at Bremerton, and Yesler Terrace in Seattle. The latter is an especially humane housing scheme with its hedge-enclosed gardens. But the most impressive projects of the decade are Moran State Park and the Reclamation Bureau's irrigation scheme in central and eastern Washington. Ellsworth Storey's structures around the lower lake at Moran State Park (1934–41) are reminiscent of an English landscape park of the eighteenth century in

Longview, c. 1928 (courtesy of Photo Collection, UW Library)

their siting, although they lack the symbolic meaning and explicit references to classicism of the latter, and instead glorify rusticity in heroic terms. The Columbia River Basin project was one of the greatest landscape transformations ever made in the Northwest. The ten dams on the Columbia River brought water and cheap power to the region. But the green cities which Lewis Mumford hoped would be created as a result of the irrigation never materialized. The inherent conservatism of so many of these public works projects is revealed in the design of the town of Grand Coulee at the base of the dam. Its plan of gently curving roads and a central parkway leading down to the river could have come straight out of the City Beautiful era.

Bathhouses, Moran State Park. Photo: Grant Hildebrand

Grand Coulee Dam (courtesy of Washington State Historical Society)

The Moderne, which was popular with architects in the thirties, made little impact on landscape design in any part of the country. Designs were invariably formal like Noble Hoggson's entry garden (1933) at the Seattle Art Museum. However, Butler Sturtevant's Pigott garden (1947) in The Highlands is a late but magnificent Moderne creation with its curving flight of stairs, rounded corners, and ribbon- and crosslet-pierced balustrade.

The development of a Northwest residential idiom by John Yeon and Pietro Belluschi in Oregon and by William Bain, Paul Hayden Kirk, and Roland Terry in Washington was paralleled by the landscape practice of John and Carol Grant. The Grants were influenced by Japanese gardens and the work of the English Arts & Crafts landscape designer Gertrude Jekyll and from these sources evolved a landscape idiom of spaces formed entirely with plant material. They advocated the use of native plants or nonnative plants of similar habit and character and emphasized the textural qualities of plants rather than their color. Like Thomas Church and other contemporary Californian designers they created illusions of greater space by the use of rhythmically flowing curves, but unlike their Californian contemporaries they rigorously eschewed architectonic devices and did not attempt to integrate interior and exterior spaces. Their superb plantsmanship was at its best on large sites, but even in small gardens such as the Meyer house (1941) in Seattle the carefully chosen planting in the courtyard and the subtle grading and planting outside complement the house beautifully.

The Grants' work established a strong sense of regional identity but its essentially conservative nature becomes apparent when it is compared with Roland Terry's own house (1937) in Seattle with its small enclosed entry and living room gardens which fuse house and garden together in a way that anticipates the work of the fifties.

By the fifties the burgeoning suburbs of Tacoma, Seattle, and Everett had adopted a pattern of development of low density, sprawling, automobile-oriented living which differed little from that of California except in specific details. Indeed, *Sunset* magazine specifically advocated Californian models for use in the Northwest. Privacy was paramount and could be easily achieved by inserting buildings into the forest. But the changed concept of the garden as an outdoor living room which became popular in California in the forties is as much a western phenomenon as it is peculiar to California. Paved patios, decks, covered porches and loggias, barbecue pits, and the use of borrowed scenery occur as frequently in Washington as they do in California. What is distinctly different, however, is the presence of the forest and the different scale that it creates, and the smaller incidence of recreational features such as swimming pools and tennis courts. This reflects not only the problems of accommodation on steep hillsides but lower levels of affluence.

In the forties and fifties there was a great fascination with geometry. Pergolas, screens, and paving projected out into the landscape, locking the houses into the trees as in the Russell house (1957)

Roland Terry house. Photo: Dearborn-Masser, 1948 (courtesy of Photo Collection, UW Library)

by William Teufel. Here as in many designs of this period the modular geometry and the extensive use of gravel suggest the influence of Japan. In the Dowell garden (1957) Tuefel treated the ground plane as an abstract three-dimensional composition of different textures stepping down toward the water and the view.

Abstract forms were also explored as in the Beryl Davis garden (1958) in Medina by Elizabeth Brazeau, which is very similar to much of the work of Garrett Eckbo and Robert Royston. Modular

Russell house. Photo: Dearborn-Masser, c. 1957 (courtesy of Photo Collection UW Library)

Dowell garden. Photo: Dearborn-Masser, c. 1957 (courtesy of Photo Collection, UW Library)

geometry was used by Roland Terry to organize a very small patio for the Hauberg house (1956) containing numerous works of art.

Yet while local designers such as Glen Hunt, William Teufel, Roberta Wightman, Elizabeth Brazeau, and Robert Chittock were exploring themes similar to those of Californian designers, it was the Californian Thomas Church who demonstrated that older traditions could still be invoked to produce fine landscapes. The Bloedel garden (1952–78) was literally hacked out of the forest,

Hauberg garden. Photo: Dearborn-Masser, 1957 (courtesy of Photo Collection, UW Library)

but it is a magnificent essay in the manner of the landscape park, although the complete acceptance of the qualities of the rough and dense native forest give a very different spatial feeling. The Wagner garden (1956–64) by contrast is a remodeling of an existing formal garden. The pavilion, quatrefoil-shaped swimming pool, and the subtle colors of the massed rhododendrons, azaleas, dogwoods, and bedding plants recall the restrained elegance of Platt's work.

It was not until the sixties that landscape designers became more consistently involved in nonresidential and larger-scale projects. Richard Haag's remodeling of the Seattle Center (1964) into a high density urban park with restaurants, shops, museums, recreational features, and amusement rides demonstrated convincingly that the European concept of a park, which had much in common with amusement parks and pleasure gardens, was an idea whose time had arrived.

Most projects, however, were suburban in nature and applied on a larger scale the concepts that had been explored in the garden. In many of these projects, such as the Ridgeway Dormitories at Western Washington University in Bellingham, also by Richard Haag, the solution was to place the buildings among the trees. At Battelle Northwest headquarters (1966–70) in Seattle, the same designer conceived an elegant landscape park with buildings beautifully sited around a small lake in an introverted landscape which is in principle no different from the private estate.

A series of designs of the late sixties explored the potentials of the mini-park, with challenging and exciting alternatives to standard play equipment. A particularly good example is Firehouse Park (1968) in Seattle, again by Richard Haag, with its careful use of old paths and basement walls and commando nets and lookout towers. Luther Burbank Park (1974) on Mercer Island by Jongejan/Gerrard, and E. J. Roberts Park (1977) in South Bend by Talley & Associates, explored similar ideas in the context of suburban sites.

The seventies have produced a series of projects of more than regional significance most of which are urban. Lawrence Halprin has designed a number of handsome fountains in such locations as the Capitol Park in Olympia and the Washington Water and Power headquarters in Spokane. But the special circumstances of a park on a concrete lid cover over the freeway in Seattle brought forth from Halprin's firm a splendid and baroque tour-de-force in which a concrete abstraction of a mountain cascade produces white noise to drown out the sounds of the freeway and invite exploration and active participation. The design is most successful in establishing visual linkages to the city but leaves much to be desired in its physical accessibility. As a prototype for solving the divisiveness created by freeways, it is likely to remain an isolated example owing to its high cost and the technical difficulties of construction.

Richard Haag and Fred Bassetti's Federal Building (1974) in Seattle celebrates movement with a series of staircases flowing down a steep hillside in a highly theatrical and baroque manner which is, however, a powerfully imaginative alternative to the conventional single-level plaza.

Luther Burbank Park

Jones & Jones's schemes for Pioneer Square and Occidental Square (1972) in the Pioneer Square Historic District are sensitive essays in a simple but vigorous style which is not historically authentic but which provides an appropriate setting for the restored buildings in this part of Seattle. The contrast with the Waterfall Park (1978) by Sasaki, Dawson & DeMay of Boston is a most telling one. Waterfall Park is a design whose sophistication seems completely out of place in the robust Pacific Northwest, particularly in the context of the period architecture of Pioneer Square.

Gas Works Park (1978) by Richard Haag is a notable example of reclamation. The former gasworks site has been reclaimed into a high density park, conceived in the spirit of the old amusement parks but accommodating many new uses. The old cracking towers serve not only as a tangible link with the past but also as a rich and complex piece of sculpture.

The new animal exhibits at the Woodland Park Zoo (1979) by Jones & Jones are designed to display animals in social groupings, in environments that replicate closely their natural habitats. The location for each exhibit was determined by a process of establishing the best "fit" between a potential bioclimatic zone and the site's existing vegetation and microclimate.

The Weyerhaeuser Company headquarters (1971) in Federal Way by Sasaki, Walker & Associates is a notable attempt at integrating a large building into a large-scale landscape. Indeed the large structure designed as a stepped dam in the center of a formal allée is as much a landscape as it is a building. The *burolandschaft* treatment of the interior spaces (a system of free interior planning that eliminates partitions) and the generous provision of planting spaces on the exterior of the building have created a fusion of building and site which though very different in its spatial

Occidental Square. Photo: Grant Jones

character from earlier residential work is nevertheless similar in purpose.

These recent projects suggest positive and exciting new directions in landscape design. But at the same time that they were being conceived it had become clear that, at least in the western part of the state, the loosely controlled growth of the past thirty years had created many social and environmental problems. The challenge of the eighties will be to address these problems, particularly the diminution of natural resources, energy, and water supply and the acceleration of urban growth, by carefully controlling

the rate, location, and quality of new development. Ultimately, some of the most significant work of the seventies may be studies that have addressed these issues such as the Nooksack River Study (1972), the Yakima River Regional Greenway Study (1978), and the Green River Study (1979), all by Jones & Jones.

If these problems can be adequately solved, it is certain that landscape design in Washington in the future will be very different from that of the past and will be more responsive to the particular characters of the regions within the state.

Gorilla exhibit, Woodland Park Zoo. Photo: Veronica Seyd

Photo History

Factor's house, Fort Nisqually, 1843. See Tacoma/Point Defiance Park. Courtesy of City of Tacoma

Slocum house, 1867. See Vancouver, 10.

Tom Crellin house, 1869. See Oysterville. Courtesy of State Office of Archaeology and Historic Preservation

St. Paul's Episcopal Church, 1870. See Port Gamble.
Courtesy of Photo Collection, UW Library

Olmstead Place, 1875. See Ellensburg.

Perkins house, 1880s. See The Palouse/Colfax.

*Colman Building, 1888. Stephen J. Meany. See Seattle/Central Downtown, 4. Photo: A. Curtis
(courtesy of Photo Collection, UW Library)*

Davidson Block, 1889. See Ellensburg.

St Michael's Episcopal Church, 1889. See Yakima/Downtown, 9.

Pioneer Building, 1889–90. Elmer Fisher. See Seattle/Pioneer Square, 4.

Ezra Meeker house, 1890. Farrell & Darmer. See Puyallup. Drawing: Carl A. Darmer
(courtesy of Architectural History Collection, UW Library)

Gamwell house, 1890–92. Longstaff & Black. See Bellingham/Fairhaven, 15.

Board of Education, originally Thurston County Courthouse, 1891–92. W. A. Ritchie. See Olympia, 20. *Courtesy of Photo Collection, UW Library*

Whatcom Museum of History and Art, 1892–93. Alfred Lee. See Bellingham/New Whatcom, 1.
Photo: Rod Slemmons (courtesy of Whatcom Museum of History and Art)

Spokane County Courthouse, 1895. W. A. Ritchie. See Spokane/City Center, 34.

Hoquiam's Castle, 1897. See Hoquiam. Courtesy of State Office of Archaeology and Historic Preservation

Patrick F. Clark house, 1898. Cutter & Malmgren. See Spokane/Browne's Addition, 2.
Courtesy of Eastern Washington State Historical Society

W. C. Wakefield house, 1898–1900. Cutter & Malmgren. See Spokane/Browne's Addition, 6.

Fairmont Cemetery Chapel, c. 1900. Kirtland K. Cutter. See Spokane/Environs, 1.

Broadway High School, 1902. W. E. Boone and J. M. Corner.
See Seattle/Capitol Hill, 66. Photo: A. Curtis (courtesy of Photo Collection, UW Library)

Hallett house, 1903. See Columbia Plateau/Medical Lake.
Courtesy of State Office of Archaeology and Historic Preservation

Thomas Bordeaux house, 1903. W. D. Kimball. See Seattle/Capitol Hill, 43.

Lowe house, 1904. See Columbia Plateau/Cheney.

W. R. Rust house, 1905. Ambrose J. Russell and Everett P. Babcock. See Tacoma/Stadium-Seminary, 20.
Photo: Albert Barnes, c. 1906 (courtesy of Photo Collection, UW Library)

Mineral Lake Lodge, 1906. See Trans-Cascade Routes and Landmarks.
Courtesy of State Office of Archaeology and Historic Preservation

Johanson house, 1909. Cutter & Malmgren. See Seattle/Capitol Hill, 1.

Pacific County Courthouse, 1910–11. C. Lewis Wilson. See South Bend.
Courtesy of State Office of Archaeology and Historic Preservation

Heffernan house, 1915. Cutter & Malmgren. See Seattle/Madison Park, 28.

Capitol Group, 1917–1920s. Wilder & White. See Olympia/Capitol Campus. Photo: A. Curtis, 1939
(courtesy of Photo Collection, UW Library)

Causland Memorial Park, 1920. Louis LePage. See Anacortes.

Capitol Theater, 1920. Frederick Mercy, Sr. See Yakima/Downtown, 5.
Courtesy of State Office of Archaeology and Historic Preservation

L'Amourita Apartments, c. 1925. See Seattle/Eastlake/Cascade, 13.

St. John's Episcopal Cathedral, 1926–54. Whitehouse & Price. See Spokane/Rockwood and Manito Park, 2.

Seattle Tower, 1928–29. Albertson, Wilson, & Richardson. See Seattle/Central Downtown, 10.
Photo: A Curtis (courtesy of Photo Collection, UW Library)

Cascade Lake bathhouses, 1930s. Ellsworth Storey. See San Juan Islands. Photo: Grant Hildebrand

U.S. Public Health Service Hospital, 1934. Bebb & Gould; John Graham, Sr. See Seattle/First Hill, 28. Photo: C. F. Todd (courtesy of Photo Collection, UW Library)

Pepsi Bottling Company, c. 1935. See Vancouver, 9.

Thiry house, 1936. Paul Thiry. See Seattle/Madison Park and Denny Blaine, 33.

Sproule house, 1936. John R. Sproule. See Seattle/Laurelhurst, 5.

Lake Wilderness Lodge, 1950. Young, Richardson Carleton & Detlie. See Lake Washington East Shore/Environs.

Hauberg house, 1954. Roland Terry. See Seattle/Madison Park and Denny Blaine, 23.

Washington Water Power Company, 1959. Kenneth W. Brooks and Bruce M. Walker. See Spokane/Environs, E.

Zema house, 1965. Gene Zema. See Seattle/Laurelhurst, 11. Photo: Roy O. Welch

Sherwood Center, 1968. Adkison, Leigh, Sims, Cuppage. See Walla Walla, 13. Photo: Roland C. Colliander

House, 1968. Hobbs/Fukui. See Mercer Island, 17. Photo: Art Hupy

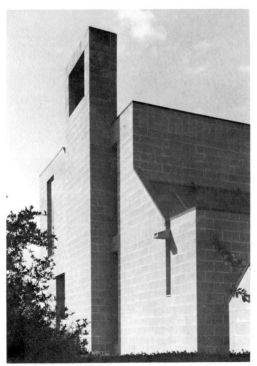

House, 1970. Olson/Walker. See Seattle/Queen Anne Hill, 19.

Weyerhaeuser Headquarters, 1971. Skidmore, Owings & Merrill. See Tacoma/Environs. Photo: Ezra Stoller

House, 1972. Wendell Lovett. See Lake Washington East Shore/Environs, 9.

Central Plaza, 1972. Kirk/Wallace/McKinley. (Also Kane Hall, 1971. Walker, McGough, Foltz, Lyerla.)
See Seattle/University of Washington. Photo: Joseph Freeman (courtesy of UW)

Tulalip Community Center, 1974. The Bumgardner Partnership. See Everett/Environs.

Social Sciences Building, 1974. Ibsen Nelson & Associates. See Bellingham/Western Washington University.

Camp Orkila, 1976. TRA. See San Juan Islands.

Arts, Music, and Drama Complex, 1977. Brooks/Hensley/Creager. See Columbia Plateau/Tri-Cities. Photo: Gordon Perry

Health, Physical Education, Recreation, and Athletics Facility, 1977. Adkison, Leigh, Sims, Cuppage. See Columbia Plateau/Cheney. Photo: Ritch D. Fenrich

House, 1979. Barnett Schorr Miller Company. See Mercer Island, 5.

Geographic Areas

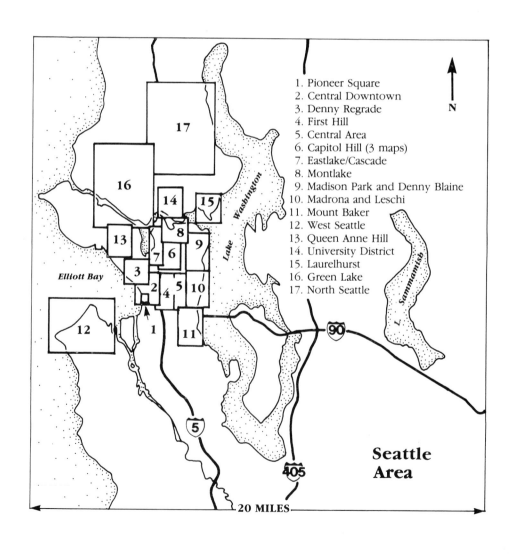

1. Pioneer Square
2. Central Downtown
3. Denny Regrade
4. First Hill
5. Central Area
6. Capitol Hill (3 maps)
7. Eastlake/Cascade
8. Montlake
9. Madison Park and Denny Blaine
10. Madrona and Leschi
11. Mount Baker
12. West Seattle
13. Queen Anne Hill
14. University District
15. Laurelhurst
16. Green Lake
17. North Seattle

N

17

16

14

15

Lake Washington

13

8

3

7 6

9

Elliott Bay

2

4 5 10

L. Sammamish

12

1

11

90

5

405

Seattle Area

20 MILES

Seattle

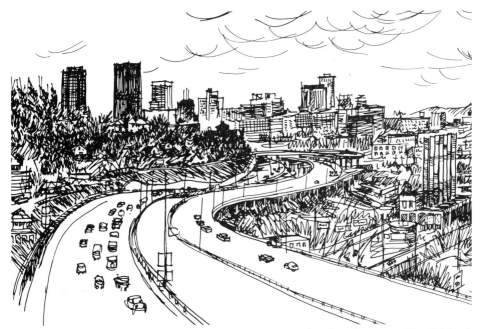

Downtown Seattle and Interstate 5, as seen from the north. Drawing: Victor Steinbrueck

Seattle, the Northwest's largest city, is blessed with a setting unsurpassed in natural splendor by any other city in the country. Located over a hundred miles east of the Pacific Ocean, out of range of its cold fogs and harsh winds, the city is still bordered by bodies of water on both sides. Puget Sound lies on the west with the generous indentation of Elliott Bay; Lake Washington lies on the east. The Lake Washington Ship Canal cuts through the city to the north linking the Sound with Lake Washington via Salmon Bay, Lake Union, Portage Bay, and Union Bay. Green Lake is another relatively large urban body of water. Altogether there is an extraordinary amount of waterfront available for private ownership and public use.

If much of Seattle's specialness as a place stems from this frequently encountered intersection of land and water, the juxtaposition of sky and mountains—the Olympics on the west, the Cascades on the east and southeast—reinforces the beholder's sense that this is a particularly favored place. Mt. Rainier has an almost palpable presence that astonishes the eye and mind, particularly when, as the skies clear, its snowy cone materializes, reducing the rest of the world to a more human scale.

Built on many hills, Seattle is a city of high bluffs, precipitous descents, and wooded ravines. As in many other U.S. cities, the resident powers have seen fit to rearrange the landscape at various times and to generally ignore the possibilities for environmental delight implicit in the topography. Seattle's gravelly, glacial geology particularly facilitated aggressive environmental design. Early downtown regrading projects were conducted along First Avenue in the 1870s and in most of the central business district after the 1889 fire. Conversion of the north-south streets into level planes which step up from the water to the top of the central ridge proceeded as downtown moved northward in the 1900s. Also in this period the whole south end of the downtown was remade with slices of land taken out between First and Beacon hills and off the top of Jackson Street. The earth was used to fill the tidal flats

between Beacon Hill and West Seattle and to provide space for the burgeoning railyards. The East and West waterways were opened south of Elliott Bay to the Duwamish River leaving between them Harbor Island, now the site of an aggressively managed, highly rationalized container port.

Denny Hill, one of the most important topographical features of early Seattle, comprised sixty-two city blocks. The top featured a famous hotel and the first city park. Under the direction of Seattle's most renowned city engineer, R. H. Thomson, the hill was leveled in several phases beginning in 1897. Sluiced down by the method of hydraulicking that Thomson observed in the

Denny Hill regrade, c. 1910 (courtesy of Photo Collection, UW Library)

California goldfields, the hill produced enough earth to fill the rest of the tidal flats and, at the same time, to furnish garden designers and nurseries with a long-lasting supply of boulders for retaining walls and rockeries.

Though downtown is the most completely man-made landscape, the residential districts to the north, south, east, and west have been relentlessly subjugated to the grid street system. Only in shoreline areas, long considered unbuildable, are winding and looping roadways likely to occur. An extensive park system, discussed by David Streatfield in his introductory essay, and the propensity of nature to pay back double any effort at landscaping, has given Seattle a garden city appearance par excellence.

That Seattle is an industrial city in addition to being a major import-export center is clear to anyone who explores the Duwamish–Green River corridor to the south or the northwest section of the Lake Washington Ship Canal, largely devoted to marine industry.

Although Seattle has the reputation of being rain drenched all year, statistics reveal that it has about the same annual rainfall as Chicago, not known for rainy weather. However, Seattle, like other northwest coastal cities, has many fewer hours of sunlight than Chicago and therein lies the reason for its sodden image. Although long periods of overcast skies with a fine rain or mist have influenced the development of a regional strain of residentially scaled wooden building, the moist air has had little effect on mainstream commercial and institutional buildings. The latter building types, adopting more advanced

technologies, have followed national patterns. Thus, Seattle's built environment is interchangeable with that of other major U.S. cities.

Predictably, the most dramatic approach to Seattle is by water. The Washington State Ferries, the major public water transportation system for the Puget Sound area, give everyone the opportunity to experience the splendid passage across Elliott Bay to the waterfront. From the bay, the city skyline appears as a man-made mountainscape of office towers rising above the hilly terrain that rolls up from the shoreline. Closer to the shore the carpet of low-rise buildings appears to blanket the slopes.

Approaching Seattle from the east is quite a different experience involving a descent from the semi-wilderness of the Cascades through the foothill regions and logged-over lands to the rural-suburban fringe of housing tracts, shopping centers, and strip development. This gradually intensifies toward the metropolitan center though it is interrupted by the broad surfaces of Lake Sammamish, Lake Washington, and other smaller lakes. Interstate 90 zips through the outskirts, crosses Mercer Island, and breaks out at Lake Washington with a panorama of the city's eastern ridge, where it dives through a tunnel and emerges just south of downtown.

From the north or south, today's traveler is likely to use Interstate 5, the 1965 freeway that bisects the city and is known in its central downtown section as "the ditch." Another alternative is U.S. 99, the old Pacific Coast Highway which for its downtown passage becomes the Alaskan Way Viaduct. Both projects

Seattle in the 1870s, looking north from First and Columbia. Photo: A. Curtis (courtesy of Photo Collection, UW Library)

have done violence to the environment. Interstate 5 performed a type of lobotomy directed at relieving what was viewed as an intense traffic disorder with little consideration of the injury that would result from severing some of the city's vital nerves. U.S. 99 created a no-man's-land between downtown and the waterfront. As of today, these environmental actions seem irreversible in spite of the band-aid of Freeway Park applied to one piece of the I-5 cut.

The history of Seattle is bound to that of the Northwest region which it has dominated for so long. The rich social history, much of it involved with the history of the labor movement, is beyond the scope of this book. For those who wish to broaden their knowledge, we recommend Roger Sale's *Seattle, Past to Present* as a comprehensive single work. Other useful sources are listed in the bibliography.

Seattle's early history is marked by isolation and the suggestion of a conspiracy on the part of the developing world to ignore her potential to become Queen City of the Northwest. The early settlers, the small band that migrated from Oregon in the late fall of 1851 to what is now Alki Point, were not so much motivated by the possibilities of developing an agreeable place to live as they were by the certainty that exploitation of the natural resources would make them rich. Possibly this narrowly defined goal was the only one sufficiently powerful to keep them going through the many ordeals of the pioneer experience. In any case, most of what was produced by the community for the first twenty years or so was for consumption in other places.

Seattle was platted in 1853. The founders, the Denny brothers, the Borens, the Bells, and Doc Maynard, divided up the flatland so that each could have access to the water. They relinquished some of the best land to Henry Yesler, who like Maynard came from Ohio, but unlike Maynard was a shrewd businessman.

Panorama from Denny Hill. Photo: Peterson Brothers, 1878 (courtesy of Photo Collection, UW Library)

(For detailed and colorful portraits of these early figures, read Murray Morgan's *Skid Road.*) Yesler's steam-powered sawmill gave Seattle its first industry. Skid Road, now Yesler Way, accommodated the logs that were skidded downhill from the wooded slopes above the mill and wharf and thence to waiting ships. This timber built a lot of San Francisco in the Gold Rush era as well as the modest town that was Seattle from 1853 to the 1880s.

A primitive-looking outpost with wooden shanties and stump-filled yards lining the rutted roads along the bay, Seattle's early growth was stunted when word of the so-called Indian Uprisings of 1855 reached potential settlers. In 1862 the population was still only 182, perhaps a tenth the size of Olympia, the territorial capital. Remote and casual as Seattle was, it won the territorial university in 1861 and put up a Classical Revival building, painted white and surrounded by a picket fence. Though

modest in size, the structure was lavishly detailed in comparison with other buildings, and imposing enough to give the settlement a serious look.

The Civil War years slowed migration to a trickle. By 1869 when the town was incorporated, its assets were the university, a hospital, a school, two churches, a bank, the sawmill, a newspaper, telegraph service, several commercial enterprises, and a collection of houses. Further development would depend, as everyone in the Northwest knew, on transcontinental transportation.

Railroad fever gripped the region in the 1870s. When the Northern Pacific chose Tacoma over Seattle for its terminus, the frustrated citizens decided to build their own line with their own hands. The line was optimistically called the Seattle and Walla Walla, but it stopped not far out of town. Still, the publicity that accrued to the city boosted its national reputation and brought additional population. Besides, the rails stretched far enough to service the nearby coal fields that were then purchased, along with the railroad itself, by Henry Villard. The entrepreneurial efforts of this future president of the Northern Pacific made Seattle a major exporter of coal—again to San Francisco—by the end of the decade.

Not till 1883 with the coming of the Northern Pacific did Seattle get securely tied to the rest of the country by rail. Ten years later Jim Hill's Great Northern arrived and finally in 1909 the Chicago, Milwaukee and St. Paul reached Puget Sound. Though the crash of 1893 slowed development the city swiftly revived and the long boom period continued. The closing decades of the century were most significant in the transformation of Seattle from a frontier town into a first-class city. Sale's book contributes importantly to unraveling how it was that Seattle beat out Tacoma and Portland even though the rails came later. He ascribes it to the economic diversity and the entrepreneurial zeal which had made Seattle the region's mercantile center by the end of the 1880s.

The 1889 fire that destroyed the city accelerated its development, as a similar fire that year did in Spokane. By the end of the 1880s, the population had leaped from 3,500 to 43,500. Cheap electricity was introduced in Seattle around 1890 to light public and private buildings and power an electric tramway. By the beginning of the twentieth century there was a municipally owned water supply, an improved sewer system, and a reconstructed waterfront beside a solidly rebuilt central business district. Railroad construction, expanding lumber mills, and fish canneries drew a broad range of

nationalities: Chinese, Scandinavians, Germans, Finns, Englishmen, Irishmen, and Canadians made up the labor market. Finally, the Alaska Gold Rush of 1897 and a barrage of propaganda put out by the Chamber of Commerce certified Seattle as Queen City of the Northwest. The "Seattle Spirit" had triumphed.

To celebrate, the city staged the Alaska-Yukon-Pacific Exposition in 1909, the year before the population hit 250,000. This boom period saw the beginning of business expansion uptown and the development of a ring of streetcar suburbs from First to Capitol Hill and Queen Anne Hill, and in the area north of Lake Union. Further away, on the shores of Lake Washington, the streetcar lines created well-to-do suburban enclaves, but the most exclusive effort of this kind was the private residential park to the north, The Highlands, laid out by the Olmsted Brothers in 1909. Although there were still large areas of undeveloped land and farms within the city limits, people increasingly chose their places of residence far from downtown.

Seattle's brush with the City Beautiful movement initiated by the Olmsted Plan of 1903 came in 1911 when the *Plan of Seattle*, commissioned by the Municipal Plans Commission from civil engineer Virgil Bogue, was published. Bogue had a national reputation as a city planner and engineer as well as firsthand knowledge of Seattle. His plan followed the format influenced by the Beaux Arts' academic planning tradition that modeled all cities after Paris with tree-planted boulevards, malls, and cross-axial vistas terminated by Neo-

Regrade on Third Avenue, looking northeast toward Marion Street. Photo: A. Curtis, 1905
(courtesy of Photo Collection, UW Library)

Classical buildings. The centerpiece of the grand design was, as elsewhere, the civic center. Both the formal conception of the civic center and its siting on reasonably priced land on the fringe of downtown, in this case the Denny Regrade area, tallied with the schemes for other U.S. civic centers, notably those of Cleveland, St. Louis, Denver, and San Francisco. Where Bogue revealed a concern for the specifics of the place was in his transportation program. Foreseeing the linear expansion of Seattle for considerable distances north and south and the complications of topography, it stressed the necessity of a rapid transit

system. Bogue's plan also endorsed the work of the Olmsteds in planning for Seattle's parklands and coastline.

Roger Sale gives an excellent analysis of the plan and its defeat in the election of 1912. For the most part it was simply too grandiose to be believable; it was produced in a vacuum and voted down by an uninformed public. Only the harbor and waterfront plan, adopted separately, was considered worthy of public expenditure. People of influence who were both knowledgeable and sympathetic to the plan failed to work for its adoption. According to Sale, their apathy was symptomatic of an anomic withdrawal from the urban scene, a civic complacency produced by the new era of technology that permitted people to live in the manicured suburban countryside and do business in the city without spending too much time in between. The population pressures of the future were as academic as the need for a civic center.

Following a boom produced by World War I, Seattle's economy slowed to a near no-growth state that lasted through the twenties and hit bottom in the thirties along with the rest of the country. Downtown grew modestly, developing a new uptown center for retail trade, but relative to the preceding boom and to what was happening to the rest of the country in the roaring twenties, the volume of building was down considerably. Suburban development consolidated

within the boundaries set in the teens. Pseudo-Tudor builder's cottages filled in pockets of undeveloped land. Again, Roger Sale gives a particularly compelling portrait of Seattle during this period as a place that was great to grow up in because the citizens tended their own gardens, literally and figuratively, maintaining a stable and geographically coherent city that knew its limits.

Children were not all that interwar Seattle nurtured. The beginnings of local culture evolved in these years. The university took its place among America's major public institutions. New centers for art, music, and the performing arts blossomed, among them the influential Cornish School. A first generation of architects born, bred, and trained in the Northwest began to practice. By the late 1930s, the first strong hints appeared of

City Hall Park. Photo: A. Curtis (courtesy of Photo Collection, UW Library)

B-29s being assembled at Boeing plant during World War II (courtesy of The Boeing Company)

the residential architecture that would bloom in the postwar years to symbolize the Northwest life style. Local designers developed it in Seattle drawing on earlier imported Craftsman, Prairie, and Shingle styles; on Oriental, especially Japanese, models; on the thirties work of Belluschi and Yeon in nearby Portland; and on versions of the European International Style much filtered by distance and the timber tradition. These years were the formative ones for Paul Hayden Kirk, Roland Terry, Fred Bassetti, and others. Very little work, though, was actually constructed before 1946.

The quiet decades between the wars laid the groundwork for later explosive growth and development. Of the several important catalysts during these years none counted for more than the successful management of The Boeing Com-

pany. Through its infancy in the twenties, the crash, and the depression, it grew to be one of the country's largest and most innovative aircraft manufacturers. Though Boeing would in time become practically synonymous with the region's economy, other productive forces were at work too, largely in the public sector. Just as Boeing prospered from military orders, so the naval rearmament of the thirties revived Puget Sound's marine industry. On the local level, public entrepreneurship at Seattle City Light developed the hydroelectric power of the Skagit River and plugged into the federally developed resources of the Bonneville Power Administration.

When war came, it triggered Seattle's second boom, one that still continues albeit unevenly. Aircraft and shipbuilding led the surge along with the direct expansion of the myriad army and navy installations around Puget Sound. Overcrowding became commonplace as war housing, jerrybuilt additions, and backyard rental units housed the thousands of immigrants. Though not a time of distinguished architecture and environmental design, the war years turned round the local economy, exposed countless service people to the pleasures of the city, and laid the basis for the postwar expansion.

The blessings of a stability produced by economic depression are easier to count in hindsight. Even so, they were quickly forgotten by Seattle after World War II. Within thirty years, the region more than doubled in population, and the city increased by roughly 50 percent. The war had started the massive migration to Seattle; the strength of the local economy kept it going. Boeing dominated this second boom. In one of the boldest and best conceived initiatives ever by that conservative species, the American corporation, Boeing successfully created the jet air transport from its experience with large military jet aircraft. In one stroke Seattle's economy emerged as an independent force in the world, no longer linked to annual defense appropriations in far off Washington, D.C.

During the second boom Seattle's economy matured. This meant internal differentiation and a strengthening of the local economy, more self-sufficiency, less dependence on other economic centers. This new status compounded the simple growth of the population by a parallel growth in relative wealth. For all but the super rich the postwar decades permitted ever increasing levels of consumption, and this seldom benefited the environment.

The major pushes of the city to the north and to the east across Lake Washington took place roughly between 1950 and 1965. By the end of that period, the anti-urban movement that began in the 1900s had come to fruition. Yet, suburbanism was branded as mindless and decried by critics as leading irrevocably to provincialism and anti-intellectualism. The morphology of postwar development with its tracts of ranch houses, open-ended commercial strips, and shopping centers had a sameness that suggested nothing more behind it than profits and inertia. Still, for all their physical monotony, many such neighborhoods have survived as pleasant living environments, simply the automobile-oriented equivalents of the earlier streetcar suburbs. Now, with mature vegetation, they have achieved as much diversity as their predecessors.

One analyst who worried about the implications of Seattle's postwar self-satisfaction with limited horizons was Constance Green, author of *American Cities in the Growth of the Nation*, published in 1957. Looking at the city's aging residents, she foresaw continuing "stand-patism" and conservatism instead of a return to the entrepreneurship and radicalism of the past. Green was wrong. Though new analysts have yet to examine just why, certain main events are clear. First, a brief recession in world air traffic dealt the local economy a fierce blow while the rest of the country still basked in Vietnam War era boom times. Staggered at first, Seattle revived as the new diversity gradually picked up the slack. In the local stereotype of the time, the unemployed aircraft engineer opened a successful health food restaurant. By the time the 1973–74 recession hit the rest of the country, Seattle was on the way up. This time revival drew on a new national mood embodied in the environmental movement. Fifteen years earlier Green had written, "the visitor will find little to remind him of the pioneer spirit that built Seattle in the wilderness." Since then Seattle has become the first choice of a new wave of urban pioneers and perhaps their favorite large American city.

The thirty-year boom was back on track, but now influenced by a minor but crucial urban revolution. Here, as in other U.S. cities, the inner core partially abandoned in the previous decades began to be resettled by a younger generation, children of the suburbs with a new taste for urban life. This rediscovery has spotlighted the old city, and the places with roots like the Pioneer Square area and the Pike Place Market. Thus, historic preservation in Seattle which began with a few lonely voices—Richard White, Ralph Anderson, and Victor Steinbrueck, among them—has been carried along by younger residents and newcomers. They have spiffed up the neighborhoods and in the process created one of the country's strongest neighborhood activist movements. The many residential architectural delights of Seattle now receive the loving care they merit. So do some of the other places, recycled schools and firehouses, gussied up satellite commercial centers, parks, even corners of downtown. The urban pioneers and their environmentalism have done well by Seattle. It may be too much to expect them also to defeat the drive toward empty monumentalism downtown.

Pike Place Market (courtesy of Seattle Post-Intelligencer)

Pioneer Square

Accounts of the original settlement of Seattle, now the Pioneer Square Historic District, are spiced with acts of bravery, aggression, open-handedness, meanness, foolishness, practicality, and eccentricity. Larger than life figures like Henry Yesler and Doc Maynard are now memorialized in buildings and streets. Though inanimate, many of the buildings in the area do have the kind of visual exuberance that evokes the city's early pluck and confidence.

Here the town of Seattle, platted in 1853, had its first center consisting of a few wooden shanties and makeshift structures around Henry Yesler's sawmill. Yesler's cookhouse, the first community building, was allegedly carved up and moved elsewhere later. By 1885 there were some 12,000 inhabitants, most of whom lived within a ten-block radius of Yesler Way. Then, on 6 June 1889, a fire ignited by glue boiling over in a basement cabinet factory destroyed twenty-five blocks, virtually the whole city. As in other such catastrophes, notably in Spokane the same year, the destruction unleashed new civic energies. Beginning that year buildings were rebuilt of masonry instead of wood. At the time of the rebuilding, the area was being regraded and raised as much as eighteen feet making some of the new three-story buildings into two-story buildings. Gradually shops moved upstairs and sidewalks covered these temporary lower levels, now a trumped-up tourist attraction called Underground Seattle.

Following the Alaska Gold Rush, 1897–1905, boom times brought down the old pioneer district. Numerous hotels, bawdy houses, gambling saloons, and other disreputable enterprises took over the old sawmill's skid road; decent businesses began to move north. By World War I, Skid Road had acquired its social meaning as a place where people not logs were on the skids.

Today we need not regret that the commercial center moved on, leaving the area to stagnate. This lack of interest and investment insured that a remarkable stand of urbanistically compatible buildings from the end of the nineteenth century would remain. Streetscapes like that from Pioneer Square south along First Avenue are rare in a modern metropolis forced to reuse the same downtown area over and over.

An artist's view of Pioneer Square, 1880s (courtesy of Photo Collection, UW Library)

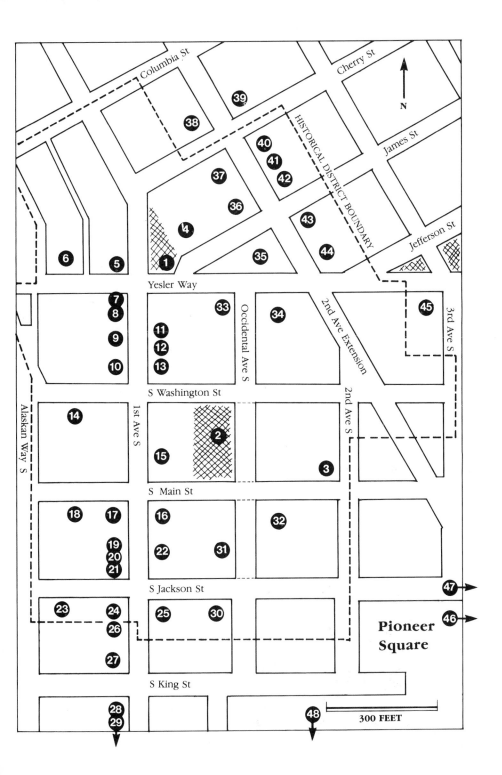

The contemporary commercial architecture of the Chicago School, created by H. H. Richardson, Louis Sullivan, Burnham & Root, and others, provided the architectural inspiration for the area's buildings. The railroads carried the stylistic seeds west through Minneapolis and St. Paul to Northwest cities like Seattle, Tacoma, and Spokane. By the 1950s and 1960s when talk of redevelopment began, there was also, fortunately, a preservation movement in progress. After a decade of battles, a civic ordinance created the Pioneer Square Historic District in 1970. This past decade has witnessed the kind of rehabilitation both respectful of the past and reflective of contemporary taste.

The district is fortunate not only in its buildings but also in its street pattern. The original survey of the Denny and Maynard plats set them askew to each other and created an irregularity in the grid that left several angular public spaces. One such is Pioneer Square, actually a triangle, which features an elaborate cast-iron and glass pergola (1) to shelter people waiting for the trolley. It was designed in 1909 by J. F. Everett and restored in 1970.

Pioneer Square, with Smith Tower in background. Photo: C. F. Todd, 1917 (courtesy of Photo Collection, UW Library)

Contemporary efforts created the main public open space, Occidental Park (2), in 1972, designed by Seattle landscape architects Jones & Jones. This robust but plain plaza fits the area well, though its attempted sculptural gazebo suffers in comparison with the old pergola in Pioneer Square; its rough cobble pavement provides a good foil for the Victorian commercial architecture. Not so fitting is the Waterfall Park (3) at the nearby northeast corner of Second and Main. Designed in 1978 by the eastern landscape architects Sasaki, Dawson & DeMay, it is an expensive and pretentious project, a small enclosed corner lot dominated by rocks and rushing water.

The following accounting of the area's buildings begins back at Pioneer Square.

4 Pioneer Building

4 **Pioneer Building,** 1889–90, rehabilitated
1970–75
Elmer Fisher; Ralph Anderson
606 First Avenue

A fitting expression of the high optimism of
the burgeoning city, piling up stone
doughnuts like lucky horseshoes to frame the
entrance. Alas, an earthquake in 1949 toppled the central square tower that was the
crowning element.

5 **Mutual Life Building,** 1892, addition 1903
Blackwell, James & Eustance, addition
only
605 First Avenue

Fanciful details on a relatively staid design
apparently a composite of several additions.
The site is that of Seattle's first community
building, Yesler's cookhouse.

6 **Traveler's Hotel,** 1914
76–78 Yesler Way

7 **Yesler Building,** 1890–95
Elmer Fisher
Yesler Way and First Avenue S

By the same architect as the Pioneer Building
and also mutilated by the 1949 earthquake.
Fisher, the major architect of Seattle's first
great building period, was a Scot who came
down to Seattle from Victoria and Vancouver,
B.C., presumably seeking ever greater opportunities. In the year after the fire he built
some fifty buildings in the city. For years it
seemed that he had vanished without a trace,
but recent information has revealed that he
ended his long career in Los Angeles working
for the firm of John B. Parkinson, whose
senior partner he himself had hired as a
draftsman in Seattle. Fisher died in Los
Angeles in 1905.

8 **Schwabacher Building,** 1890
Elmer Fisher
105–7 First Avenue S

A major outfitting firm for the Yukon Gold
Rush; the building's ground floor has been
altered.

9 **Terry-Denny Building,** 1889–90
109–15 First Avenue S

A monumental central bay, originally the
hotel entrance, recalls former pretensions.

9, 8, 7 Terry-Denny, Schwabacher, and Yesler buildings

10 Maynard Building

10 **Maynard Building,** 1892, rehabilitated
1975–76
A. Wickersham; Olson/Walker
119 First Avenue S

The most sophisticated of the Chicago School
buildings in the area, it is true to the Sullivanesque principle of weaving spandrel and
pier to create a refined and structurally
expressive design. Also an award-winning
rehabilitation.

11 **Lippy Building,** 1900 or 1902
E. W. Houghton
108 First Avenue S

12 **The City Club,** 1906
112 First Avenue S

13 **State Hotel,** c. 1890
H. Steinman
114–16 First Avenue S

14 **St. Charles Hotel,** 1889
81–85 S Washington Street

15 **Grand Central Building,** 1889, rehabilitated 1971
Ralph Anderson & Partners, rehabilitation
208–20 First Avenue S

Site of John Squire's Opera House and one of
the initial rehabilitation projects that turned
the public attention to the possibilities for
making old buildings as amenable as new.

15 Grand Central Building

16 **Globe Hotel,** 1890
William E. Boone
105–7 S Main St

Romanesque Revival Style missing its cornice
as are many of the district's buildings.

17 **Bread of Life Mission,** 1889
91–99 S Main St

18 **Our Home Hotel,** 1895
15–85 S Main Street

19 **Maud Building,** 1889
309–11 First Avenue S

20 **Squire Building,** 1900
C. H. Bebb
317 First Avenue S

21 **Smith Building,** 1900
Max Umbrecht
323 First Avenue S

22 **Seattle Quilt Building,** 1904
Boone & Corner
316 First Avenue S
A clean expression of the structural frame.

23 **Schwabacher Hardware Warehouse,**
1905 or 1909
Boone & Corner
S Jackson Street below First Avenue

24 **Pacific Marine Building,** 1905
Boone & Corner
SW corner First Avenue S and S Jackson
Street

Note the Sullivanesque frieze around the entrance. Terra cotta companies produced this
kind of ornament by the foot to touch up
appropriate areas of otherwise unadorned
commercial buildings

24 Pacific Marine Building

25 **Wax & Raine Building,** 1904
101 S Jackson Street

26 **Seller Building,** 1906
A. Warren Gould
409–17 First Avenue S

27 **Hambach Building,** 1907
Saunders & Lawton
419 First Avenue S

28 **Seattle Hardware,** 1904
A. Wickersham
First Avenue S and S King Street

Referenced to the work of Louis Sullivan, but
much simplified; compare with (10).

29 **Flatiron Building** (formerly Triangle
Hotel), 1908–10, 1979
C. A. Breitung; remodeled by Tonkin
& Greissinger
551 First Avenue S

It may be hard to believe, but this tiny structure once combined commercial uses in the basement and on the first floor with an eight-room hotel above.

30 **Shorey's Book Store,** c. 1925
119 S Jackson Street

A banal block with patches of lovely, whimsical ornament.

31 **Waltham Block,** 1890
311–13 Occidental Avenue S

32 **State Building,** 1890
Elmer Fisher
300–12 Occidental Avenue S
Handsome Chicago School commercial design with the ground floor intact but a somewhat mutilated top.

33 **Korn Building,** 1890
Elmer Fisher
119 Yesler Way

34 **Smith Tower Annex** (formerly Seattle National Bank Building), 1890
John Parkinson
102–8 Occidental Avenue S

A fine example of Romanesque Revival styling used to dignify and embellish the practical and mundane plans of the typical block building with mercantile space on the ground floor and cubbyhole offices above. Although the building may have had a more elaborate cornice before the earthquake, the corner entrance is the focal point for historicist ornament that in the Middle Ages would have adorned a private palace rather than a commercial one. The fenestration is carefully orchestrated from floor to floor to give rhythm and variety.

35 **Sinking Ship Garage,** 1965
Mandeville & Berge
Yesler Way, James Street, and Second Avenue

A striking but uningratiating structure that replaced the more appropriately styled Seattle Hotel.

34 Smith Tower Annex

36 **Butler Block,** 1893
John Parkinson
NW corner Second Avenue and James Street

Formerly a fine hostelry, the building is missing its two upper floors and an impressive ballustraded cornice that strengthened its resemblance to a Renaissance palazzo.

37 **Bailey Block,** 1889–91
Saunders & Houghton
615–23 Second Avenue

Romanesque Revival with a heavy masonry character. Charles Bebb, later of the firms of Bebb & Mendel and Bebb & Gould, was the designer.

The following three buildings indicate by their size, scale, styling, and location the shift northward of the twentieth century central business district.

38 **Hoge Building,** 1911
Bebb & Mendel
Cherry Street and Second Avenue

Built on the site of Seattle's first home, the Carson Boren cabin, this building is a good example of the influence of the Ecole des Beaux Arts on early skyscraper design. The eclectic Classic styling is carried out in the then fashionable materials of tan terra cotta and brick, also used on the Alaska Building across the street.

39 Dexter Horton Building. Photo: A. Curtis (courtesy of Photo Collection, UW Library)

39 Dexter Horton Building, 1922–24
John Graham, Sr.
NE corner Second Avenue and Cherry Street

More restrained and businesslike than its neighbors, the notched plan enhanced rental space by providing equal light and air for more interior spaces. Ivory was a popular color for terra cotta office buildings of the twenties. On the north side giant Doric columns of granite express the original height of the lobby and tie the building to its granite-faced base.

40 Alaska Building, 1904
Eames & Young
618 Second Avenue

Downtown's first steel-framed skyscraper and a dramatic contrast with the old-style Bailey Block.

41 Corona Hotel (or Oriental Building), 1903
Bebb & Mendel
606–10 Second Avenue

Fine Sullivanesque ornament.

42 Hartford Building, 1929
John Graham, Sr.
600–4 Second Avenue

A gray block retrieved from anonymity by fine ornament from the Art Deco vocabulary of the 1920s. The design is clearly from the same drawing board as the former Great Northern Building uptown, and also provides an instructive comparison with its older neighbor, the Corona Hotel.

43 Collins Building, 1893
520–24 Second Avenue

Fine brickwork in the Romanesque Revival idiom.

44 Smith Tower, 1914
Gaggin & Gaggin
Yesler Way and Second Avenue

When completed this was the highest building west of the Mississippi and remained so for many years. Smith, a typewriter magnate, built the tower to anchor downtown near its starting place. The idea failed, but the design of the tower has the kind of authority that still makes it one of the city's most interesting buildings. One presumes the design was loosely based on Sienese palazzi but it is the monotonous if truthful expression of the structural frame with every windowed space rented for human occupancy that conveys the size of the investment and hence power behind this building. The interior is a priceless period piece in every detail especially the marble and tile surfaces used in public areas.

45 Frye Apartment Hotel, 1911
Bebb & Mendel
223 Yesler Way

A functional and unpretentious design until the eye reaches the top where it is riveted by a collection of splendidly over-scaled decorative motifs. As a way of visually bringing the building down to the ground, this approach was used in tall commercial buildings across the country; nearly every medium-sized city has or had a few.

At the edge of the district are the two railroad stations, for so long symbols of urban progress. King Street Station (46), Third Avenue South and South King Street, was built in 1906 and designed by Reed & Stem for James J. Hill and the Great Northern. Next door Union Station (47), Fourth Avenue South and South Jackson, was completed in 1911 and designed by D. J. Patter-son to serve the Northern Pacific, Milwaukee, and Union Pacific. The King Street Station remains in much reduced service for Amtrak passengers. These two stations mark the point at which the city stopped and tidal mudflats took over. Back in the 1880s the first Northern Pacific trains reached Seattle from the south on a trestle across these flats. In subsequent years, all sorts of tracks, yards, and terminals gradually caused the entire area from Airport Way and Interstate 5 to the present waterline to be filled.

With the obsolescence of center city rail facilities, the area is slowly being put to other uses. This explains the presence of the King County Stadium (48), or Kingdome, which is situated on King at the end of Second Avenue and looms up over everything in the area. Designed by Naramore, Bain, Brady & Johanson and completed in 1976, it has been variously called the orange squeezer, the hat box, the pill box, and other endearing epithets. There is no doubt that the structure's scale is an environmental affront to the district, however reasonable was the reuse of the derelict railroad yard area.

46 King Street Station. Photo: A. Curtis, 1912 (courtesy of Photo Collection, UW Library)

48 Kingdome (courtesy of King County Stadium)

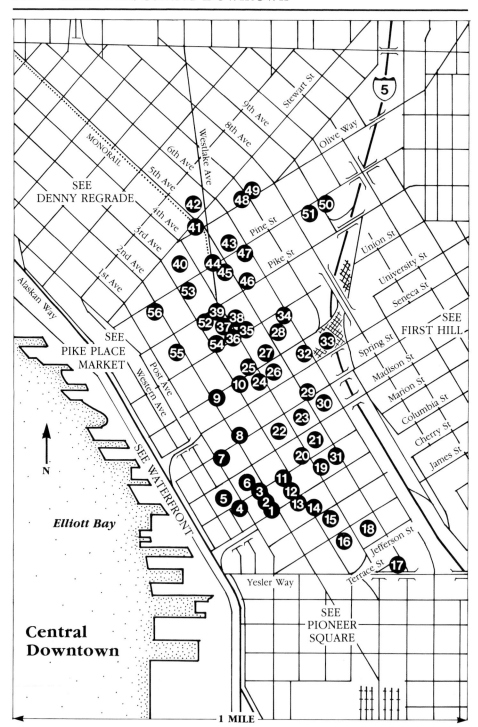

Central
Downtown

Central Downtown

The central business district continued to move northward after World War I. Even taller buildings were erected, generally fronting on the north-south streets that between 1892 and 1911 had been graded, lowering their levels sometimes as much as twenty-six feet. Streetcar lines crisscrossed the area with some like the Madison, James, and Yesler Way lines providing major service to suburban areas by 1888. Today's office towers are behemoths that dwarf the early skyscrapers in all dimensions and rarely convert to a human scale at the pedestrian or street level. Streetscapes like those found in the Pioneer Square district have been traded in for skyscapes that give a mighty city image from across the water or from freeways and airplanes. From a number of vantage points such as an approaching ferry or Gas Works Park on Lake Union, the city is a comely garden of form. Construction of the Alaskan Way Viaduct, Highway 99, in the 1950s walled off most of downtown from the waterfront, a tragedy for which there is little hope of remedy. The 1963 cut through the city made by Interstate 5 created a moat along the other side of the business district that is just as irreparable in spite of the admirable Freeway Park, a band-aid connection to First Hill. The downtown buildings, in a range of international

Downtown Seattle, with Alaskan Way Viaduct in foreground. Photo: Julius Shulman

styles, are generally best seen from several blocks away to understand their massing and design. Although some have interesting street-level plazas, street-level commercial activity is sparse. Consequently, at night and on weekends this part of downtown is relatively deserted.

1   **Norton Building,** 1959–60
    Bindon & Wright; Skidmore, Owings & Merrill; sculpture by Philip McCracken
    801 Second Avenue at Columbia Street

    The first of the city's aluminum and glass curtain-walled office towers, kin to the nationwide work of Skidmore, Owings & Merrill at this time. At sixteen floors high, this was the first structure to put the nearby Exchange Building in the shade. The crispness of the curtain wall along with the aloofness of the tower and its glazed lobby at the back of the plaza heralded the postwar corporate image.

2   **Bank of California Building,** 1916
    John Graham, Sr.
    815 Second Avenue

    Sandwiched between two office buildings, this Classic Revival bank has a fine high and airy interior in the Beaux Arts tradition. The exterior terra cotta cladding does a remarkable job of imitating granite.

3   **Exchange Building,** 1930
    F. W. Grant; John Graham, Sr.
    821 Second Avenue

    Designed as the new home for the stocks and commodities exchanges, the building opened its doors as the effects of the depression began to be felt locally. Consequently it was the tallest downtown structure until the post-World War II period. It follows the fashionable set-back style of the 1920s, with verticality emphasized by accentuation of the structural piers and recession of the nonstructural spandrels. Derived from the then fashionable vocabulary of ornament now called Art Deco or Zigzag Moderne, the decorative detail, particularly that of the entrance, is outstanding. The dark marble lobby with elaborate gilt ceiling has a curving elevator wall which has the practical advantage of making all the elevator doors visible at once.

3 Exchange Building

4   **Colman Building,** 1889, 1904, 1930
    Stephen J. Meany; August Tidemand; Arthur B. Loveless
    811 First Avenue

    Built by a prominent early Seattle capitalist, Laurence J. Colman, the building was once appended to an important wharf complex. Colman acquired the property by beaching a ship there long enough to establish legal title;

4 Colman Building. Photo: A. Curtis (courtesy of Photo Collection, UW Library)

the building was constructed over the hull. The 1889, Romanesque Revival design with a massive central tower fell victim to the 1893 depression; only the first two stories were completed as drawn. In 1904 Tidemand completed the building in the more austere style of the later Chicago Skyscraper School. In 1930, Arthur B. Loveless did a major remodeling that encorporated elements from Art Deco styling in the glazed street canopy and in the entrance and lobby; he also redesigned the dock, now destroyed. Scenes of Northwest occupations by sculptor Dudley Pratt adorn the entrance of the bank at the building's southeast corner.

5 **Old Federal Office Building,** 1932–33
James A. Wetmore, supervising architect
900 block of First Avenue

Whether or not it was intentional, this building-as-a-snow-capped-mountain is particularly appropriate for Seattle. The massive, stepped, brick-faced structure with light colored terra cotta capping for the piers and summit fills the site in an impressive way. The then expensive aluminum window frames and spandrels are an indication of the period's interest in new metals, metal alloys, and reflective materials characteristically used in Moderne buildings.

6 **Federal Office Building,** 1974
Fred Bassetti & Co.; John Graham & Co.; Richard Haag Associates, landscape architects
First to Second Avenue between Marion and Madison Streets

As the only contemporary office tower with a tiled, hipped roof, the building has a vaguely Mediterranean cast. This elongated palazzo for the federal bureaucracy also has a distinctive wall system composed of interlocking, prefabricated concrete pieces. The interior reveals a regional concern for the warmth of wood and for wood joinery. Outside, the designers have made every effort to enhance the street-level experience. An elaborate composition of steps and landings embellished by sculptures by Noguchi, Balazs, and McCracken cascades down either side of the building while the restrained landscaping of the Second Avenue plaza and the human scale of the entrances underscore the building's public nature.

7 **Holyoke Building,** 1889–90, 1980
Bird & Dornbach; Olson/Walker, rehabilitation
107 Spring Street

Under construction at the time of the great fire, this building was one of the first to be completed afterward. Like many of the business blocks of the period, this one was designed in a free version of the Romanesque, a style that was thought to express vitality and stability, desirable qualities both in business and in downtown.

The blocks across First Avenue retain much of the character of early downtown Seattle in the remaining turn-of-the-century buildings. Ideally, future development would incorporate their facades and thus preserve a significant piece of the city's heritage.

8 **National Bank of Commerce** (now Rainier Bank), 1908
1100 Second Avenue

Another of Seattle's striking terra-cotta-sheathed buildings. It was originally built as the J. A. Baillargeon Co. department store.

9 **Commercial Building** (formerly Majestic Theatre), 1909
E. W. Houghton
1222 Second Avenue

A fragment from the turn-of-the-century downtown, and one of several theaters by this noted architect.

6 Federal Office Building. Photo: Julius Shulman

10 Seattle Tower. Photo: A. Curtis (courtesy of Photo Collection, UW Library)

10 **Seattle Tower** (originally Northern Life Tower), 1928–29
Albertson, Wilson & Richardson; Joseph Wilson, principal designer
1218 Third Avenue

Seattle's most distinctive Moderne skyscraper, described by Albertson as "rising out of the ground, not as sitting traditionally on the surface. . . . The piers are conceived of as mounting and surmounting surges decreasing upward in motion and vigor, finally coming to rest against the block of the top story. . . . Possibly this creates a feeling of upward motion and aspiration . . . from the grading of the brickwork from darker at the bottom to lighter at the top. . . . Mt. Rainier is white at the top with perpetual snow and grades in strength of color downward into the deep evergreen of the forests below." We wish they would wash the building so we could see this poetic aspect of it. Tunneling through the ground floor the lobby of lustrous, dark marble walls and shimmering gilt ceiling is well worth traversing from one entrance to the other. The building was once lit by more than two hundred flood units concealed in the set back spaces. A

light show simulating the aurora borealis illuminated the exterior and, as an advertising brochure stated, "added assurance that one's office location will not be forgotten."

11 **Seattle Trust Court,** 1977
Ralph Anderson & Partners; T. William Booth, supervising architect
SW corner Third Avenue and Marion Street
Marion Building, 1916, 1976–78
Joseph Williams, rehabilitation
SE corner Second Avenue and Marion Street

A low-rise building with an open shopping court that is one of downtown Seattle's most popular open spaces; orientation away from the wind and weather has much to do with its success. The court's suburban character is the result of the scale and the use of a tiled, hipped roof. Maintaining a storefront tradition, the design acknowledges the corner location with a column out front and the entry set back from it on the diagonal. Downhill is the Marion Building, a handsome and civil design that, along with 814 and 804, its two neighbors to the south, was rehabilitated to provide attractive interior spaces for a restaurant and other uses as well as circulation to the

11 Seattle Trust Court. Photo: Robert Strode

top level and the Seattle Trust Court. The walls of the Second Avenue concourse have frescoes by John T. Jacobsen depicting themes from the exploration and settlement of Puget Sound.

12 Seattle Credit Union, 1979
Hobbs/Fukui
NW corner Third Avenue and Columbia Street

One of the most recent downtown buildings, the design reflects the ideas of the 1970s in combining precast concrete wall panels with flush glazing in different proportions according to the orientation; the south wall, appropriately, has the most glass. While the street level has a closed, nonpublic character, the north elevation thoughtfully provides the Seattle Trust Court users with updated Art Deco motifs to look at instead of a blank wall.

13 Chamber of Commerce, 1924
Schack, Young & Myers; Harlan Thomas & Associates
219 Columbia Street

An urbane design loosely derived from Byzantine or Italian Romanesque or both, the basilica type with its welcoming entrance and regional sculptures was a good match for the evangelical Chamber of Commerce, a powerful early Seattle institution. TRA, descendants of Schack, Young & Myers, occupy the rehabilitated upper floors. They deserve a hand for restoring the street-level arcade as well. The sculptural frieze by Charles Morgan Padelford to either side of the main entrance refers appropriately to Northwest history.

14 Arctic Building, 1917
A. Warren Gould
NE corner Third Avenue and Cherry Street

Renaissance Revival Palazzo in ivory colored terra cotta with confectioner's touches of aquamarine and rose. The decoration detail speaks of a time when architects thought about eye-catching regional details. Don't miss the walrus heads, sadly stripped of their tusks after the '49 earthquake, or the restored Dome Room.

15 Public Safety Building, 1946
Naramore, Bain, Brady & Johanson; Young & Richardson; B. Marcus Priteca
604 Third Avenue

Many architectural talents went into making

this rather bland expression of governmental bureaucracy. Though the northeast plaza has a rather barren, unwelcoming quality, it is a potentially attractive public amenity and will be useful if Seattle's downtown population grows according to predictions.

16 King County Courthouse, 1912–16,
remodeled 1960s
A. Warren Gould; Henry Bittman; Paul Delaney; Harmon, Pray & Dietrich
500 block of Third Avenue

The design reveals a shift in the courthouse image for large cities from a monumental temple of justice to that of an office building. Use of the time-worn Classic vocabulary and U-shaped plan makes the building more compatible with the Frye Hotel across the park than with the Public Safety Building next door.

13 Chamber of Commerce. Photo: Hugh Stratford

17 Old Public Safety Building, 1909,
rehabilitated 1977–78
Wilson & Loveless
400 Yesler Way

A benchmark rehabilitation under the Federal Tax Incentive program offering useful comparison with (15), in terms of the changing scale of such public agencies in a growing metropolis.

18 **King County Administration Building,**
    1971
    Harmon, Pray & Dietrich
    East side, 500 block of Fourth Avenue

A bewildering image for county government,
the building overpowers its neighbors in this
architectural zoo that comprises Seattle's civic
center. On the whole, these few blocks of
public buildings reveal both the increasing
gigantism of governmental bureaucracy and
the failure to utilize the urban design process
to humanize it all.

19 **Rainier Club,** 1904, addition 1929
    Kirtland K. Cutter; Bebb & Gould
    Fourth Avenue and Columbia Street

The suburban, residential character of this
exclusive club, even more pronounced before
the north section was added, was perfectly
logical before Interstate 5 severed its historic
link with First Hill, Seattle's first suburb,
where many of the original members lived.

19 Rainier Club

20 **Y.M.C.A.,** 1930
    Albertson, Richardson & Wilson
    909 Fourth Avenue

Elegant brickwork and a rich copper roof give
this simplified Tudor Revival building a kin-
ship with the more romantic Rainier Club.

21 **Bank of California,** 1973
    John Graham & Co.
    Fourth Avenue and Marion Street

An office tower that was slenderized through
its composition, with three laminated tower
sections of different heights. Warm toned,

triangular panels face the piers and contrast
with darker windows and spandrels em-
phasizing the vertical and giving the structure a vertical, tapering appearance. The
design makes little use of its contact with
the street.

22 **Seattle First National Bank,** 1969
    Naramore, Bain, Brady & Johanson
    1001 Fourth Avenue

A block-square fortress of polished granite
surmounted by a bronze-colored, monolithic
tower. Structural elegance in the tradition of
Mies van der Rohe finds expression in the
treatment of each face of the tower as a rigid
frame, or Vierendahl truss. The corner columns taper to reflect the diminishing loads
toward the top. The enormous lobby is preceded by a sloping, raised plaza with a
monumental sculpture, *Vertebrae*, by Henry
Moore. For about a decade this building was
the city's major corporate symbol. If future
projects proceed to completion, it will no
longer be the giant of the forest. One of its
competitors, at least in respect to scale, will
be the Seafirst Fifth Avenue Plaza by 3-D of
Houston with developer Gerald Hines.

22 Seattle First National Bank. Photo: Morley Baer

23 Seattle Main Public Library, 1959
Bindon & Wright; Decker, Christensen &
Kitchin
1000 Fourth Avenue

A period piece of late 1950s Americanized
International Style design with Le Corbusian
massing and a rich palette of typical materials: exposed aggregate concrete of all types,
graph-paper curtain walls, mosaicked round
columns and terrazzo floors. The building
fulfills its public responsibility better than
most by offering usable landscaped spaces on
both street levels and a number of art works:
bronze fountain and entrance gates by George
Tsutakawa, glass and bronze screen by James
FitzGerald, copper screen by Glen Alps, and
figures by Ray Jensen in the courtyard off the
upper level.

The blocks bounded on the south by
Seneca Street, on the north by Union
Street, and on the east and west by the
alleys dividing Fifth and Sixth and Third
and Fourth avenues comprise the University of Washington's Metropolitan
Tract. The university's involvement
with this significant piece of downtown
began in 1861 when the Denny and
Terry families donated a logged-over
ten-acre knoll for the site of the Territorial University that Senator Arthur
Denny had proposed. When, in 1895,
the university moved out to its new
campus, the Board of Regents was faced
with the problem of how to deal with a
large property that was well on the outskirts of town. The regents' wish to keep
the tract undivided delayed development until after downtown began to expand in the early 1900s. At that time
interest on the part of local entrepreneurs hinted at the area's potential for
generating revenues. In 1904 the tract
was leased to the Metropolitan Building
Company for fifty years. The leasee was
required to improve it with permanent
buildings that would, upon expiration

*Metropolitan Building Tract, looking northwest on Univer-
sity Street. Photo: A. Curtis (courtesy of Photo Collection,
UW Library)*

of the lease, revert to the university.
Metropolitan hired the New York firm
of Howells & Stokes to prepare a plan for
the tract's development. Described as
"comprehensive and symmetrical," the
plan reflected the Beaux Arts ideals of
the City Beautiful movement. A central
plaza, University Place, was to be carved
out of two large structures on either side
of University Street; uniform office
building facades lined Fourth Avenue
close to trolley lines, and apartment
buildings with garden courts were slated
for the eastern edge of Fifth Avenue.
Between 1909 and 1929 significant

pieces of the plan were carried out. The now destroyed White-Henry-Stuart Building was erected along the east side of Fourth; the still standing Cobb Building initiated development of the west side of Fourth followed by the adjoining annex and the Douglas Building. Although most of the other buildings—the Metropolitan Theater, the old Olympic Garage, and the Stimson and Skinner buildings—deviated stylistically from the original format, the last project of the company's leasehold, the Olympic Hotel, was stylistically sympathetic. In 1954 the tract was leased by Unico Properties. Beaux Arts ideals were supplanted by those of Modernism, which stressed architectural individuality rather than homogeneity. Demand for new office space and increasing occupation of Fourth Avenue by financial institutions were reflected in Naramore, Bain, Brady & Johanson's Plan 2009, formulated in the late 1960s.

Since then dramatic changes have occurred. Instead of the former emphasis on unity through physical design and an overall massing of buildings, the area has been opened up in the center leaving the older structures as strong edges to contain the space. The current approach also stresses the tract's complicated economic functions. A rich mix of uses continues. Fourth and Fifth avenues are lively shopping corridors linking the tract with the retail core to the north, while to the south Fourth Avenue is a strong spine linking the major financial institutions. Yet without any effective visual links between the parts, it has become increasingly difficult to tell where the tract begins and ends. The present challenge is to reinforce the continuity of this historic urban space.

24 The Financial Center. Photo: Art Hupy

24 **The Financial Center,** 1972
Naramore, Bain, Brady & Johanson
1215 Fourth Avenue

A warm colored, rough concrete tower with 3-D punch card walls that was the first product of the architects' Plan 2009. The siting on the south side of the block so as not to hide the Seattle Tower was a commendable idea, but the resulting plaza is a rather lifeless space mostly providing access to the Olympic Hotel skywalk.

25 **Cobb Building,** 1910
Howells & Stokes
NW corner Fourth Avenue and University Street

Originally built for medical and dental offices, the Cobb Building complemented the now demolished White-Henry-Stuart Building across the street. The fashionable combination of brick and terra cotta embellished with Classical detail was flavored with touches of regionalism in the eight Indian heads that punctuate an upper story frieze. The building turns the corner graciously, and the reconstructed interior of the Seafirst bank is worth seeing.

26 Olympic Hotel, 1924–29
George Post & Co.; Bebb & Gould
Fourth Avenue and Seneca Street

A remnant, like the Cobb Building, of the original architecture of the Metropolitan Tract designed by prominent New York architects with their home town in mind. A major city landmark, the hotel is now being refurbished so that its interiors will once more be as resplendent as they were at its opening, 6 December 1924.

27 Rainier Tower, 1977
Minoru Yamasaki; Naramore, Bain, Brady & Johanson
1200 Fourth Avenue and University Street

An engineering extravaganza consisting of an office tower balanced on top of a 121-foot base embedded in an unimaginable amount of concrete below grade. The structure's theoretical underpinning is that towers are more responsible to the urban matrix when they take up as little land as possible in the crowded city center. The plaza development attempts a streetscape composition through varying shop fronts. Informally terraced spaces allow some interesting views framed by the curve of the pedestal. An underground shopping mall terminates in the One Union Square Building of 1980, designed by TRA.

28 Skinner Building, 1926
R. C. Reamer
Fifth Avenue from University to Union Street

A stripped, tile-roofed Mediterranean palazzo clad in warm Wilkeson sandstone. The design departs from the format prescribed for the tract by Howells & Stokes and exemplified by the Cobb Building and the Olympic

27 Rainier Tower (courtesy of Office of Urban Conservation)

28 Skinner Building. Photo: A. Curtis (courtesy of Photo Collection, UW Library)

Hotel, but the block-long facade provides an urbane backdrop for elegant street-level shops. The Fifth Avenue Theatre's oriental decor—allegedly an authentic replica of traditional Chinese timber construction of the Forbidden City—reflects the exoticism of 1920s movieland.

29 **IBM Building,** 1963
Minoru Yamasaki; Naramore, Bain, Brady & Johanson
1200 Fifth Avenue

A delicately scaled and detailed, medium sized office tower with a ground level arcade that foreshadowed the Rainier Tower. The usually shaded, northside plaza with a fountain by James FitzGerald benefits from the openness of the upper terrace of the Plymouth Congregational Church. The integrated siting of these buildings is a worthy moment of urban design in the area.

30 **Federal Courthouse,** c. 1935
Louis A. Simon
Fifth Avenue and Madison Street

An architectural expression of governmental austerity befitting the depressed times in which it was built. The color scheme of rust red and gray was fashionable. The building's Classical lineage is revealed in its symmetry, central massing, and vertical strip windows defining voids between blank walls that suggest piers; it presides with dignity over a formally landscaped open space with ceremonial stairs.

31 **First United Methodist Church,** 1907
James Schack and Daniel Huntington
811 Fifth Avenue

An example of the small-scale institutional buildings that used to occupy large parts of downtown when there were still people living there and the urban fabric extended unbroken to First Hill.

32 **Plymouth Congregational Church,** 1967
Naramore, Bain, Brady & Johanson
Sixth Avenue and University Street

A formal yet playful building with an asymmetrical arrangement of rounded and square volumes that reflects its interior functions. The urban design contribution of the western terrace is noted in (29).

33 Freeway Park (courtesy of Seattle Parks and Recreation)

33 **Freeway Park,** 1976
Lawrence Halprin & Associates; Angela Danadjieva, project designer
Park Place Building, 1972
The Callison Associates
Sixth Avenue and Seneca Street

At an approximate cost of $14.5 million Seattle has bridged a bit of the disastrous freeway ditch with surely the most luxurious minipark anywhere. The central cascade and water element provide a man-made mountain trail experience for urban mountaineers in the shadow of the office tower mountainscape of the city center. Another ironic touch is the aquarium-like window at the bottom of the cascade through which passing autos are viewed like exotic fish. The east side continuation of the park over the public garage is an uneventful promenade. Only time will tell if the lush planting, selected for high pollution tolerance, will prosper in the inimical atmosphere. The popularity of the park attests to the desperate need for such an amenity in this part of town.

34 Washington Athletic Club, 1930
Sherwood D. Ford; Don Clippenger, designer
Sixth Avenue and Union Street

A commanding, centrally massed, stepped block with fine naturalistic ornament, much of it from the Art Deco vocabulary.

Seattle's principal retail shopping area takes up the blocks just south of where the street grid bends at Stewart Street; the district extends east-west from about Second to Sixth Avenue. The first retail palace to move uptown was Frederick & Nelson, formerly located in the early retail core area around Second and Madison. Mr. Frederick acquired the block site of the Westlake Market because of its easy access for delivery vehicles and customers. Other retailers moved to the area following the 1918 completion of the new Frederick & Nelson store, described as the Marshall Field of Seattle. Largely built up by the mid-thirties, the district is, to a remarkable extent, architecturally intact. The triangular plot at the end of Westlake Avenue between Pike and Pine and Fourth Avenue is the area fulcrum, a site now ripe for a major unifying urban design project. At this writing it is not clear what the final form of development will be. Terra cotta, the most popular exterior material of the teens and twenties, is the area's most common building material. Since it could be easily cast and was relatively inexpensive, designers were free to embellish otherwise monotonous steel-framed structures with luxurious-appearing decorative detail. The district is therefore a fine hunting ground for ornament buffs.

35 Pacific Savings (formerly Great Northern Building), 1928
R. C. Reamer
1404 Fourth Avenue

A suave gray block with fine foliate friezes.

36 1411 Fourth Avenue Building, c. 1930
R. C. Reamer
NW corner Union Street and Fourth Avenue

High quality design by one of Seattle's most interesting architects. The entrance sign was designed by Lloyd Lovegren; the elegant lobby was sympathetically remodeled by Fred Bassetti in the late 1960s.

36 1411 Fourth Avenue Building

37 Washington Building, 1960
Naramore, Bain, Brady & Johanson
1325 Fourth Avenue

A gleaming, marble-faced, curtain slab astride a glass cage lobby enriched by a bronze sculpture by James FitzGerald.

38 People's National Bank Headquarters, 1974
The Richardson Associates
1400 Fourth Avenue

A snow white corporate palace that cuts through the block and has a sunken forecourt on the Fifth Avenue side.

39 Joshua Green Building, 1913
John Graham, Sr.
SW corner Pike Street and Fourth Avenue

One of the area's notable terra cotta blocks.

38 People's National Bank Headquarters. Photo: Michael Burns

40 Bon Marche, 1929–early 1930s
John Graham, Sr.
Third to Fourth Avenue between Pine and Stewart Streets

A block-size, irregular box decorated with finely scaled ornamental motifs and a handsome metal canopy skirting the ground floor. The fifth floor was added in the early 1930s; the interior has also undergone several remodelings.

41 Times Square Building, 1916
Bebb & Gould
Fourth to Fifth Avenue between Olive Way and Stewart Street

A diminutive, lantern-like, flatiron building richly detailed in the academic Classic mode of the Beaux Arts.

41 Times Square Building. Photo: A. Curtis (courtesy of Photo Collection, UW Library)

42 Washington Plaza Hotel, 1969
John Graham & Co.
Fifth Avenue and Westlake Avenue

Nicknamed the corncob building, the hotel also alludes in its form to a giant fluted column. A second tower is slated to join this one; two may be too many.

43 **Frederick & Nelson,** 1918, 1950
John Graham, Sr.; John Graham & Co.
Fifth Avenue and Pine Street

Designed by the firm that has produced major components of downtown, the building had its monumental Classical cornice removed when upper floors were added in 1950. Today it has a more simplified and Modern format while retaining enough detail to recall its historic importance to the retail core.

43 Frederick & Nelson (courtesy of Office of Urban Conservation)

44 **Monorail Terminal,** 1964
Westlake Mall

The Seattle World's Fair (see Denny Regrade, 29) explains the existence of this exotic fragment of possible future. By all means take the brief ride.

45 **Nordstrom,** 1973
Skidmore, Owings & Merrill; Roland Terry
Fifth Avenue, Pine to Pike Street

What was originally three buildings has been collapsed into one and given a new, warm colored, terrazzo skin. Remnants of the old structures poke through the top at the south end. The curved, metal canopy has become a logo for the store.

46 **Coliseum Theater,** 1916
B. Marcus Priteca
Fifth Avenue and Pike Street

An exotic—even extraterrestrial—terra cotta confection by the Northwest's leading theater architect. Unfortunately, the dome that originally occupied the hollow over the marquee is gone; the neon sign is also a later, somewhat jarring addition.

47 **Shafer Building,** c. 1920
Sixth Avenue and Pine Street

A clearly expressed, steel frame office building with tasteful terra cotta cladding.

48 **Pacific Northwest Bell Building,** 1970
Naramore, Bain, Brady & Johanson
Seventh Avenue and Olive Way

49 **The Music Hall** (formerly Mayflower Theater), 1928
Sherwood D. Ford
702 Olive Way

Less encrusted than the Coliseum, but similar in its effort at the exotic.

50 **Paramount Theater,** 1929
B. Marcus Priteca
Ninth Avenue and Pine Street

A more restrained and more monumental building than the Coliseum or the Music Hall, the building gives importance to an otherwise nondescript area.

45 Nordstrom. Photo: Fred Milkie

51 **Pande-Cameron, Inc.**, 1928
Henry Bittman
815 Pine Street

A small box with an arresting amount of rich terra cotta detail.

52 **Woolworth's,** c. 1935
Third Avenue and Pike Street

A stock company design in the Moderne Style that was repeated across the country.

53 **Olympic Tower** (formerly United Shopping Tower), 1929
Henry Bittman
Third Avenue and Pine Street

A gray terra cotta block with a polygonal Art Deco crown now being restored by Charles Kober as headquarters for Olympic Savings.

54 **Joseph Vance Building,** 1930
John Graham, Sr.
Third Avenue and Union Street

Another terra cotta block with a notable, over-scaled frieze.

55 **J. C. Penney Building,** 1930
John Graham, Sr.
Second Avenue and Pike Street

More design in Moderne terra cotta on a much remodeled building.

56 **A. E. Doyle Building,** (formerly J. S. Graham Department Store), c. 1915, interior remodeling 1973
Doyle & Merriam; Ibsen Nelsen & Associates
SW corner Second Avenue and Pine Street

Lavishly detailed as a Venetian Renaissance palazzo by the prominent Portland architect whose name graces the building since its remodeling.

56 A. E. Doyle Building. Photo: Jim Ball

Waterfront

The waterfront, severed from the city by the Alaskan Way Viaduct (U.S. 99), has the traditional attractions of restaurants and boating and fishing piers. In the past decade it has gained other amenities, namely the Public Aquarium and the Waterfront Park funded by the 1968 Forward Thrust bonds. Considerable renovation has taken place along the stretch from Yesler Way, site of Henry Yesler's 1853 sawmill, to Pier 70 at the foot of Broad Street. To the northwest beyond Pier 70 is the new Myrtle Edwards Park engineered by Kelly, Pittelko, Fritz & Forsen, and Jongejan/Gerrard, landscape architects. The park has a massive stone sculpture by Michael Heizer. Proceeding from north to south the major waterfront sights are:

Pier 70, 1972
Barnett Schorr & Co.
Foot of Broad Street

A subtly colored, appropriately low-key rehabilitation of this substantial wooden pier building, formerly the storage warehouse for the Ainsworth and Dunn tuna cannery, now a shop and restaurant complex. The bar at the end has an attractive interior and view over Elliott Bay.

American Can Company, 1924, remodeled 1942, 1976–77
O. B. Preis, engineer; Andrew Willatsen; Ralph Anderson & Partners
2601 Elliott Avenue

A fine industrial vernacular structure rehabilitated as a merchandise mart closed to the public, with an interior three-story court.

Old Spaghetti Factory, 1902
Saunders & Lawton
Elliott Avenue and Broad Street

Originally the Dunn Tin Storage Warehouse, this brick and heavy timber, post-and-beam structure was rehabilitated by the Dunn family in 1970 as a restaurant, with office space above.

Pier 64, c. 1930

An imposing and well-maintained facade fronts for the Princess Marguerite Shipping Line, formerly the Canadian Pacific steamship terminal for the famous cruise line to Victoria, British Columbia, and beyond.

Public Aquarium, 1975–76
Fred Bassetti & Co.
Piers 59–61

A complex and interesting solution to the problem of putting fish on display.

Waterfront Park, 1974
Al Bumgardner Partnership; bronze fountain sculpture by James FitzGerald and Margaret Tomkins
Piers 59 to 57

A somewhat truncated version of the original design which was to have floating concrete pads just offshore accessible to pedestrians by means of ramps.

Fire Station No. 5, c. 1960
Durham, Anderson & Freed
Foot of Madison Street

Open to the public, this station has two fireboats serving Elliott Bay.

Pier 70

Public Aquarium. Photo: Roy Montgomery

Waterfront Park. Photo: Mary Randlett

Pike Place Market

One of Seattle's most famous cultural and commercial institutions, the Public Market began in 1907 when Mayor Charles H. Burnett proclaimed "Market Day" in support of a free market for farmers to sell their produce direct to consumers. From 1907 to 1917 permanent buildings with stalls replaced the produce wagons. The Corner Market Building, at Pike Place and First Avenue, was built in 1912 from a design by Thomas & Grainger; John Goodwin, an engineer, designed the Public Market's upper concourse and shopping arcade at that time. But overall the market grew by accretion, creating a rabbit warren structure that rambled down the hillside and spilled over into support structures across the street. By 1927 there were more than four hundred farmers selling at the Pike Place complex. The Sanitary Public Market was erected in 1910. The major developers were John and Frank Goodwin and Joe Desimone; their architect was Andrew Willatsen.

During World War II the number of farmers declined, other kinds of merchandise began to appear, and the Market was increasingly viewed as a shabby place with a questionable economic base. Besides, the urban renewal era with its grandiose schemes was beginning, and so-called blighted areas like the Market and the Pioneer Square district were attractive targets. The long battle to protect the Market has been told many times. Its chief protagonist, architect Victor Steinbrueck, led the organization of the Friends of the Market. They insisted, as had the famous Northwest painter Mark Tobey, that the Market was a way of life essential to Seattle's history and future. In the November 1971 municipal general election the Friends of the Market's initiative to protect the Market's traditional character and use was passed. It established a seven-acre historic district administered by a twelve-member citizen commission with the aid and cooperation of the City Department of Community Development. With the new local priorities, and a now enlightened federal program, Pike Place has been designated an urban renewal project. This permitted federal aid to finance the recently completed rehabilitation by George Bartholick of the upper concourse and shopping arcade. The Public Market Center occupies two floors below the street level. The Pike Market Hill Climb Corridor (1978), designed by Sanders & Gorasht and Portland landscape architect Robert Perron, is a long sequence of stairs that connects the upper levels with the waterfront area below.

Corner Market Building. Photo: A. Curtis, 1912 (courtesy of Photo Collection, UW Library)

Altogether the Market with its assemblage of merchants, people of all kinds, spaces, smells, visual delights, and general clamor beggars description. Mark Tobey captured much of its atmosphere in his many drawings and paintings of the place and its denizens. Recently Victor Steinbrueck published his drawings of the place. Though the local truck farmers no longer dominate trade, some remain, and a welter of new types has appeared. The total richness must be experienced, preferably again and again, to realize that such places can never simply be preserved. Instead, care and concern are needed to insure that the Market continues to exist; it will survive only the most gentle modifications. The admirable restoration by George Bartholick that strengthened the structure and otherwise just freshened things up is complemented by a growing number of rehabilitated buildings and interiors. Two that are most compatible with the utilitarian, industrial character of the Market are the Soames-Dunne Building, 1916 Pike Place, a straightforward 1976 rehabilitation of a concrete and heavy timber frame structure by Arne Bystrom, and Gretchen's Restaurant at 94 Stewart Street, with a 1979 interior by the Barnett Schorr Company that successfully fuses basic Market style with a contemporary high-tech approach to hardware and materials. The Pike and Virginia Building (1978) at that address is a private condominium and commercial development by Olson/Walker that continues the area's industrial-commercial aesthetic. Other plans include more housing, the partial restoration of the Stewart Hotel at 76 Stewart Street, and a park over a garage at the end of Virginia Street.

Pike and Virginia Building. Photo: Dick Busher

Denny Regrade

This flat and geographically featureless area, occupying the blocks northwest of the retail shopping area and extending along the waterfront to the foot of Queen Anne Hill, was once dominated by Denny Hill. Too steep for horse drawn vehicles, the hill effectively blocked city expansion. Only Belltown, the claim of pioneer William Bell on the southwest slope of the hill, developed as a community with a commercial center of its own based on the shipbuilding industry.

In 1892 R. H. Thomson became city engineer. Having witnessed in the California Gold Rush country the power of water to move earth, Thomson was inspired by the formidable challenge of Denny Hill to try regrading it by the hydraulic method. The leveling took place in two stages, the first from 1902 to 1911 and the second in 1929–30.

Using millions of gallons of water a day from Lake Union, the hill was sluiced down into Elliott Bay. The expectation was that this tabula rasa would then burst forth with buildings. In 1911, for example, the ambitious Bogue Plan, inspired by the national City Beautiful movement, proposed a Civic Center at Fourth Avenue and Blanchard. But, in reality, the city neither at that time nor in the depression years had the economic capability to support an expanded high-density commercial district. Instead the Regrade developed as a service area for downtown composed of auto showrooms, small manufacturers' outlets, new businesses, and enterprises like printing. Low rent was key. Since low land values seldom generate custom-designed commercial architecture, the old Regrade buildings are mostly built

Old Washington Hotel atop Denny Hill. Photo: A. Curtis, c. 1905 (courtesy of Photo Collection, UW Library)

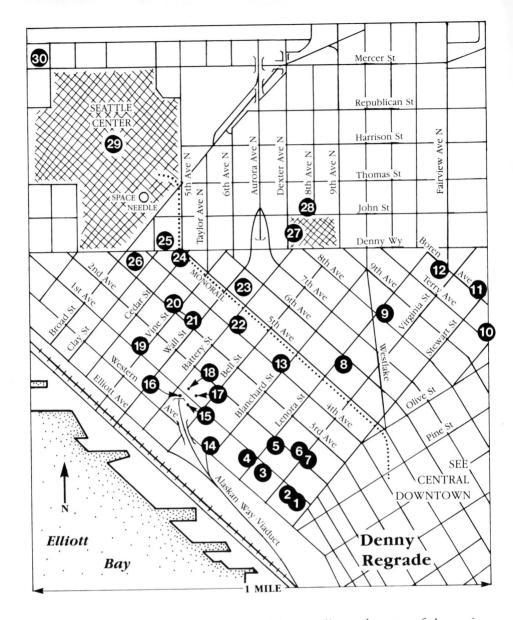

from stock plans. Whether they be turn-of-the-century wood frame buildings, medium-sized brick apartment buildings from the teens and twenties, or commercial buildings of the same vintage, they are modest in aspiration and achievement. Lovers of vernacular and catalogue design will enjoy exploring the area.

The overall mundaneness of the environment here heightened the impact of the area's one extravagant chunk of comprehensively planned, generously financed development, the Seattle Center. Constructed in the early 1960s to house an internationally certified world's fair, the Center was supposed to catalyze development in this downtown area.

Seattle Center. Photo: Steve Meltzer (courtesy of Seattle Center)

Though the fair was a success, it did not directly trigger much other than motel building. In the years since, it has been converted to a multi-purpose civic entertainment, culture, sports, and recreational facility that is an important metropolitan amenity.

In 1974, the Seattle Department of Community Development produced a plan for a new in-town residential community in the Regrade along with a variety of business and commercial enterprises. Landscape open spaces were keyed to new land-use zoning. Though the plan has had little visible effect so far, recent development indicates that downtown is at last really boiling over. A series of glassy medium-rise buildings by developer Martin Selig—see the pair of irregular rhomboids at Fourth and Blanchard—mark the beginning of the Manhattanization process. Should the demand for office space prove to be limited, residential development may give the area the welcome mix of occupancy and use projected by the 1974 plan. Whether or not the vision of the plan becomes a reality will depend on the willingness of the private sector to treat the Regrade as more than just real estate.

A word about getting around the Regrade must stress that its flatness does not make the area easy to navigate by car. In addition to the usual one-way street problem, Aurora Avenue, one of the major arterials, is a rarely penetrable concrete moat. The driver is frequently enraged by seeing his destination close by and not being able to get there. The skewed grid also creates some discontinuities. Walking is not really a solution because of the size of the area and the current lack of pedestrian amenities. Studying the map is our only suggestion. The one positive transportation note in the Regrade is the monorail connection between downtown and the Seattle Center, a leftover from the fair and a pleasant if truncated public conveyance.

1   **Alaska Trade Building,** 1909
    J. O. Taft
    1915–19 First Avenue
    One of the first steel and concrete structures
    in the Pike Place Market area.

2   **Butterworth Building,** 1903
    John Graham, Sr.
    1921 First Avenue

3   **Heman Building,** 1904
    2021 First Avenue

4   **Guiry Building,** c. 1895
    2101–5 First Avenue

5   **Crystal Swimming Pool,** c. 1915
    B. Marcus Priteca
    2033 Second Avenue
    The corner piece of this frothy building was
    once as the illustration shows. Now there's a
    worthy restoration project.

*5 Crystal Swimming Pool. Photo: A. Curtis, 1916 (courtesy
of Photo Collection, UW Library)*

6   **Calhoun Hotel,** 1918
    2000 Virginia Street

7   **Moore Theatre and Hotel Building,** 1908
    E. W. Houghton
    1932 Second Avenue
    Built in 1908 for the 1909 Alaska-Yukon-
    Pacific Expo tourist trade, the theater interior
    is vaguely Egyptian Revival.

To the northeast is an area of later, larger
buildings, a smattering of which call for
attention:

8   **United Airlines Building,** 1965, remodel-
    ed 1975
    C. Lindsey; Roland Terry
    2033 Sixth Avenue

9   **Johnson Hudson Dealer** (now Westlake
    Chevrolet), 1928
    2030 Eighth Avenue
    Colorful twenties terra cotta ornament.

10 **King County Medical Services Building,**
    1964
    Grant, Copeland, Chervenak & Associates
    1800 Terry Avenue
    A representative sixties contemporary low-
    rise office structure.

11 **Church,** c. 1910
    1900 Stewart Street
    A Craftsman-Gothic Revival church kin to
    the spirit of Norway Hall.

12 **Norway Hall,** 1915
    Engelhardt Sonnichsen
    2015 Boren Avenue
    A praiseworthy effort by a Norwegian born
    and trained architect to express traditional
    building forms and details in order to make
    visiting or transplanted Norwegians feel at
    home. The hall was commissioned by the
    Sons and the Daughters of Norway, fraternal
    societies organized by immigrants on the
    Pacific coast between 1903 and 1906. It for-
    merly had carved dragons on each of the major
    gables.

13 **Otis Elevator Building,** 1923, 1980
    Remodeled by T. William Booth
    2200 Fourth Avenue
    Built from the same stock plans used by the
    company all over the country.

14 **Pike Place Market Livery Stable,** c. 1910
    2200 Western Avenue
    A fine and substantial utilitarian structure
    erected for the farmers of the Pike Place Mar-
    ket with a horse's head signaling the nature of
    its use. It was once the largest stable of its
    kind west of the Mississippi.

Belltown: the old commercial district retains several buildings from its once independent days.

15 **Dr. Bradish Office Building,** c. 1890
2319 First Avenue

16 **Leader Building,** 1890
2323 First Avenue

Former home of an early Seattle newspaper.

17 **Barnes Building** (formerly Odd Fellows Hall), 1888
Elmer Fisher
2320 First Avenue

18 **Austin A. Bell Building,** 1889
Elmer Fisher
2326 First Avenue

Named for a member of the pioneering family who developed Belltown, and designed like the Barnes Building by Seattle's most prominent post-fire architect.

19 **New Pacific Apartments** (formerly Pacific Hospital), 1904
2600 First Avenue

A fairly standard vernacular commercial building which was actually built as a hospital and nursing school.

20 **Apartments,** c. 1910, rehabilitated 1970
Norman Aehle, renovation
2600 Third Avenue

Commendable and successful rehabilitation in an area where there are several well kept apartment buildings from the same period.

21 **Farwest Lithocraft Building,** 1937
J. Lister Holmes
Third Avenue and Wall Street

A modest but well-designed 1930s building by a prominent early modern architect.

18 Austin A. Bell Building

14 Pike Place Market Livery Stable (courtesy of Office of Urban Conservation)

22 **Fire Station No. 2,** 1920
D. R. Huntington
Fourth Avenue and Battery Street

A frank expression of the structural frame and a characteristic approach of Huntington, who served for many years as the city architect.

23 **Post-Intelligencer Building,** 1948, re-modeled and upper floor 1978
Lockwood-Greene; Naramore, Bain, Brady & Johanson
521 Wall Street

Designed by New York architects as the result of a national competition, the building speaks of the power of the big city newspaper symbolized by the revolving globe.

23 Post-Intelligencer Building

24 **Tillicum Place,** 1912, redesigned site 1975
James A. Wehn, sculptor; Jones & Jones, landscape architects
Denny Way and Cedar Street

When dedicated, the statue of Chief Sealth and the fountain, the city's oldest, stood on the edge of a meadow used by the Indians as a gathering place. The monorail trains now whiz by.

25 **KOMO Broadcasting Studio,** 1948, re-modeled 1974
Austin Co.; Naramore, Bain, Brady & Johanson
Fourth Avenue N and Denny Way

Seattle's best Streamline Moderne building sensitively remodeled just as the style has come into fashion's limelight again.

25 KOMO Broadcasting Studio. Photo: Jim Ball

26 **KIRO Radio and TV Station,** 1965
Fred Bassetti & Co.; Richard Haag, landscape architect
Fourth Avenue and Denny Way

Neo-Liberty Italian influence in a design very characteristic of this firm's work during the 1960s.

27 **Denny Park, Park Department Head-quarters,** 1890, 1948
Young, Richardson, Carleton & Detlie
Denny Way between Dexter and Ninth Avenues N

The city's oldest park, rebuilt after the regrade, is a verdant oasis in a desert of asphalt parking lots and motels. The Park Department Headquarters Building is an informal and gracious building embodying the spirit of the Americanized International Style. It has weathered well and contributes to the amenity of the park.

28 **Lutheran Church,** 1939
Bjarne Moe
NW corner Eighth Avenue N and John Street

An interesting brick church reminiscent of early modern Scandinavian and Dutch brickwork.

29 **Seattle Center,** 1960–64
Paul Thiry, supervising architect; Lawrence
Halprin, exposition landscape architect;
Richard Haag Associates, reuse plan land-
scape architects
Broad and Mercer Streets; First Avenue N and
Fifth Avenue N

Site of the 1962 exposition dedicated to Century 21 symbolized by the Space Needle, not
as significant an engineering feat as the Eiffel
Tower, but still not a bad if belated symbol
for the culture that produced Buck Rogers
and Amazing Comics. Victor Steinbrueck designed the Space Needle for the office of John
Graham, Jr. Supervising architect Paul Thiry
planned the site around the existing Armory,
High School Memorial Stadium, and Civic
Auditorium, the latter remodeled into an
Opera House by Chiarelli and Priteca. The
rest of the Century 21 complex, including the
Playhouse, Exhibition Hall, and Parking
Garage, was designed by Kirk/Wallace/
McKinley. The complex that best captures
the Expo spirit is the Pacific Science Center,
formerly called the Federal Science Pavilion,
by Naramore, Bain, Brady & Johanson with
Minoru Yamasaki & Associates. The gleam-
ing white court with its crystalline neo-
Gothic towers is an appropriate architectural
fantasy and perfectly characteristic of
Yamasaki's design taste.

Nearby is an ingenious sprinkler fountain by
Jack Overhoff of the office of Lawrence Halprin, landscape architect for the fair. Another
feature, the monumental concrete and colored glass organ-fountain extravaganza, is the
work of Japanese designers Kazuyuki Mat-
sushita and Hideki Shimizo. Between 1962
and 1964, seventy-four acres of the site were
relandscaped by Richard Haag, who added
the many trees and covered walkways.

29 Space Needle, with Pacific Science Center in foreground

29 Playhouse. Photo: Hugh N. Stratford

30 Hansen Baking Company, 1973–74
Harry B. Rich; Jongejan/Gerrard, landscape
architects; Hoyt & Lee, developers
100 Mercer Street

This whole block was originally owned by the
Hansen family whose bakery occupied the
circa 1900 brick building at the corner of
Mercer Street and First Avenue North. To
create the present shopping and restaurant
complex with its central landscaped court
required the removal of two buildings from
inside the block. Otherwise the context is
intact with a new structure at the corner of
Mercer and Warren Avenue. Delightful surprises await the visitor, such as Sunday's Restaurant inconspicuously housed in a former
Gothic Revival church that has retained its
high airy interior and stained glass windows.
Another fine and spirited interior is that of
O'Shaughnessey's Bar and Restaurant, by
Business Space Design.

30 Hansen Baking Company

First Hill

The name is doubly significant. Immediately adjacent to downtown, First
Hill was settled first by the wealthy and
socially prominent, the first families of
Seattle, developing a character like that
of Nob Hill in San Francisco. The first to
come, it was also, in a sense, the first to
go as new suburbs opened and it became
less desirable to live so close to
downtown. Today the area demonstrates
nothing so much as a conflicting set of
land uses and scale of development. A

residential and institutional patchwork
covers the hill. Medical institutions
dominate the central-western part. The
hospitals—there are six plus numerous
clinics, offices, and labs—have created
campuses as has Seattle University.
None of them intersect or otherwise
seem to support each other in an environmental sense. At the south end is a
low income housing project, Yesler Terrace, which also has its own precinct.
Because of all this, the tourist must use

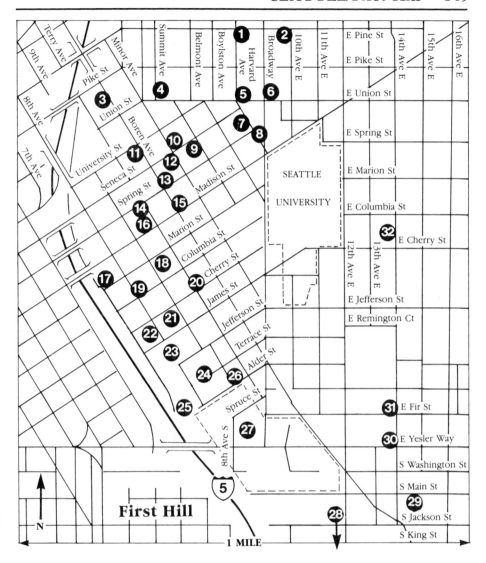

considerable imagination to reconstruct the era of simple opulence that the name implies. In fact, this first era began to vanish about 1908 when two of the hospital sites, for Cabrini and Swedish hospitals, were acquired. Large apartment houses also appeared at this time. In addition to First Hill, one also hears the northern part called "Pill Hill" for the concentration of medical facilities and the southern part called "Profanity Hill" because of the pioneers' reaction to climbing the muddy, steep grade on Yesler Way.

Today, First Hill is severed from downtown by Interstate 5. Until the opening of the Freeway Park there was no gracious way to bridge the gap for the many apartment dwellers who were stranded on the other side of the concrete river. The park is no real solution to the problem, but over the years the community on the hill has developed both an autonomous nature and strong links to the developing central area.

1 **Masonic Temple,** 1915
Saunders & Lawton
801 E Pine Street

2 **Odd Fellows Temple,** 1908
C. A. Breitung
915 E Pine Street

Two impressive Renaissance Revival Style designs.

3 **Ward House,** 1882
1423 Boren Avenue

A transitional design with both Italianate and Eastlake details, almost the last of its kind in the city.

4 **Summit Grade School,** 1905
James Stephen
1415 Summit Avenue

Designed by the school district architect from 1899 to 1908 who was responsible for the many new schools and additions that were needed to serve the city's increasing population during those boom years, the building

4 Summit Grade School

has been rehabilitated in an exemplary way. For other similar works by Stephen, see the Latona School in Wallingford and the University Heights Elementary School in the University district.

5 **Firehouse No. 25,** 1908
Somervell & Cote
Harvard Avenue at Union Street

6 **Johnson & Hamilton Mortuary,** 1909
Daniel R. Huntington
1400 Broadway

7 **First Baptist Church,** 1908–12
U. Grant Fay with Russell & Babcock
Harvard Avenue and Spring Street

A notable Perpendicular Gothic Revival church.

8 **Scottish Rite Temple,** c. 1910
Broadway, at Harvard Avenue

A prominently sited example of Beaux Arts, eclectic Classic design.

9 **Evangeline Young Women's Residence,** 1927
Huntington & Torbitt
1215 Seneca Street

Originally the Piedmont Hotel designed in late Mission Revival Style out of California.

10 **Stimson-Green House,** 1899–1901
Cutter & Malmgren
1204 Minor Avenue

Occupied from its completion to 1914 by the C. D. Stimson family and from then to 1975 by the Joshua Green family, both prominent early industrialists, this mansion belongs to a dwindling stand inspired by the European Arts & Crafts movement. Kirtland K. Cutter, one of the state's most prominent architects with an office in Spokane, executed a number of these somber baronial homes (see Spokane section) for which he also designed furnishings. The interior with its fine fireplaces by Cutter is worth a visit, which may be arranged through the Historic Seattle Preservation and Development Authority.

11 **Sunset Club,** 1916
Somervell & Cote
1021 University Street

A compatible use for this former Georgian Revival Style mansion

12 **Dearborn House,** c. 1909
1117 Minor Avenue

Now rehabilitated as offices, this domestic building helps retain the original character of the block.

13 **Roman Catholic Archbishop's Residence** (formerly W. D. Hafins House), 1902
A. Spaulding and Max Umbrecht
1104 Spring Street

A design that would have been at home in F. L. Wright's Chicago even with the exotic Venetian Gothic touches on the porches and conservatory. It has belonged to the Diocese since 1920.

13 Roman Catholic Archbishop's Residence

14 **The Baroness,** 1930
Schack, Young & Myers
1005 Spring Street

A fine Moderne work with exemplary ornament.

15 **Stacy House,** 1889
1004 Boren Avenue

A much altered late nineteenth century mansion, now the University Club.

16 **Hotel Sorrento,** 1908
Harlan Thomas
Madison Street at Terry Avenue

A distinctive Mediterranean Style design with an urbane forecourt, this hotel had the first rooftop restaurant in Seattle.

17 **Naramore, Bain, Brady & Johanson Office Building,** 1950
904 Seventh Avenue

The architects' office.

18 **St. James Cathedral,** 1907, remodeled 1917
Heins & LaFarge; John Graham, Sr.
Ninth Avenue and Marion Street

An imposing Neo-Baroque design which lost its dome when it collapsed under a snow load in 1916. Somewhat to the detriment of the building's image, a flat roof replaced the dome. The adjacent parish school was designed by the Beezer Brothers, while the complementary Catholic Diocese Chancery, at 907 Terry Avenue, was built in 1905 and remodeled in 1937 by Paul Thiry.

18 St. James Cathedral. Photo: Arthur Warner (courtesy of Photo Collection, UW Library)

19 **Thiry Architectural Offices,** 1946
800 Columbia Street

Another well-designed small office building still occupied by its designer.

20 **Frye Art Museum,** 1952
Paul Thiry
704 Cherry Street

International Style design similar to Thiry's Museum of History and Industry.

21 **German Club,** 1886
613 Ninth Avenue

Built by the Prusch Brothers for office and ballroom space.

22 Trinity Episcopal Church, 1891, restored
1903
John Graham, Sr.
609 Eighth Avenue

Another of First Hill's prominent cultural
landmarks, this rough cut stone church is
reminiscent of the English country parish
church. It was restored by Graham, who also
designed the rectory following a disastrous
fire in 1901. Many of the stained glass windows are original; the interior is worth seeing.

22 Trinity Episcopal Church

23 Jefferson Terrace, 1967
Kirk/Wallace/McKinley
800 Jefferson Street

A public housing project for the elderly.

24 Harborview Hospital, 1931
Thomas, Grainger & Thomas
325 Ninth Avenue

Impressive Moderne design with a finely detailed entrance. Although there have been
many mediocre additions over the years, the
mountain-like mass with its stylized craggy
brick walls is still a major city landmark. The
form is echoed by that of the 1934 U.S.
Public Health Service Hospital similarly
sited on Beacon Hill. The nurses' residence
across the street is by the same architects.

23 Jefferson Terrace. Photo: Hugh N. Stratford

*24 Harborview Hospital. Photo: C. F. Todd (courtesy of
Photo Collection, UW Library)*

25 Harborview Medical Center View Park and Parking Garage, 1974
Joyce/Copeland/Vaughan/Nordfors;
Richard Haag Associates, landscape architects

Interstate 5 right-of-way between the hospital and the freeway retaining wall; a fine piece of interstitial urban design.

26 Fire Station No. 3, 1903
30 Terry Avenue

Architecturally harmonious with the early mansions of the area, the station is now used by the city.

27 Yesler Terrace Low-Rent Public Housing Project, 1941
W. Aitken, W. Bain, J. T. Jacobsen, J. Lister Holmes, and G. W. Stoddard; Butler Sturtevant, landscape architect
903 Yesler Way

Simple dark-stained wooden boxes with flat overhanging roofs, minimal entrances, and windows ganged at the building corners; beautifully staggered on the hillside site to provide views, gardens, and privacy. This exemplary low-cost housing was the city's first federally sponsored slum clearance project. Open space, play areas, and common facilities are other important components of this planned community, the creation of Jesse Epstein, director of the Seattle Housing Administration through the 1940s. Yesler Terrace, which remains the best low-cost housing in Seattle, represented the finest flowering of early Modern movement social and design ideals. Some of the entranceways have been remodeled in ways unsympathetic to the original design character.

28 U.S. Public Health Service Hospital (formerly Marine Hospital), 1934
Bebb & Gould; John Graham, Sr.
1131 14th Avenue S

An outstanding, nearly unaltered complex of Zigzag Moderne buildings that crowns Beacon Hill and complements Harborview Hospital on First Hill. The complex consists of six two-story buildings, originally quarters for officers and nurses, grouped around the hospital, and a sixteen-story tower flanked by T-shaped wings with a banded, horizontal treatment. A rich palette of brick and terra cotta is used in a variety of floral, zigzag, and woven patterns. Lighting, fenestration, and other details have an admirable consistency and verve. It all takes place in a park-like setting.

28 U.S. Public Health Service Hospital. Photo: C. F. Todd (courtesy of Photo Collection, UW Library)

27 Yesler Terrace

29 Seattle Buddhist Church, 1914
Yoshio Arai
1427 S Main Street

A combination of traditional Buddhist elements, such as curving eaves and decorated roof ridge and gable bracing, with conventional construction. The interior has the traditional altar, screens, and other furnishings.

30 St. George Building, 1909
105 14th Avenue

A good example of the type of early twentieth century commercial building in an eclectic, Beaux Arts–influenced style which is well scaled for the street.

31 Washington Hall of Danish Brotherhood, 1908
Victor Voorhees
153 14th Avenue at E Fir Street

A bizarre combination of Mission Revival and Flemish vernacular styles.

32 Coca Cola Bottling Plant, 1939
Graham and Painter with Sheldon
1313 E Columbia Street

Pop bottling plants were a rising building type in the 1930s. Consequently, most of them are reliably Moderne. This one, though not streamlined, is still identifiable. Architect Sheldon was the company designer from Atlanta.

Central Area

Between downtown on the west and the slopes above Lake Washington on the east, Capitol and First hills on the north and south, lies a rather featureless area largely developed over the first decades of the century. At that time streetcar lines crisscrossed this centrally located zone making it an ideal place for the sort of eleemosynary institutions that could not compete for downtown land but needed accessible sites. It still serves this function as well as providing homes for many inner-city residents.

1 Temple de Hirsch Sanctuary

1   Temple de Hirsch Sanctuary, 1960
B. Marcus Priteca; Detlie & Peck
E Pike Street at 16th Avenue

A real period piece of religious architecture; the stained glass is worth seeing from the interior.

2   Cherry Hill Neighborhood Center (formerly Firehouse No. 23), 1909, rehabilitated 1970
Everett & Baker; T. Bower
18th Avenue and E Columbia Street

A good example of Seattle's successful rehabilitation program for historic structures that no longer suit their original function. Adjacent is Firehouse Park (1968) by Richard Haag Associates.

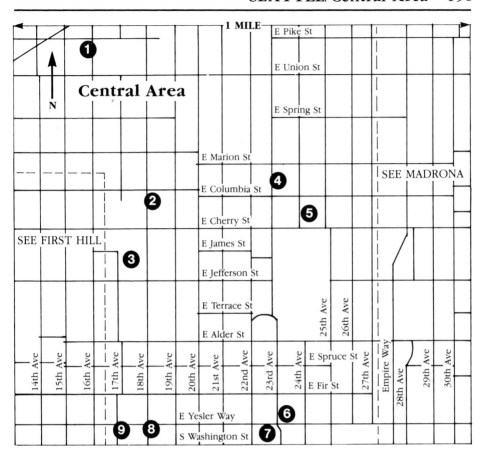

Central Area

N

SEE MADRONA

SEE FIRST HILL

E Pike St
E Union St
E Spring St
E Marion St
E Columbia St
E Cherry St
E James St
E Jefferson St
E Terrace St
E Alder St
E Spruce St
E Fir St
E Yesler Way
S Washington St

14th Ave, 15th Ave, 16th Ave, 17th Ave, 18th Ave, 19th Ave, 20th Ave, 21st Ave, 22nd Ave, 23rd Ave, 24th Ave, 25th Ave, 26th Ave, 27th Ave, Empire Way, 28th Ave, 29th Ave, 30th Ave

3   **Providence Hospital,** 1911
     Somervell & Cote
     17th Avenue and E Cherry Street
     An early city hospital and a landmark of the
     area.

4   **Victorian Row,** c. 1890
     East side 23rd Avenue at E Marion Street
     A row of almost miniature-scale late
     nineteenth century houses with the kind of
     wooden fancywork that was produced by the
     advanced tool technology of the times. Re-
     habilitated by the Historic Seattle Preserva-
     tion and Development Authority.

5   **Horace Mann Elementary School,** 1902
     Saunders & Lawton
     2410 E Cherry Street
     A utilitarian building putting up a good Co-
     lonial Revival front.

5 Horace Mann Elementary School

6   **Douglass-Truth Branch Public Library,**
    1914
    Somervell & Cote
    23rd Avenue and E Yesler Way
    One of many well-designed branch library
    buildings with a proper civic presence even in
    this nondescript setting.

7   **Fire Station No. 6,** 1931
    Dudley Stewart
    23rd Avenue and E Yesler Way
    Moderne styling with a fine zigzag patterned
    transom—a municipal structure that serves as
    a counterbalance for the library across the
    way.

7 Fire Station No. 6

8   **Bryant Manor** (two-story part only), 1971
    Townland Corp.; site planning by Buildings
    Systems Development; Boeing Company,
    developer
    1831–39 E Yesler Way

    The two-story part of this structure consists of
    a heavy concrete frame within which are two
    layers of conventional two-story wooden row
    houses. One set has front doors at ground
    level; the other set has front doors on an open
    gallery or "street in the sky" at the third-floor
    level. The project was designed as part of
    Operation Breakthrough, an abortive U.S.
    government exercise in technological innova-
    tion. The two-block open area surrounding
    Bryant Manor was cleared, urban-renewal
    style, to form Edwin T. Pratt Park.

9   **Langston Hughes Cultural Arts Center,**
    c. 1912, rehabilitated 1970
    B. Marcus Priteca; Streeter/Gorasht
    17th Avenue S and E Yesler Way
    Another admirable rehabilitation of a visually
    prominent building for a new community
    use.

Capitol Hill

The name reveals pioneer Arthur Denny's first ambition for the area, part of
which he platted prior to 1861 before
Olympia's claim to the state capitol was
secure. Although this aspiration came to
nothing and little development occurred
over the next thirty years, the potential
of the hill was fast realized with the
coming of the electric street railways
around the century's turning. At this
time Capitol Hill succeeded First Hill as
the favored zone of residence of the
wealthy; in fact, "second hill" might
have been a good name had it not been
imperative for such places always to be
first. Although the area was built up
thereafter at a steady pace, for topographical and other reasons local
neighborhoods evolved that preserve
their separate identities to this day.

A most influential factor in the hill's evolution was the amount of land taken from potential development as early as 1876 when the park department purchased 140 acres from J. M. Colman. Few improvements were made until 1885 when the Seattle Cemetery, located on Denny Hill, was moved, and the Washelli Cemetery was created to accommodate the bodies. Lakeview Park (47), established in 1887, was incorporated by the Olmsted Brothers in their 1903 park plan; later the name was patriotically changed to Volunteer Park to honor Spanish American War soldiers. The handsome brick water tower was built in 1907; the conservatory in 1910. By then these major focal points, the park and the cemetery, divided the area into two prototypical urban neighborhoods. On the west side, right next to downtown, lay a zone of exclusive residence for those who controlled the city's wealth. On the east side, one found the democratic ideal of the single-family-home neighborhood for white-collar wage earners who worked downtown and depended on mass transit.

The residential zone on the western side of the hill remained prime until the suburban exodus, particulary after World War II, siphoned off many of its elite residents. Before the new urbanites of the late 1960s could reclaim the hill, Interstate 5 cut across the western side, taking its toll of substantial homes and mansions. Today, although the area has suffered badly from freeway blight, it is once again desirable and much quiet refurbishing goes on. In the western part, from Highland Drive to Roy Street, the

Volunteer Park. Photo: Veronica Seyd

neighborhood has been laid out to accommodate the changing terrain by interrupting the grid street system. Larger lots even when the grid is in force combine with diagonal streets and irregular parcels to produce one of the loveliest of Seattle's residential environments.

To the east, the blocks immediately south of Volunteer Park became an enclave for the wealthy with a private gate at 14th and Roy that admitted the Cobbs, the Whites, the Stuarts, the Skinners, and other prominent names to Millionaire Row. Here large houses were tightly packed in rows facing the streets suggesting that the sale of valuable land was the primary reason for development, not the creation of an ideal living environment.

About 1905 developer J. A. Moore, backed by eastern money, planned the Capitol Hill Addition, a streetcar suburb on the east side of the hill served by the 19th Avenue line. One of the most intact of this characteristic type of urban landscape, the addition is a showcase for the Colonial Revival house type nicknamed the "Classic Box." The

Classic Box

whole gamut of variations on the theme—elaborate roof brackets, projecting square corner bays, Moorish keyhole windows, and a rich variety of leaded glass—can be found in the blocks between East Galer and Mercer streets and 15th and 23rd avenues. The student of this period will also find here other favored styles of the times such as the porticoed mansion type with Classic details and the New England gambrel-roofed, shingled cottage.

In addition to topographical features, religious institutions have played their part in the development of the hill. On the east side, the Holy Names Academy (58) was a dominant institution in 1908. St. Joseph's Church (57) was built nearby in 1932. On the west side, St. Mark's Episcopal Cathedral (13), 1926–30, provides a major focus, while to the south is St. Nicholas, 1932–38, the Russian Orthodox Cathedral (65).

Skirting the western edge of the hill and continuing south is a broad, relatively flat area of mixed residential, institutional, and commercial development; population pressures show up in the increase in multi-unit buildings. Broadway, the traditional main street, at one time had a major streetcar line. Later automobile dealerships moved in. Now, more diversified, the street is still the main artery. Nearby is the area's most memorable street intersection, symbolically speaking, Harvard Avenue and Republican Street.

North Capitol Hill

The northernmost section of the hill, amputated from the rest by a freeway cut, has a quiet, park-like ambiance.

1   Johanson House, 1909
    Cutter & Malmgren
    2800 Broadway E

    An excellent example of the Swiss Chalet for the founder of the Swedish Hospital.

1 Johanson house

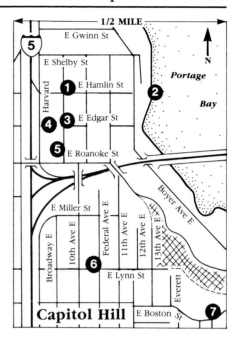

2   Hamlin Pier Houseboats, c. 1974
    Grant Copeland
    Foot of E Hamlin Street

    Contemporary houseboats in the cut-out box or contemporary cubist style.

2 Hamlin Pier houseboat

3   St. Patrick's Rectory and Office (formerly, a private house), 1915
    Andrew Willatsen
    2702 Broadway E

    A half-timbered Tudor design attributed to Andrew Willatsen.

3 St. Patrick's Rectory and Office

4   **House,** c. 1905
    2706 Harvard Avenue E

A stately mansion in the Classic Revival Style, balanced by the California Mission Revival Style house at 2612 Harvard.

4 House

5   **"Ole" Hanson House,** c. 1910
    Elmer Green
    2609 Broadway E

A timbered-up Craftsman Style house for a former mayor. Next door is its twin, stripped of decorative detail.

6   **E. E. Vogue House,** 1918–19
    Andrew Willatsen
    1016 E Lynn Street

A Prairie Style house reputedly designed on speculation for the Long Building Company by Seattle's noted Wright disciple.

6 E. E. Vogue house

7   **Nichols House,** 1939
    Paul Thiry
    1600 Boston Terrace E

A notable example of the European-born International Style by one of Seattle's first Modern architects.

7 Nichols house

Central Capitol Hill

The main part of the hill includes the upper class district on the west side, the park and the enclave south of it, and the more middle class Capitol Hill Addition east of the park. These areas are discussed in the introduction to Capitol Hill.

8   **Rhodes House,** 1911
    A. Warren Gould
    1901 10th Avenue E

    A Mediterranean Renaissance Revival mansion in terra cotta with a formal garden. Extensive reforming of the site and a massive retaining wall were necessary to create this fine Beaux Arts composition.

8 Rhodes house

9   **Streissguth House,** 1961
    Daniel M. Streissguth
    900 E Blaine Street

    Using the contemporary approach to hillside design, this boxy but elegant shingled house steps down the slope using part of the upper ground level for a courtyard.

10 **John Leary House** (now the Episcopal Diocesan Offices), 1903–4
    J. Alfred Bodley, with John Graham, Sr., supervising architect
    1551 10th Avenue E

    English Arts & Crafts Style with the fifteen-acre site designed appropriately as a deer park. Distinctive massing and an impressive stone entrance composition mark this baronial mansion. A famous stained glass window by New York's Tiffany Company, formerly in the house, is now in the Burke Memorial Washington State Museum on the University of Washington campus.

10 John Leary house

11 **Pierre P. Ferry House,** c. 1905
    John Graham, Sr.
    1229 10th Avenue E

    Home of Leary's partner and brother-in-law, this less formal half-timbered house reflects the more local approach of its designer. A beautiful stained glass window graces the north elevation.

12 **House,** c. 1918
    David Myers
    1000 E Garfield Street

    The half-timbered style with vigorous detailing of the entrances.

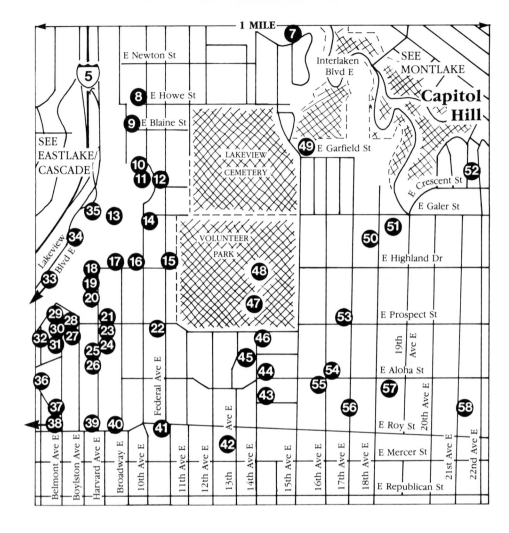

13 St. Mark's Episcopal Cathedral, 1926–30, addition 1958

Bakewell & Brown; E. F. Champney, supervising architect; addition by Young, Richardson, Carleton & Detlie
1245 10th Avenue E

The stark modernity of this poured concrete, Neo-Byzantine design is due to the onslaught of the depression which halted construction at Phase I. The interior, an immense masonry box, has an almost breathtaking brightness and airiness. Bakewell & Brown was a well-known San Francisco firm.

13 St. Mark's Episcopal Cathedral

14 Collins House, 1910
Walter Oates
1254 10th Avenue E

Mediterranean Revival design on a lavish scale.

15 Scheetz House, 1914
Somervell & Cote
1204 Federal Avenue E

A fine Georgian-Federal Revival design whose central, Palladian window and portico were treated in a highly personal way. This is one of the many fine period revival homes along Federal Avenue East from about Blaine to Prospect.

15 Scheetz house

16 Smith Townhouses, 1979
Olson/Walker
10th Avenue E and E Highland Drive

17 Sam Hill House, 1909
Hornblower & Marshall
814 E Highland Drive

A concrete adaptation of an eighteenth century manor house. Hill reused the design for his Columbia River plantation house, Maryhill.

18 M. C. Bain House, 1938
William Bain
1157 Harvard Avenue E

A Colonial Revival cottage representative of a very popular residential style of the 1930s.

19 C. J. Smith House, 1907, remodeled 1937
Cutter & Malmgren; Carl Nuese, designer
1147 Harvard Avenue E

One of the many local designs that reflect American admiration of the work of the English architect Richard Norman Shaw.

20 Brownell-Bloedel House, 1910
Carl Gould
1137 Harvard Avenue E

Georgian Revival Style untypically sheathed in large, Northwest, natural wood shingles. The architect was one of Seattle's leading eclectic stylists.

21 E. W. Cummings House, 1904
Francis H. Perkins
1108 Harvard Avenue E

An elegant example of the elaborate Classic Box, the standard design type on the other side of the hill.

22 Frederick Hurlbut House, 1914
Andrew Willatsen
1015 E Prospect Street

Half-timbering used to express modular construction. A hint of Prairie styling in the window muntins contributes to the linear quality of the elevations.

23 C. E. Farnsworth House, 1910
Somervell & Cote
803 E Prospect Street

Another variation on the solid half-timber theme.

24 Peeples–Huessy House, 1909
James H. Schack
948 Harvard Avenue E

A very large Swiss Chalet, well detailed with impressive timbers from the good old days. Influence from the California Arts and Crafts movement is evident in the use of Batchelder tiles inset above the garage doors.

25 Garber House, 1922
Schack, Young & Myers
937 Harvard Avenue E

A well-built Tudor Style mansion designed by a long-enduring Seattle firm now called TRA (The Richardson Associates).

26 R. D. Merrill House, 1909–10
Charles A. Platt
919 Harvard Avenue E

The Georgian mode restrained and modified by one of the most prominent eastern architects of the day. A formal garden and carriage house, visible on Boylston Avenue East, complete the Beaux Arts composition. This is Platt's only west coast work.

26 R. D. Merrill house

27 Holmes—Paterson House, 1905
J. Alfred Bodley
1025 Boylston Avenue E

One of the area's most idiosyncratic designs in a Colonial/Craftsman mode that looks back to the English work of Charles F. A. Voysey.

28 J. A. Kerr House, 1910
Blackwell & Baker
1105 Boylston Avenue E

A rather conventional half-timbered house in a lovely landscaped setting.

29 O. D. Fisher House, 1909
Beezer Bros.
1047 Belmont Place E

30 O. W. Fisher House, 1913
Beezer Bros.
1039 Belmont Place E

This and (29) demonstrate that talented hands could work forceful improvisations on what was often a dry, convention-bound style.

31 McVay House, 1911
Andrew Willatsen & Barry Byrne
1025 Belmont Place E

A strong, unconventional combination of the shingled Craftsman Style and the Prairie School.

32 Bower/Bystrom Houses, c. 1900, remodeled 1978–79
Arne Bystrom, renovation
1022 Summit Avenue E

A pair of Colonial Revival houses, one of which has been respectfully remodeled by the architect-owner; the other is nicely intact and makes a useful comparison.

32 Bower/Bystrom houses (courtesy of Office of Urban Conservation)

30 O. W. Fisher house

33 Architect's Office, 1946
Terry, Tucker & Shields
914 Lakeview Boulevard E

A planar composition tied to the site with fieldstone walls, recalling Frank Lloyd Wright and one of the several currents of Modernism.

34 Edgar Clise House, c. 1895
1218 Lakeview Boulevard E

A well-preserved and well-decorated late nineteenth century house.

35 Egan House, 1958
Robert Reichert
1500 Lakeview Boulevard E, accessible from the south via Belmont Avenue

One of Seattle's most arresting houses with a distinctive form that expresses its interior organization in which levels, like graduated trays, diminish in size as they rise. With its clear geometry climaxed by a totemic wooden flag, the house is a perfect foil for the wooded glen. Other Reichert houses are on Queen Anne Hill (**27**) and in North Seattle (**7**).

35 Egan house (courtesy of Office of Urban Conservation)

36 Summit Tower Apartments, 1974
The Bumgardner Partnership
766 Belmont Avenue E

Contemporary shingled apartments that harmonize in scale and appearance with the older neighborhood context.

37 Apartments, 1929–30
Fred Anhalt, developer; Ed Dofsen, designer
710, The Belmont Apartments; 730, Oak Manor; 750 Belmont Place E

A cluster of apartment buildings in an Old English or Norman Provincial Style, much favored by Anhalt, well designed for a difficult site.

37 Apartments

38 Belroy Apartments, 1931
William Bain & Lionel Pries
703 E Roy Street

Bottom-of-the-depression design in the early Modern idiom. The saw-toothed west elevation has bays angled to catch the view.

39 Cornish School of the Allied Arts, 1921
Albertson, Wilson & Richardson
710 Harvard Avenue E

One of the city's major cultural institutions is located in this quietly elegant building of Mediterranean persuasion. Cast terra cotta ornament reveals its consecration to the arts, whose history in Seattle would not have been so rich without the school's multi-faceted program. Among its talented faculty was the Northwest's leading painter, Mark Tobey. Those who are interested in reading more should consult Roger Sale's *Seattle, Past to Present*.

40   North Broadway Shopping Center, 1931
Arthur Loveless
711 Broadway E

This group of shops and apartments around a court proves that straitened depression-era budgets did not necessarily defeat good design. Though given an English Cottage look, the complex is quite Modern in its economy of detail and functional plan. An interesting cinder-concrete block was used in place of stone. The court is intimately scaled with round stair towers and balconies providing the proper dose of the picturesque. The Russian restaurant is an original tenant.

40 North Broadway Shopping Center

41   Apartments, c. 1930
Fred Anhalt, developer; Ed Dofsen, designer
1005 and 1014 E Roy Street

Anhalt was the developer-builder of a series of remarkable city apartment houses done with style and practicality. At 1005 East Roy, the apartments have up to nine rooms with two baths and a fireplace. Unusual for the time is the underground parking. Anhalt developed an uncommon sound-proofing system that consisted of double floors; because the top floor was not tied to the structure, it did not

transmit sound. Interior walls were also doubled. The choice of English or French Provincial styles permitted the use of picturesque round towers into which the apartments opened, a device that eliminated long stair halls. Brick bearing walls are a foot thick; roofs are either slate or hand-split shakes.

42   House, c. 1915
627 13th Avenue E

A fine example of the Japanesque bungalow.

43   Thomas Bordeaux House, 1903
W. D. Kimball
806 14th Avenue E

Casting about for ways to describe the various half-timber styles then in vogue, the 1913 Seattle edition of *Homes and Gardens of the Pacific Coast* detected a Tyrolian influence in this large house enlivened by a decorated tower.

43 Thomas Bordeaux house

44   Cobb House, c. 1910
Bebb & Mendel
1409 E Aloha Street

A fusion of the spirit of the German Black Forest and the English Arts & Crafts movement was one of the specialties of this prominent turn-of-the-century architectural firm.

45   House, 1902
923 14th Avenue E

A characterful variation on the English Arts & Crafts theme.

46 House, c. 1910
1409 E Prospect Street

The way that this vast Colonial Revival house overpowers its site suggests that it used the park as a borrowed setting.

47 Volunteer Park (originally Lakeview Park), 1887

See Capitol Hill introduction for description, dates, and discussion of the park's development.

48 Seattle Art Museum, 1932
Carl Gould
Main park drive

Presented to the city by Dr. Richard Fuller and his mother, the museum's major collections are the Fullers' outstanding collection of Asian art and many notable works by contemporary Northwest painters. A proto-Modern design, the building reveals its Beaux Arts academic origins in its symmetrical composition and massing; it should be compared with the architect's other work in this mode, the Seattle Times Building at Fairview Avenue North and John Street. On the terrace in front of the building is Isamu Noguchi's *Black Sun*, a granite doughnut through which the Space Needle can be seen, miniaturized like an approaching U.F.O. The entry garden, designed in the 1930s by Noble Hoggson in the Moderne mode, shows the influence of this style of landscape architecture.

East of Volunteer Park lies the less pretentious but still aggressively middle class Capitol Hill Addition discussed in the introduction to the overall district.

49 Louisa Boren View Park, 1975
Victor Steinbrueck; Lee Kelly, sculptor
15th Avenue E, E Garfield Street, Olin Place

One of the small parks funded by Forward Thrust. In addition to a variety of places for viewing, there is a handsome Cor-Ten sculpture. The designer cut down maintenance by restricting the lawn to a free-form, curbed area beyond which native clover takes over. Random sandstone blocks echo the cemetery and protect corners.

50 Houses
1200 block 18th Avenue E
An exemplary row of Classic Boxes.

51 Isaac Stevens School, 1906
James Stephen
19th Avenue E and E Galer Street

A huge wooden Colonial Revival School, handsomely painted. Kin to it and by the same architect are the Green Lake Elementary School (Green Lake, 6) and the Frantz H. Coe Elementary School (Queen Anne Hill, 26).

48 Seattle Art Museum. Photo: John Davidson, 1933 (courtesy of Photo Collection, UW Library)

51 Isaac Stevens School

55 House, 1902
747 16th Avenue E

Two lavishly detailed and generously proportioned Colonial Revival houses. Number 747 is distinguished by a handsome, carved foliate frieze and elegant shallow bays on the ground floor.

56 Houses
700 block 17th Avenue E

A notable ensemble of streetscape and houses.

57 St. Joseph's Catholic Church, 1932
Albertson, Wilson & Richardson; Joseph Wilson, designer
732 18th Avenue E

A richer sheathing was intended for this stripped Gothic design, but the depression limited its decorative expression to sparing but effective cast concrete detail. The interior is also interesting for its proto-Modern expression. For other works by this architect see the Cornish School (39) and the Seattle Tower (Central Downtown, 10).

58 Holy Names Academy, 1908
C. A. Breitung and T. Buchinger
728 21st Avenue E

A landmark and one of the city's most imposing institutional buildings in the academic Beaux Arts Style.

52 House, c. 1915
Ellsworth Storey
1614 21st Avenue E

The client for this house was a jeweler which may explain its idiosyncratic decorative detail. A strong horizontal emphasis given by deep overhangs and a flat roof makes a bow to Frank Lloyd Wright and the Prairie School architects.

53 Bucklin House, c. 1905
1620 E Prospect Street

A fine example of the Queen Anne–Colonial Style with a garland frieze below the cornice, Palladian windows, and beautiful leaded glass on the ground floor.

54 Megrath House, 1906
904 16th Avenue E

53 Bucklin house

57 St. Joseph's Catholic Church

58 Holy Names Academy. Photo: A. Curtis, 1908 (courtesy of Photo Collection, UW Library)

59 **Earthstation No.** 7 (formerly Firehouse No. 7), 1920
402 15th Avenue E
One of Seattle's commendable rehabilitations of outmoded public buildings.

60 **Group Health Hospital**, 1961
The Richardson Associates
16th Avenue E between E Thomas Street and E Denny Way

61 **Apartment House**, c. 1935
Fred Anhalt, developer; Ed Dofsen, designer
SE corner E John Street and 14th Avenue E

62 **Two Houses**, 1895, 1898
133 and 203 14th Avenue E
Turn-of-the-century houses representative of the type that once dominated the area.

63 **Capitol Hill United Methodist Church**, 1906
128 16th Avenue E
Creditable Gothic Revival design with an interesting plan that accommodates the main auditorium space on the bias with the external cruciform mass. The church's founders included pioneer John Denny and the Reverend Daniel Bagley.

64 **First Church of Christ Scientist**, 1914
Bebb & Mendel
1519 E Denny Way
A Neo-Classic design of Indiana limestone and New Hampshire granite with a richly appointed and detailed interior.

Capitol Hill, South of Roy Street

As the introduction to Capitol Hill suggests, this mixed-use area ties the swankier parts of the district to downtown.

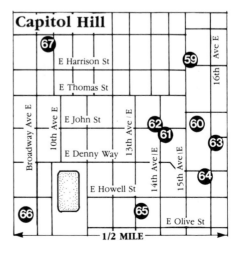

65 St. Nicholas Russian Orthodox Cathedral, 1932–38
Ivan Palmov
1714 13th Avenue

Seattle's first Russian church was established in 1898. Although St. Nicholas and St. Spiridon (Eastlake/Cascade, 5) both date from much later times, they perpetuate the traditional image of the multi-domed, eastern church.

66 Seattle Central Community College, 1973
Kirk/Wallace/McKinley
1718 Broadway

A Neo-Brutalist or Formalist work, depending on your verbal preference, by the firm responsible for "Red Square" on the University of Washington campus and for a large number of delightful residential-scale designs. The buildings replace the old Broadway High School, a Romanesque Revival complex of which a fragment remains at East Pine Street and Broadway in the form of the rehabilitated auditorium. The final design utilized the Romanesque Revival Style entrance facade of old Broadway High as the front for its Renaissance Revival Style back.

66 Seattle Central Community College

67 Midwestern Three-Decker Apartment Houses, c. 1915
SW corner 10th Avenue E and E Republican Street

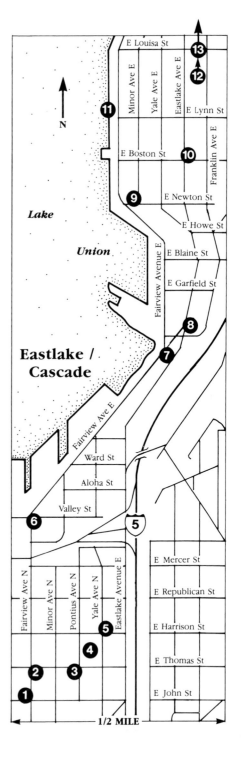

Eastlake/Cascade

In contrast to Lake Washington, the shores of Lake Union have been almost totally consumed by industry, as anyone who attempts to walk around the lake will find out. Beginning with the David Denny lumber mill of 1886, this waterfront has played an important part in Seattle's history.

Both Cascade and Eastlake were early residential districts, but only a few early houses survive. One which echoes the past is at 2622 Franklin Avenue East (c. 1893). The generally unprepossessing quality of Eastlake and Cascade, now totally a mixed-use area, camouflages some nifty architecture.

1 **Seattle Times Building,** 1930
R. C. Reamer
Fairview Avenue N and John Street

A good example of the Moderne Style in its classic phase; note the fine grill work on the entrance and the use of the upper part of the facade as a dignified sign for the building.

2 **Social Security Building,** 1959
Waldron & Dietz
230 Fairview Avenue N

Contemporary American design reflecting the principles of the European International Style with a flat-roofed cubistic form and a dramatic glazed entrance.

3 **Immanuel Lutheran Church,** 1907–12
Watson Vernon
1215 Thomas Street

4 **School District Shops and Warehouse,** c. 1955
Thomas to Harrison Street, Pontius Avenue N to Yale Avenue N

A rare concrete-shell structure from the era when such structures were in fashion. Compare with the Concrete Engineering plant in Tacoma and Pioneer Junior High School in Wenatchee.

5 **St. Spiridon Orthodox Cathedral,** 1938
Ivan Palmov
Yale Avenue N at Harrison Street

This and (3) above are remaining landmarks of the district's Russian and Scandinavian immigrant communities, once settled here. With its white and blue onion domes, tiny St. Spiridon enlivens the view from the freeway.

1 Seattle Times Building

5 St. Spiridon Orthodox Cathedral

6   **Craftsman Press** (formerly Ford Motor Assembly Plant), 1913
John Graham, Sr.
Fairview Avenue N and Valley Street

Early industrial design by this prominent local architect who designed Ford plants in other parts of the country as well.

6 Craftsman Press

7   **City Light Lake Union Steam Plant,** 1911
Daniel R. Huntington
Between Eastlake Avenue E and Fairview Avenue E

A landmark of the city's industrial development; the first generator used run-off water from the Volunteer Park reservoir.

8   **Architect's Office,** 1960
Steinhart, Theriault & Associates
1264 Eastlake Avenue E

A Miesian glass box on a stone pedestal dramatically cantilevered over a manicured garden on the slope below.

9   **Architect's Office,** 1961
Kirk/Wallace/McKinley
2000 Fairview Avenue E

Community Psychiatric Clinic, 1962
Kirk/Wallace/McKinley
2010 Fairview Avenue E

Two refined expressions of the wooden post-and-beam pavilion; the matchstick quality of the structural expression is a hallmark of Paul Hayden Kirk's work.

Eastlake is a favored place for architects' offices in renovated older buildings as well as new. The Bumgardner Partnership is at 2021 and John Morse & Associates at 2033 Minor Avenue East.

10   **Architect's Office and Gallery,** 1961
Gene Zema
200 E Boston Street

Contemporary design in the Northwest timber tradition. Originally the architect's home it is now an office and gallery, with an ideal architectural setting, for Japanese folk arts.

9 Architect's Office

The Lake Union houseboat community (11) is one of the most fully developed on the Seattle waterways. It stretches north from the end of Newton Street nearly continuously to the freeway bridge. Although their tenure has been periodically threatened, the residents are community-conscious and active, as witnessed by street-end parks at Newton, Lynn, and Roanoke. At Hamlin there is a contemporary houseboat development largely designed by James Jessup, whose office and home are on one of the boats. Other contemporary designs are scattered throughout the community. Although stylish and smooth they often loom too large, overwhelming their smaller, more shanty-style neighbors. Lovers of vernacular design will find the old houseboats an endless visual pleasure.

12 **Apartments,** 1929
Paul Thiry
2717 Franklin Avenue E
Moderne styling enlivens an otherwise utilitarian brick building.

13 **L'Amourita Apartments,** c. 1925
2901–15 Franklin Avenue E and E Shelby Street
Exuberant Mission Revival which catches the eye even from the freeway.

13 L'Amourita Apartments

Montlake

Christened Montlake in 1909 by developers Corner and Hagen to conjure up for future residents the desirable combination of mountains and water, this area in fact is chiefly characterized by its parkland and water frontage boundaries. Two of these, Interlaken Boulevard to the southwest, and Lake Washington Boulevard, which runs through the University of Washington Arboretum on the east (see Madison Park, 11), were part of the Olmsted Brothers' Park and Recreation Plan of 1903. Apparently this famous eastern firm utilized an earlier bicycle path laid out by mayor-engineer George Cotterill. The beautiful Arboretum is the product of later Olmsted planning; much of its landscaping and development was completed during the depression by Works Progress Administration labor.

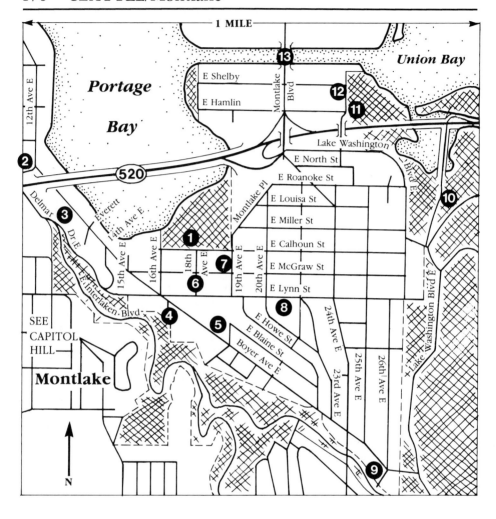

Architecturally the area is typically Seattle: modest, without monuments, but with decent builder's houses (6), and some representative architect-designed houses (2, 3, 4, 7 and 8). The real environmental accomplishments in Montlake are early products of the neighborhood activism that has recently become a Seattle trademark (1 and 10).

1 **Montlake Playfield and Community Center,** 1931, 1976
Harry B. Rich, community building; Jongejan/Gerrard, landscape architects for recent improvements
E Calhoun Street between 15th and 19th Avenues E

The existence of this amenity and its initial development in 1931 memorialize the early neighborhood activism of Montlake's inhabitants. Part of the site was formerly a commercial dahlia bed and part is fill into Portage Bay, the adjacent lobe of Lake Union.

The fill for Montlake Playfield displaced a considerable houseboat settlement along the shore. Some of this floating settlement remains on the other side of the freeway viaduct. Closest in are a set of very modish seventies houses floating on concrete pads and looking most unlike the traditional shanty-style Seattle houseboat dwelling. West Montlake Park off Delmar near the crossing of the freeway and Interlaken Boulevard provides a splendid vantage point from which to see all of this. The first two houses below practically border the park.

5 St. Demetrios Greek Orthodox Church

2   **A. Gunby House,** c. 1930
    J. T. Jacobsen
    118 E Roanoke Street

    An early Modern design that uses wood to express both Scandinavian and Northwest regional influences.

3   **A. Mason House,** 1952
    Victor Steinbrueck
    2525 Boyer Avenue E

    A good example of postwar Modern functionalist design with its minimal, open plan expressed by the compact, boxy form.

4   **Stephens House,** 1970
    Gene Zema
    2181 Boyer Avenue E

    A shed roof with a reverse shed dormer and encircling covered decks add to the regional character of this dark-stained, woodsy house by an architect who has contributed to the Northwest timber tradition.

5   **St. Demetrios Greek Orthodox Church,** 1962
    Paul Thiry
    2100 Boyer Avenue E

    A crossing of traditional and contemporary design ideas. The striated brick walls are effective foils for the white vaults.

6   **Builder's Cottages,** c. 1920–40
    E Lynn to E McGraw Street, 16th to 19th Avenue E

    A particularly fine stand of vernacular permutations of the Tudor Style.

6 Builder's Cottage

7   **Johnston House,** 1964
    Norman Johnston
    2401 19th Avenue E

    An elegant, modular box not in the Northwest tradition.

8   **Hews House,** 1913
    Andrew Willatsen
    2021 E Lynn Street

    Now nearly impossible to see, this is one of Willatsen's best works in his characteristic, Wright-influenced Prairie School Style.

9   **Boyer House,** 1907
Norman Lacey, builder
1617 26th Avenue E

One of the most interesting of the masonry and half-timbered residences in Seattle. Its designer is, alas, unknown. The siting, arrangement of porches and roofs, and mighty masonry work on the ground floor recall the Ames Gate Lodge by H. H. Richardson.

10   **R. H. Thomson Freeway Stub,** 1969
Evergreen Point Freeway at the Arboretum

The latest monument to local activism this stub was originally to have continued south blasting through the Arboretum and Montlake. Arrested at this point, devoid of traffic and noise, it makes a kind of heroic junk sculpture. At its round pillared feet an extension of the Arboretum features a pedestrian ramble along footbridges over Union Bay's marshes. Known as the Foster Island Trail, it is accessible from the east side of the museum site (11).

11   **Museum of History and Industry,** 1950, additions 1958, 1961, 1970
Paul Thiry; 1950 and 1970 additions by Naramore, Bain, Brady & Johanson; 1961 addition by J. Lister Holmes
2161 E Hamlin Street

A stucco and wood-frame modular pavilion vaguely reminiscent of the Miesian approach and well suited for exhibition space. The museum's permanent exhibits feature local history in pioneering and the maritime and aviation industries.

11 Museum of History and Industry. Photo: C. F. Todd, 1951 (courtesy of Photo Collection, UW Library)

12   **Houlahan House,** 1915
2159 E Shelby Street

Seattle's historic goal of linking Lake Washington with Puget Sound was finally accomplished for sea-going vessels with the completion of the Lake Washington Ship Canal in 1917. The Portage Canal had been built years earlier, in 1885, to accommodate log rafts and small boats from Henry Yesler's sawmill on Union Bay. A circuit walk beginning in a westerly direction from Montlake Boulevard near the bridge down East Hamlin Street goes past the Seattle Yacht Club, designed by John Graham, Sr., about 1920, through the West Montlake Park and along the canal, returning by way of the Lake Washington Canal Walkway to the Museum of History and Industry. It provides a range of scenic pleasures on an intimate scale that is hard to match.

13   **Montlake Bridge,** 1925
Blaine & Associates; Carl Gould
Montlake Boulevard

A valuable urban design element for the district. The "Gothicky" towers were designed by the university architect, Carl Gould, to harmonize with the campus buildings.

13 Montlake Bridge

Madison Park and Denny Blaine

The northernmost of the Lake Washington shoreline suburbs south of Union Bay derives its name from the late nineteenth century amusement park erected at the end of the Madison Street cable car line. The line was laid on an 1864 road built from downtown which extended Madison Street out to the lakeshore. There, Judge McGilvra, who had practiced law with Abraham Lincoln in Chicago before coming west, donated twenty-one acres of his very large lakeside estate as a public park in order to promote his adjoining real estate development. The cable car company owners built the amusement park to increase business. The Pioneer Association Hall (1), built and given to the city by McGilvra and Sarah Denny in 1910, now serves the city as a community center and museum. It is located at 43rd Avenue East and East Blaine Street.

A pleasant, low-profile shopping area occupies the last blocks of Madison across from the park and tennis court. Apartment houses cluster along the lakeshore. One of the most environmentally sensitive of these is the Lake Court Apartments (2), at 2012–20 43rd Avenue East, designed by leading early-modern architect Paul Thiry and completed about 1936. Its French Provincial farmhouse styling is appropriate for the courtyard plan. West of the shore via Newton Street is Canterbury, a post–World War II tract identifiable by its curved street plan. Houses range from the late fifties to the present; many are elaborately landscaped. Like the modern tracts in the communities across the lake, Canterbury is a good place to study the evolution of the contemporary house

in Seattle. A few houses are pointed out here; nearly all are worth looking at.

3   House, 1963
Gene Zema; Charles Stoll, landscape architect
2233 40th Avenue E

4   House, 1964
Gene Zema
2256 38th Place E

This house and (3) above are exemplary modern designs in the Northwest timber tradition.

4 House

5   House, 1956
William Bain
2151 38th Avenue E

6   House, 1963
Robert Shields
2201 40th Avenue E

7   House, 1964
Nelsen, Sabin & Varey
3827 E Crockett Street

The rest of Madison Park north of Madison Street is packed with generally less distinguished development. Two noteworthy houses are:

8   House, 1979
Lee Copeland
1615 39th Avenue E

9   **Samuel Hyde House**, 1908
Bebb & Mendel
3736 E Madison Street

An imposing Colonial Revival house.

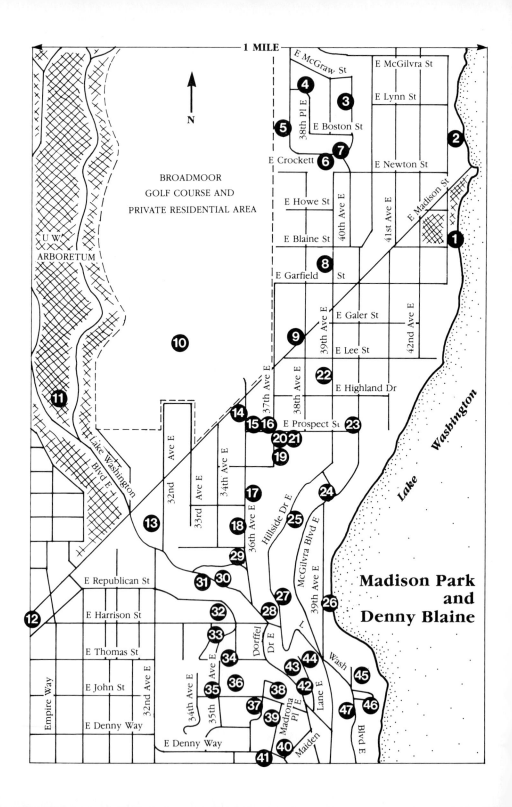

9 Samuel Hyde house

East of Madison Park lies the exclusive and private residential park called Broadmoor (10), opened in 1927 and designed by Vernon Macon for a tract of land originally owned by the Puget Mill Company. Representative of a fashionable type of land development for the affluent—the country club within the city—it has maintained much of the natural setting. Many houses here were designed by Seattle's leading architects, but they are not listed in this guide since Broadmoor is closed to the public.

Further east is the Arboretum (11), the University of Washington botanical reserve. It functions as one of the chain of parks and boulevards incorporated by the Olmsteds and their successors into the greenbelt that extends from Puget Sound to the shores of Lake Washington. The Arboretum land was also acquired from the Puget Mill Company about 1900 by the University of Washington. In addition to some fine scenic effects and special gardens such as the Japanese garden, there is a 1900 viaduct, designed by W. R. B. Willcox, crossing Lake Washington Boulevard, and near the Madison Street entrance a rustic gardener's cottage of 1927 by Loveless & Fey.

12 Spot Cleaners, c. 1900
Signs by artist Luban Petric
27th Avenue E and E Madison Street
This much "signed" building may look ad hoc but it is actually the work of a respected artist who turned the small commercial enterprise into a creditable pop art creation.

12 Spot Cleaners

13 Fire Station No. 34, 1971
Hobbs/Fukui
633 32nd Avenue E

13 Fire Station No. 34. Photo: Art Hupy

The Washington Park residential area lies south of Madison Street and north of the ravine edging Lake Washington Boulevard. Although development did not begin until after the turn of the century, it now has the classic look of mature subdivisions of its kind across the country. Stately trees line the streets, which generally follow the grid pattern. Large houses are set back on their lots, with carpet-like lawns embowered with lush foundation planting. Much of the landscaping is professionally maintained. This is not an area for eccentric or dramatic architecture, but the appreciator of eclectic residential design from about 1900 to the mid-1930s will be rewarded by a tour. Mixed in with the rest are some outstanding examples of Modern design from the post–World War II period. Altogether it is one of the richest architectural concentrations easily visible from the street in the whole Northwest. We call your attention to the following general selection:

14 **Alexander Pantages House,** 1909
Wilson & Loveless
1117 36th Avenue E

An inventive variation on the half-timbered theme with overtones of the California Mission Revival that originally left the wooden features such as the window framing elements dark, giving the whole facade a more dramatic linear organization. The original owner was a nationally renowned vaudeville impresario.

14 Alexander Pantages house. Photo: A. Curtis, 1912 (courtesy of Photo Collection, UW Library)

15 **House,** 1936
Victor N. J. Jones
3602 E Prospect Street

A cubistic International Style house in concrete with nautical overtones—it was once painted a crisp white rather than eye-ease green.

16 **Lea House,** 1909
Bigger & Warner
3620 E Prospect Street

The enduring Colonial Revival mode with attention paid to historical correctness.

17 **Ames House,** 1907
Bebb & Mendel
808 36th Avenue E

A stately Colonial Revival mansion now the residence of the president of the University of Washington.

17 Ames house (courtesy of Photo Collection, UW Library)

18 **Holmes House,** 1930
J. Lister Holmes
615 36th Avenue E

Stripped Norman Provincial Style by an architect who turned to the Modern idiom in the next decade.

19 **House,** 1928
William Bain
1002 37th Avenue E

Tudor Revival or "Jacobethan" by one of the founders of the prominent contemporary firm Naramore, Bain, Brady & Johanson.

20 **House,** 1950
Terry, Tucker & Shields
3717 E Prospect Street

The Modern ideal of the one-floor plan is dramatically stated in this postwar house projected on stilts over its sloping site.

21 **House,** c. 1910
Andrew Willatsen
3727 E Prospect Street

Another of the handful of Prairie Style houses designed by an architect who had firsthand experience in the office of Frank Lloyd Wright.

22 **McDonald House,** 1948
Paul Thiry
1217 39th Avenue E

An understated, even bland, application of the principles of the Modern movement.

23 **Hauberg House,** 1954
Roland Terry
1101 McGilvra Boulevard E

A cubistically massed, formal, and refined design; a fine example of the full-blown Americanized International Style.

23 Hauberg house

24 **Preston House,** 1959
Terry, Tucker & Shields
745 McGilvra Boulevard E

Early postwar Modern house design with careful attention paid to the use of materials and siting.

25 **Two Houses,** c. 1935
Thiry & Shay
626 and 630 Hillside Drive E

Small-scale International Style.

26 **House,** 1932
T. Haire
420 39th Avenue E

Pioneering Moderne Style design.

27 **Hobbs House,** 1975
Hobbs/Fukui
530 Hillside Drive E

Architect Hobbs's own house designed in a taut and complicated form for a very difficult site, best seen from below on McGilvra Boulevard. For comparison see the other partner's house at 182 35th Avenue East.

27 Hobbs house. Photo: Art Hupy

28 **Heffernan House,** Helen Bush Parkside School, 1915
Cutter & Malmgren
408 Lake Washington Boulevard E

A fine Tudor Revival mansion designed by the famous Spokane firm that also did the Stimson-Green house on First Hill.

29 **Weyerhaeuser Experimental House,** 1935
R. C. Reamer
545 36th Avenue E

A prototype design from a Weyerhaeuser-sponsored effort to use wood products, particularly the new plywood. Similar designs were built on Capitol Hill and at the 1937 Chicago World's Fair, but this is the only one known to remain.

28 Heffernan house

29 Weyerhaeuser experimental house (courtesy of Office of Urban Conservation)

30 House, 1941
J. Lister Holmes
433 Lake Washington Boulevard E
Early Modern design.

31 House, 1976
Chelminiak & Hayden
499 Lake Washington Boulevard E
Neo-Corbusian formalism initiated by Richard Meier, Gwathmay/Siegel, and others of the New York 5 School; an easily visible example of this fashionable style.

32 Helen Bush Parkside School, 1936–60s
J. T. Jacobsen, John Morse, John Scott, and others
405 36th Avenue E
One of the area's prominent landmarks, this modern school has grown by structural accretion over the years. The oldest parts are the classroom sections on the south and north sides. Miller Hall is by John T. Jacobsen.

In 1901, the Denny Blaine Addition south of Harrison Street was platted and developed by Elbert Blaine. It included small parks, winding streets, and romantic sites. This and the Mount Baker area are the best places to see the work of Ellsworth Storey, one of Seattle's most important early twentieth century architects. He worked in the Craftsman aesthetic as did Bernard Maybeck, Julia Morgan, and others in the San Francisco Bay area, and the Greene Brothers in southern California. Storey came to Seattle from Chicago with his wife and parents, for whom he designed houses (43) on land purchased about 1903 in the newly developed Denny Blaine Addition. An important advertisement for his work, these buildings attracted other clients moving into the new area. In addition to Storey's houses it includes much the same spectrum of residential design as does the whole district south of Madison.

33 Thiry House, 1936
Paul Thiry
330 35th Avenue E
An early Modern expression of the European
International Style, built by a pioneering
Modernist for himself. Compare with (34)
and (35) below.

33 Thiry house

34 Edwards House, 1936
Paul Thiry
303 35th Avenue E
See (33) above.

35 House, c. 1936
Paul Thiry
3410 E John Street
Another example of Thiry's early International Style work.

36 Two Houses, 1908
Ellsworth Storey
219 and 221 36th Avenue E
Two good examples of Storey's work in the
Craftsman idiom.

37 House, 1973
Olson/Walker Associates
187 37th Avenue E at E John Street
A contemporary shingled wood box disappearing into the trees.

38 House, 1910
3270 E High Lane
A design reflecting Storey's work.

39 Elmer C. Todd House, 1906
Ellsworth Storey
123 Madrona Place E

40 Denny Blaine Shelter, c. 1901
E Denny Way and Madrona Place E
Originally built by Blaine's company as a
combination real estate office and streetcar
passenger shelter, this rubblestone-based
pavilion with peeler logs supporting a gabled
roof with exposed rafters epitomizes the
Craftsman design ethic. As built it was enclosed with clapboards and had diamond-panel windows.

*40 Denny Blaine shelter. Photo: Anders Wilse, c. 1901
(courtesy of Photo Collection, UW Library)*

**41 Episcopal Church of the Epiphany,
Chapel and Rectory,** 1911, 1922
Church by Whitehouse & Price; chapel and
rectory by Ellsworth Storey
E Denny Way and Madrona Place E
Both the chapel and the church emphasize
craftsmanship; the rectory is a handsome
Shingle Style design with a subtle south
elevation. The interiors are worth seeing for
their detail and furnishings, particularly the
church altar.

41 Chapel

42 **House,** 1909
Ellsworth Storey
232 Dorffel Drive E

Craftsman Style with an eccentric plan and clipped hedging that makes a nice mustache over the door.

43 **Two Houses,** 1903, 1905
Ellsworth Storey
260 and 270 Dorffel Drive E

The most famous of Storey's houses and his first work in Seattle, these houses, connected by a gallery, were for his family (no. 260) and his parents (no. 270). They reflect the best of the unpretentious Craftsman spirit and should be compared with the work of Northern California architects Bernard Maybeck and Julia Morgan.

43 260 Dorffel Drive E

44 House (courtesy of Photo Collection, UW Library)

44 **House,** 1925
Loveless & Fey
300 Maiden Lane E

One of the many English Cottage Style designs, always well sited and well executed, by Arthur B. Loveless.

45 **House,** c. 1955
Lionel Pries
230 40th Avenue E.

An interesting design by an important architect and educator; but not very easy to see.

46 **House,** 1932
A. H. Albertson
154 Lake Washington Boulevard E

Tudor Revival, or English Cottage, was perhaps the most enduring residential style of the Seattle area from the turn of the century to the pre–World War II period. Compare this house with the work of Arthur B. Loveless and with many, many others, unidentified and too numerous to enumerate, in the more affluent and older residential neighborhoods.

47 **Blaine House,** c. 1900
171 Lake Washington Boulevard E

Home of Elbert Blaine, important early Seattle developer, one of the pair for whom the Denny Blaine area is named.

Madrona and Leschi

The Madrona district, beginning at East Howell Street and extending south to Leschi, was homesteaded by the Randell family. Through the efforts of a real estate company that in the 1890s built a streetcar line from downtown to the shore with the predictable amusement park at the end, the community began to grow. The amusement park buildings gradually disappeared. The boathouse, built by the Works Progress Administration in 1941, was rehabilitated by Arne Bystrom in 1971 as a dance studio. Completion of Lake Washington Boulevard in 1910 connected Madrona Park to the others in the Olmsted plan. Winding along the shore much of the way from Madison Park to Mt. Baker, this well-mannered drive is the major organizing element for the lake-oriented area which extends east to about 30th Avenue. Frink Park occupies the steep, wooded slopes west of Leschi Park. Originally platted for private use by Judge Thomas Burke in 1883, then purchased by Francis G. Frink, educator and legislator, it was given to the city as a park in 1906 and remains in a natural state. The flatter area at the top of the ridge from about 30th to 33rd Avenue was developed earlier than much of the slope. The cross streets, East Terrace and East James, have some late nineteenth century Victorian styles that are not in evidence nearer the lakeshore. Leschi, the southernmost community before the Lacey V. Murrow floating bridge, bears the name of the ill-fated chief of the Nisqually tribe, native of the area. Chief Leschi's history, as it relates to the state of Washington, is told most movingly by Norman Clark in his bicentennial

history of Washington. The present Leschi Park, established in 1908, overlooks the marina, an important component of this major water recreation area.

1   **House, c. 1915**
    SW corner 37th Avenue and E Olive Street
    A letter-perfect Japanese bungalow.

2   **House, 1914**
    Ellsworth Storey
    3852 E Olive Street

    A shingled Colonial Revival house similar to contemporary work by Julia Morgan in Berkeley, California.

3   **Two Houses, 1914**
    Ellsworth Storey
    1618 and 1622 40th Avenue

    This pair of houses, with compatible but not identical designs, was clearly designed to go together. The stacking of gables along a diagonal roof line as in 1622 is a hallmark of Storey's work.

3 1622 40th Avenue

4   **Firehouse No. 12, 1919**
    Daniel R. Huntington
    E Union Street and 33rd Avenue
    A successful reuse of an obsolete structure.

5   **House, 1916**
    1100 38th Avenue
    A fine Craftsman Style bungalow.

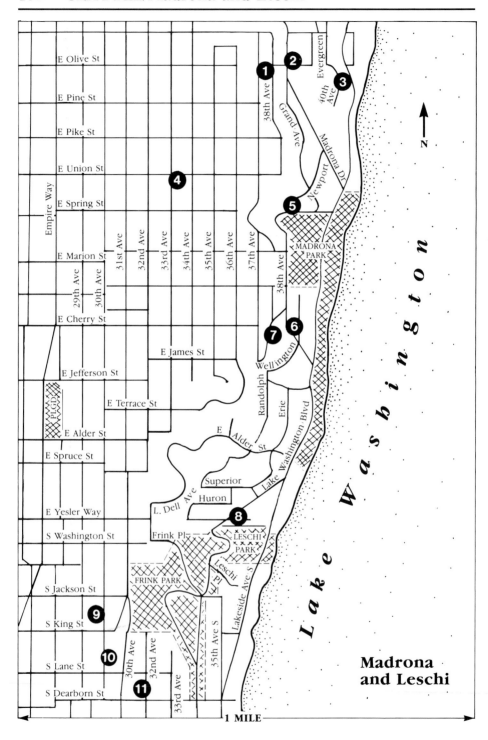

Madrona
and Leschi

6　**House,** 1964
Ralph Anderson & Partners
702 38th Avenue

Dramatically sited contemporary design
using wood expressively to heighten the effect
of structure. The formal T-plan, broad overhanging eaves, and emphasis on verticality
are hallmarks of Anderson's work.

7　**House,** 1962
Victor Steinbrueck
626 Randolph Place

Understated contemporary design that retreats gracefully into its setting.

8　**McKnight House,** 1914
100 Lake Washington Boulevard

Built as a family-owned hotel and restaurant
by Leschi Amusement Park to serve the trade
that came out to the shore on the Yesler Way
streetcar line, built in 1888, from Pioneer
Square.

9　**Judge Ronald House,** 1883, remodeled
1889
421 30th Avenue S

A Virginia architect restyled this house to
make the judge, also from the South, feel
more at home.

10　**House,** 1938
Paul Thiry
530 30th Avenue S

Another early Thiry house to be compared
with (33), (34), and (35) in Madison Park.

11　**House,** 1947–48
Paul Hayden Kirk
725 32nd Avenue S

A prototype modern house built by this famous Northwest architect for his brother,
now insensitively painted to obscure the simple post-and-beam structural aesthetic which
at the time marked it as avant-garde.

10 House

11 House

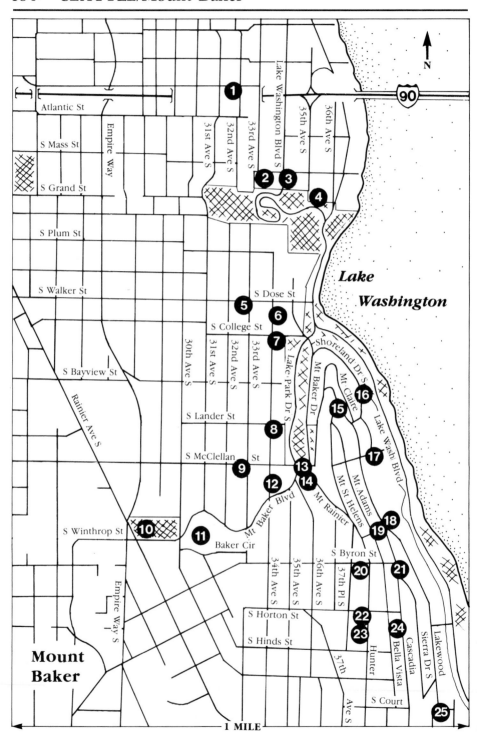

Mount Baker

In this early planned residential community, the neighborhood layout exhibits a number of laudable turn-of-the-century planning principles such as generous allotment to parks, landscaped boulevards, and streets laid out to reflect the topography. Extending roughly from the floating bridge south to Charlestown Street, this topography features a north-south ridge running along 31st Avenue and over to Mt. Baker Park, and another ridge between the park and the shore along Mt. St. Helens Place and Hunter Boulevard. The eastern slopes have striking views. Much of the sensitive siting is the work of the Olmsted Brothers, who were hired to plan the area by the Hunter Company, developers of the Mount Baker Addition; Colman Park is also their work. Three companies had platted their adjacent holdings in the early 1900s: the York Addition owned by G. M. Taggert in 1902, the Dose Addition owned by Charles Dose in 1906, and the Hunter Company Addition in 1907. By 1910 the companies had successfully promoted the area as an attractive zone of better residence. As was typical of the best suburban development of this period, the environment was thought to be conducive to community life.

The Mount Baker Park Improvement Club, established in 1909, built its clubhouse in the area designated for commercial development. Active community cooperation ensued; the neighborhood blossomed like a rose, with an annual rose show to prove it. By 1910 a streetcar line ran down 31st Avenue and over to the median strip on Hunter Boulevard. Schools were established and the area grew solidly until the 1930s depression and World War II period. Although the Lacey V. Murrow Bridge of 1940 disrupted the continuity of the lakeshore communities, Mount Baker remains a distinctive urban area well worth exploring.

1   **Thompson Laturner House,** 1897
    3119 S Day Street
    One of the area's few remaining large, towered Queen Anne villas.

2   **Stricker House,** 1968
    Milton Stricker
    3303 S Massachusetts Street
    A striking Wrightian design by a former fellow at F. L. Wright's Taliesin West.

2 Stricker house

3   **Cottage Group,** 1911
    Ellsworth Storey
    1706–10 Lake Washington Boulevard S

4   **Cottage Group,** 1915
    Ellsworth Storey
    1800–16 36th Avenue S

Though unpretentious in design, these two groups of cottages are among Seattle's most interesting and famous buildings. Designed "to be nice low-cost rental homes in a good neighborhood" in the words of Storey, who designed and owned them, they exemplify the kind of straightforward, functional, and structurally sophisticated building that is so deceptively simple as to invite the label of shanty or shack. The 20 × 32 foot, four-room units were set on timber posts and beams on concrete foundation blocks. They are single-wall construction with a single thickness of 1 × 6 inch, tongue-and-groove fir boards set inside the studs. The front porches have slatted screens with an effective thickthin pattern. Exposed roof framing and simple casement sash set in the structural module complete a good-carpenter image that is absent in many more visually elaborate designs. Walking down the hill past the second group of houses, the visitor is happily deceived into thinking they are staggered on the site. Instead it is the path that winds, a perfect and simple approach to giving variety to a house row.

5   **House, c. 1915**
Ellsworth Storey
SW corner 33rd Avenue S and S Dose Terrace

6   **House, 1928**
2212 34th Avenue S
Eccentric styling with a touch of French chateau.

7   **Evans House, 1915**
Ellsworth Storey
2306 34th Avenue S

An arresting design with a strong diagonal emphasis worked into the fused gable on the first and second floor. Compare this house with 1622 40th Avenue (Madrona, 3).

7 Evans house

8   **Dyer House, 1922**
Ellsworth Storey
2704 34th Avenue S

A handsome Swiss Chalet type with fine roof brackets and decorative wood detail. Storey felt that this style was appropriate to the locality.

9   **House, 1926**
Ellsworth Storey
SW corner 33rd Avenue S and S McClellan Street

A Prairie Style bungalow.

10   **Boy Scouts of America Headquarters Building, 1959**
Ibsen Nelsen & Associates
3120 Rainier Avenue S and Empire Way S

A handsome institutional office building in the contemporary Northwest idiom.

11   **Franklin High School, 1912**
Edgar Blair
3013 Mt. Baker Boulevard S

A very large, eclectic Classic institution, and an appropriately scaled landmark to terminate this Olmstedian boulevard with its tree-lined median strip. Unfortunately the building received an inappropriate addition in the 1960s.

12   **Two Houses, c. 1920**
2820 and 2823 34th Avenue S

Two more interesting bungalow designs across the street from each other.

13   **Mount Baker Commercial Center, 1928**
John Graham, Sr.
2803–9 Mt. Rainier Drive S

A brick business block topped off with an Art Deco, terra cotta ornamental design.

14   **Mount Baker Community Club House, 1914**
Charles Haynes
2811 Mt. Rainier Drive S

An informal wooden building with a rustic cast appropriate for its role in this early planned suburb.

15   **House, 1908**
2601 Cascadia Avenue S

16   **Bowles House, 1925**
Arthur B. Loveless
2520 Shoreland Drive S

A handsome, rambling English Cottage or Tudor Revival house with an impressive orange shale roof.

10 Boy Scouts of America Headquarters Building. Photo: Art Hupy

14 Mount Baker Community Club House

16 Bowles house

17 R. C. Force House, 1908
Saunders & Lawton
2810 Cascadia Avenue S

18 Dr. Bouffler House, 1925
Somervell & Putnam
3036 Cascadia Avenue S

A loosely eclectic design with a vague Mediterranean quality.

19 Stuart House, 1913
Elmer Green
3105 Cascadia Avenue S

A huge bungalow with Craftsman elements writ large.

20 Mount Baker Presbyterian Church, 1924
Albertson, Wilson & Richardson
3201 Hunter Boulevard S

Based on Early Christian church architecture with fine brick work and detail.

21 Two Houses, c. 1915
3208 and 3212 Cascadia Avenue S

A pair of small Craftsman bungalows.

22 Peterson House, 1913
A. Peterson
3303 Hunter Boulevard S

A design that gains drama from the expressive structural treatment of the two-story front porch.

23 Two Houses, c. 1915
3317 and 3319 Hunter Boulevard S

More heavy-timbered expression, similar to the Peterson house and perhaps by him.

22 Peterson house

24 **A. E. Lyon House,** 1907
    3311 Cascadia Avenue S
    Impressive and well-sited Colonial Revival
    design.

25 **House,** c. 1925
    SE corner of S Court Street and Lakewood
    Avenue S
    Derived from the Cottswold cottage type
    with a splendid shingled roof rolled at the
    eaves.

West of Mount Baker across Empire
Way at the corner of 24th Avenue and
Grand Street lies a fine contemporary
church.

26 **Japanese Presbyterian Church,** 1963
    Kirk/Wallace/McKinley
    1801 24th Avenue S
    A delicately articulated structure with the
    affinities for Japanese wood joinery that are
    hallmarks of Paul Hayden Kirk's work.

26 Japanese Presbyterian Church

Lake Washington Boulevard South and Columbia City

Lake Washington Boulevard continues
south along the Olmsteds' lakeshore
parkway. It terminates at Seward Park, a
large, natural area on a peninsula jutting
into Lake Washington. Seward Park is
part of the Olmsted plan, and remains,

but for the cars and roads, largely as
originally laid out. It exemplifies the
large-scale pastoral landscape park so
central to Olmstedian design. Once it
actually was an island, but construction
of the canal to Lake Union and the Sound

Lake Washington Boulevard South

lowered the water level of the lake sufficiently to expose a connecting stem of land. A narrow belt of middle class residential development follows the lakeshore southward for some miles. Columbia City is the major neighborhood in the area. Paralleling the lake but a bit inland lie the main southeastern arterials, Rainier Avenue and Empire Way, leading to the industrial suburbs of the Renton area. Predictably this is an area of mixed uses, modest dwellings, and the vernacular architecture of the commercial strip. The pre–World War II public housing community of Holly Park is the area's most consequential landmark.

Along Rainier Avenue South from Alaska to Dawson Street between 35th and 39th avenues is the heart of Columbia City, incorporated in 1893 and annexed by Seattle in 1907. The Seattle, Renton & Southern Railway completed its seven miles of track on Rainier Avenue in 1891; land speculation began

shortly thereafter, and Columbia grew prosperous from the railroad traffic and the sale of timber from the surrounding forests. Today, the tracks are gone and a collection of modest business blocks from the turn of the century and later, along with the erstwhile Columbia Hotel (1892), attests to this originally independent town. One of the nicest things about Columbia City is the park, or village green, which has a small but important-looking Carnegie Library of 1914.

Columbia branch, Seattle Public Library

Congregation Ezra Bessaroth. Photo: Art Hupy

House, 1972
David Hewitt
4927 49th Avenue S

Designed by the architect for himself.

Congregation Ezra Bessaroth,
Durham, Anderson & Freed
5217 S Brandon Street

Rough-sawn, dark-stained cedar boards sheathe the battered walls of this dramatic concrete structure—an eye-catcher by the side of the road.

House, 1957
Paul Hayden Kirk
5756 Wilson Avenue S

Modest-appearing from the road, this house steps down the slope and features a dramatic interior garden court lit by a clerestory. The recessed entrance is accented by a stone wall of Oregon basalt, a favorite material of Kirk's and one that he used often as a foil for lighter wood and glass construction.

Two Houses, c. 1925
Arthur B. Loveless
7126 and 7140 55th Avenue S

The first house belonged to the architect. Both are examples of the kind of gracious and well-sited Period Revival design that characterized Loveless' work.

Holly Park, 1943
John Paul Jones, Fred Ahlson, and Paul Thiry;
John R. Sproule, designer; Butler Sturtevant,
landscape architect
S Holly Street and 28th Avenue S

Another notable wartime public housing project to be compared with Yesler Terrace. Two- and four-unit apartments, brightly colored wooden cubes with mono-pitch roofs and the aesthetic of the Modern movement, are well sited on curving streets. The project has a spacious suburban quality, enhanced by playgrounds and community facilities. Perhaps most important, it is well maintained.

Holly Park

Boeing Field and Georgetown

Six and one-half miles south of downtown in the Duwamish River plain, the long narrow strip of Boeing Field, the King County Airport, parallels Interstate 5. Constructed in the 1920s it became the municipal airport and was the central flying field of the Seattle region for many years. In the 1930s the Boeing Airplane Company moved much of its operations here and today it continues to dominate the area. On the east side of the field is the Red Barn, Boeing Building 105, moved here in the 1970s from the port area to be restored by Ibsen Nelsen & Associates as a museum for the nation's oldest continually operating air-frame manufacturer. This two-story wooden structure, originally a boat house, was rented by William E. Boeing beginning in 1915 and used for the construction of the company's early planes. At 7755 East Marginal Way South is the Boeing Company Administration Building, circa 1935, a fine, late Moderne work. Further north at 6800 East Marginal Way South is the Hat and Boots Restau-

Boeing Company Administration Building (courtesy of Office of Urban Conservation)

rant, shaped like same and recently refurbished in the wave of enthusiasm for pop architecture. At the intersection of East Marginal Way South and Corson Avenue is the Seattle Water Department Operations Center (1972) by the Burke Associates. A late Brutalist work, the building has a forecourt fountain with a striking and appropriate sculpture.

To the north is Georgetown, where the buildings of the 1893 Seattle Brewing and Malting Company, 6004 Airport Way South, dominate the old town center. An early satellite settlement of Seattle, Georgetown boomed before and dur-

Hat and Boots Restaurant (courtesy of Office of Urban Conservation)

ing World War I. Like Ballard and Fremont, Georgetown and its environs have a wealth of industrial architecture waiting to be discovered and appreciated. Of particular historical interest is the 1906 Georgetown Steam Plant, a reinforced concrete frame structure in a stripped Classic Revival style at the northeast corner of the King County Airport. Designed by the Stone and Webster Engineering Corporation of Boston, it was originally built and operated by the Seattle Electric Company. In 1951 it was purchased by Seattle City Light.

Georgetown Steam Plant (courtesy of Office of Urban Conservation)

West Seattle

Alki Point was the original place of settlement for the handful of pioneers who later moved to Elliott Bay to found Seattle. The settlement was christened New York after the Terry brothers' home state, but diminished horizons led to the name "Alki," meaning "by and by" in Chinook. Most of the pioneers later moved to Seattle, but Charles Terry stayed on for a while in New York–Alki to manage his store and lumber pier. Competition from Yesler's mill, and a windstorm that destroyed the pier, caused him to move to Seattle, ending the white settlement of the point for about thirty-five years. In 1888, Puget Sound's first ferry line was established between Seattle and Duwamish Head to the northeast of Alki; the dock was near the present east end of Southwest Atlantic Street. A beach road was laid over to

Alki Point, which became popular for Sunday excursions.

By the time West Seattle was incorporated in 1902, there was a summer cottage settlement in Alki and a thriving commercial-industrial center around Duwamish Head with fishing canneries, warehouses, taverns, etc. When West Seattle was annexed by Seattle in 1907, the electric railroad indirectly spawned the Luna Amusement Park on Duwamish Head. It enjoyed an era of popularity until about 1912, but burned in 1931. One of the most praiseworthy events in the city's history was the donation by Ferdinand Schmitz of fifty acres for a true wilderness park, the only piece of the virgin timber that once covered Seattle left undisturbed. Public utilities and facilities came slowly, with the first school established in 1912. Because of the steep grade of Duwamish Head, transportation was also limited. Older development along the shoreline on picturesque view sites contrasts with that of the more recent past and present on the flat highland known as Admiral. California Avenue is the major commercial street.

1   **Hainsworth House,** 1907
John Graham
2657 37th Avenue SW
Originally part of the large estate of a major developer, William Hainsworth.

2   **House,** 1911
Andrew Willatsen
2715 Belvedere Avenue SW
Shows the strong influence of F. L. Wright on his former draftsman, who contributed a number of Prairie Style houses to Seattle suburbs.

3   **West Seattle High School,** 1917
Edgar Blair
Walnut Avenue SW and SW Stevens Street
A strong functional design by an architect who initiated steel framing in Seattle schools.

4   **Admiral Twin Theatre,** 1938
B. Marcus Priteca
2343 California Avenue SW

Moderne design by Seattle's leading theater designer, who also designed the Coliseum downtown.

5   **West Seattle Public Library,** 1910
Somervell & Cote
2306 42nd Avenue SW
One of the many branch libraries by this firm.

6   **Lamphere House,** 1973
Ralph Anderson & Partners
Edgewood Avenue SW
Designed by one of the leading proponents of the Northwest timber tradition.

7   **House,** 1910
1305 Sunset Avenue SW
An experimental concrete house remodeled by Donald Avery.

8   **House,** 1916
1414 Sunset Avenue SW
Designed as a replica of a Swedish house.

9   **Potter House,** c. 1915
1439 Sunset Avenue SW
A subtly composed Craftsman Style house.

10   **Kennedy House,** 1909
Wilson & Loveless
1620 47th Avenue SW

Luna Park (courtesy of Photo Collection, UW Library)

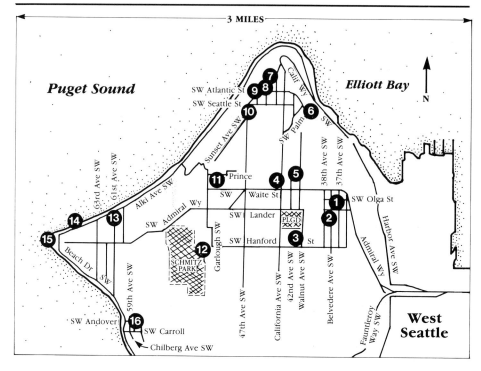

11 **Wilson House,** 1908
Joseph Wilson
5037 SW Prince Street

Sophisticated eclectic design by the principal designer of the Seattle Tower in the firm of Albertson, Wilson & Richardson.

12 **House,** 1958
5231 SW Forest Street

A sensitively sited house with a strong Wrightian cast.

13 **Bernard House, Fir Lodge,** 1903
2717 61st Street SW

A prominent landmark built from logs salvaged from Alki beach. A block south at 6301 Southwest Stevens Street, also from 1903, are the stables of this former mini-estate, now a house also on a corner lot.

14 **Carkonen Apartments,** 1979
Olson/Walker
3033 Alki Avenue SW

Blue and white triplexes sited offshore.

15 **Alki Lighthouse,** 1916
Alki Point

16 **House,** 1904
4004 Chilberg Avenue SW

A fine Craftsman cabin.

14 Carkonen Apartments

Queen Anne Hill

The only Seattle neighborhood named for an architectural style, Queen Anne Town, as it originally went, took its name from the great number of towered villas built on its slopes around the turn of the century. So few remain that the name is no longer as meaningful. Arriving almost simultaneously with the other earliest settlers, in 1853, Thomas Mercer had come from the East to claim 320 acres of the hill which he called simply "Eden." Not that the name meant anything sacred. With the aid of others, Mercer began logging off the west side of the hill where the logs could easily be floated to the water. Later, David Denny's mill on the south shore of Lake Union promoted logging on the east side. By the time the hill became officially part of Seattle in 1891, several civic improvements had taken place. The First Street Cable Railway Company had extended service to the top of Queen Anne Avenue where a commercial district was established. In 1891 Kinnear Park was planned on the wooded slope looking over the Sound to the city. This park was the terminus of the North Seattle Electric line.

In the decades around the century's turning, the southern part of Queen Anne Hill became a prime residential area. The 1903 Olmsted plan recommended a 150-foot-wide tree-lined boulevard to circle the hill. In 1906 residents demanded such a drive and got the stretch of Queen Anne Boulevard on the west side. Curving and tree-lined Bigelow Avenue on the east side is another segment of the Olmsted plan. Other small parks which grace the older residential area are Kerry Park, given by Albert Sperry Kerry and his wife in 1907, and the Reginald Parson estate garden, now public. Building activity on the hill has proceeded in predictable ways with the prime view areas increasingly the target for high-rise apartment blocks, while the upper, flat areas retain a low-density character with modest, single-family houses.

1 **Public Schools Administration Building,** 1947
J. Lister Holmes & Associates
815 Fourth Avenue N
A well-detailed building in the post–World War II modern aesthetic. The different functions of the building are expressed by changes in scale, structure, and use of material.

1 Public Schools Administration Building (courtesy of Seattle Public Schools)

2 **Aloha Terrace Apartments,** c. 1950
200 Aloha Street
An uncommon approach to a hillside site.

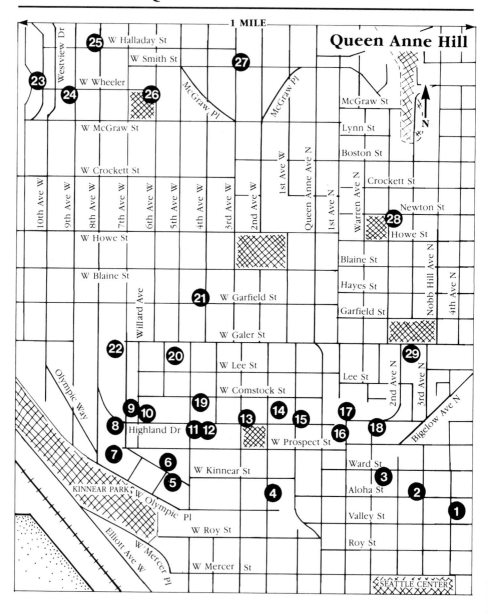

The lower slopes of Queen Anne Hill, especially along Highland Drive, were favored by the wealthy in the first period of development from about 1890 to 1910. East of Queen Anne Avenue from Prospect to Lee Street is an area worth exploring for the number of substantial eclectic homes that dot the hillside. Alas, most of the towered villas that inspired the hill's name are gone.

3   House, 1974–80
    Bruce Goff
    173 Ward Street

    Originally a lapped-cedar-sided house of a
    conventional sort, this has now been trans-
    formed into a dazzling, somewhat space-age
    dwelling by the wizardry of Bruce Goff,
    most of whose work is in the Midwest.

4   Two Houses, c. 1890
    912 and 918 Second Avenue W

    Two fine shingled Queen Anne Style houses.
    The Ankenny house, at 912, has a particu-
    larly nice medley of rounded forms interlock-
    ing with a gambrel roof that has a subtle
    eyebrow dormer.

5   House, c. 1915
    Andrew Willatsen
    515 W Kinnear Place

    This and two other houses on Kinnear, 320
    and 218, are modest Prairie Style houses with
    Willatsen's signature details.

6   House, 1889
    520 W Kinnear Place

    A well-maintained Queen Anne villa.

6 House

7   House, c. 1915
    715 W Prospect Street

    A small shingled bungalow with some
    Japanese influence.

Beyond the Betty Bowen view point
park (8) at the end of Highland, designed in 1977 by Victor Steinbrueck,
the tree-lined stretch of Queen Anne

Boulevard has retaining walls at Seventh
and Eighth avenues designed by
W. R. B. Willcox in 1913 with brickwork set in rough concrete to make a
simple but effective pattern. The composition of steps, railings, and lights is
also well handled to create an inspiring
work of civic design.

9   Pifer House, 1970
    Ralph Anderson & Partners
    1217 Willard Avenue W

    Another box-like design with an exaggerated
    vertical volume.

9 Pifer house

10 Parson House, 1905
    Somervell & Cote
    618 W Highland Drive

    The estate that donated the lovely garden
    next door to the public.

11 Kerry House, 1906
Bebb & Mendel
421 W Highland Drive

Similar to (12); the roof has been unfortunately altered.

12 Stimson House, 1910
Bebb & Mendel
415 W Highland Drive

A ponderous half-timbered design with a massive cut-granite ground floor, certainly expressive of wealth and social position. Bebb & Gould designed many houses for Seattle's first families, generally in variations of the half-timbered theme that was a legacy of the English Arts & Crafts movement.

13 Black House, 1912
Andrew Willatsen
220 W Highland Drive

Though the ground floor has been slightly altered in respect to material and window sash, the design preserves its strong Prairie School character identified by the low-pitched, broadly overhanging gable roof, the band of second-story windows tied to a belt course, and the large, boldly framed ground floor windows. Willatsen was briefly in partnership with Barry Byrne; both worked in Frank Lloyd Wright's Chicago office.

13 Black house

14 Victoria Apartments, 1921
John Graham, Sr.
100 W Highland Drive

A very large Tudorish apartment block well composed around a court; Seattle's first condominium.

15 Ballard House, 1906
DeNeuf and Heide
22 W Highland Drive

An elegant Neo-Georgian or Colonial Revival house.

16 Chappel House, 1906
Edgar A. Matthews
21–23 Highland Drive

A highly decorative use of nonstructural half-timbering and a sprightly variety of forms; Matthews was a San Francisco architect.

16 Chappel house

17 House, 1965
Ralph Anderson & Partners
18 Highland Drive

A formal, vertical box, dramatic in its simplicity. Accentuated vertical volumes and broad roof overhangs with somber, monochromatic color schemes are typical of Anderson's work of this period. See also Pifer house (9) at the other end of Highland Drive.

17 House

18 **Riddle House,** 1893
   E. W. Houghton
   153 Highland Drive

Seattle's best example of the Queen Anne–Shingle Style composed of interlocking rounded spatial volumes and a general use of Colonial forms and detail.

18 Riddle house

19 **House,** 1970
   Olson/Walker
   411 W Comstock Street

An interesting contemporary house in concrete block.

20 **West Queen Anne Elementary School,** 1896, 1916
   Skillings & Corner
   515 W Galer Street

A significant city landmark and focal point on the hill, the school is one of two intact pre-1900 structures still in use by Public School District #1. The simplified, vaguely medieval styling gives the building a dignified domestic presence. The 1916 wing is harmonious with the original construction.

21 **Queen Anne Library,** 1913
   Somervell & Thomas
   400 W Garfield Street

A pleasantly scaled public building in the same stylistic line of descent as the elementary school.

22 **Three Houses,** c. 1930
   1423 and 1429 Seventh Avenue W and 1423
   Eighth Avenue W

A group of period revival houses which point up the flexibility of period revival design; the last house is a particularly interesting amalgam of 1904 Romanesque Revival and 1930s Mediterranean styling.

20 West Queen Anne Elementary School

The block bounded by Newton and Boston streets between 13th and 14th avenues is a remnant of the 1890s development of the hill.

23 Mayor Cotterill House, 1910
2501 Westview Drive W

A shingled Craftsman Style house of woodsy simplicity built for one of the city's most famous mayors, who supported the outdoor life by personally laying out an extensive system of bicycle trails still in use.

24 House, 1910
Andrew Willatsen
2433 W Wheeler Street

Another house in the F. L. Wrightian manner.

25 Seventh Church of Christ Scientist, 1926
Thomas, Grainger & Thomas
2555 Eighth Avenue W

An effectively scaled and decorated Neo-Byzantine–Early Christian Revival church design.

25 Seventh Church of Christ Scientist

26 Frantz H. Coe Elementary School, 1907
James Stephen
Sixth Avenue W between W McGraw and W Smith Streets

One of the group of monumental wooden schools done in Colonial Revival or Mission Revival Style by Stephen, official school district architect. For others see Capitol Hill, the University District, First Hill, and the Green Lake area.

27 House, 1958
Robert Reichert
2500 W Smith Street

Designed by the architect to house himself, his mother, and a pipe organ, the structure was shaped by the necessity of accommodating the pipes and providing a proper musical setting. Originally the house was painted in an abstract, black and white pattern. Though this early use of super graphics was a success in the architectural world, it was not so in this otherwise conventional neighborhood. Perhaps some day the graphic format will be restored.

27 House

28 Wilke Farmhouse, 1898
1902 Second Avenue N

A relic of the vanished past, this pioneer farmhouse was erected to advertise the skills of its building contractor–owner. Together with its outbuildings, this farm witnesses to a semi-agrarian life on what was then the edge of town.

29 Queen Anne High School, 1909
James Stephen
215 Galer Street

The most visible landmark on the hill, second only to the television tower.

Magnolia Bluff

Ceded to the Secretary of War in 1895, the area now called Magnolia Bluff became Camp Lewis in 1916 during the World War I buildup. The end of the point remained an active military base, Fort Lawton, until its demobilization in 1970. Now most of the area occupied by the fort has been turned over to the city for Discovery Park. An ambitious development plan conceived in 1972 by the respected eastern landscape architect Dan Kiley is only partly realized. When it is completed it will be the first new Olmstedian-scale public open space since Seattle's first wave of park development. In one small portion of the park leased for ninety-nine years to the United Indians of All Tribes Foundation stands the Daybreak Star Arts Center (1977). Designed by Arai/Jackson in collaboration with Lawney Reyes, this impressive timbered building makes use of traditional Northwest Indian forms and motifs.

Like Queen Anne Hill, Magnolia ranges from an exclusive marine view residential development in the southwest portion to an uneventful flatland area to the northeast merging with the industrial strip along Salmon Bay. Mayor Cotterill rode his bicycle along the Sound, and the Olmsted Brothers recommended this track as part of the parkway system, but there was little building until the post–World War I period. The curving waterside drives, particularly Magnolia Boulevard and Perkins Lane, afford fine views and occasional glimpses of interesting houses, but it is difficult to be an architectural sightseer in the area. Three easily seen and notable buildings are:

Catherine Blaine Junior High School, 1952 J. Lister Holmes & Associates; Robert Dietz & Charles MacDonald
2550 34th Avenue W

An outstanding example of the large public school in the full-fledged postwar Modern idiom with natural lighting through sawtooth skylights, antiglare ceiling baffles, window walls, modular construction, and a division of building units according to their function. Recreation facilities are shared with the Parks Department as a community service.

Daybreak Star Arts Center

Magnolia Branch Library, 1974
Kirk/Wallace/McKinley
2801 34th Avenue W

An informal public building graced by a clear, post-and-beam structure, abundant natural light, and a generally open, welcoming ambiance.

Magnolia Branch Library

Runions House, 1972
Ralph D. Anderson
2587 Magnolia Boulevard W

A striking design in wood on a small, triangular site.

Runions house. Photo: Julius Shulman

Ballard

Platted in 1887, Ballard remained an independent town until 1907. Like Fremont, its original industry was milling lumber; its first citizens were Midwest lumbermen who moved to the Northwest as the Great Lakes timber stands gave out. Once Ballard was known as the "Shingle Capital of the World." Somewhat later it became a Scandinavian enclave and the home of a fishing fleet. Although architecturally unprepossessing, the old commercial district has a contextual importance that the community is wisely seeking to preserve through the creation of a historic district along Ballard Avenue between Market Street and Dock Place. Lining the street are mostly brick buildings dating from about 1900. An urban design plan by Folke Nyberg will organize street refurbishing and introduce the district by a sign and monument incorporating the cast-iron columns from the old city hall. An unusual aspect of the plan is that the electric street wiring will not be put underground. The architect and the community felt that cheap power from the overhead wires had contributed much to Ballard and should be preserved as a historic feature.

The Ballard entries appear on the Green Lake map.

1 **Stimson Mill Office,** c. 1913
Cutter & Malmgren
2116 Vernon Place

A sedate design with a residential character by this famous Spokane firm.

2 **Ballard Fire Station No. 18,** 1911
Bebb & Mendel
NW Market and Russell Avenue NW

A monumental brick building with the character of a German Räthaus. It was rehabilitated by the Historic Seattle Preservation and Development Authority in 1977.

3 **Puget Sound Mutual Savings Bank,** 1973
Kirk/Wallace/McKinley
5512 22nd Avenue NW

The Hiram M. Chittenden Locks,
1911–16
Lake Washington Ship Canal at Puget Sound
(off the map)

The idea of connecting Puget Sound with Lakes Washington and Union first received federal recognition in 1867, but realization awaited the construction of permanent masonry locks in 1911–16. Achievement of the project was primarily the work of Hiram M. Chittenden, district engineer for the U.S. Army Corps of Engineers from 1906 to 1908 and a man of many accomplishments. His design of the locks and 1907 report on the whole project persuaded Congress to adopt it. Construction of the eight-mile channel regulated the levels of the inland waters, raising the level of Salmon Bay and lowering that of Lake Washington twenty feet. One of Seattle's major tourist attractions, the locks operate free of charge day and night. The sur-

Hiram M. Chittenden Locks. Photo: A. Curtis, 1921 (courtesy of Photo Collection, UW Library)

rounding park with the Carl English Memorial Gardens provides an added attraction. In cooperation with the Corps of Engineers, the Seattle Garden Club inaugurated, in 1958, a further beautification of the eight-mile stretch of canal banks called Canal Parkway which provides paths and view parks. The lock buildings, constructed by the Corps in 1914–16, were designed by Carl Gould in a style gently reminiscent of Parisian Art Nouveau.

Hiram's Restaurant, 1977
Barnett Schorr & Co.
5300 34th Avenue NW (off the map)

Originally designed using the Butler system, this corrugated metal building fits well in its industrial context. The interior is particularly successful, while the site affords diners a grandstand view of shipping activity on the canal.

Hiram's Restaurant

In the northwest section of Ballard at 3306 Northwest 71st Street is the 1908 Norvell House, a late Queen Anne villa with a strong Swiss chalet character and some extraordinary gingerbread.

Fremont

A former 1880s mill town with a still strong and independent community spirit, Fremont is currently seeking to revitalize its historic business center at the foot of the 1916 Fremont Bridge.

Architecturally the area has little to offer the monument-minded tourist. The most distinguished buildings are those in the old center on the blocks bounded by Evanston, 36th, Aurora, and 34th—also an area for crafts and antiques shops.

On the south side of 34th Street at Fremont Avenue is a particularly fine and appropriate sculpture titled *Waiting for the Interurban*, by Richard

Beyer. On rainy days you almost feel like giving the figures a ride.

The Fremont entries appear on the Green Lake map.

1   **Fremont Building,** 1901
    3427 Fremont Avenue N

2   **J. P. Dean Building,** 1906
    3500 Fremont Avenue N

    Two of the most characterful of the old commercial buildings which together make a winning ensemble.

3   **Fremont Public Library,** 1921
    Daniel R. Huntington
    731 N 35th Street

    A Carnegie grant made this compact design echoing the California Mission Style possible. The interior is also worth viewing.

Waiting for the Interurban. *Photo: Linda Reed*

4   **B. F. Day School,** 1891–92
John Parkinson
3921 Linden Avenue N

The city's oldest school still in operation.

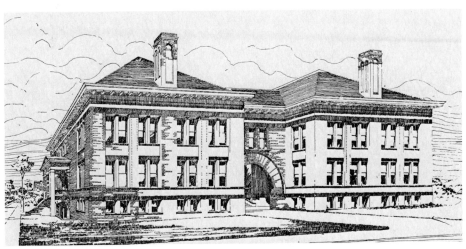

4 B. F. Day School (courtesy of Photo Collection, UW Library)

Wallingford

Platted in the 1880s as a residential district, the eastern part of this hill on the north shore of Lake Union was named after developer John Wallingford, while the western part was called Latona by its developer, John Moore, after a Lake Union passenger launch. The two communities grew together and were annexed by Seattle in 1891. Development of Woodland, the proverbial amusement park, was concurrent with the running of trolley lines along Woodland Park Avenue connecting Fremont with Green Lake in 1889 and with the park in 1893. Soon a transportation network encircled the area. In 1893, David Denny built the wooden Latona Bridge, now the site of the I-5 bridge, for his Third Avenue Street Railway Company. The Seattle, Lake Shore & Eastern Railroad ran on the north shore of the lake. The 1916 Fremont Bridge was preceded in 1900 by a wooden trestle bridge. Such a network also promoted growth of the kind of industry along Lake Union's north shore that discouraged upper middle class settlement. A gas works, a garbage incinerator, tar and asphalt companies, and various wood products factories caused the sort of pollution that made living in Wallingford hazardous to health. By 1956, when the gas works shut down because of increased use of natural gas, a large number of residents had already moved out in the post–World War II suburban exodus. In recent years, Wallingford has shared the urban resettlement pattern of the older inner city suburbs. In 1973 an organized and vocal community defeated the development of a shopping center on the grounds of the Home of the Good Shepherd at North 50th Street and Sunnyside. Now this 1906 institutional

2 Gas Works Park

building designed by C. Alfred Breitung has been converted into a community and arts center with its generous grounds preserved as open space. The majority of Wallingford's buildings are builder's bungalows with a few Victorian residences scattered throughout the area. Entries appear on the Green Lake map.

1 **Latona Elementary School**, 1906, 1927
James Stephen; Edgar Blair
NE 42nd Street and Fifth Avenue N

This is the only one of Stephen's great wooden school buildings to incorporate Queen Anne towers. Highly visible from Interstate 5 just north of the bridge.

1 Latona Elementary School. Photo: Webster & Stevens (courtesy of Photo Collection, UW Library)

2 **Gas Works Park**, 1978
Olson/Walker; Richard Haag Associates, landscape architects
Lake Union off Northlake Way

One of the most inspiring of preservation projects, Richard Haag's design and patient planning for this former industrial sink have resulted in a major waterside park. The now grassy point jutting out into the lake is presided over by the remaining collection of industrial dinosaurs that formerly produced gas. Much credit goes to Haag for seeing the iron-age complex as an aesthetic resource and for providing a splendidly simple, minimal maintenance format to show it off. Beside the ever fascinating views of the sailboats on Lake Union and the cityscape across the water, major attractions include the Play Barns and the recycled boiler house and exhauster buildings. Here the machinery has been brightly

painted and serves as the most indestructible jungle gym ever. To the west, an artificially made mound created by site excavation has an autonomic sun dial on top created by Charles Greening.

At 4416 Wallingford Avenue North is the 1904 Interlake School (3) one of the dozen or so designed by James Stephen that are still in use. For another in the same area see the Latona Elementary School.

3 Interlake School. Photo: A. Curtis, 1904 (courtesy of Photo Collection, UW Library)

University District

Development of the university district came logically with the university's move from downtown to its present site in 1895. Growth was not particularly oriented to the institution until after the Alaska-Yukon-Pacific Exposition of 1909 when the campus itself began to grow. The twenties boom established the business district along University Way from about 40th to 50th Street. It is presently occupied by small retail businesses catering to the campus population. The northern boundary of the district, Ravenna Boulevard and the Ravenna-Cowen Park (1), is mentioned in the Olmsted Brothers' plan of 1903.

From an urban design standpoint the area presents a clear image marked by memorable landmarks. From the I-5 freeway which forms the district's western boundary, the earlier Gothic landmark of the Blessed Sacrament Church (1910) at 5041 Ninth Avenue Northeast has been joined by the banal Safeco high-rise office building at 45th Street and Brooklyn Avenue in demarking the skyline. Within the area, 17th Avenue and Ravenna Boulevard provide memorable passages leading north then west from the university campus. Ravenna-Cowen Park is bridged by the graceful concrete 15th Avenue viaduct which keeps cars out of that quiet precinct.

Population pressures have resulted in multi-unit residential development through much of the district though a sizable area of single-family homes exists north of 50th Street. University Way, known as "The Ave," has become a lively strip of youth- and singles-oriented eateries, boutiques, and stores which seem to be regularly remodeled and enlarged. The Northlake Urban Renewal Project of the late 1960s resulted, typically, in a nondescript, desolated area of parking lots and miscellaneous structures in the shadow of the freeway bridge. Compared with older parts of the campus community, there is a notable lack of "place" here.

1 **Ravenna-Cowen Park**
NE 58th to 62nd Street, Brooklyn to 24th Avenue NE

Privately owned in the 1880s by W. W. Beck, who named it for the Italian city, Ravenna Park was served by the Ravenna Park or East Lake streetcar line and also the University line late in the decade. In 1889 Beck installed benches and pavilions and made pathways among the giant, first growth cedars. In 1907 Charles Cowen gave the city twelve acres to the west. In 1911 the city acquired Beck's land through condemnation and, with astonishing ease, began cutting down the giant trees to provide funds for the park department. Today the park is certainly pleasant enough; Ravenna Boulevard, a segment of the Olmsted parkway system, cuts across the northern part of the university district in a picturesque way.

2 **Annie and Homer Russell Houses,** 1904
F. A. Sexton
5803 and 5727 8th Avenue NE

Two chalets in the Craftsman Style built from builder's plans by a pioneer woman doctor and her son. An expressionistic use of wood is evident in the over-long logs crossing at the corners, and porch posts with the knots left unplaned. In true Craftsman tradition the chimneys are made of neatly stacked river boulders.

3 **Two Houses,** c. 1910
5260 16th Avenue NE and 5269 17th Avenue NE

Two vernacular houses whose builders clearly thought in terms of the-more-style-the-better. The 16th Avenue house is a collision between the Queen Anne Colonial and the

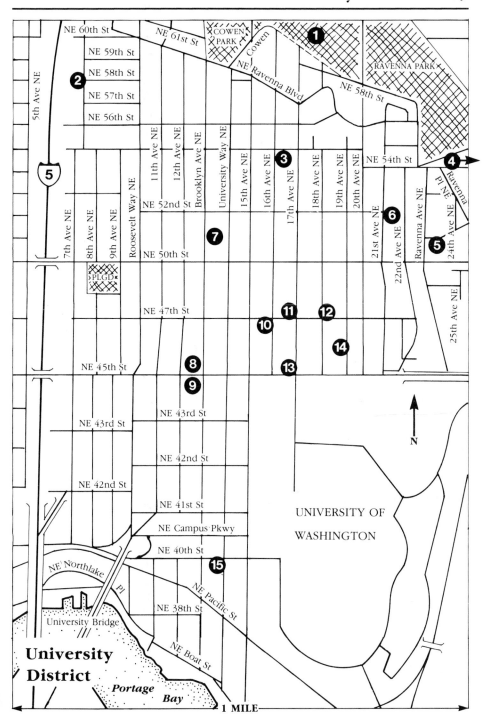

3 5269 17th Avenue NE

Bungalow; around the end of the block, the other is a Missioned-up Classic Box.

4   **Deluxe 2 Restaurant,** 1972, remodeled 1976
Barnett Schorr
NW corner NE 54th Street and 26th Avenue NE

5   **Blakely Psychiatric Clinic,** 1956
Paul Hayden Kirk
2271 NE 51st Street
One of many small medical clinics designed by Kirk in the postwar period as post-and-beam modular pavilions of glass and wood often with basalt rock screen-walls.

5 Blakely Psychiatric Clinic

6   **Steps and House Group**
NE 52nd Street between 21st and 22nd Avenues NE
The steps and a group of Craftsman Style cottages to the south form an attractive ensemble of vernacular urban design.

7   **University Heights Elementary School,** 1902
Bebb & Mendel
5031 University Way NE

A vast wooden Mission Revival school handsomely painted. This and some other Seattle public schools built in the teens form a remarkable but unfortunately dwindling group of monumentally scaled wooden structures in Colonial Revival styles. See also the 1906 Latona School, at Northeast 42nd Street and 5th Avenue North; the Isaac Stevens School (Capitol Hill, 51); the 1902 Green Lake Elementary School (Green Lake, 6); and the West Queen Anne Elementary School (Queen Anne, 20) by James Stephen, school district architect from 1902 to 1910.

7 University Heights Elementary School

8   **Meany Hotel** (now University Tower Hotel), 1931
R. C. Reamer
4507 Brooklyn Avenue NE
A striking early Modern design with glazed corner bays that give every room a dramatic view.

9   **Safeco Building,** 1973
Naramore, Bain, Brady & Johanson
4347 Brooklyn Avenue NE
A restrained, precast concrete office tower which when viewed in conjunction with the Meany Hotel offers interesting comparisons between the economy of the 1930s and that of the 1970s.

10   **University Presbyterian Church,** 1916
Ellsworth Storey
NE 47th Street and 16th Avenue NE
Storey had a personal way with the half-timbered style as can be seen by the interior as well as exterior of this residentially scaled church with a thoughtfully designed lychgate at the street.

8 Meany Hotel (courtesy of Photo Collection, UW Library)

10 University Presbyterian Church

11 **Sigma Nu House,** 1926
Ellsworth Storey
1616 NE 47th Street

An idiosyncratic design with Wrightian overtones.

12 **Alpha Tau Omega House,** 1929
Lionel Pries
1800 NE 47th Street

A rare work by a local architect whose most significant contribution to the field was his

11 Sigma Nu house

years of teaching at the University of Washington Department of Architecture.

13 **Phi Gamma Delta House,** 1927
Mellor, Meigs & Howe, with J. Lister Holmes
5404 17th Avenue NE

A unique west coast work by a famous Philadelphia firm demonstrating the national sway of the Tudor Revival at this time.

14 **Campus Christian Ministry,** 1967
Nelsen, Sabin & Varey
3525 19th Avenue NE

An award-winning design with a courtyard scheme.

15 **Man Bites Dog Restaurant,** 1978
Barnett Schorr Miller Company
SW corner University Way and N 40th Street

An exemplary small-scale demonstration of late-1970s High-Tech design; it is destined to disappear in ten years.

15 Man Bites Dog Restaurant

University of Washington

The Northwest's first and largest university now occupies over six hundred acres of land extending north from Portage and Union bays. As the Territorial University it occupied one building on a ten-acre site downtown at Fifth Avenue and University Street where the Olympic Hotel now stands. This first structure was a porticoed, Classic Revival block with a cupola and white picket fence, as someone quipped, "to keep the stumps from getting out." Records show that a carpenter, John Pike, was paid for the building's design, probably from a pattern book, and construction. Instruction began in November 1861 with thirty-seven pupils, thirty-six of whom were below college level.

Insufficient funds plagued the administration until the mid-1880s when enrollment accelerated. When the site became inadequate, the regents considered moving out of the center of the expanding city. A first plan, drawn up by architect William E. Boone for the Board of University Land and Building Commissioners, shows a half-dozen or so buildings informally set around a loop road near the Northern Pacific tracks, still visible in the U-shaped circulation routes at the bottom of the campus. The plan was never realized and the board itself was abolished by the 1893 legislature. A regents' committee was then authorized by the legislature to proceed with a new plan. This one located the

Territorial University building (upper right), 1870s (courtesy of Photo Collection, UW Library)

Denny Hall. Photo: James O. Sneddon (courtesy of UW)

first building, Denny Hall, on newly acquired high ground to the north overlooking Lake Washington and facing the old Seattle-Snohomish Road. Designed by Saunders & Lawton, the building was started in 1894 and was largely complete by 1895 when the new campus opened. By 1896, two dormitories, Lewis and Clark halls, designed by Josenhans & Allen were built.

Soon after, Professor A. H. Fuller of the College of Engineering was asked to make a plan to accommodate the existing structures and provide for future growth. This scheme, later called the Oval Plan, laid out an ellipse that encompassed the first three buildings plus Science Hall, now Parrington, and a power house later destroyed by fire.

In 1904, the Olmsted Brothers prepared a plan retaining the oval as the Arts Quadrangle and siting other buildings to the south around a Science Quadrangle. This scheme was swept aside the next year when the planning began for the 1909 Alaska-Yukon-Pacific Exposition, inspired by Portland's 1905 Lewis and Clark Exposition. After consider-

able lobbying of the state and federal government, the fair became a reality in May 1908 when Congress voted an appropriation for the federal buildings and exhibits. Previously, in 1906, largely through the efforts of University Professor Edmund S. Meany the regents agreed to have the fair on a 250-acre part of the campus if it would result in improvement of the grounds and several new permanent buildings.

J. C. Olmsted of the Olmsted Brothers' firm began the landscape design in 1906 with both the expansion of the university and the scenic possibilities of the site in mind. In keeping with the aesthetic preference of the times, the slope was cleared of its dense fir and cedar forest and graded to receive a formal design of walks, pools, fountains, and gardens. Dazzling floral displays, a major feature of the landscaping, were rearranged during the run of the fair to delight the public. To assist in this transformation of the landscape into an eastern garden-esque setting, a greenhouse and nursery were built where over 200,000 plants were propagated. Much of the extensive engineering of the site was necessary to provide a circulation system for the great number of fair visitors. Pieces of its patterns are identifiable in the present campus, the most obvious and impressive being the Rainier Vista with the Drumheller Fountain and what remains of the great rose garden. When the mountain is "out," as they say, this is one of the most memorable places to see it. Other surviving elements are Campus Parkway, which was the original main access to the Expo grounds, and the curving paths on the east side of the campus.

Alaska-Yukon-Pacific Exposition. Photo: R. T. Jones, 1909 (courtesy of Photo Collection, UW Library)

Supervising architects for the Expo were Howard & Galloway, a San Francisco firm (John Galen Howard was campus architect for the University of California, Berkeley, at that time). In general the exposition architecture had the exotic stage-set qualities considered essential for the success of such undertakings. Of the four new permanent buildings left when the fair closed, only the old Architecture Hall, built as a museum, survives today. It was designed by Howard in a relatively staid, eclectic Classic Style.

Again the Olmsted Brothers were hired to adapt the Expo ground plan to the needs of the campus. From 1911 to 1914 they evolved a plan adopted in 1915 after some modifications by the local architectural firm of Bebb & Gould. This plan, featuring Academic and Science quadrangles set nearly at right angles to each other, underwent further revision by the same firm in 1933–34. It con-

tinued in force until after World War II when the greatest growth in the university's history took place. The architect chiefly involved with alterations and additions to the plans was John Paul Jones of Bebb & Jones.

During this last period of growth an architectural commission appointed by the regents was established in 1957 to guide campus development. Past professional members of the commission have included William W. Wurster, Pietro Belluschi, Minoru Yamasaki, and Hidao Sasaki. Today the growth rings have finally reached the limits of the land. The first ring, outside Stevens Way, has been mainly given over to the expansion of science and engineering facilities that witness the enormous investment of federal money here as in other major U.S. universities following World War II. The northeast corner has been the site of dormitory expansion. East of Montlake Boulevard are the athletic facilities,

South Campus area. Photo: James O. Sneddon, 1972 (courtesy of UW)

while the so-called South Campus area is the location of the health sciences and hospital complex, with the marine sciences at the edge of Portage Bay. In recent years some development has taken place in the southwestern blocks, generally on a smaller scale.

Despite much filling in of open spaces with buildings, the central core of the campus still bears the stamp of the original plan with its quadrangles meeting at the brick-paved Central Plaza framed by principal university facilities. The main entrances from Campus Parkway and Memorial Way converge here and link up with the open-ended axis of Rainier Vista. Although there has been no master plan for landscaping, the legacy of the A.Y.P. Expo combined with development of specific areas has endowed the campus with a lush landscaped setting. Architecturally, the buildings on campus reflect the range of styles fashionable over its lifetime. Dis-

continuities of style are softened by the use of brick as a basic building material, resulting in a more or less uniform palette and texture, at least for the central campus.

Maps of the University of Washington campus are available at the Visitor Information Center, 4014 University Way Northeast. The buildings listed on this campus tour are located by the coordinates on the official map. It also identifies the buildings by name in an alphabetical listing.

The campus tour starts with the original hilltop campus accessible by Memorial Way, a gracious tree-lined avenue that also provides access to the 1962 Burke Memorial Washington State Museum by James J. Chiarelli, a memorial to Judge Thomas Burke (1849–1925), a pioneer civic leader, by his wife, Caroline McGilvra Burke. Along with the fine collection of Northwest

Indian artifacts is an architectural relic, the large stained glass Tiffany window that was formerly in the Leary house (Capitol Hill, 10). Opposite the museum is the old Observatory (1895) by Charles W. Saunders.

Denny Hall, 1894–95, 1956–57
Saunders & Lawton; interior remodeled by Grainger, Thomas & Barr
6-L

A chateauesque design, one of the nineteenth century's many stylistic cross-currents, was no doubt considered most appropriate to crown the new campus site. Arthur Denny, one of Seattle's founders, donated 8⅔ acres of the university's original 10-acre tract.

Lewis and Clark Halls, 1896
Josenhans & Allen
6-N

Two very plainspoken designs that suggest a lean budget for early university housing. Named for the explorers, the buildings were originally dorms for men and women, respectively.

Parrington Hall, 1902
Josenhans & Allen
8-K

Apparently designed to complement Denny Hall and named posthumously for the famous professor of English, Vernon L. Parrington.

Central Plaza (colloquially, Red Square), 1972
Kirk/Wallace/McKinley
9-K

Beneath this vast, brick-paved space is the Central Plaza Garage; the soaring campanile in the northwest corner also functions as part of its ventilation system. On the plaza's western edge the Edmund S. Meany Hall for the Performing Arts (1974), and the Odegaard Undergraduate Library (1972) by the same firm, are massive brick structures with a formalist expression that give this campus entrance a fortified aspect. Other buildings are: Kane Hall (1971) by Walker, McGough, Foltz, Lyerla; the Administration Building, by Victor N. Jones, anachronistically designed in 1949 in the Gothic Revival mode; and the Suzzallo Library, named for the fifteenth president, Henry Suzzallo, and built in 1923–27 from a design by Bebb & Gould, with Carl Gould

Central Plaza and Kane Hall. Photo: Joseph Freeman (courtesy of UW)

Suzzallo Library. Photo: James O. Sneddon (courtesy of UW)

as principal designer. The 1950 addition is by Bindon & Wright. This design set Collegiate Gothic as the official style of the new campus plan following the A.Y.P. Exposition. The library's elaborate, spiky detail contributes to a wedding cake effect intensified by the severity of the rest of the buildings on the square. The sculptures above the entrance, Thought, Inspiration, and Mastery, are by Tacoma artist Allan Clark. The graduate reading room is worth seeing.

Rainier Vista, 1909
Olmsted Brothers
15-N

From the steps above the cross-axial path called Grant Lane, Rainier Vista sweeps down to the lake providing a majestic view even when Mt. Rainier is not out to top it off. The buildings that frame the vista—Johnson and Physics, Bagley and Guggenheim—were designed by John Graham, Sr., in a modernized version of Collegiate Gothic and built from 1928 to 1937. Physics Hall has a 1960 addition by Durham, Anderson & Freed. This firm also designed the Atmospheric Sciences/Geophysics addition to Johnson Hall, completed in 1970. The Drumheller Fountain and surrounding rose gardens are the residue, along with the vista itself, of the A.Y.P. Expo.

Gowen-Smith, Savery, Raitt, and Miller Halls, 1916–39
Bebb & Gould (Gowen is by A. H. Albertson)

Music and Art Buildings, 1949–50
Whitehouse & Price
7, 8–L, M, N

Northeast of the Central Plaza is the original Academic Quadrangle laid out by Bebb & Gould in their 1915 plan. Raitt Hall (1916) was the first built, and Gowen-Smith (1939) the last of the group. Although these classroom buildings share the Collegiate Gothic idiom, they are different from each other and distinguished also by a variety of ornamental detail that rewards scrutiny. Alonzo Victor Lewis, sculptor of the gargoyles on both Savery and Miller, must have seen his work as a contemporary challenge, since he endowed his characters with a range of modern emblems that included gas masks. Similar concerns affected Dudley Pratt, sculptor of the twenty-eight gargoyles on Smith. Raitt Hall, originally Home Economics, was graced with designs by Carl Gould showing women in a variety of domestic labors performed under the guidance of a lone male holding a stone tablet. Times do change. In addition to the visual surprises, the landscaping of the quad is appropriately formal and most lovely in its spring flowering. The much later Music and Art buildings by the well-known master of Neo-Gothic styling, Spokane architect Harold Whitehouse, harmoniously complete the quad.

Academic Quadrangle. Photo: John A. Moore (courtesy of UW)

Hutchinson Hall, 1927
Bebb & Gould
5-M

The School of Physical Education housed in Neo-Gothic dignity with an interesting plan and some walls made largely of windows to create high, daylit interiors.

Hutchinson Hall. Photo: James O. Sneddon (courtesy of UW)

Dormitories
Hansee Hall, 1935, John Graham, Sr.; McCarty Hall, 1959–63, Young, Richardson, Carleton & Detlie; Haggett and McMahon halls, 1963 and 1965, Kirk/Wallace/McKinley
3-M

Concentrated northeast of Stevens Way, this group of dormitories ranges from gracious Tudor Revival to a variety of contemporary structural expressions in concrete.

Hansee Hall. Photo: James O. Sneddon (courtesy of UW)

Faculty Center, 1960
Victor Steinbrueck and Paul Hayden Kirk
10-O

A well formulated and executed design in the Americanized International Style tradition of Mies van der Rohe that manages to be both formal and informal at the same time. The dining area takes advantage of the panoramic view of the mountains and Lake Washington. Downstairs a lounge is embellished with wood balusters salvaged by Victor Steinbrueck from Ellsworth Storey's "Hoo Hoo," or Forestry Building.

Faculty Center. Photo: Richard S. Heyza

Student Union Building (the HUB), 1977
Joyce/Copeland/Vaughan/Nordfors
10-N

The original building was dramatically transformed by the 1977 remodeling that added a glazed gallery along Stevens Way which opens into an interior dining hall/ballroom space. Mezzanine decks, crisp white detail, sinuous metal pipe railings, and a high-toned color scheme give the sort of nautical note that often marks this current revival of the Streamline Moderne.

McMahon Hall. Photo: John A. Moore (courtesy of UW)

The various departments of engineering are concentrated in the southwestern part of the campus. Architecturally notable buildings are:

Engineering Library and Loew Hall, 1965
Fred Bassetti & Co.; Richard Haag Associates, landscape architects
11-O

Designed in a personalized version of the Italian Neo-Liberty Style, one of the several crosscurrents of contemporary architecture and a hallmark of this firm.

Sieg Hall, 1960
Harmon, Pray & Dietrich
11-M

A contemporary attempt to harmonize with the Gothic Revival styles of the upper campus, done in a now dated fashion by filling in the expressed structural frame with exposed aggregate panels.

Aerospace and Engineering Research Laboratory, 1969
The Richardson Associates
12-N

A handsome and well-detailed design in the contemporary Formalist mode.

Aerospace and Engineering Research Lab.
Photo: Hugh Stratford

Electrical Engineering Building, 1948
Paul Thiry; addition by Carlson, Ely & Grenstad; relief sculptures by Everett Du Pen
13-N

An early post-World War II Modern design that reflects European influence as well as the work of Walter Gropius at Harvard.

Nuclear Reactor Building, 1960
TAAG: The Architect Artist Group (Lovett, Streissguth, Zema, Torrence)
13-O

Roberts and More Halls, 1921, 1946
Bebb & Gould; Bebb & Jones
14-O

Sylvan Theater, 1911
13-N

Tucked into the slice of land between Electrical Engineering and the Rainier Vista is a rustic interlude where the four hand-fluted cedar columns from the original Territorial University Building are enshrined. The scroll capitals are fiberglass replacements for the original carved cedar caps that rotted away.

On the east side of Montlake Boulevard the formerly marshy edges of Union Bay have been transformed into an enormous physical education and sports layout dominated by the monumental Stadium. Other facilities include Edmundson Pavilion (1928) by Bebb & Gould, and Canoe House, constructed by the U.S. Navy as a seaplane hangar in 1918. The building illustrates a rare structural response to a new challenge; no other examples of this hangar type are known of in the state.

Stadium, 1951
Stoddard & Huggard; Sigmund Ivarsson, structural engineer
16-Q

A steel balcony and roof structure cantilevered over the earlier stadium. Access is provided by two monumental, spiral pedestrian ramps of reinforced concrete. The cantilever has a span of 145 feet; the stadium has a capacity of 55,000.

Stadium

Along the west side of Montlake Boulevard and Rainier Vista, the outer ring of building beyond Stevens Way continues. Outside of it are yet another couple of rings on land originally cut off by the railroad tracks.

Winkenwerder and Bloedel Halls, 1963, 1970
Robert Chervenak & Associates
15-M

Two fine examples of the contemporary wooden post-and-beam structural aesthetic that seem particularly appropriate for the Forestry departments. A landscaped, paved court links them to the earlier, traditionally styled Anderson Hall (1925), designed by Bebb & Gould.

Health Sciences Building, 1950–65
Naramore, Bain, Brady, & Johanson

University of Washington Medical School Teaching Increment, 1973
Naramore, Bain, Brady, & Johanson
15-K

A massive complex linked to the University Hospital that creates a solid wall of building south of Pacific Street. These structures witness some of the changes that the Modern Style underwent from the post-World War II period to the present. The well-scaled western portion of the complex with brick-faced walls and ribbon windows is cut through in the middle to provide a welcome break in the building mass and a view toward the water.

College of Fisheries Center, 1951, 1968–69
Young & Richardson; Ralph Anderson & Partners
18-K

South Campus Center, 1974
The Bumgardner Partnership
17-J

Built to serve the expanding South Campus population, the design expresses the complex program of such a facility by incorporating a range of spaces from offices, seminar rooms, lounges, and vending areas to a dramatic conservatory-like cafeteria opening onto an outside dining court. The interior use of wood as a warm decorative surface contrasts happily with the brute concrete.

Oceanography Laboratory and Marine Sciences Building, 1967
Liddle & Jones, Richard Haag Associates, landscape architects
16-I

Kincaid Hall, 1971
John Morse & Associates; Clayton and Jean Young
13-J

Penthouse Theater, 1940
U.W. Physical Plant Department
13-J

Pacific Apartments, 1960
Bassetti & Morse
13-I

The earliest of the distinctive and influential series of residential compounds by this firm (see also Bellingham and Ellensberg). Though strikingly modern in 1960, they have now acquired a regional, vernacular quality that speaks well for the original design intentions.

South Campus Center. Photo: Art Hupy

West of 15th Avenue the university has crept out into the previously privately owned blocks along the now abandoned Northern Pacific tracks. Much of this area which had been occupied by modest, even marginal business facilities was cleared via the urban renewal bulldozer. This explains its present look. Campus Parkway remains a reminder of the Alaska-Yukon-Pacific fair, its monumental ambitions aided by two recent structures, Condon and Terry-Lander halls.

Computer Center, 1977
Ibsen Nelsen & Associates
13-G

Benson Hall, 1966
Bindon, Wright & Partners
13-K

Guthrie Hall, 1973
Bindon, Wright & Partners
12-J

Architecture Hall, 1909
Howard & Galloway
11-J

Home Management House, 1942
John R. Sproule
11-J

Gould Hall, 1972
Daniel Streissguth and Gene Zema with Grant Hildebrand, Dale Benedict, and Claus Seligmann
11-I

Built to house the related disciplines of architecture, urban planning, landscape architecture, and building construction, this cast concrete structure has a dramatic, skylit interior court around which are ranged the department offices and studios. The design reflects a contemporary approach to public buildings as enclosed open space.

Henry Art Gallery, 1927
Bebb & Gould
9-J

Schmitz Hall, 1969
Waldron/Pomeroy
9-I

Hughes Playhouse, 1931, remodeled 1966
Arthur B. Loveless; Ibsen Nelsen & Associates
8-H

A pleasant eclectic brick structure with an entryway mosaic by Mark Tobey, the building was originally a garage that Loveless remodeled for the old Seattle Repertory Theater of Burton and Florence James.

Gould Hall. Photo: Ari Cowan (courtesy of UW)

Condon Hall, 1974
Mitchell/Giurgola with Joyce/Copeland/
Vaughan/Nordfors
8-F

Contemporary smoothed-off Brutalism by a
well-known eastern firm as principal designers.

Condon Hall. Photo: John A. Moore (courtesy of UW)

Terry-Lander Hall, 1959–63
The Richardson Associates
10-G

Applied Physics Lab, 1956, 1964
W. Alexander Trimble; Al Bumgardner
10-F

A skilled remodeling of an older but interesting
building.

Mercer Hall, 1970
Royal A. McClure Company
11-F

Laurelhurst

Laurelhurst was laid out by Mayor Cotterill. The older development is on the
upland; the lakefront features mostly
modern houses with some from the
1920s. Enlightened subdivision planning of later times blessed the lower
elevations near the water with streets
that follow the terrain. This last generation has witnessed construction by architects of a number of houses for themselves. On the whole Laurelhurst has the
character of a special enclave cut off from
more banal development by the major
arterial of Sand Point Way and bounded
on two sides by water.

1   **Battelle Memorial Institute,** 1966–70
Naramore, Bain, Brady & Johanson; Richard
Haag Associates, landscape architects
4000 NE 41st Street

A group of pavilions with a strong oriental
cast beautifully nestled in a serene and
lushly landscaped block-sized site; a perfect
environment for an institute for the study of
human affairs. Along with the more ambitious, more remotely located Weyerhaeuser
Headquarters (see Tacoma/Environs), this is
the best northwestern example of the contemporary corporate campus for higher echelon white collar workers. In contrast to
Weyerhaeuser, it is a product of local design
talents, demonstrating the degree to which
Washington can hold its own on the national
design scene. As at Weyerhaeuser the landscape architect's contribution is pivotal.

2 **Houses,** c. 1950
3830 and 3850–54 Surber Drive NE

A group of exemplary wooden post-and-beam houses of the kind that were often designed by architects for small builder's tracts in the immediate post-World War II period.

3 **House,** 1974
The Hastings Group
3905 NE Belvoir Place

A cut-out, shed-roofed vertical box in the 1970s mode, nicely sited on a tight lot.

4 **Houses,** c. 1925
Henry Hodgson, builder
3911, 3914, 3922, 3935, 3952 NE Belvoir Place

A group of well-crafted cottages with a rich mix of materials and imagery of the French Provincial, Norman-Flemish farmhouse persuasion that might be summed up as Mother Goose.

5 **Houses,** 1936
John R. Sproule
3927 and 3933 NE Belvoir Place

Number 3927 is a fine example of the European International Style with white cubistic forms and crisp detail. Number 3933 is a more Americanized, Wrightian adaptation of the same aesthetic.

5 3927 NE Belvoir Place

6 **House,** 1961
Nelsen & Sabin
3201 W Laurelhurst Drive NE

A quietly elegant design in dark-stained wood with a hip roof, showing the Japanese influence on contemporary Northwest design.

1 Battelle Memorial Institute. Photo: Art Hupy

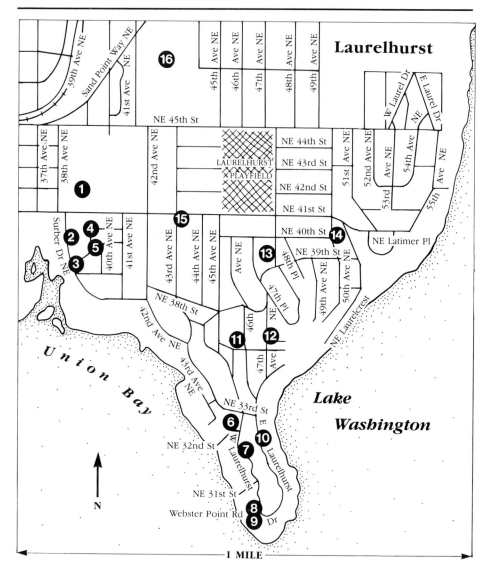

7 **Lionel H. Pries House,** 1946, second floor
   addition c. 1965
   Lionel Pries; Myer Wolfe
   3132 W Laurelhurst Drive NE

   Now all but hidden in foliage, this was the
   home of a highly creative designer and
   influential teacher.

8 **Gurvich House,** c. 1960
   Lionel H. Pries
   3006 Webster Point NE

9 **House,** c. 1960
   Nelsen & Sabin
   3011 Webster Point NE

   By the same architects as (6) above.

10 **House,** c. 1925
   3054 E Laurelhurst Drive NE

   Though undocumented this half-timbered,
   Tudorish house suggests the hand of Arthur
   B. Loveless.

7 Lionel H. Pries house

11 Zema House, 1965
Gene Zema
3522 46th Avenue NE
Designed by the architect for himself, this
house and (13) below exhibit Zema's
characteristic design format, strongly
influenced by the Oriental and Northwest
traditions of timber construction.

11 Zema house. Photo: Ray O. Welch

12 Gerald Williams House, 1978
TRA
4720 NE 36th Street
A well-composed design with Neo-Corbusian
forms in latticed wood.

12 Gerald Williams house. Photo: Christian Staub

13 House, 1967
Gene Zema
3919 48th Avenue NE

14 Jacobson House, 1973
TRA
3935 51st Avenue NE
A well-composed, crisply detailed house
using the long mono-pitch roof to provide a
stepped sequence of spaces and natural light
for the interior.

14 Jacobson house. Photo: Hugh Stratford

15 House, c. 1950
Milton Stricker
4300 NE 41st Street
A flat-roofed, postwar ranch house with a
modular rhythm and the living section plat-
formed over a lava boulder base.

16 **Children's Orthopedic Hospital**, 1953,
  expansion 1972–76
  Young, Richardson, Carleton & Detlie; expansion by Naramore, Bain, Brady & Johanson
  4800 Sand Point Way NE

A large hospital complex designed and built over a period of about twenty-five years with changes in style duly recorded. The recently finished section housing out-patient and in-patient areas is cast-in-place, sandblasted concrete, stained with a light acrylic paint. The finish enhances the Neo-Corbusian Brutalist sculptural format. Both parts of the hospital are good examples of the design approach of their times.

16 Children's Orthopedic Hospital. Photo: Jim Ball

Green Lake

In a city that appears to have more usable waterfront per resident than most others in this country, Green Lake is still an urban wonder. A remnant of a glacially formed drainage system, Green Lake began silting up long before man appeared on the scene. However, man's plans for the lake after it was acquired by the city in 1905 have included additional filling that has much diminished its size. The major fill was recommended by the Olmsted Brothers to provide a boulevard around the lake.

Since trolley lines already ran along the shore, space for the roadbed was gained by diking and filling Sawmill Cove, thus closing off the outlet to Ravenna Ravine. Subsequently the lake water began to turn truly green with algae. The recent policy of daily pumping of surplus reservoir water through the lake has finally rectified the situation and restored the lake as a major recreational center. The only part of the lakeshore that remains relatively untouched is the site of a small former amusement park, West Green Lake. South of this area, Guy Phinney developed his large estate with a zoo, conservatory, playfields, etc., all on his own trolley line to Fremont. The city purchased Phinney's estate in 1900. At present the Woodland Park Zoo (1) is being extensively redesigned by Jones &

Green Lake
with Ballard, Fremont
and Wallingford

Jones. A drive around the lake and its residential area reveals a solid community with many of its institutions naturally oriented toward the water. The lakeside park itself has become a premier jogging and bicycling course.

2 **House,** 1909
5858 East Green Lake Way N

A prominent Colonial Revival design, or Classic Box.

3 **House,** c. 1890
2159 N 61st Street

4 **House,** c. 1890
2153 N 62nd Street

Two gracious, late nineteenth century houses.

5 **House,** 1948
McCallum, engineer
6602 East Green Lake Way N

An International Style house of reinforced concrete designed by the owner.

6 **Green Lake Elementary School,** 1902
James Stephen
2400 N 65th Street

Compare this with the half dozen others by
Stephen, who was the official school district
architect in the early part of this century.

6 Green Lake Elementary School

7 **Green Lake Methodist Church,** 1903
N 65th Street and First Avenue NE

Picturesque massing, cyclopean masonry,
and good stained glass tie this church to the
Arts & Crafts movement.

8 **John Marshall Middle School,** 1927
F. A. Naramore
NE Ravenna Boulevard and NE 68th Street

A dominant landmark on the tree-lined
boulevard that is one of the major urban design elements linking Green Lake to Ravenna
Park and to the university via 17th Avenue
Northeast.

9 **Fire Station No. 16,** 1928
Daniel R. Huntington
6846 Oswego Place NE

10 **Green Lake Public Library,** 1910
Somervell & Cote
7364 East Green Lake Drive N

Mediterranean and Chicago School influences
combined to produce a properly civil institution. Compare this with the University
Branch Library of the same year.

10 Green Lake Public Library

11 **Green Lake Christian School,** 1916
7514 Orin Court

A shingled Craftsman school.

12 **Twin TeePees Restaurant,** 1934
Holtzheimer, builder
7201 Aurora Avenue N

A California curiosity prefabricated in concrete and trucked to this site on the Pacific
Highway; another reminder of this remarkable early automobile-strip development.

12 Twin TeePees Restaurant. Photo: June Layton

13 John B. Allen Elementary School, 1904, 1918
James Stephen; Edgar Blair
6601 Dayton Avenue N

14 Nyberg house

At 2265 North 56th Street there was once a simple, concrete-block store that over some years has been recycled into a remarkable contemporary house (14) by its owner and architect, Folke Nyberg. The influence of early Modernism traceable to Scandinavian roots is combined with a contemporary concern for using salvaged materials and a sure touch with scale and detail.

North Seattle

Post—World War II expansion gobbled up the land north of Green Lake in a mindless way. Single family, automobile-oriented tract housing larded with commercial strip development extended for miles. In this respect Seattle was no different from other U.S. cities; in fact, this kind of suburban sprawl is as American as apple pie. Architects and planners later expressed horror over this rape of the virgin landscape that had once held such potential for enlightened improvement over the monotony of the old streetcar suburbs. But criticism has somewhat abated with the passage of time and the capacity of mature vegetation to disguise and diversify the scene. There is much for the observer of environmental development to study, although the architectural rewards are few and far between. Unfortunately, one of the area's most interesting developments, The Highlands, an exclusive residential park laid out by the Olmsted Brothers in 1909, is closed to the public. For a description of it, see the introductory essays to this guide. On the edge of The Highlands is the Seattle Golf and Country Club, designed in 1909–10 by Spokane's Kirtland Kelsey Cutter, and one of the grandest examples in the Northwest of the half-timbered, mountain chalet-resort. Though this is a private club, it is possible to see the exterior from the club driveway and parking lot.

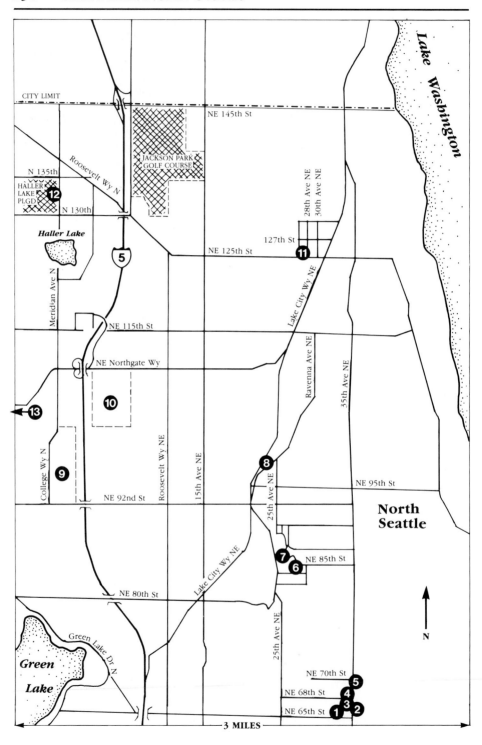

Lake Washington

CITY LIMIT

NE 145th St

JACKSON PARK
GOLF COURSE

N 135th

Roosevelt Wy N

HALLER
LAKE
PLGD

12

N 130th

28th Ave NE

30th Ave NE

Haller Lake

127th St

11

NE 125th St

5

Meridian Ave N

Lake City Wy NE

NE 115th St

NE Northgate Wy

Ravenna Ave NE

35th Ave NE

13

10

College Wy N

Roosevelt Wy NE

15th Ave NE

9

NE 92nd St

8

25th Ave NE

NE 95th St

**North
Seattle**

NE 85th St

7

6

Lake City Wy NE

NE 80th St

N

Green Lake Dr N

25th Ave NE

**Green

Lake**

NE 70th St

5

NE 68th St

4

3

2

NE 65th St

1

◄———————— 3 MILES ————————►

1   **Washington Children's Home,** 1973
    The Mithun Associates
    330 NE 65th Street

    A nicely sited group of wooden pavilions that
    exude a noninstitutional appeal.

2   **University Unitarian Church,** 1960
    Paul Hayden Kirk
    6556 35th Avenue NE

    A delicate tour de force of wood by an ar-
    chitect deservedly famous for his elegant use
    of the material.

2 University Unitarian Church

3   **The Theodora,** 1965
    Robert Chervenak & Associates
    6559 35th Avenue NE

    Another well-articulated wooden structure
    built as a residence hall for the Volunteers of
    America.

4   **Northeast Branch Library,** 1954
    Paul Thiry
    6801 35th Avenue NE

    A fine expression of the Modern post-and-
    beam, screen-walled pavilion with an open,
    airy, light-filled interior. The group of struc-
    tures around this intersection illustrates the
    range of expression in wood explored by con-
    temporary Northwest architects.

4 Northeast Branch Library. Photo: Art Hupy

5   **Medical Clinic,** 1961
    Gene Zema
    6850 35th Avenue NE

6   **House,** 1961
    Nelsen, Sabin & Varey
    2503 NE 85th Street

    Another notable design by a firm that con-
    tributed substantially to the development of
    Modern residential design in the Northwest.

7   **House,** c. 1970
    Robert Reichert
    26th Avenue NE

    An arresting design by Seattle's least conven-
    tional architect. See also his own house on
    Queen Anne Hill (27), and Capitol Hill (35).

7 House

8   **Weight-Watchers Building,** 1975
    Joyce/Copeland/Vaughan/Nordfors; Tom
    Berger, landscape architect
    9700 Lake City Way NE

    An L-shaped, shingled building presenting a
    wall-like form to the street; behind, the site
    slopes down to a lovely court and a flowing
    stream across which is a small parking ter-
    race. The thoughtful landscaping has pre-
    served part of an orchard.

9   **North Seattle Community College,** 1974
    Mahlum & Mahlum
    College Way N between N 92nd and N
    103rd Streets

    Brutalist concrete aesthetic used for a formal
    megastructure, or single building campus.

9 North Seattle Community College

12 Helen Madison Swim Center, c. 1972
Kirk/Wallace/McKinley
Meridian Avenue N at N 134th Street

An impressive contemporary public facility with a handsome interior, one of several swim centers funded by the 1968 Forward Thrust bond issue.

12 Helen Madison Swim Center

10 Northgate Shopping Center, 1950
John Graham & Company, first development
First to Fifth Avenue NE and NE Northgate Way

The Northwest's first regional shopping center.

11 Lake City Library, 1965
John Morse & Associates
12501 28th Avenue NE

A pleasantly landscaped, low brick building with a shingled mansard roof. The sculpted entrance gates are by George Tsutakawa.

13 Viewland Hoffman Receiving Substation, 1979
Hobbs/Fukui
NW corner Fremont Avenue N and N 105th Street

A public utility designed to fit as unobtrusively as possible into a residential setting. Artist participation made possible by the One Percent for Art program helped convert a jungle of machinery into colorful sculpture.

13 Viewland Hoffman Receiving Substation. Photo: Art Hupy

Mercer Island

Mercer Island was once unglamorously known as East Seattle, but following the opening of the Lacey V. Murrow Memorial Bridge in 1940 and the substantial development of the 1950s, it was incorporated as Mercer Island City. The bridge itself is worth noting. Designed by Washington State Highway Department engineers with Lloyd Lovegren as architectural designer, it is built of concrete pontoons anchored to the lake bottom and carries a four-lane roadway more than a mile long. Steel bridges at either end make the transition from float to land. At the Seattle end the concrete tunnel entrance was designed by Lovegren and the low relief sculpture by James FitzGerald.

Tunnel entrance, Seattle end of Murrow Bridge

Geographically the island consists of a broad, level plain bordered by more or less steep slopes and bluffs. Mercer Way circles the island on the mid-contours below the plain. Most of the island's remarkable sequence of post–World War II woodsy northwestern houses are situated on minor cul-de-sac streets off of this main loop. Public facilities, including a characteristic set of public schools, run down the center of the island connected by Island Crest Way.

Tract houses and less ambitious residential designs occupy most of the interior plain. No downtown exists—in this sense it is the perfect suburbia—the few car-oriented shopping plazas and strips occur naturally near the freeway interchanges across the north end.

The island is not easy to navigate even with a good map. As is typical of the region, streets start and stop in the grid with no indication of where they resume. Although most streets and avenues are numbered, they can be difficult to sort out, particularly when they curve and wind. Still, Mercer Island has special architectural treasures for those who persevere. Homeowners have pursued landscaping with such zeal, and nature has been so prolific in response, that houses are vanishing year by year from public view. We offer the following selection, still visible at this writing, from a field of residential design ranging from the fifties to the present. Many well-known architects' work can be observed and compared. The entries are organized according to a counterclockwise circuit via Mercer Way.

1   **House,** 1958
    Paul Hayden Kirk
    2711 60th Avenue SE

    A dark, one-story pavilion behind glass and lattice patio screens, this is one of many designs from the hand of perhaps the most prolific and famous of the Northwest residential architects.

2   **House,** 1968
    The Bumgardner Partnership
    3009 60th Avenue SE

    Tasteful addition to one of the island's few early twentieth century houses.

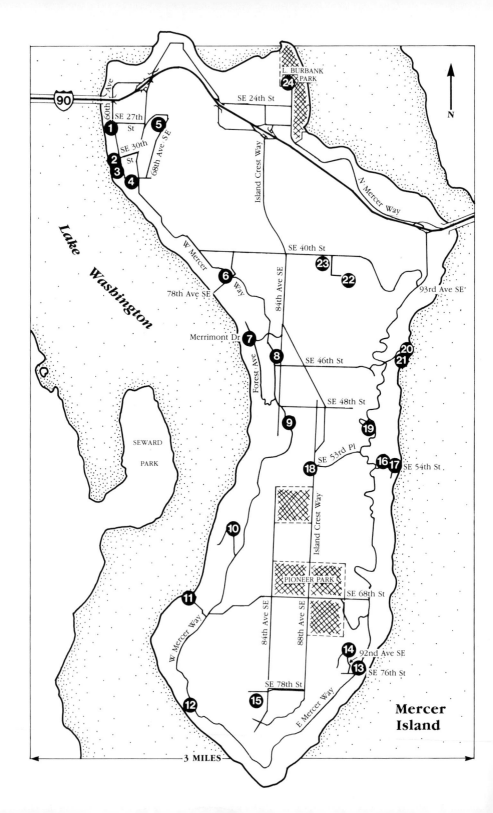

3 **House,** 1963
Al Bumgardner
3019 60th Avenue SE

Another house by a well-known residential designer, this one in a less woodsy, stone and flat-roof manner.

4 **House,** 1959
Nelsen & Sabin
6105 SE 32nd Street

A two-story, gray brick and half-timbered stucco villa by yet another prominent firm which started in the postwar period.

4 House

5 **House,** 1979
Barnett Schorr Miller Company
2768 68th Avenue SE

A recent work that reflects both fashionable eastern trends and a reaction to the traditionally darker timber houses of the Northwest.

5 House

6 **House,** 1957
Chiarelli & Kirk
4157 West Mercer Way

Deep in the shade, a fragile stick pavilion.

7 **House,** 1960
The Bumgardner Partnership
4429 Forest Avenue SE

The roof form especially evokes the Japanese contribution to Northwest design.

8 **House,** 1966
Gene Zema
4518 West Mercer Way

Zema ranks with the other form-makers of the Northwest contemporary house style represented so well on Mercer Island, here in a quiet chalet deep in the woods.

9 **House,** c. 1960
Paul Hayden Kirk
4848 West Mercer Way

10 **House,** 1969
Ralph Anderson & Partners
6007 79th Avenue SE

A small tract extends from West Mercer Way to 77th Avenue at the shore. Several houses are speculative designs by Anderson interspersed with others of less architectural distinction. Of interest is the increase in house size from the fifties to the sixties.

11 **House,** 1973
Olson/Walker
7428 SE 71st Street

An ambitiously sculptural design by a firm that rose to prominence in the early seventies.

12 **House,** 1950
Chiarelli & Kirk
7829 West Mercer Way

A most fragile, modular post-and-beam pavilion steeped in a wooded site. The stick-like structure and slender trees have all but grown together.

13 **House,** 1969
Wendell Lovett
7545 East Mercer Way

13 House. Photo: Christian Staub

14 House, 1968
Wendell Lovett
7446 92nd Avenue SE

Two exemplary designs which fully express the change of formal vocabulary from the structural to the sculptural and volumetric. These are both the work of an important teacher and contributor to the Northwest contemporary house. Contrast with Lovett's earlier design (**20**).

15 Lakeridge Elementary School, 1954
Bassetti & Morse & Aitken
8215 SE 78th Street

Flat-roofed pavilion classroom elements with pipe columns and covered walks, a true period piece, well maintained and landscaped.

16 House, 1968
The Bumgardner Partnership
9428 SE 54th Street

17 House, 1968
Hobbs/Fukui
5411 96th Avenue SE

A firm which, like Olson/Walker, has worked successfully with the vertically interlocking spatial concept of the late sixties and early seventies. The exteriors of these houses can only hint at the complexities that lie within.

18 Island Elementary School, c. 1960
SW corner Island Crest Way and SE 53rd Place

Bar joists and a sawtooth roof make this suburban school design a period piece of the postwar decades.

19 House, 1973
Wendell Lovett
5003 East Mercer Way, off main road on the East Mercer Highlands Road

The most recent of the Lovett houses visible from a public thoroughfare.

20 House, 1959
Wendell Lovett
4456 Ferncroft Road

A pure International Style house of the type labeled affectionately Harvard box. Designed by the teacher-architect whose continuously up-to-date later work is typified by (13), (14), and (19) above. This and the Kirk house in the next entry sit side by side on the water's edge at the end of a private drive off Ferncroft.

21 House, 1960
Paul Hayden Kirk
4458 Ferncroft Road

A comparison of these houses illustrates the difference between the effect of the European-born International Style on eastern-educated architects like Wendell Lovett and the influence of the Japanese and Northwest timber tradition on the work of locally trained Paul Hayden Kirk.

17 House. Photo: Art Hupy

22 **Mercer Island High School,** 1958
Bassetti & Morse
9100 SE 42nd Avenue

This multi-purpose building uses a hyperbolic-parabola roof structure, a fashion of the times.

21 House

23 **Mercer Island District Swimming Pool,** 1973
Kirk/Wallace/McKinley
8815 SE 40th Street

Stylish mono-pitch shed. The pool structure occupies the same superblock central facility site as the high school above, North Mercer Junior High, and Island Crest Elementary School. The resulting large educational park is another archetypal fifties–sixties suburban form.

24 **Luther Burbank Park,** 1974
Jongejan/Gerrard
West of 84th Avenue SE and north of I-90

Long planned, this suburban waterfront park typifies the best current design standards for such facilities.

24 Luther Burbank Park

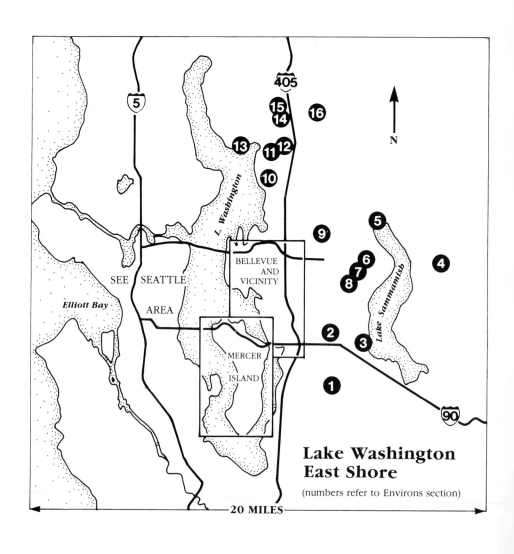

405

5

16

15
14

13

11 12

10

L. Washington

9

5

BELLEVUE
AND
VICINITY

6

7

8

4

SEE   SEATTLE

Elliott Bay

AREA

2

3

Lake Sammamish

MERCER

ISLAND

1

90

N

Lake Washington
East Shore

(numbers refer to Environs section)

◄── 20 MILES ──►

Lake Washington East Shore

Before World War II, development on the east shore of Lake Washington was typical of the kind of rural-suburban fringe around most U.S. cities. Communities were few and discreet in size and shape. A slow transition from stump farming to exurban development had been under way for about thirty years. Kirkland and Renton, to the north and south, were towns established in the late nineteenth century for industrial purposes. The King County coal mines southeast of Renton provided Seattle with a major export product to sell to Portland and San Francisco in the late 1870s and 1880s. From Seattle to Renton, the area's first railroad, constructed by James Colman and originally planned to run all the way to Walla Walla, carried the coal and contributed to Seattle's growing hegemony over the region.

Ferry service connected residents of the exurban eastern lakeshore communities to Seattle from a terminal in what is now the Medina City Hall, but most east shore traffic was better served by private or rented boat. Seemingly remote and blessed with an idyllic environment, the shore was selected shortly after the turn of the century as the site for the mildly utopian Beaux Arts Village (Bellevue, 1). Founded in 1908 as the Western Academy of the Beaux Arts, it was a far-flung spawn of the European Arts & Crafts movement. Founders Alfred T. Renfro, architect-writer-photographer-artist, and Frank Calvert, newspaper cartoonist, borrowed money from Medina millionaire E. W.

Johnston to set up a corporation and buy land where they hoped artists and craftspeople would live and work in harmony with nature. A fifty-acre tract with 1,100 feet of beach and dense stands of cedar and fir was platted into 114 small home sites and a waterfront park. Ten acres were set aside in Atelier Square for studios and workshops. The natural landscape was disturbed as little as possible by the Craftsman Style bungalows and narrow curbless streets which even today scarcely accommodate an automobile. The first house, for Renfro, was built in 1909; by 1919 there were twenty-two. But the village turned out to be more bourgeois than bohemian, more populated by art lovers than art makers, since the latter could scarcely afford to live there. In 1925 Atelier Square was sold and is now developed like the rest of the village. This is not to say that the Beaux Arts Village looks like the rest of the Bellevue area of which it is now a part. Anachronistic perhaps, it is still an object lesson and a good place to start a tour. A quiet rusticity reigns; contemporary houses sit easily beside the old homes; the whole is homogenized by nature.

In 1939, construction of the Lacey V. Murrow Memorial Bridge to Mercer Island and the span across the East Channel opened the east shore to development. The war intervened and little building ensued until the postwar boom decades. Then a whole series of instant suburbs—Kenmore, Juanita, Hunts Point, Medina, Clyde Hill, and Bellevue—spread themselves over the unresisting landscape. A Bellevue Chamber of Commerce brochure averred that new residential communities were mushrooming artistically in the natural splendor of forested, water-rich terrain. Along the lakeshore of Medina and the points this was true because large lot zoning ensured settlement of the affluent and preservation of the trees and natural setting. Though most of the shoreline is relentlessly private, some snippits of public access beach on Juanita, Moss, and Meydenbauer bays are easily accessible to plebeian folks. As to the rest of the area, the observer may judge for himself.

Certainly the privately landscaped subdivisions of the boom period, now almost thirty years old in some cases, have been softened by or have even disappeared in vegetation. With the passage of time it becomes increasingly difficult to track the phenomenal development paradoxically described in earlier times as the rape of the landscape. The tourist driving along well-tended winding roads in residential areas developed in the fifties and early sixties finds them pleasantly punctuated with appropriately scaled schools and churches in parklike settings. These oases do not occur just at the water's edge, but in fact throughout the inland area. Crisscrossing freeways have assisted this pattern. More importantly they have assisted development on a scale so vast that it bewilders and distresses those with prior knowledge of the place who see how it might have been planned otherwise.

The grid street plan originally laid over the whole area has fallen prey to skip-stop or leap-frog development. For those unfamiliar with the area, this makes for some of the most frustrating driving imaginable. Streets may run for miles but are interrupted periodically where topographical features or undeveloped land intervenes. The visitor is well advised to get a good road map and consult it frequently.

The postwar years also witnessed a few carefully planned developments. Hilltop Community (Environs, 1) was organized by a group largely composed of architects and University of Washington faculty who, between 1947 and 1950, acquired a sixty-three-acre site southeast of Factoria for $15,000 with the help of the Federal Housing Administration. The community goals were: to preserve a parklike setting rich in native plants and animals; to breathe clean air at 1,000 feet altitude; to maintain scenic views by running wires underground and judiciously pruning vegetation; to maintain family privacy by providing relatively large lots—three-quarters to over an acre; and to maintain a picnic ground, grassy playfield, frog pond, and thicket for secret children's trails. To these ends 3.8 acres were set aside for the central park and playfield, 12.9 acres for a green belt park, and 6.8 acres for a country road. The cost per family was $2,000 plus a lot of sweat equity.

The architecture of Hilltop is archetypal 1950s, informal, imaginative, and intended for comfortable living, not display. The image was that of the one-story or split-level, flat-roofed wooden house generally termed "ranch," using contemporary materials. All were custom designed. Hilltop echoed similar developments that sprouted near San Francisco, Boston, and elsewhere, places with a higher concentration of architects than the country's average. Though viewed as prophetic at the time, their planning ideals did not square with the profit incentive of real estate interests and the construction industry, which have traditionally viewed land as a commodity, not an instrument for social planning. The success of Hilltop is uncontested. One measurement of this is the fact that it is all but invisible. Houses designed by some of Seattle's best known architects, Perry B. Johanson, John Morse, Fred Bassetti, Paul Hayden Kirk, and Wendell Lovett, have disappeared into the well-tended landscape. Like the Beaux Arts Village, it is an object lesson at this stage, a place to see how healthy the environment can be after the hand of man has touched it.

While Hilltop and Beaux Arts Village exhaust the east shore communities with utopian aspirations, a number of fine, small, post–World War II developments by merchant builders and developers suggest that some of the idealists' influence infected the more commercial world. Among the examples noted in the pages that follow are Norwood Village (Bellevue, 29), Surrey Downs (Bellevue, 25), Sherwood Forest (Environs, 6), and Little Finn Hill (Environs, 11). More recently condominium type developments have continued the tradition of symbiosis between sensitive land planning and sound current architecture. Representative of these designs are Lockwood Townhouses (Bellevue, 4), Bellefield Park (Bellevue, 28), Sammamish Shores (Environs, 3) and Sahalee Village (Environs, 4).

Surrey Downs (Bellevue, 25)

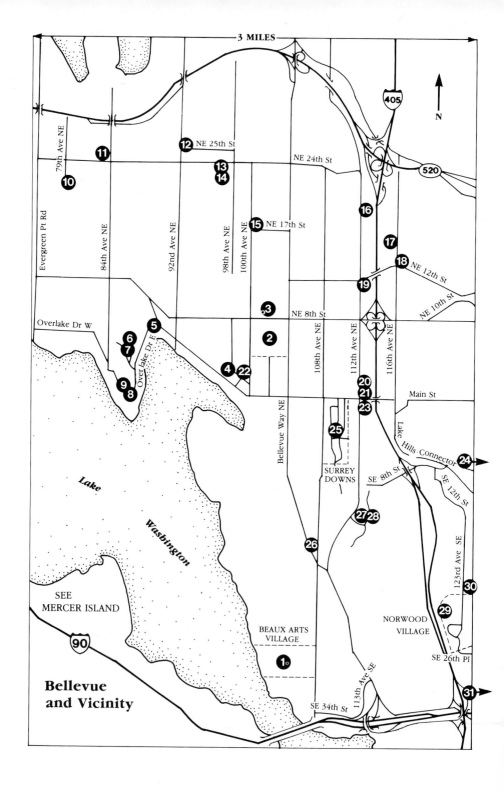

Bellevue
and Vicinity

Bellevue and Vicinity

Bellevue, the largest community on the east shore, epitomizes the "slurb," or unplanned urban-suburban development, of the post–World War II boom. The long-range plan in 1953 when the town was incorporated expressed the then revolutionary philosophy that public streets were dedicated to the movement of automobile traffic and that parking was the responsibility of property owners. As a result, central Bellevue is a vast asphalt and concrete desert divided into superblocks with off-street parking and buildings aggressively different from their neighbors. The residential areas range from monotonously individualistic to carefully planned landscape ensembles. Here as elsewhere in the suburban world of the fifties and sixties institutions provide the best examples of public-oriented design. In sum, the areas present the kind of drab but mainstream American urban matrix that northwesterners used to derisively associate with Los Angeles. In truth Bellevue has no real heart of town, but part of Main Street west of Bellevue Way has been spruced up as one and does have the look of an older suburban shopping street.

1 **Beaux Arts Village,** 1908
West of 108th Avenue SE, north of I-90
See introduction to East Shore above.

2 **Bellevue Shopping Square,** 1946
Moore & Masser; Bliss Moore Jr. & Associates
NE 4th to 8th Street, 100th Avenue NE to Bellevue Way
An early suburban shopping center.

3 **Bellevue Village Shopping Center,** 1968
Mithun & Associates
102nd Avenue NE and NE 8th Street, Bellevue

A pleasant and well-tended, small, open mall across from the older square and representative of later taste. Clustered shops are housed in modular post-and-beam units with shingled roofs and beam ends extended to form covered walks, all nicely landscaped.

4 **Lockwood Townhouses,** 1972
Mithun & Associates
111–407 98th Avenue NE, Bellevue
An exemplary development of vertical and diagonal wood-sided townhouses with steep mono-pitched roofs on a tight site well planned to retain privacy.

4 Lockwood Townhouses. Photo: Art Hupy

The following houses are a sampling of the best of contemporary Northwest residential design in an ideal suburban setting. They are in the town of Medina which adjoins Bellevue and occupies some of the choice shoreline real estate.

5 **House**, 1966
The Bumgardner Partnership
8846 Overlake Drive E, Medina

6 **House**, 1970
Kirk/Wallace/McKinley
8105 NE Fifth Street, Medina

7 **House**, 1970
Kirk/Wallace/McKinley
8605 NE Fifth Street, Medina

8 **House**, 1962
Nelsen, Sabin & Varey
760 Overlake Drive W, Medina

8 House

9 **Living for Young Homemakers House**, 1957
Paul Hayden Kirk
107 Overlake Drive W, Medina
See entry (24) for another design by this sponsor of architectural prototypes.

9 Living for Young Homemakers house. Photo: Dearborn-Masser

10 **House**, 1966
The Bumgardner Partnership
2038 79th Avenue NE, Medina

11 **Wells-Medina Nursery**, 1968
Gene Zema
8300 NE 24th Street, Medina

An expressive wood structure for a building type particularly appropriate to this lush, green world.

12 **House**, 1969
Hobbs/Fukui
9210 NE 25th Street, Clyde Hill

A multi-faceted, gray-stained wood box with a shed roof, well done by a firm that rose to prominence in residential design in the late sixties and seventies.

12 House. Photo: Art Hupy

13 **Clyde Hill Fire Station**, 1967
Mithun & Associates
9615 NE 24th Street, Clyde Hill

Styles in fire stations change like everything else. Compare this one with the new Bellevue facility (26) by the same firm.

14 **Clyde Hill Elementary School**, 1952
Naramore, Bain, Brady & Johanson
98th Avenue NE and NE 24th Street, Clyde Hill

A prototypical design for a building type that was a standard component of postwar communities like Clyde Hill.

15 **Bellevue Presbyterian Church,** 1955
Mithun, Ridenour & Cochran
1720 100th Avenue NE, Bellevue

A well-sited, big, wood shingled, A-frame tent with side walls of colored glass in narrow sashes and enameled panels, and walls of field stone. Mithun's design is very representative of the times when churches, like schools, filled the institutional needs of new communities, and also representative of the sure handed touch of Bellevue's leading design office.

Another building type that boomed in the postwar decades was the small, suburban medical clinic. From clinics and medical offices the type mutated into more general purpose office groups but usually retained hints of the Northwest contemporary residential quality that infused the best early examples. Architects such as Paul Hayden Kirk and Omer Mithun have worked extensively in this field. The following buildings are representative of their work.

16 **Everwood Park,** 1976
The Mithun Associates
2000–50 112th Avenue NE, Bellevue

Sensitive siting which accommodates several office buildings designed in low-key variations on the timber theme; the central building houses the office of The Mithun Associates where a steep mono-pitch roof permits a glazed wall for the drafting room on the other side.

17 **Middleton, Berner & Wood Medical Building,** 1974
Ralph Anderson & Partners
1551 116th Avenue NE, Bellevue

A new departure for the combination medical center and office park whereby the buildings are nestled in a wooded landscape. Anderson's cross-axial, gabled roof composition continues the Northwest's expressive timber tradition.

18 **Family Medical Center,** 1960
Paul Hayden Kirk
1200 116th Avenue NE, Bellevue

19 **Bellevue Medical-Dental Center,** 1962
Mithun & Associates
1100 112th Avenue NE, Bellevue

20 **Office Building,** 1970
Omer Mithun & Associates
220 112th Avenue NE, Bellevue

21 **Zylstra Building,** 1969
Omer Mithun & Associates
222 112th Avenue NE, Bellevue

Two exemplary variations on the contemporary concrete office building theme that suggest the architectural meaning of today's more urbanized and cosmopolitan east shore.

14 Clyde Hill Elementary School. Photo: Jim Ball   *16 Everwood Park. Photo: Art Hupy*

22 **Youth Eastside Service Building** (formerly
First Baptist Church), 1905
James Stephen
315 100th Avenue NE

A fine shingled Craftsman Style building by
an architect known chiefly for his Seattle
schools of the same period.

23 **Holiday Inn**, 1970
Omer Mithun & Associates
11211 Main Street, Bellevue

A two-story rambling motel of tilt-up, concrete party-walls with wood-stained siding,
very untypical of Holiday Inns.

24 **House**, 1960
Paul Hayden Kirk
220 130th Avenue SE, Bellevue

A prize-winning design—the best in wood
for the money—for the *Living* magazine
Wood Research House by one of the leading
residential architects of the postwar period.
(See also Bellevue, 9.)

24 House. Photo: Vern and Elizabeth Green

25 **Surrey Downs**, 1952–55
Omer Mithun
109th and 110th Avenues SE off Main Street,
Bellevue

About forty of the houses in this tract were
built from three basic designs furnished the
developer by the architect. They are some of
the best and most representative of postwar
small tract housing design. A knowledgeable
architectural tourist will immediately recall
the work of Anshen & Allen and Jones &
Emmons for Joseph Eichler in California, or
that of Charles Goodman around Wash-

ington, D.C. Another feature, not true
of larger tracts lacking custom design, is that
every tree on the site was saved.

26 **Firehouse**, 1976
The Mithun Associates
Bellevue Way SE, Bellevue

Streamline Moderne revival well done.

27 **Bellefield Office Park**, 1972
Ralph Anderson & Partners
1309 114th Avenue SE, Bellevue

Wood, flat-roofed, modular pavilions with
raised concrete frames set in a lovely landscaped parkland reclaimed from a bog. The
site planning is exceptional and blends well
with the adjacent wildlife and plant preserve.

27 Bellefield Office Park

28 **Bellefield Residential Park**, 1972
The Mithun Associates
Across from the office park

Equally fine site planning for a planned unit
development of elegant, restrained, and
woodsy townhouses.

29 **Norwood Village**, 1951
Chiarelli & Kirk; Bassetti & Morse; site planning by Gardner & Hitchings
Access from I-90 at I-405 interchange to 128th Avenue SE, follow signs to Woodridge Park

Originally a cooperative, finally financed under Federal Housing Administration Title

28 Bellefield Residential Park. Photo: Art Hupy

8 loans, the Veteran's Mutual Building Association was formed in 1946. Five basic houses were designed by the architects listed above for the owner's choice; construction began in 1951. The nucleus of the tract, around the hilltop, has wooden mailbox shelters that say Norwood Village and streets that follow the contours of the hills. The modest houses, staggered along the streets and generally sited above street level, have the modular, post-and-beam structural expression with exposed beams ends, banded windows, integrated carport, and white painted trim which identifies them as vintage postwar Modern design.

30 **Woodridge Elementary School,** c. 1955
SE 20th Street and 23rd Avenue SE in Norwood

A vintage Modern finger-plan school with signature details of the period such as covered walkways framed with bar joists.

31 **East Shore Unitarian Church,** 1957
Bassetti & Morse
SE 32nd Street between 125th and 128th Avenues SE in Norwood

A broad, low-pitched gable roof anchored to the ground gives the effect of a great sheltering tent.

Environs

The development of the east shore communities has now extended back ten miles or more to the far side of Lake Sammamish and runs more or less continuously from north to south the length of Lake Washington. In common with other new suburban landscapes the few notable works of environmental design are widely scattered and often hard to locate. Those listed below sample the more interesting examples. For people who wish to seek them out we recommend using a well-detailed road map in addition to our general location map (see page 238) and addresses.

1   **Hilltop Community**, 1947–50
    Fred Bassetti, Perry Johanson, Paul Hayden
    Kirk, Wendell Lovett, John Morse, and
    others
    South end of 150th Avenue SE

    Described in the introduction to the east
    shore communities (page 240). To find Hill-
    top go south 1.6 miles on 150th Avenue
    from the I-90 interchange, following the
    fairly obvious main route even though street
    names change until finally you reach the loop
    at the top of the hill where 150th ends.

2   **Bellevue Community College**, 1971
    Naramore, Bain, Brady & Johanson
    3000 145th Place SE, Bellevue

    A ninety-five acre, wooded campus with a
    well-integrated plan and snappy design.

Lake Sammamish is the largest of several
inland lakes east of Bellevue. To the
south on the west shore is the Sammamish Shores Condominium (3), a
well-designed complex by The Mithun
Associates completed in 1972. Near the
east shore is Sahalee Village (4), 1971,
by the same firm, also worth seeing. At
the north end is Marymoor Park (5), a
King County park with a master plan by
Richard Haag Associates.

6   **Sherwood Forest**, c. 1955
    159th to 162nd Avenue NE, NE 24th to NE
    28th Street, Bellevue

    Another post–World War II small tract
    which used some prototype designs by Paul
    Hayden Kirk.

7   **Unigard Building**, 1974
    Naramore, Bain, Brady & Johanson
    NE 24th Street and 156th Avenue NE,
    Bellevue

    Massive, low concrete blocks stepping up the
    slope.

8   **Overlake Park Presbyterian Church**,
    1958, additions 1964 and 1973
    The Mithun Associates
    1836 156th Avenue NE, Bellevue

    Although obvious by now, it is still impor-
    tant to pay tribute to the consistently fine site
    design and the solid architecture done by this
    firm. The building design seems to have
    evolved from an earlier church (Bellevue, 15),
    drawing more on Japanese sources for this
    high-peaked, gable-roofed structure sweep-
    ing down low to the ground with side screen
    walls of colored glass.

9   **House**, 1972
    Wendell Lovett
    4256 132nd Avenue NE, Bellevue

    A sculptural, volumetric design with the fine
    detail and hand-crafted interior typical of this
    famed Northwest designer. The house actu-
    ally stands far back from 132nd Avenue on an
    unmarked group driveway.

9 House

10 **Peter Kirk Building**, 1891
    Seventh Avenue NE and Market Street, Kirk-
    land

    A nineteenth century commercial island in
    the post–World War II sea. Peter Kirk was an
    early developer whose interests lay in the coal
    mines and ironworks of King County. The

7 Unigard Building. Photo: Niranjan Benegal

10 Peter Kirk Building

three buildings—formerly four—at this crossroads symbolized a commercial empire and a new urban center Kirk named for himself that got nowhere at the time.

11 **Little Finn Hill,** c. 1950
Paul Hayden Kirk; Robinson Homes, developer
NE 112th and 113th Streets from 100th to 106th Avenue NE, Kirkland
A small builder's tract with houses from prototype designs by Paul Hayden Kirk; 10161 Northeast 113th Place represents a typical example. Lots were $1,000; houses cost $11,000. Dick Robinson, the builder, worked several years as architectural draftsman for Kirk.

12 **Alexander Graham Bell Elementary School,** 1967
Kirk/Wallace/McKinley
11212 NE 112th Street, Kirkland

13 **House,** 1972
Kirk/Wallace/McKinley
8221 NE 117th Street, King County
The latest phase in the residential work of this firm.

14 **Juanita High School,** 1972
Kirk/Wallace/McKinley; Richard Haag, landscape architect
10601 NE 132nd Street, Juanita area of King County
A formal design with windowless buildings intended to create a sealed learning environment—theoretically. It is carefully landscaped all the same.

15 **Helen Keller Elementary School,** 1970
Joyce/Copeland/Vaughan/Nordfors
NE 140th Street and 108th Avenue NE, King County

16 **John Muir Elementary School,** 1971
Joyce/Copeland/Vaughan/Nordfors
NE 140th Street and 132nd Avenue NE, King County
Like (15) above, this school represents a flexible approach to a building system using various levels of site and factory fabrication to suit a variety of educational specifications.

Off the map about ten miles southeast of Renton is the former Gaffney's Lake Wilderness Lodge (1950), now serving as a University of Washington conference center. Conceived by Young, Richardson, Carleton & Detlie, the design won several awards. It is a striking structure with a broadly-pitched gabled roof built into the side of the slope and a glazed wall facing the lake. The public space, high, open, and airy, focuses on a three-story-high thunderbird totem pole, carved by Dudley Carter. A grace-

13 House. Photo: Hugh N. Stratford

Lake Wilderness Lodge

full, open-tread, open-string spiral stairway with metal railing leads up to the mezzanine. To reach the lodge, take the Renton-Maple Valley Road (Route 169) southeast from Renton; continue south on Witte Road to Southeast 248th Street, and take the Gaffney Road to the shore of Lake Wilderness where signs indicate the way. On the lakeshore is a beach and park facility, the first phase of the King County Parks and Recreation Department Lake Wilderness park plan, designed by Calvin/Gorasht and completed in 1973. This playful, sculptural building in gray-stained vertically sided wood is as well suited to the lakeshore as the earlier lodge, with its quarter-century-old, different design concept.

Auburn

The city is situated about midway between Seattle and Tacoma on Route 405, a major railroad division point. The Northern Pacific came through in 1883; the railroad depot on C Street attests to its historic presence. The City Hall, 25 West Main Street, of about 1923 was designed by Andrew Willatsen. A modern addition on the outskirts is the Red Barn Ranch (1973), by Hobbs/Fukui, a well-designed facility in the contemporary Northwest timber idiom.

Red Barn Ranch. Photo: Art Hupy

Sea-Tac Airport

Sea-Tac Airport (courtesy of Port of Seattle)

First conceived as a modern replacement for Boeing Field, the Seattle-Tacoma International Airport was finally designed to serve as the major regional facility. Its recent master plan and terminal development result from a cooperative effort between The Richardson Associates and the planning staff of the Port of Seattle. Though tightly constrained by the circumstances of the surrounding area—uncontrolled commercial development, highway connections, topography, and limited acreage—the plan calls for phased growth through 1985. Its centerpiece is the present airport terminal complex, expanded from the 1949 passenger terminal to include satellite concourses and aircraft loading positions, and one of the most expressionistic, high-density parking facilities to be seen at any airport. From the air the overall terminal has a butterfly form. From the ground, and particularly inside, the design is a very carefully executed example of the mainstream Academic Formalist branch of the American International Style. Below ground the various units of the terminal are connected by a remote controlled mini-subway system which ranks as one of the first people-movers in the country.

Route 99 gives access to Sea-Tac. This is the original Pacific Highway completed as a two-lane paved road before 1920. Needless to say it is much modified in the vicinity of the airport. In contrast to the sprawl of aggressively contemporary motels and hotels near the terminal, older sections of Route 99 both to the north toward Seattle and south toward Tacoma preserve some of the characteristics of the pre-freeway era.

Airport parking terminal. Photo: Hugh Stratford

Tacoma

Long before such momentous events in the white man's history of Tacoma as the arrival of the Northern Pacific railroad from Kalama in 1873, the area had a special significance for the Puyallup Indians. Legend has it that the Indians called the mountain whose ethereal presence commands the city on clear days, Tahoma, meaning "nourishing breast." Near the Puyallup's burial ground in the vicinity of the former Northern Pacific Headquarters Building there was, allegedly, a sacred rock so large that it could not be moved when Pacific Avenue was graded in 1873–74 in the preparation of the new townsite. As one of many insults, the newcomers buried the rock beneath the street which they built to serve their own sacred interests. Later

they themselves felt shunted aside when their mountain was unpatriotically named Rainier after a foreign naval officer. An account of the unavailing efforts to restore the mountain's name along with other treasures of local lore appears in Murray Morgan's *Puget's Sound*.

American settlement started in 1852 during a boom in the Puget Sound lumber business. After vacating to Fort Steilacoom briefly during the Indian hostilities, settlers returned to their homesites and the lumber milling revived. Over the next decade a number of settlers staked homestead claims, including Job Carr's at Chebaulip, later to be Old Tacoma. By the end of the 1860s, General Morton Matthew

View from Tacoma City Hall. Photo: Alvin Waite, 1894 (courtesy of Photo Collection, UW Library)

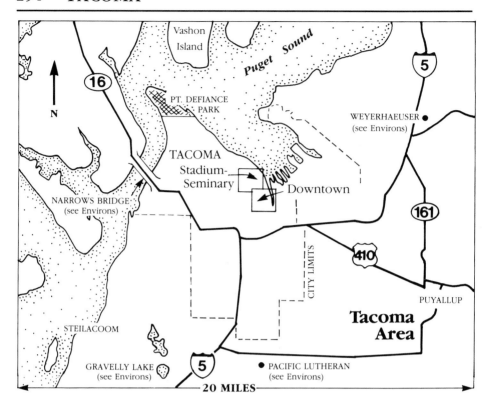

Tacoma Area

20 MILES

McCarver and his speculator colleagues bought out Carr's claim, platted a townsite, lured in a major lumber mill, and set the stage for Tacoma's victory in the Puget Sound Northern Pacific terminal location sweepstakes.

The course of Pacific Avenue, still the principal downtown artery, was first determined along with other streets in the New Tacoma townsite in an 1872 plan commissioned by the Northern Pacific's site committee from James Tilton, who had been Governor Stevens' surveyor general. Even as Tilton was finishing up, the approaching national depression toppled the Northern Pacific's eastern financial wizard, Jay Cooke. It became easier to sell land than railroad bonds. The Tacoma Land Company was forthwith created with Charles B. Wright, one of Cooke's most trusted associates, as president. Later Wright also assumed the presidency of the Northern Pacific, thus becoming Tacoma's most powerful paternal figure.

Desperately in need of working capital, Wright and his cohorts turned to Frederick Law Olmsted, the nation's most prominent landscape architect-planner, famous for transforming difficult terrain, to whip up an eye-catching scheme for the townsite that would ensure quick sales. In the six allotted weeks, Olmsted and his engineer, G. K. Radford, work-

Pacific Avenue in 1889 (courtesy of Photo Collection, UW Library)

ing from sketches and contour maps since time did not permit a site visit, produced a dazzling plan. Whereas Tilton's plan had used a standard grid system slightly modified by two north-south diagonal avenues that conceded the difficulty of the direct east-west grade, Olmsted's was a cat's cradle of streets following the hill's contours. Presented to the public a week before Christmas, 1873, the plan drew ambivalent reactions at best. Newspaper coverage revealed the public's dismay in statements which acknowledged that Olmsted had put on paper "the most astonishing plat of a town ever seen. . . . There wasn't a straight street, a right angle or even a corner. The blocks were shaped like melons, pears and sweet potatoes. One block, shaped like a banana, was 3,000 feet long." The lack of four-way intersections was particularly distressing to speculators, who regarded the corner lots produced by this configuration as essential to successful real estate promotion. "No one could sell a crooked lot to an honest Iowa farmer. The plots must be rectangular and there must be plenty of corner lots for the prairie states people to purchase sight unseen."

In boom times the railroad officials might have held the strength of their convictions and given the Olmsted Plan a fair run. As it was, with financial losses mounting, confidence in Olmsted's vision vanished. About a month and a half later, he and his plan were dropped from consideration. The unexecuted plan, now in the Washington State Historical Society Museum in Tacoma, has provoked continuing speculation concerning what the city's fate might have been had it been developed as "the most picturesque city in the world."

Tacoma Hotel (courtesy of Photo Collection, UW Library)

Theodore Hosmer, C. B. Wright's brother-in-law, sent west to manage the Tacoma Land Company's affairs, hired William Isaac Smith, an engineer who specialized in lighthouses, to clean up the plan. By April 1874, the company was ready to put the downtown section on sale. The final plan was so conventional as to elicit no public comment. Wright himself bought a corner lot, and, to bolster confidence, commissioned the first brick business block. This was the first of many gestures that inscribed Tacoma with his family name, including such notable landmarks as the Annie Wright Seminary and Wright Park. The family continued residence in Philadelphia where Wright responded to Hosmer's requests for various of the town's needs, such as land for the new city hall or construction of the splendid, company-owned Tacoma Hotel on the bluff above the city. (Destruction of this remarkable Chateauesque Style pile designed by the famous Sanford White of McKim, Mead & White in New York must rank as one of the great tragedies of the 1930s.)

As the 1870s wore on and the Northern Pacific added no more track to the Tacoma-Kalama line there was talk of demanding forfeiture of the company's land grant. To keep things moving, Wright bought land in the Wilkeson coal fields due west of the city and laid a spur line to the port. As a result, Tacoma became a leading coaling station on the west coast. But the honor of completing the transcontinental line fell not to Wright, Tacoma's fairy godfather, but to the hated Henry Villard, who in 1883 linked the Northern Pacific's eastern section with Portland via the Oregon Railroad & Navigation Company tracks in the Columbia Gorge. Somewhat anti-climactically, the completion of the Cascade Division in 1886 finally brought eastern rails directly to Tacoma, but by this time Seattle had begun the aggressive diversification of its economic base that would allow it to eclipse Tacoma as the foremost city of the region.

What had originally attracted the railroad's attention to Tacoma was its great, natural, deepwater harbor. Since the Indians owned the tideflats, the initial railroad-oriented development was restricted to the western bank of Commencement Bay between Old and New Tacoma. This development determined the location of the Northern Pacific Headquarters Building on the bluff above, and, across Pacific Avenue, the site of the City Hall on company-donated land. These two institutions marked the northern end of the central business district just as Union Station anchored the southern end. Commercial interests gradually moved north from the turn-of-the-century center near the station to where they remain today between Thirteenth and Ninth streets. With the consolidation of Old and New Tacoma in 1884, the city settled into its first boom period, still very much a railroad company town. Until the depression of 1893 Tacoma grew dramatically, boasting of its fine homes and neighborhoods. Some of these residential areas have retained their character to this day, especially the Stadium-Seminary district between New and Old Tacoma, but also Hilltop, directly west of the central business district; Fern Hill in South Tacoma at a crossroads of Indian and Hudson's Bay Company trails; McKinley Hill, an early working-class neighborhood south of

the central business district; and South Tacoma, originally Excelsior, which became an adjunct to the Northern Pacific shops in 1891. In general, the topography determined the areas developed for industry, railroading, commerce, and residence as well as the general north-south growth of the city.

Five years of hard times ended with the 1898 Klondike Gold Rush, but thereafter the major expansion took place in Seattle not Tacoma. Although a land commission set up after 1900 led to the acquisition of private land in the tideflats, the industrial development that has subsequently consumed the area did not really begin until World War I with the construction of extensive temporary shipbuilding ways. At the same time Fort Lewis expanded to become a major contributor to the Tacoma economy, a role it continues to play along with the other military facilities it spawned, McChord Air Force Base, Madigan Army Hospital, and Mt. Rainier Ordnance Depot. All of this complex lies south of Tacoma along Interstate 5.

In the 1920s the Northern Pacific moved its western headquarters to Seattle. Downtown Tacoma began its long decline in spite of such revitalization efforts as the 1925 Winthrop Hotel, the Medical Arts Building of 1931, and the growth of wood products industry administration, especially the Weyerhaeuser headquarters which was scattered through several downtown buildings. Wood interests became increasingly in evidence with the kraft mills on the Puyallup estuary contributing to the aroma of Tacoma. The Port of Tacoma, smaller industries related to the port, the wood products industry,

Medical Arts Building

and others needing extensive level, accessible land developed on the former Puyallup mudflats.

The automobile had an early and powerful effect on Tacoma. Beginning as early as World War I the city was a car and bus oriented place. Later, in the 1920s, the Pacific Highway, Route 99, sliced right through town paralleling the Northern Pacific tracks. The powerful magnet provided by the military bases south of town encouraged strip development. Even today in backwaters along the South Tacoma Avenue part of Route 99, the careful observer can discover a characterful, 1930s strip commercial ruin or two, such as the Coffee Pot at number 2102 and the single-structure, brick, Moderne motel next door.

Suburbanization began early too. Most of the upper income housing constructed during the 1920s and 1930s occurred in amenable, auto-oriented areas, especially the lake district southeast of

Tacoma between the city and the military bases (see the discussion of Gravelly Lake in Streatfield's introductory essay). Shipping began to expand too. Sprawl was well established when World War II halted city building and at the same time enormously stimulated the local economy. The military bases expanded; the shipyards reappeared; industry boomed with such opportunities as the expansion of Boeing; war housing was built. Much of this development was temporary and is now long gone.

Postwar suburbanization has cemented Tacoma into the sprawl that extends with few interruptions throughout the Puget Sound area. The city's economy too is now integrated into that of the larger region. The old central areas of Tacoma exist now in a rather coequal way with such new centers or districts as those along Federal Way (old Route 99) east of town, the Puyallup Valley to the southeast, Parkland and Spanaway to the south, and the really considerable infilling and intensification of development in the lakes area. Interstate 5 now serves and stimulates development in both the Federal Way and lakes areas. Perhaps the crowning event in the suburbanization of Tacoma, certainly in terms of the superb resulting environmental design, was the recent removal of the Weyerhaeuser Corporation headquarters from downtown Tacoma to a palatial new setting in the Federal Way area.

The Weyerhaeuser move simply put an exclamation point on a long, leveling process that has also suburbanized Tacoma's central business district. The decision continued the downtown decline following World War II that resulted from private disinvestment, and government action as well. Public urban renewal had been proposed as the remedy for inner city blight, a remedy perhaps worse than the disease. A 1944 City Center Plan suggested razing the blighted blocks and creating green belts around downtown; in 1963 the San Francisco firm of Rockrise & Watson proposed the Broadway Pedestrian Mall now complete. Though much of the old business district was demolished, the preservation movement, gathering force from the bicentennial and the current phenomenon of urban resettlement, or gentrification, has had an impact on Tacoma, both downtown and in the old, inner city suburbs. The Old Tacoma City Hall Historic District was the first so designated in the city. Just north of downtown the Stadium-Seminary dis-trict contains most of the city's architecturally valuable houses. It too benefits from the preservation and resettlement movements.

In the old days Tacoma aimed to surpass Seattle as the state's Queen City. At present, as Murray Morgan sees it, the goal is not to surpass but to become something more than a satellite, to wit, a place with a personality of its own, "a city small enough for people to say hello on the downtown streets, a city where it is safe to walk at night and a morning's drive takes you to mountain or ocean, a city of easy access to parks and playgrounds, and to the more metropolitan delights of Seattle: in short, a pleasant place to live" (*Puget's Sound*, p. 332).

Broadway Pedestrian Mall and Pantages Theater. Photo: Jerry Timmons (courtesy of City of Tacoma)

Downtown

1 **Union Station,** 1901–11
Reed & Stem
Pacific Avenue between S 17th and S 20th
Streets

Anchor for the south end of Pacific Avenue
downtown and symbol of Tacoma's primacy
as a railroad center at the turn of the century,
this opulent, eclectic, Neo-Baroque structure
with a great copper-faced dome awaits restoration, cries out for it in fact.

1 Union Station

2 **Nineteenth Century Commercial Buildings**
West side of Pacific Avenue between S 17th
and S 20th Streets

A sampling of fine, late nineteenth century
commercial warehouses, Tacoma's early
commercial center. Some were designed by
one of Tacoma's first architects, C. August
Darmer.

3 **Tacoma Light and Water Company Puri-
fier Building,** 1884
2203 S A Street

A significant example of industrial architecture and the only remaining structure of the
original gas works complex that provided the
city's first dependable gas lighting.

4 **Pacific National Bank of Washington,**
1969
Skidmore, Owings & Merrill
Pacific Avenue between S 12th and S 13th
Streets

A handsome, contemporary office building.
The loads from structural, concrete mullions
are collected by enormous beams at the base of
the building permitting a clear-span interior.
The well-appointed lobby and banking floor
are worth a visit for the artwork which includes, on the banking floor, the dramatically
placed sculpture *Myth of the Sea* by Portland
sculptor Hilda Morris. The Pacific Avenue
plaza has a sunken shopping court with an
elegant stair spiraling down beside a patterned mosaic pool and fountain.

4 Pacific National Bank of Washington.
Photo: Edmund Y. Lee

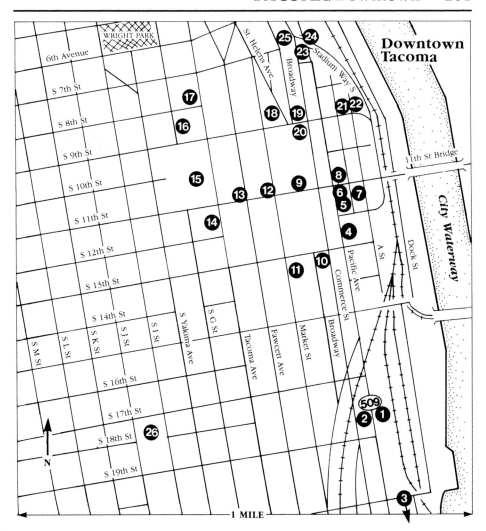

5 **Tacoma Art Museum** (formerly National Bank of Washington), 1919
Alan Liddle, remodeling
NE corner S 12th Street and Pacific Avenue

A restrained, eclectic Classic Revival building which was given to the city and became the Tacoma Art Museum when the bank moved to its new building across the street. It presently exhibits the city's permanent art collections. Across Pacific, to the west, is a recently constructed mini-park and fountain designed by James McGranahan Associates.

6 **Puget Sound National Bank,** 1909–11
Heath, Gove & Bell
1119 Pacific Avenue

A former symbol of Tacoma's prosperity and holder of one of those height records—the tallest building west of the Mississippi when completed in 1911—that used to mean progress. The design is rooted in the Chicago School skyscraper aesthetic.

7   **Federal Building and Post Office,** 1908–10
James Knox Taylor, supervising architect,
U.S. Treasury Department
A Street between S 11th and S 12th Streets

A building in the Roman-Classical Revival mode traditionally used for federal buildings after its triumph at the Chicago World's Fair of 1893. The first session of the Federal District Court took place 20 September 1910.

7 Federal Building and Post Office. Photo: Don Hines (courtesy of City of Tacoma)

8   **Bank of California Building,** 1928
John Graham, Sr.
Pacific Avenue between S 10th and S 11th Streets

Another office building of eclectic Classic persuasion. It was constructed of Wilkeson sandstone quarried east of Tacoma in Pierce County in pieces of sufficient size to make the pediment and the five drums of each of the facade's four Ionic columns. These were set in place without mortar. Graham's firm, located in Seattle, was one of the largest and most prominent in the Northwest. It continues as John Graham & Company.

From the corner of Market and 11th Street looking east towards the Eleventh Street Bridge a cluster of Chicago School

8 Bank of California Building (courtesy of City of Tacoma)

buildings enlivens the vista. These include the former Bon Marche at 11th and Broadway Plaza, the Washington Building at 11th and Pacific Avenue, and the Perkins Building at 11th and A Street.

9   **Broadway Plaza,** 1969–72
Harris, Reed & Litzenberger
Broadway between S 9th and S 13th Streets

This pedestrian shopping mall was first proposed in 1963. The format, with fountains, play areas, grassy mounds, and sitting areas protected by glass covered canopies, is reminiscent of many urban renewal projects across the country. The two parking garages (1966–67) on Pacific Avenue, designed by Lea, Pearson, & Richards, connect with moving sidewalks, allowing easy access up the steep slope between Pacific Avenue businesses and the mall. The plaza extension to the south is by Wilsey & Ham. While the Broadway Mall seems technically more ambitious than most such "pedestrianization" schemes, it achieves neither memorable urban design quality nor the economic rebirth originally intended—which was almost certainly an impossible objective.

10 **Pacific Northwest Bell Headquarters,**
1976
Harris, Reed & Litzenberger
1313 Broadway

Across from the Broadway Plaza this stylish
mirror-clad prism is graced by Thomas
Morandi's sculpture, *The Sun King*, at its
western entrance.

11 **Bicentennial Pavilion,** 1976
Robert B. Price & Associates
SE corner Market and S 13th Streets

A publicly funded, faceted concrete auditorium with angled skylights built specifically for the bicentennial. The pleasant
forecourt with fountain is a welcome civic
amenity. Experiments are under way in the
building to test the feasibility of using solar
energy for public purposes.

11 Bicentennial Pavilion

12 **Topping Motors,** 1975
James McGranahan Associates
NW corner Market and S 11th Streets

A snappy design for a building type that
needs one.

13 **Samson Hotel,** 1891
1156 Fawcett Avenue

An interesting expression of masonry forms
executed in wood, this rectangular structure
is notable for its size and is easily recognized
by the two large octagonal towers rising from
the third floor and the large Richardsonian
style arches on the south and east facades. The
Samson is the second oldest and last all-wood
hotel of Tacoma's early expansion.

14 **Public Library** (Carnegie Library), 1903,
addition 1959
Jardine, Kent, Jardine; addition by A. Gordon Lum
SE corner S 11th Street and Tacoma Avenue

An eclectic Classic Revival building of
Tenino stone and yellow brick. Originally it
was topped by a dome, which was removed
after earthquake damage in 1947. This portion of the library building now houses the
Northwest Collection of the Tacoma Public
Library.

15 **County-City Building,** 1958
930 Tacoma Avenue S

A classic example of fifties Corporate International Style and a miniature of the mold set by
Detroit's 1950 City-County Building,
pivotal more as a building type than as an art
form.

16 **IBM Building,** 1963
Krona, Ziegler & Associates
615 S Ninth Street at S G Street

A correct, glass, curtain-wall box in the
Americanized International Style.

16 IBM Building

13 Samson Hotel

17 **Central Administration Building,** Tacoma
Public Schools, 1912
Heath, Gove & Bell
Tacoma Avenue between S Seventh and S
Eighth Streets

Strong Collegiate Tudor Style with a rather
diminishing Yamasaki-Gothic porch addition. A prominent landmark, this was the site
of Tacoma's first secondary school.

18 **Medical Arts Building** (now City Hall),
1930
John Graham, Sr.
700 block Market Street at St. Helens
Avenue

The city has recently acquired this intact Art
Deco skyscraper for use as the City Hall. The
decor of abstract, floral forms is repeated in
terra cotta, wood, plaster, marble, and metal.
The lobby with three-story spiral stairway is
worth seeing. A much simplified example of
this style with decorative reliefs about transportation can be seen in the Bekins Building
at 615 Tacoma Avenue South.

19 **Winthrop Hotel,** 1925
W. L. Stoddard
NE corner S Ninth Street and Broadway

One of Tacoma's earliest urban renewal
projects, this hotel was built on the site of the
earlier Chamber of Commerce Building. It is
now divided into apartments for senior citizens.

20 **Pantages Theater/Jones Block,** 1918
B. Marcus Priteca
909 Broadway Plaza

Designed by the official architect for the Pantages Theater Company, this building has
two florid, gleaming terra cotta facades and
one of white glazed terra cotta tiles patterned
to create an architectural mural. Renovation
plans, when implemented, will provide a performing arts center for Tacoma and the southern Puget Sound region.

21 **Tacoma Savings and Loan,** 1958
Lea, Pearson & Richards
NW corner S Ninth and A Streets

A well detailed and proportioned 1950s
curtain-wall pavilion with a rich use of materials typical of the period: aluminum, glass,
and black marble on the exterior; black-
veined white marble gracing the interior.
South across Ninth Street is the original
Tacoma Savings and Loan Building. Constructed in the 1890s, it is being renovated
for a travel agency on the main floor and
apartments above.

22 **Tacoma Totem Pole,** 1903, restoration
1976
Alaskan Indians; restoration by Douglas
Granum, Northwest Woodcarving
Firemen's Park, S Ninth and A Streets

When originally raised in 1903 this totem
pole was advertised as being the tallest in the
country. It was funded by William Shead and
Chester Thorne, who wanted Tacoma to have
a finer pole than the one stolen by Seattle and
placed in Pioneer Square. The symbols in the
pole depict a general religious history of the
Eagle Clan.

20 Pantages Theater. Photo: Don Hines (courtesy of City of Tacoma)

The Old City Hall Historic District in downtown is the city's first designated commercial historic district. Boundaries are Firemen's Park on the east; Ninth Street on the south; Broadway on the west; and the Old Elks Temple, Old City Hall, and the Northern Pacific Headquarters Building on the north. The structures within the district illustrate the attempts of early developers to create a solid family-oriented business community in the Puget Sound wilderness. The physical growth of this area of Tacoma depicts a broad range of economic activities—transportation, housing (hotels), government, theaters and halls, and printing—radiating from the headquarters of the Northern Pacific Railroad Building. South of the district more traditional retail and banking activities predominated. The liveliness of this area as an early company town was nurtured by whisky row, on the east side of Pacific.

23 Old City Hall, 1893, renovation 1972
Hatherton & McIntosh; Barnett Schorr Co.
S Seventh Street and Pacific Avenue

Originally designated for the Chamber of Commerce building, this site was later swapped with the city for one closer to the center of economic activity. The design intended for the Chamber of Commerce was used with modifications producing a building with little relation between exterior design and interior layout. Contemporary sources described the Old City Hall as Italian Renaissance, perhaps referring to the Sienna City Hall. Though the irregular site may have been partly responsible, there seems to be no explanation for the facade's being broken into pieces. The terra cotta ornament, copper-sheathed roof, and fine roman brickwork exemplify Tacoma's awareness of the need for substantial buildings. After the city vacated the building in 1959, it stood vacant until renovation began in the early 1970s. The Barnett Schorr Company created an interior

that affords dramatic vertical and horizontal vistas for shops and restaurants. The structural system of the renovation follows the engineering diagram with remarkable honesty, using beams and columns of varying sizes to match the loads.

24 Northern Pacific Headquarters Building, 1888
Charles B. Talbot
S Seventh Street and Pacific Avenue

A dignified Italianate building designed by the railroad's official architect and rounded off at one end to fit the site. The railroad's headquarters overlook the Northern Pacific "halfmoon yards," still located below. The newer grain terminal once was the site for the railroad's busy wharves.

25 Elks Temple, 1916
Edward Frere Champney
565 Broadway

Eclectic Classic styling was common for such civic institutions. This one is nicely wedged on a difficult site. The "Spanish Stairs" to the south were designed as a fire escape from the Elks Temple and have served as a means of pedestrian access between Broadway and Commerce Street. They are being restored with public funds. To the north of the Elks Temple is the University Union Club.

23 Old City Hall

Along the west edge of downtown a ridge beginning at Wright Park (see Stadium-Seminary district, 1) forms a backdrop against which the central area is silhouetted when you approach on Interstate 5 from Seattle or Sea-Tac. On its crest one landmark dominates for better or worse.

26 St. Joseph's Hospital Addition, 1976
Bertrand Goldberg
1718 S I Street

The overscaled, curiously shaped forms of this structure follow the trademark curves of this Chicago designer. The original hospital was completed in 1913.

East of downtown lie the broad mudflats of the estuary. This has become the principal industrial district and port of the Tacoma region. Pulp mill smells, endless plumes of process steam, dockworks, a great silver hemispherical storage shed, and other utilitarian signs provide convincing evidence of the world's work in progress. In the middle of all of this is at least one notable piece of design.

Concrete Engineering Co., c. 1950
Arthur Anderson, structural engineer
1123 Port of Tacoma Road

A range of concrete shells creates a barrel-vaulted structure that expresses a favorite 1950s architectural motif.

South of downtown, Interstate 5 mostly parallels the old railroad and Pacific Highway path. The interchange serving central Tacoma peels off in a bit of freeway spaghetti. It contrasts with the older highway engineering of the South 34th Street Bridge (1947) passing overhead. A fine "gothicky" spire dominates the skyline here.

Holy Rosary Church, 1920
Lundeberg & Mahon
512 S 30th Street

A prominent and scholarly Gothic Revival church sited at the end of the long axis of Tacoma Avenue. It was the last church in Tacoma to hold services in German.

Concrete Engineering Co.

Stadium-Seminary Historic District and Adjacent Area

Earliest of Tacoma's more well-to-do residential neighborhoods, the area is now a historic district named for the two landmarks delineating its eastern and western boundaries. Both are characterful buildings contributing grace and institutional dignity to the neighborhood. The southern boundary of the official district is North Yakima Avenue. Many fine examples of residential architecture from the early 1890s to modern times, in addition to the State Historical Society, Wright Park, and mature street landscaping throughout, make this an ideal area to tour on foot. A number of other interesting designs appear immediately south of the district, and are included among the entries below.

In addition to being the site for the city's most interesting collection of houses, this district represents quite an achievement in the annals of gridiron street plans. It was platted on the open land remaining between Old Tacoma, which had been carefully laid out to the compass points, and New Tacoma, which the Northern Pacific engineers had squared up with the shoreline along which the tracks ran. The surveyor for the present Stadium-Seminary district deftly connected the streets of both prior plats by cranking his grid over to a new orientation, which rather nicely relates to the bluff line. Streets run without offset or discontinuity through the shifts in the grids. Anyone familiar with places like Bellingham and Portland, Oregon, where offset street geometries abound, will appreciate this neatly cranked plan.

1 **Wright Park and Seymour Conservatory,** 1890, 1907
E. O. Schwagerl, landscape architect
S Fourth and S G Street

The twenty-seven acres of Wright Park were donated to the city in 1886. Landscaping began in 1890 from a design done two years earlier. The park combines exotic trees, picturesque statuary, and water features with one of the few surviving turn-of-the-century glass and steel conservatories in the West.

1 Seymour Conservatory. Photo: Albert Barnes, c. 1907 (courtesy of Photo Collection, UW Library)

2 **First Presbyterian Church,** 1925
Cram, Goodhue & Ferguson; Sutton, Whitney & Dugan, associates
Division Street and Tacoma Avenue South

An impressive composition in a medley of Mediterranean Medieval styles from an eastern office with a major national reputation especially for serious Gothic Revival design such as the unfinished Cathedral of St. John the Divine in New York.

3 **Henry Drum House,** c. 1895
9 St. Helens Avenue

A design exhibiting the period's fascination with expressed decorative structure infilled with a variety of wood sheathing, horizontal channeled siding, cut shingles, vertical tongue and groove, etc.

4 **Blackwell House,** c. 1900
401 Broadway

A large Colonial–Queen Anne Style dwelling.

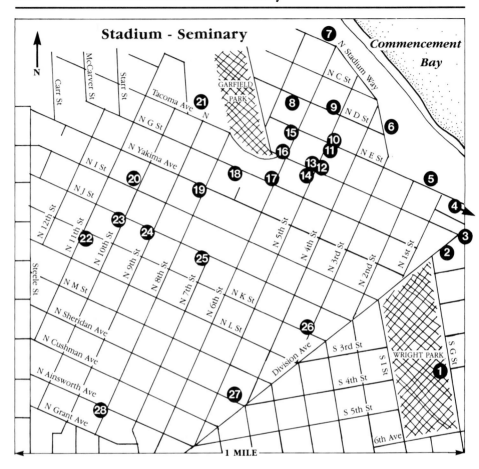

Stadium - Seminary

Commencement Bay

5   **Stadium High School,** 1891, remodeled
1906
G. W. and W. D. Hewitt; remodeled by
Frederick Heath
111 N E Street

Conceived as the Tacoma Land Company
Hotel in Bruce Price's Canadian Pacific
Railroad Chateauesque Style, this project
was halted midway by the depression of
1893. The design was reworked and completed in 1906 as the grandest high school on
the west coast. The adjoining Stadium Bowl,
a dramatic piece of environmental design
tucked neatly into its ravine, was another of
Heath's projects and was the first of its kind
on the west coast. It was dedicated in 1910.

*5 Stadium High School. Photo: Boland (courtesy of Tacoma
Public Library)*

6 **Washington State Historical Society and Museum,** 1911, addition 1973
Bullard & Hill; addition by Lea, Pearson & Richards
315 N Stadium Way

Classic Revival with a contemporary Formalist addition. The old and new portions of the building are connected by an interior open courtyard which is four stories high and topped by a skylight. The society was established in 1891 and designated the first state historical society by the legislature in 1903.

7 **House,** 1970
Olson/Walker
729 N Stadium Way

Contemporary design by a Seattle firm.

7 House

8 **Hewitt House,** 1925–36
Delano & Aldrich
616 N D Street

English Cottage Style by a prominent eastern architectural firm.

8 Hewitt house

9 **House,** c. 1915
508 N D Street

A brick and stucco bungalow straight out of the pages of Gustav Stickley's *Craftsman* magazine.

10 **Gower House,** 1905
Ambrose J. Russell and Everett P. Babcock
417 N E Street

Colonial Revival Style.

11 **Vaeth House,** c. 1895
Ambrose J. Russell and Everett P. Babcock
422 N E Street

Queen Anne villa.

12 **Hyde House,** c. 1910
425 Tacoma Avenue N

Craftsman Style.

13 **Dixon House,** c. 1915
501 Tacoma Avenue N

A handsome, large Craftsman house featuring a dramatic, asymmetrical gable form recalling the Prairie School houses, and nice detailing including a band of decorative tiles.

13 Dixon house

14 **House,** 1903
C. August Darmer
SW corner of N Fifth Street and Tacoma Avenue N

Colonial Revival Style.

15 **Arkley House,** c. 1915
602 N E Street

Northwest Half-timbered Style.

16 House, c. 1930
517 N Sixth Street

White brick Moderne with an attractively planted site.

16 House

17 House, c. 1915
N Sixth and N G Streets

Prairie School–influenced bungalow.

18 House, c. 1956
718 N G Street

Flat-roofed, wide-eaved Modern.

19 House, c. 1910
802 N Yakima Avenue

Towered Medieval cottage with a great high-peaked gabled roof.

20 W. R. Rust House, 1905
Ambrose J. Russell and Everett P. Babcock
1001 N I Street

A large Georgian Colonial Revival house for Rust, the founder of Ruston, who came to Tacoma in 1889 to manage the Ryan Smelter.

21 Annie Wright Seminary, 1924
Sutton & Dugan
827 Tacoma Avenue N

A gracefully sited Collegiate Gothic or Tudor Style campus with a boldly dormered roofscape, a genuine area landmark. Named for donor Charles Wright's daughter, it was one of the first schools in Tacoma.

22 House, c. 1905
1022 N K Street

Colonial Revival monumentalism of the sort responsible for Tacoma's earlier reputation as a city of stately homes.

23 St. Patrick's Convent, c. 1959
1001 N J Street

A contemporary brick and shingle complex now used as a business college. Near St. Patrick's and a couple of blocks east (see 25) are a couple of fine rows of turn-of-the-century, stripped Eastlake builder's houses.

24 Immanuel Presbyterian Church, 1909
901 N J Street

A Mission Revival church with Arts & Crafts leaded windows.

25 Henry Rhodes House, c. 1905
701 N J Street

An exemplary Shingle Style house. More turn-of-the-century houses nearby on J Street.

26 Christ Church (Episcopalian), 1927, 1971
Addition by Paul Thiry
310 N K Street

The older Parish Hall, a representative brick structure of the period, has been overruled by the expressionistic concrete addition.

20 W. R. Rust house. Photo: Albert Barnes, c. 1906 (courtesy of Photo Collection, UW Library)

24 Immanuel Presbyterian Church

27 Murray house

27 **Murray House,** c. 1905
402 N Sheridan Avenue

Colonial–Queen Anne Style with a dramatically exaggerated gabled roof and remarkable dormers.

28 **House,** c. 1892
1601 N Eighth Street

Known locally as the Dutch Embassy it is one of the earliest residences in the area.

Just west of the Stadium-Seminary district described above, a more modest area of about the same vintage contains relatively few designs that merit attention here other than a public building or two and the University of Puget Sound.

Engine House No. 9, c. 1910
611 N Pine Street

Tacoma's earliest surviving fire station exhibits a strong residential character; only a discrete sign and oversize garage doors identify its function.

Weyerhaeuser Mansion, now part of Commencement Bay Campus of the University of Puget Sound, c. 1905

A very correct Period Revival Style, Tudor country house it merits comparison with the splendid Frank estate in Portland, now the campus of Lewis and Clark University.

Old Tacoma

The historical importance of Old Tacoma, the birthplace of the city, is attested to by markers in the area for firsts: Job Carr's 1864 log house and post office; the first school, frame house, sawmill, hotel, and hospital. Before Carr's arrival, Nicholas De Lin, a Swedish immigrant and industrial entrepreneur in these parts (see Steilacoom), erected the first water-driven mill in 1852. He also ran a brewery, a barrel factory, and a salmon packing plant. In 1861 he sold out and moved to Portland, where he met General Morton Matthew McCarver and told him about the area. McCarver was associated with a group of roving entrepreneurs who were in the business of creating cities and were scouting the Northwest for a fitting terminus for the Northern Pacific. After hearing De Lin's account, the general bought the claim and left forthwith for the site on Commencement Bay. There in 1868 he platted a townsite of about twenty blocks, first named Commencement City and later Tacoma after the legendary name of the mountain.

When New Tacoma was platted in 1873, the older settlement became Old Tacoma, an unpopular decision forced on the residents by the powerful railroad interests. The competitive spirit flourished between the two towns until the arrival of transcontinental rails and subsequent incorporation in 1884. Little remains but St. Peter's, Old Tacoma's one significant landmark, to reveal the architectural character of the original settlement. The mills, fisheries, and boatworks which flourished along the waterfront have mostly gone, but the plain walk-to-work town which grew up on the gentle slope above the shore gives an authentic sense of the turn-of-the-century image.

St. Peter's Episcopal Church, 1873
Starr Street between N 29th and N 30th Streets

A simplified Gothic Revival, board-and-batten church, the city's first, St. Peter's also served as a community center. Its most memorable feature is the bell tower, a vine-covered cedar tree trunk topped by a half-ton bell donated by Sunday School children in Philadelphia. When first raised and still bare, the bell tower was publicized as the oldest in the world.

St. Peter's Episcopal Church

Slavonian Hall
N 30th Street near Carr Street

A cultural landmark registering the importance of the settlement of Slovenian fishermen in Old Tacoma at the turn of the century.

West of Old Tacoma the same street grid continues through a modest, mid-twentieth century residential area, the new home for old St. Luke's.

St. Luke's Episcopal Church, 1882
N 36th and Gove Streets
A Gothic Revival design based on that of an English parish church admired by C. B. Wright's daughter, Annie, and funded by him for $35,000 as a memorial to his wife. When it was demolished on its downtown site at Sixth and Broadway in 1936, the pieces were numbered and moved to the present site where it was rebuilt with some modifications and rededicated in 1947.

To the northwest of Old Tacoma, Ruston Way borders Commencement Bay. Beside it run the railroad tracks which serve the curious half-mile-square, encapsulated industrial municipality of Ruston formed around a great metal smelter and marked by a 500-foot stack. Much of the bayside shows only ruins of former activity but for one small, elegant, contemporary structure:

Robert B. Price Office, 1973
Robert B. Price
4303 Ruston Way
A modest, but stylish Northwest contemporary office structure on a waterside site by and for one of Tacoma's most prominent architects.

Robert B. Price Office

Ruston Way leads to Point Defiance Park.

Point Defiance Park

Although Point Defiance was reserved for the military as early as 1866, there was no immediate use for it. In 1888, the city was given the authority to occupy it, and in 1905 it was deeded to the city and laid out as a park by Hare & Hare, landscape architects of Kansas City. Stretching over 638 acres and surrounded on three sides by Puget Sound, the park is famous for its virgin wilderness and beautiful viewpoints. Principal features are: the Rose and Japanese gardens; the Municipal Boathouse; a replica of Job Carr's log cabin, originally built in 1864 and moved to the park in 1917; and Owen Beach. The Western Washington Forest Industries Museum, Camp Six, has a collection of original examples of movable steam-powered logging equipment assembled and interpreted within a natural forest area.

Most important, architecturally, is Fort Nisqually, built in 1833 by the Hudson's Bay Company to the south near Old Fort Lake in DuPont, and reconstructed in the park from 1933 to 1939. Of the several buildings assembled within the stockade, the 1843 Granary, one bastion, and the factor's house were sufficiently intact to be incorporated in the reconstruction. The Granary, in fact, is the only surviving original example of the French-Canadian post-and-sill construction used in the Hudson's Bay forts of the period (see also Fort Vancouver). This method employed posts that were set in ground sills and slotted to receive hewn wall planks laid in horizontally. The remaining buildings though totally or primarily reconstructions serve very well to demonstrate the construction and design characteristics of this interesting vernacular building tradition.

The Ruston Smelter and its mini-town form the gateway to the park and provide a striking counterpoint to its verdant scenic delights.

Granary, Fort Nisqually (courtesy of City of Tacoma)

Factor's house, Fort Nisqually (courtesy of City of Tacoma)

Environs

Water bounds Tacoma on two sides. Expansion of suburban environs has thus been restricted to the east side of Commencement Bay, the Puyallup Valley, and to a broad south-facing fan of development that includes Steilacoom, Fort Lewis and the other military installations, the lakes area, and the southeastern plain facing distant Mt. Rainier. Ranging clockwise from Dash Point a belt of suburban development, largely post–World War II vintage, lies half hidden in second growth forest and spreads to Federal Way, Interstate 5, and beyond. Hidden too are some few items of architectural interest, principally workmanlike Northwest style contemporary houses and the public schools that serve them. These include some vintage finger-plan fifties and sixties designs of Robert Billsborough Price, among them the similar Illahee and Sacajawea junior high schools, the latter

right on Dash Point Road. However, the one most compelling environmental design work of the region and one of the finest architectural and site design moments in the West stands invitingly revealed to the I-5 traveler. Especially southbound motorists can expect to catch at least a fleeting glimpse of the Weyerhaeuser Headquarters Building.

Weyerhaeuser Headquarters Building, 1971
Skidmore, Owings & Merrill; Sasaki, Walker & Associates, landscape architects
East of I-5 off Route 18 at the S 348th Street interchange

In his introductory essay David Streatfield wrote that it "is a notable attempt at integrating a large building into a large-scale landscape. Indeed the large structure designed as a stepped dam in the center of a formal allée is as much a landscape as a building. The *burolandshaft* treatment of interior spaces (a system of free interior planning that eliminates partitions) and the generous provision of planting spaces on the exterior of the building have created a fusion of building and site. . . ." The building boasts also of a fine group of spe-

Weyerhaeuser headquarters. Photo: Ezra Stoller

cially commissioned works of art by Mark Adams, J. B. Blunk, Helena Hernmarck, and Gordon Newman. The San Francisco office of Skidmore, Owings & Merrill under design partner Charles Bassett and designer Richard Foster executed the Weyerhaeuser project.

The southeastern quadrant of suburban development seems too new and too nondescript to be worthy of exploration except as a document in mainstream development vernacular. Closer in to town on the main stem south from central Tacoma lies yet another attractive campus, this one notable for effective remedial landscape design.

Pacific Lutheran University, 1890
Master plan by Richard Haag Associates
Park Avenue S at Garfield Street about eight miles south of downtown and two blocks west of Pacific Avenue

A rather miscellaneous collection of modest buildings transformed into an agreeable campus by effective master planning and landscape design. Haag as well did the entrance mall, central plaza, and detailed landscape design for several of the newer buildings. The graphics and signing are well done too. Among the buildings of Pacific Lutheran are Harstad Hall, designed by August Heide and begun in 1891; a fine large church, Trinity Lutheran, interesting mostly for its high, narrow, Scandinavian-looking nave; Mortvedt Library (1967) by Bindon & Wright; the University Center Building (1970) by Wright, Gildow, Hartman & Teagarden; and Olson Physical Education Building (1969) by Robert Billsborough Price.

The lakes area southeast of Tacoma contains a number of interesting tidbits. Streatfield in his introduction mentioned the Olmsted Brothers design of the Thornewood Estate gardens at American Lake. The grand house by Kirtland K. Cutter remains, but the gardens are now largely dismembered and overgrown. Nearby lies Gravelly Lake, a favored site for stately homes of wealthy Tacomans since the early twentieth century. The drive around the lake was laid out by the Olmsted Brothers too. Second growth forest and rich understory vegetation make the lake and its surrounding development all but invisible today. Around these lakes and the others nearby a prosperous but chaotically sprawled suburban center has grown up, reputedly the largest unincorporated urban area in the state. It exhibits most of the familiar features of such development including that Northwest phenomenon, the proliferation of expressively woodsy contemporary branch banks.

Off Phillips Road Southwest lies a state game farm and fish hatchery well worth a visit for its own sake, especially the teeming trout ponds terraced down through the steep little draw. The acute observer can catch just a glimpse of the region's only Frank Lloyd Wright house, the considerably altered house of 1943–53 hidden in the woods across the Steilacoom Creek from the state lands.

To the west Tacoma is limited by the waters of the Narrows. The traveler can view the Olympic Mountains beyond, or cross over the Narrows on the structure that replaced Galloping Gertie, a suspension bridge notorious for its spectacular demise: only 130 days after opening, it collapsed from wind-induced vibration in one of history's most dramatic structural failures. The new bridge is safe.

Puyallup

First settled in the 1850s, the original village, Franklin, was platted by Ezra Meeker in 1887 and incorporated as Puyallup in 1890. The major historical and architectural landmark is the Ezra Meeker house designed by the Tacoma firm of Farrell & Darmer, and built by the illustrious pioneer in 1890. Meeker's many-sided life included the roles of farmer-inventor, merchant-banker, and promoter of roads, railways, and the hop industry. When the latter failed, he devoted himself to memorializing and marking the Oregon Trail. To publicize this cause he followed the trail across the continent by ox team, automobile, railroad, and airplane. The refurbished seventeen-room mansion is open to the public. The exterior com-

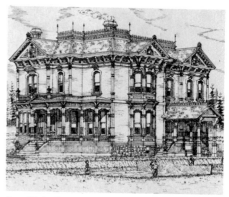

Ezra Meeker house. Drawing: Carl A. Darmer (courtesy of Architectural History Collection, UW Library)

bines a picturesque massing of gables and bays with Italianate detail. The High Victorian interior reflects the fashionable Eastlake Style.

Eatonville

On Paradise Road, Route 161, six miles northwest of Eatonville is the Northwest Trek, a wildlife preserve devoted to native Northwest animals, designed in 1975 by TRA with Jones & Jones, landscape architects. An ambitious work of environmental design, the six hundred acres have a number of buildings in addition to landscape elements such as overlooks for the bear and wolf areas. Buildings include Reception, Interpretive Center, a covered Amphitheater, and Multipurpose and Transportation centers.

Northwest Trek. Photo: Tom Upper

Steilacoom

On the shore southwest of Tacoma and just north of Fort Lewis is the town of Steilacoom, one of the oldest settlements in the state. On the road into town a State Historical Marker commemorates Byrd's Mill Road, established by the Oregon Territorial Legislature in 1852 as a military road. An important pioneer highway, it was the only route of escape from the Puyallup Valley to Fort Steilacoom during the so-called Indian Uprisings of 1855. Fort Steilacoom, 1849–68, now the site of the Western State Hospital, Fort Steilacoom Community College, and Fort Steilacoom Park, was established just inland from the town site after Fort Nisqually was attacked by Indians. The town was staked out in 1851 as a donation land claim by Captain Lafayette Balch, one of many sea captains from Maine who made their fortunes plying the trade lanes from the east to the west coast around the Horn. Balch put up a "large business house" using a wood frame he brought up from San Francisco. In the next three years small factories, a brewery, and a small mill were built by Nicholas De Lin, entrepreneur of Old Tacoma as well. Business must have been good in Steilacoom because by 1859 there was another store, three hotels, and a busy little port. Reputedly the town was even one of the several considered as a terminus for the Northern Pacific Railroad.

Actually neither the railroad nor any great number of people came here in the last decades of the nineteenth century. It remained in suspended animation until recently. Now a historic district, the community retains much of its early character along with several of the state's oldest residences.

Nathaniel Orr House and Orchard, 1857
1811 Rainier Street

A wood frame house put together with wooden pegs and square nails and sheathed with clapboards painted white, the structure shows the simplified Greek Revival influence that marked the early houses modeled after those left behind in New England. Orr brought with him tree stock that created the orchard by the house and supplied much of Puget Sound's orchard stock. In addition Orr made a variety of wood products including cabinets, wagons, and coffins. The house is open to the public; check days and times.

Captain Bartlett House, c. 1865
Stevens Street at Sixth Street

Philip Keach House, 1858
1802 Commercial Street, near Main Street

The above two houses are examples of vernacular building similar to the Orr house.

Philip Keach house

Waverly House, 1891
Commercial Street at Wilkes Street

A Queen Anne villa built by E. R. Rogers, now restored and open as a restaurant.

Steilacoom Catholic Church, 1855
1810 Nisqually

A small white-painted wooden building originally built at Fort Nisqually and moved here nine years later. It was once the center of Catholic missionary activity in the area.

Town Hall, c. 1915
Main Street and Lafayette

A simple, wood frame building which houses the historical museum with a good collection of photos showing old Steilacoom.

Recently at least one new residential building has attempted to make instant history by aping some traditional features while neglecting essentials like generous ceiling heights and double-hung wooden windows.

Nearby on the grounds of Western State Hospital a group of officers' houses, circa 1860, remains to hint at the pioneer importance of Fort Steilacoom and the essentials of mid-nineteenth century vernacular house design.

Officer's house, Fort Steilacoom (courtesy of State Office of Archaeology and Historic Preservation)

Olympia

Perhaps five hundred years before the white settlers discovered the Deschutes Falls, the Nisqually Indians ranged over the area establishing a fishing and foraging camp and possibly a permanent village called Shehtsamish at the mouth of the river. Other Indian terms applied to the area, namely "Tumschuck" and "Tum wa ta," Chinook jargon that later became Tumwater. While the abundance of fish and game attracted the Indians, it was the falls' potential as a power supply that lured white settlers to change the scene from primitive wilderness to industrial enterprise.

In 1845 a group of pioneers led by Michael Simmons finished the last leg of their journey over the Oregon Trail by moving up from Vancouver to the Deschutes Falls. They proceeded against the advice of the Hudson's Bay Company but with enough provisions on company credit to last the winter. Simmons named the settlement New Market, signaling new competition for the Hudson's Bay Company. Of the three sections—the Upper, Middle, and Lower Falls—the last was the site of most of the nineteenth century industrial development. In 1846, the Simmons party built a log grist mill at the base of the falls on the river's west bank; in 1847 they built a sawmill, the first of many that operated in the area. In that year the settlement increased its numbers by the addition of the Crosbys from Maine. Members of this clan, more than twenty-four strong, bought the Simmons mills and claim in 1849 and proceeded to establish many businesses in the town.

By 1863 the community was called Tumwater. In the 1870s a number of small factories were established there that expanded with the coming in 1878 of a fifteen-mile railroad spur from Tenino to Olympia that connected to the Northern Pacific. Of the many pioneer industries only that devoted to brewing beer survives. The Olympia Brewing Company purchased the buildings originally constructed by the Capital Brewing Company over a period from 1896 when the first beer flowed to 1905–7 when the old brewhouse and the original building were built. The company was founded by Leopold E. Schmidt, who learned brewing in his native Germany and was persuaded to move his Montana brewery to Tumwater after tasting its artesian well water. Prohibition put the brewery out of business, but today the industry is well established again. The brewhouse, designed by Vilter Manufacturing Company, Milwaukee, Wisconsin, sits in picturesque serenity on Capitol Lake, created in 1949 by the damming of the Deschutes River. This unforgettable visual prospect is impossible to miss going south on Interstate 5, but to get to the site is a test of ingenuity. Going south take Exit 103; follow Second Street to Custer Way; turn right and then immediately left to the Olympia Brewing Company. Going north on Interstate 5 take Exit 103 to the frontage road and turn into the brewery at the third right. From Olympia go south on Capitol Way around the end of Capitol Lake and left on Custer Way to the brewery.

Brewhouse

The brewhouse, a six-story brick structure in a simplified Italianate Style, is the most prominent building in the present complex, although the same basic design was used in a five-story building nearby. To the south of the brewery is the Leopold Schmidt house, called "Three Meter" for its distance from the brewery. Built around 1905, it is a shingled Colonial Revival manor house with a 1920s Craftsman Style wing. The whole precinct is well maintained by the company and worth a tour. Also of interest is the Tumwater Falls Park across the river. Pathways lead to the various points of interest which include a 300-foot-long concrete fishway (1952), two holding pens, and an extensive system of ladders that are all part of the Deschutes River salmon run. The middle falls area retains the stone foundations from the first electrical power plant of 1883, and the lower falls are spanned by a replica of the original wooden truss bridge. A concrete observation deck below the falls gives the visitor a spectacular view of the cascading water and a chance to imagine how the Michael Simmons party felt on seeing it in 1845.

In 1957, Interstate 5 pursued its relentless way, taking the heart of old Tumwater and radically altering the topography of the historic area. Consequently, there is much to imagine and little to see in the recently established historic district. Most significant is the Nathaniel Crosby III house (1858), right on the edge of Interstate 5 immediately east of the big interchange with State Route 101. The way to get there defies description though. It *is* accessible from the north frontage road reached from Exit 103 on Interstate 5 northbound only. The Crosby house design has a mixture of Greek and Gothic Revival elements, the latter being the scalloped barge boards probably added in the 1880s. Alterations to the house are minor; the back porch has been closed in and a front porch balustrade removed. Restored and refurbished, the house is now the property of the Daughters of the Pioneers and is open to the public.

Crosby house

Three-quarters of a mile east of the brewery lies an imposing three-story Dutch Colonial Revival house (1914) by Joseph Wohleb at 1100 Carlyon Avenue. It occupies a three-acre site with a small lake. Originally it formed the centerpiece of

Cloverfields, a progressive dairy farm established by General Hazard Stevens, son of the first territorial governor, on his father's donation land claim. A gambrel-roofed barn, silos, and outbuildings also remain. For other Wohleb houses see (14) and (15) below. To reach Cloverfields turn east from Capitol Way, or Boulevard, on Carlyon Avenue one-quarter of a mile north of Custer Way, which is the access to the brewery.

To the north, Smithfield, named for the 1846 land grant given to Levi L. Smith, was renamed Olympia in 1849 after Smith's death. Allegedly, Isaac Ebey, the energetic customs collector from Port Townsend, persuaded Edmund Sylvester, the heir to Smith's claim, to name the place for the splendid panorama of mountains the site enjoyed. The town developed quickly in the early 1850s with the agitation for establishment of a separate territory north of the Columbia. In 1853 Olympia was named the territorial capital; in 1854 Governor Isaac L. Stevens convened the first territorial legislature, and five years later the town was incorporated with a population of 1,489, making it the largest settlement in the territory. An 1869 view of downtown shows a collection of wood buildings on and near the wharf that stretched out into Budd Inlet.

The only early building of architectural note was apparently the 1856 wood-frame capitol in frontier Georgian Style. The building was sited on the heights where the present capitol now stands; it doubtless was isolated for some time since the main business of the town was not government, as it is today, but shipping and lumbering. Even now

First State Capitol Building. Photo: A. Curtis, c. 1902 (courtesy of Photo Collection, UW Library)

downtown retains much of its old orientation to the inlet, where the lumbering and oyster packing industries are located. The modest scale of development contrasts sharply with the fast growing governmental campus on the hill.

Although downtown retains very few of its early vernacular commercial buildings, the first residential tracts east and southeast of the commercial center around the wharves and on the western edge of the inlet have a smattering of recently restored, mid to late nineteenth century houses. Later residential development filled in these areas, spreading south of the capitol campus and across the inlet bridge to the west bluff during the major growth periods of the two world wars. Principal arteries are Fourth Avenue and Capitol Way. Tours start with the capitol campus and continue with a list of the main structures of architectural interest in the rest of the city.

Capitol Campus

Work on the permanent capitol began in 1893. The design was the result of a national competition won by the New York architect Ernest Flagg. In 1894, with only the foundations completed, a national depression, a gubernatorial veto, and attempts to move the capitol elsewhere stopped construction. Pressed for space the state rented the Thurston County Courthouse in 1901, and added a wing to house the legislature. By 1909 when political and economic conditions had improved, the legislature authorized completion of the building stipulating that the completed foundations be used.

By this time the building was too small. Flagg, consulted about changing the design, suggested a group rather than a single large building. The solution had the advantage of permitting incremental construction in response to need. Instead of appointing Flagg as architect, the Capitol Commission invited two sets of designs in a new nationwide competition of 1911, one for the Temple of Justice and the other for the Group Plan. The New York firm of Wilder & White submitted the winning designs for both commissions to a jury of Charles Bebb from Seattle, Kirtland Cutter from Spokane, and William Faville from San Francisco.

The landscape plan by the Olmsted Brothers featured a terrace behind the Temple of Justice. Two monumental stairways down the hill to an artificial lake were part of the previous Wilder & White plan and were never built. A grand esplanade was planned to link the

Capitol Group. Photo: A. Curtis, 1939 (courtesy of Photo Collection, UW Library)

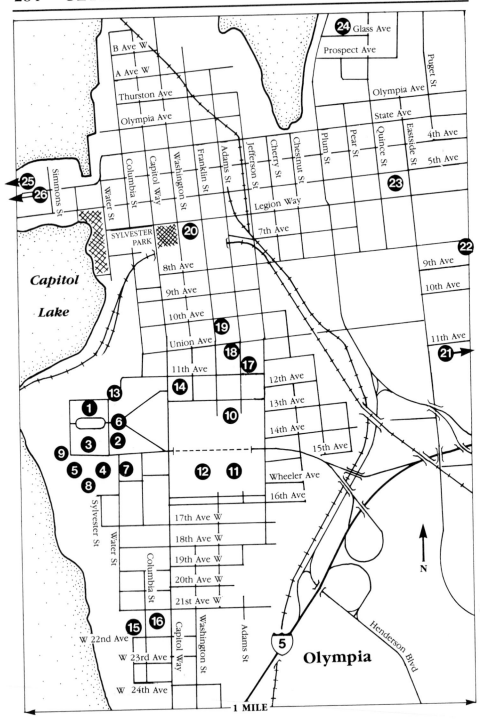

group to the new railroad station near downtown and provide the main approach. The lake was created with the damming of the Deschutes in 1949; it has an attractive parkway along the west shoreline and a small park at the northeast corner. But the rest of the scheme aborted, leaving a railroad yard in place of the esplanade. Still, the general landscaping contributes substantially to the successful City Beautiful movement image projected by the symmetrically composed, Neo-Classical buildings. While the complex may not remind us, as the November 1915 *American Architect* suggested, of the Acropolis at Athens, the view of the domed Legislative Building from across Capitol Lake epitomizes the American ideal image of government.

The most convenient approach to the eight-acre campus is from Capitol Way. Curbside parking in the area makes a walking tour convenient. The earlier western part of the campus is the location of the Capitol Group, designed initially by Wilder & White in a severe Roman Classical Revival Style. Local architect Joseph Wohleb continued the style in his work, but the rest of the buildings show a progression to a variety of proto-Modern styles in the twenties and thirties and finally to the straightforward corporate Modern Academic Style of the 1956 General Administration Building. Chronologically, the more notable and interesting buildings are as follows:

1   **Temple of Justice**, 1917–20
    Wilder & White
    A colonnaded building sheathed as are all the structures in Wilkeson sandstone; notable interiors are the State Supreme Court Room and the Law Library.

2   **Insurance Building**, 1921
    Wilder & White
    Though it was the second building of the group to be finished, the design departs from the Classical approach in the interior and reflects a more contemporary styling.

3   **Legislative Building**, 1922–28
    Wilder & White
    The centerpiece of the Capitol Group with a Doric colonnaded base rising to a dome encircled by a Corinthian colonnade. Though the building walls are brick, the footing for the dome is a 130-foot-square reinforced concrete mat with four massive concrete piers 19-foot square. Periodic earthquake damage has caused some structural alterations but the building exterior is unchanged. The interior of the rotunda, faced in Alaskan Tokeen marble, has an almost vertiginous effect, well calculated to overawe the visitor. To the west of the rotunda is the House Chamber; to the east, the Senate Chamber. They are worth seeing as is the State Reception Room to the south with its parquet floors, marble walls and fireplaces, crystal chandeliers, and rich furnishings.

4   **Public Lands, Social Security Building**, 1937
    Joseph Wohleb

5   **Public Health, House Office Building**, 1940
    Joseph Wohleb
    This and (4) are composed of square end pavilions connected diagonally by curved, colonnaded sections that frame the Legislative Building forecourt and the axis to the Library. The interiors reflect the current Moderne decor while the exteriors continue the Neo-Classic styling.

6   **War Memorial Fountain and Monument**, 1938
    Alonzo Victor Lewis

7   **Institutions Building**, 1934
    Joseph Wohleb
    Moderne Style, then in fashion, is used here on the exterior and interior because the building was not part of the main group originally designed by Wilder & White.

8   State Library Building, 1959–61
Paul Thiry

A contemporary colonnaded pavilion set temple-like on a stepped base; the design maintains an admirable continuity with the earlier buildings. Directly in front of the Library is the territorial sundial, a hand-hammered brass bas relief by John W. Eliot. Centered in the middle is a fountain with a bronze sculpture of seagulls and salmon by Everett Du Pen. The gracious, light-filled interior has more artwork: a free-standing mosaic wall by James FitzGerald at the left of the main entrance and a mural by Mark Tobey in the room to the left. Downstairs in the Washington Room are mural paintings by Kenneth Callahan.

8 State Library Building (courtesy of State Office of Archaeology and Historic Preservation)

9   Governor's Mansion, 1908, interior remodeled 1974
Russell and Babcock; Ibsen Nelsen & Associates

The oldest building in the precinct, this Georgian Revival Style mansion was to be demolished and replaced by an office building complementary to the Insurance Building.

East of Capitol Way a contemporary complex of buildings reflects the drift of the bureaucracy. The new campus, approximately the same size as the old one, has a rational separation of vehicular and pedestrian traffic with the cars stored in a garage-podium, out of sight instead of blemishing the order of the plan as they do on the old campus. The restrained, regular, and rhythmic facades of the new structures bespeak the recently evolved Modern Academic Style for governmental and other kinds of institutional buildings. They are set about a broad, modular square punctuated by works of art and landscape elements atop the garage-podium. Though both campuses have a dignified monumentality, their scale is quite different. Changing facts of building economy are also revealed in the use of precast concrete in place of cut stone though at a comparable cost.

10   Office Building No. 2, 1974
The Richardson Associates

10 Office Building No. 2. Photo: Tom Upper

11 Highways Administration Building. Photo: Tom Upper

11 Highways Administration Building, 1974
The Richardson Associates

12 Fountain, 1974
Lawrence Halprin & Associates

A playful concept in this otherwise most serious place: the passerby is lured inside a
concrete-walled maze by seeing jets of water
rise up and disappear in different rhythms.

On the north edge of the capitol campus
is a sweet little turn-of-the-century conservatory (13) set against the bland bulk
of the fifties General Administration
Building. Across the street effectively a
part of the campus is:

14 Thurston County Courthouse, 1930
Joseph Wohleb
1110 Capitol Way

14 Thurston County Courthouse

A proto-Modern, stripped Classic block with
a Beaux Arts plan and massing, and ornament
from the Art Deco vocabulary.

South of the campus, wedged on the
ridge between the lake and the freeway,
is a quiet residential enclave of mostly
modest teens and twenties houses. Two,
however, are worthy of special note.

15 C. J. Lord House (now State Capitol
Museum), 1923–25
Joseph Wohleb
211 21st Avenue W

An eclectic work combining various Mediterranean elements in what was loosely known as

*15 C. J. Lord house (courtesy of State Office of Archaeology
and Historic Preservation)*

the "California Style" in the 1920s. The grounds were landscaped in the traditional gardenesque style by a Kew Gardens gardener from London, England. Given to the state in 1939 by the family of C. J. Lord, a banking magnate and foremost citizen, the building was remodeled as a museum in 1940. The ground floor interior is little changed; the upper floor has been altered for exhibition purposes.

16 **Henry McCleary House** (now location of State Office of Archaeology and Historic Preservation), 1923–25
Joseph Wohleb
111 21st Avenue W

An imposing Jacobean-Renaissance Revival mansion allegedly commissioned by McCleary to surpass the Lord house nearby, designed by the same architect. The interior is a showcase of American woods and reflects McCleary's background and lumbering interests. The building is now owned by the Washington Farm Bureau.

16 Henry McCleary house (courtesy of State Office of Archaeology and Historic Preservation)

Back on the north side of the Capitol Campus most of the remaining entries date from the nineteenth century and some are among the oldest buildings standing in the state.

17 **IBM Office Building,** 1975
Business Space Design
410 11th Avenue

Contemporary streamlining in a stepped out, corduroy concrete block with a rounded stair tower and mirror glass.

17 IBM Office Building. Photo: Dick Busher

18 **Olympic Collegiate Institute**
1055 and 1059 Adams Street

Two substantial frame buildings sheathed in clapboards that look as though they were shipped out from New England to house this early effort at higher education in the Puget Sound region.

19 **Dr. Alan H. Steele House,** 1870
1010 Franklin Street

A basic pioneer box graced with a front porch, this house belonged to a New England physician who served as post surgeon at Fort Dalles and Fort Steilacoom and became, upon retirement, a leading citizen of early Olympia.

20 **Board of Education** (originally Thurston County Courthouse, later State Capitol Building), 1891–92, annex 1905
W. A. Ritchie
Franklin to Washington Street, Legion Way to Seventh Avenue

One of several county courthouses designed by Ritchie (see also Port Townsend and Spokane), this one in the Romanesque Revival Style. The fusion of the massive stone entrance arches with the rounded tower bases is particularly well done. Originally the structure had a polygonal central tower, destroyed by fire in 1928, that doubtless heightened its authoritative image. The 1949

20 Board of Education (originally Thurston County Courthouse), c. 1892 (courtesy of Photo Collection. UW Library)

earthquake took the turrets. In 1905, when the courthouse became the City Hall, the west wing received an architecturally compatible addition.

21 **William G. White House,** 1893
1431 11th Avenue

A Queen Anne villa with a three-story square corner tower, plentiful wood fancywork, and a nice modern gazebo. Built by the original owner, the house once overlooked Swantown Slough, an inlet of Puget Sound since filled. Swantown itself was an early platted suburb of Olympia.

21 William G. White house

22 **Patnude House,** 1893
Charles Patnude
1234 Eighth Avenue

A story-and-a-half Downingesque cottage with ornamental barge boards and other appropriate Gothic Revival detail mixed with bay windows and porches that are later stylistically and probably are additions. Charles Patnude was a builder by trade who worked on many of Olympia's major public buildings and had a brick kiln on the site of the Armory.

23 **Armory,** 1939
Eastside Street between Fifth Avenue and Legion Way

A notable example of the classic phase of the Moderne Style which stamped innumerable buildings funded by the Public Works Administration in the 1930s; this one is replete with an F.D.R. dedication plaque inside.

23 Armory (courtesy of State Office of Archaeology and Historic Preservation)

24 **Bigelow House,** 1854
918 Glass Avenue

A design combining both Greek and Gothic Revival elements but chiefly representative of the A. J. Downing cottage, a popular rural-suburban dwelling type broadcast across the country by means of pattern books including those of Downing, who first promoted the cottage ideal. The owner, Daniel R. Bigelow, was a pioneer lawyer and member of the first territorial legislature. Alterations to the house include the removal of some of the porches.

25 House, c. 1880
747 W Bay Drive

A two-story, bracketed Italianate villa on a site commanding a fine view of the city and Budd Inlet.

26 Lane House, 1891
1205 W Bay Drive

Another house with a fine hillside site and a sweeping veranda from which to observe the activity on the inlet. The house is an interesting combination of earlier Gothic Revival styling in the three high-peaked gables with later Queen Anne elements such as the polygonal bay and veranda.

Environs

Northwest of Olympia on the way to the Evergreen State College is a recently built, sprawling, suburban residential area. At 505 Division Street, north of the main commercial strip on Harrison, is Evergreen Village (1972), designed by Robert B. Price & Associates and landscape architects Richard Haag Associates. Financed by the F.H.A. Section 236 program, the complex consists of 180 units on eighteen acres broken up into nine village-like communities clustered around courtyards. It is simple, woodsy, and pleasant.

The Evergreen State College

As the first four-year college established by the state of Washington in the twentieth century, Evergreen benefited from a kind of comprehensive planning unheard of when the majority of the state's higher educational institutions were conceived. In 1967, four years before the college opened, the Board of Trustees employed planning consultant Roger Malik of Arthur D. Little, Inc., to study alternative sites in southwestern Washington and develop an educational plan. These studies resulted in the choice of one thousand acres of second growth forest on the waterfront about three miles northwest of Olympia. The educational plan was designed to permit students to create their own curricula, to benefit from interdisciplinary communication with faculty and other students, and to be able to earn credit while working in internships outside the college.

The architectural expression of this philosophy, though not radically different from that of other more traditional institutions, was the result of a joint venture between engineer-planners Durham, Anderson & Freed, and landscape architects Eckbo, Dean, Austin &

Williams. They worked under the review of a committee of luminaries composed of Hugh Stubbins and Dan Kiley, architect and landscape architect respectively, and Frederick Mann, for many years the university architect for the University of Washington.

The master plan conceived of the college as a pedestrian complex with a compact academic core sited within a loop service road connected by a parkway to the world beyond. Landscaped parking lots and village-like residential groups are accessible from the loop road. A sports area occupies the eastern corner of the campus. The core buildings group around a central mall and adjacent landscaped courts. Broad overhangs and covered walkways give protection from rain and reinforce the core's interconnectedness. Where feasible, exterior circulation continues right through buildings, as exemplified in the design of the Student Activities Building.

The buildings were designed by a selection of well-known Washington architects. Though their individual expression ranges over the gamut of late 1960s stylistic currents, master plan design guidelines produced some threads of unity within the diversity. Warm-toned, concrete-framed academic buildings and rich brick pavement textures tie things together. The contrast between the design of Evergreen and that of the other major higher learning centers in the state emphasizes the special qualities of the instant campus, at once a programmed congruity and an almost forced variety. Within the academic core the sameness-variety tension produced a somewhat hard-edged visual environment perhaps, but outside the core moderation returns. There the careful overall conservation of the natural flora and the gentle topography achieve an exemplary expression of the ideal landscape for the academy cradled by pristine nature. Excellent grounds-keeping emphasizes the pristine character.

The following list of buildings begins with the central mall. A campus map is available in the Library.

Student Activities Building. Photo: Art Hupy

Daniel J. Evans Library. Photo: Art Hupy

Daniel J. Evans Library, 1971
Durham, Anderson & Freed

Student Activities Building, 1972
Kirk/Wallace/McKinley

This is perhaps the most interesting of the campus buildings. It adopts the interior street idea very much in the air at the time of its design and achieves with it a far more humane college design than the same firm's work at the University of Washington central campus.

College Recreation Center, 1972
Robert B. Price & Associates

Lecture Hall, 1971–72
Harris, Reed & Litzenberger

Science Lab, Phase I and Phase II, 1973
Naramore, Bain, Brady & Johanson

Seminar Building, 1972
The Bumgardner Partnership

Communications Lab, 1973
Walker, McGough, Foltz, Lyerla

Covered Recreation Pavilion, 1973
Robert B. Price

Shop and Garage, 1971
Bennett & Johnson

Residence Halls, 1971–72
The Bumgardner Partnership

Modular Housing, 1971
Quinton Budlong

Science Lab. Photo: Niranjan Benegal

Bainbridge, Vashon, and Bremerton

Bainbridge Island, directly across the Sound from downtown Seattle, and Vashon Island, offshore between Seattle and Tacoma, have been developed as semi-suburban rural retreats serviced by the steady green and white boats of the Washington State Ferries system. Bainbridge functions largely as a weekend and exurban hideaway for affluent Seattleites, and has functioned this way for a long time. As such it is the site for much serious residential architecture and garden design—almost all of it invisible to the public. For this reason the architectural visitor is largely stymied. The Bloedel Garden which now belongs to the University of Washington can be visited with prior permission, and as David Streatfield's essay suggests it is an important monument.

Vashon, while larger, is somewhat less conveniently located, and, perhaps as a consequence, is more rural and modestly exurban. Here too fine houses exist, but they successfully hide from public view.

Beyond Bainbridge on the Kitsap Peninsula a number of formerly quiet lumber, fishing, and farming villages are being swallowed by the gradual spread of urbanization. The U.S. Navy is largely to blame for this. Both the main Puget Sound base and shipyard at Bremerton, a sprawling, rather characterless town, and the super-secret Trident submarine base under construction on the Hood Canal have gradually taken over the economy of the peninsula. Environmental delights are limited to the dwindling pastoral countryside, punctuated occasionally by picturesque villages like

Ferry (courtesy of Washington State Ferries)

Poulsbo, and the mysterious forms that clutter the great shipyards. (The U.S.S. Missouri, a real World War II battleship, can be visited at Bremerton.)

Port Gamble and Port Ludlow

About eight miles northwest of Kingston (the west terminus of the Edmonds ferry) on State Highway 104 is Port Gamble. A restored historic district, this tiny hamlet might be taken for a west coast Williamsburg except that it is also an active lumber port with a still operating mill visible from the main street. Most of its residents work for Pope & Talbot, one of the Northwest's major forest products firms, which was founded here in 1853 as the Puget Mill Company. Founders Andrew Pope and William Talbot came from East Machias, Maine, where their families were in the New England lumbering industry. The two men came by ship to San Francisco and thence to Puget Sound, in search of a mill site. They chose a large spit of land well sited on deep water with boundless timberland as a backdrop. Because of the phenomenal demand for lumber in San Francisco, the mill boomed right away as did Yesler's mill in Seattle. By 1856 it ran night and day; by 1858 the company bought the nearby Port Ludlow mill.

St. Paul's Episcopal Church

Most of the company's employees came from Maine. In fact, Port Gamble was consciously styled after East Machias with simple wood-frame, gable-roofed houses for the workers lining streets planted with sugar maples from seeds sent out from the East. In 1870 this creation of a New England landscape in the Northwest wilderness was crowned by St. Paul's Episcopal Church, copied from the East Machias parish church.

In the succeeding century, Pope & Talbot expanded throughout the West, diversifying and becoming a land de-

velopment firm as well as forest products manufacturer. In the late 1960s it began restoration of Port Gamble, a project that has resulted in the rehabilitation of St. Paul's along with more than thirty-six of the town's buildings. Historic homes such as the Thompson house, built in 1859 with an 1872 addition, the Drew house of 1870, the Jackson house of 1871, and the Walker-Ames house, a large Queen Anne villa of 1887, have been refurbished and are marked with plaques that tell their history. The 1876 Odd Fellows Hall is the second oldest in the state. With Ralph Anderson as consulting architect, the Company Store, originally built in 1853 and rebuilt in 1914, has been rehabilitated to serve also as the company museum. Among the more recent buildings, the 1906 Land Company and Post Office in the California Mission Revival Style is a pleasant intrusion into the New England scene.

The visitor to Port Gamble will not find a tourist-oriented setting with chic shops and restaurants; their absence contributes to the quiet authenticity of the place. There is a pleasant park for picnics after or before a walk around the town which should include a visit to the old cemetery.

Across the Hood Canal and some ten miles northwest of Port Gamble is Port Ludlow, a second-home community built and managed by Pope & Talbot. Formerly this site had, in addition to a sawmill built in the early 1850s, Admiralty Hall, the Italianate villa with sweeping veranda and cupola that General Manager Cyrus Walker built for himself when his Port Gamble house burned in 1885. The diversifying Pope & Talbot Company husbanded its enormous holdings of cut-over land until, in the 1960s, the second-home recreational community boom gave Port Ludlow a new life. The company commissioned Naramore, Bain, Brady & Johanson to design the first part of this 3,000-acre resort complex. This firm completed in 1969 the community facility called the Harbormaster Building, and the Admiralty, a 125-unit condominium complex with some single residences. The Port Ludlow Beach Club, designed by The Bumgardner Partnership, was built in 1972. A year later the Bay Home group designed by Robert E. Cooper & Associates was built. Much more is projected for the future. These initial facilities, designed in the contemporary Northwest timber tradition, are well sited and felicitously express regional ideals.

Port Ludlow Beach Club

Harbormaster Building. Photo: Art Hupy

Port Townsend

One of the most dramatic boom-to-bust stories in the history of the Northwest belongs to Port Townsend. Founded in April 1851 (six months before Alki Point in Seattle) by Alfred Plummer and Charles Bachelder, the settlement promised a bright future because of the convenient harbor and great timber resources which would supply the building needs of San Francisco. Several months later the first pair of settlers were joined by Francis W. Pettygrove and Loren B. Hastings from Portland. The quartet of pioneers proceeded to start up the town, registering claims and platting 144 blocks, 220 feet square, in 1852. The removal of the customs district headquarters from Olympia to Port Townsend in 1853 and the establishment of a marine hospital in 1855 made the name "Key City of Puget Sound" seem appropriate.

Soon the specter of the transcontinental railroad began to afflict the Northwest. Seattle and Portland competed with Port Townsend as likely sites for the terminus. Portland won the Union Pacific, Tacoma the Northern Pacific, leaving Seattle and Port Townsend to brood over their misfortunes and try to build a railroad on their own. Though none of their schemes succeeded, the end of the 1880s witnessed an unprecedented optimism about the future of Puget Sound cities. Real estate speculation was rampant. The Oregon Improvement Company, a subsidiary of the Union Pacific, acquired the interests of the Port Townsend Railroad Company with the promise of having twenty-five miles of track ready by 1 September 1890. This action produced an almost instant city between 1888 and 1890. Water Street, now a historic district, was lined with impres-

Port Townsend in the early 1890s (courtesy of Photo Collection, UW Library)

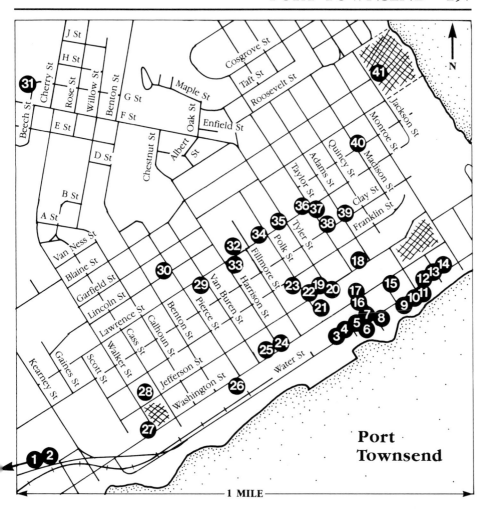

Port
Townsend

sive business blocks, most of them un-finished and unoccupied above the second floor despite solid-looking facades.

The extent of the town's expectations is also evident in the broad scattering of ample 1880s houses over the plateau above the business district. The monumental scale of the courthouse and customs house contradict the low density, rural-settlement aspect of their immediate vicinity. Clearly the visitor's initial view of Port Townsend, after passing the castellated form of the Manresa Castle on the neighboring hill, was meant to have a full complement of turrets and battlements to go with an expanded downtown and a bustling fishing and lumbering port, all wreathed round with smoke and steam from the iron horses that powered the economy.

In November 1890 the boom collapsed. The Oregon Improvement Company went into receivership, and the next years witnessed such a sharp decline that by 1893, according to James G. McCurdy's account in *By Juan de Fuca's Strait*:

Four of the six banks passed out of existence; the three street car lines ceased operations and pulled up their tracks; and from a city of over 7,000 inhabitants, the population dwindled to less than 2,000. . . . Suicides were common. Large brick buildings went to the county for non-payment of taxes.

Today, Port Townsend's calamitous past seems fortunate. Saved from progress, the Victorian city was preserved nearly intact. Now, about one hundred years after the beginning of the benighted boom, the city is having a renaissance, fixing up the old buildings and welcoming tourists, who are grateful that its future never arrived.

1   **Manresa Castle** (formerly Charles Eisenbeis House), 1892
    A. S. Whiteway
    Sheridan Street

    Pioneer merchant and real estate entrepreneur, Eisenbeis was one of the city's most important citizens. Perhaps the urge to build a castle came from memories of his native Prussia. Manresa Castle was originally brick from Eisenbeis' own brickyard. It was stuccoed over when a dormitory wing was added by the Jesuits in 1928. It is now a restaurant and hotel.

2   **J. C. Saunders House**, 1891
    Edward A. Batwell
    Cleveland Street just off Highway 20

    A fine Queen Anne villa built by a banker and customs official. The design is a transitional one, moving from the earlier medievalized Queen Anne to the later combination with Colonial Revival. This is particularly noticeable in the dormer window and porch detailing.

A booklet, "Port Townsend Illustrated," first published by the Leader Publishing Company in 1890 and now locally available in a reprint, gives a good idea of the "dream city." Though not all of the buildings in the engravings

were built, the pictures help to fill in the missing parts. Since many of the town's early entrepreneurs built the business district, the custom of imprinting the building with the owner's name and the date helps to make the history more personal. Stylistically the buildings conform to the high Victorian commercial-industrial aesthetic that found in medieval architecture the qualities of solidity and permanence likely to inspire confidence in capitalism. Faced with brick or stone, these wood-frame and masonry structures were adorned with classically derived detail with a stamped, linear quality. Pressed metal was commonly used for the ornamental features such as the cornices and window detail. The Port Townsend Foundry opened in 1883 and furnished cast-iron columns and other details for many of the buildings. With few exceptions the buildings of note are all on Water Street.

3   **Pioneer Building**, 1889
    Whiteway & Schroeder
    1014 Water Street

    Actually two buildings erected as a joint venture by the State Bank of Washington and F. W. Pettygrove, the Pioneer Building is a mixture of Renaissance and Romanesque Revival Style in brick and cast stone.

2 J. C. Saunders house (courtesy of Photo Collection, UW Library)

4 **Captain Tibbals Building,** 1889
Whiteway & Schroeder
NW corner Water and Tyler Streets

5 **James & Hastings Building,** 1889
Fisher & Clark
NE corner Water and Tyler Streets

A remarkably intact structure designed with a favored late nineteenth century prototype, the Italian Renaissance palazzo, in mind.

5 James & Hastings Building

6 **Sterming Block,** 1889
Whiteway & Schroeder
Water Street

7 **Mount Baker Block,** 1890
Whiteway & Schroeder
NW corner Water and Taylor Streets

Originally planned as a five-story hotel, the structure was reduced to four stories by hard times. The style is an eclectic mix of Renaissance and Romanesque Revival modes; the strong cornice line below the fourth story is clearly scaled to support two more stories.

8 **Hastings Building,** 1889
Elmer Fisher
SE corner Water and Taylor Streets

Originally the most lavish of the three local buildings designed by Elmer Fisher, who was busy building the Pioneer Building in Seattle

at the same time. Like the Pioneer Building, this corner block has an interior, skylit court. Most of the facade is sheathed in sheet metal formed to mimic the masonry details of the nineteenth century's idea of Italian civic architecture of the Renaissance period. Perhaps one day the ornate corner cupola will be restored.

9 **C. F. Clapp Building,** 1885
Water Street

A fine example of the kind of decorative cast-iron facade applied to a brick structure that was a common element in nineteenth century commercial streetscapes. In this case the facade was cast by the Washington Iron Works in Seattle, not by the Port Townsend Foundry.

10 **Waterman and Katz Building,** 1885
Water Street

11 **N. D. Hill Building,** 1889
Elmer Fisher
SE corner Water and Quincy Streets

Another of Port Townsend's major buildings by the famous Seattle architect Elmer Fisher, the Hill Building illustrates the rhythmic, modular quality of nineteenth century commercial buildings and their potential for creating an impressive streetscape.

11 N.D. Hill Building

12 **Franklin House,** 1886
Water Street
This spartan structure was the first brick hotel in town.

13 **Fowler-Caines Block,** 1889
Whiteway & Schroeder
NW corner Water and Madison Streets

14 **City Hall,** 1891
Batwell & Patrick
NE corner Water and Madison Streets
The truncated appearance of this building is explained by the fact that storm damage caused the removal of the gable-roofed attic story and square corner tower, which originally gave the design an Old English Revival look. Also housed here is the Historical Society Museum, well worth a visit for its collection of artifacts and furniture, including a bedroom suite from the Newsom Brothers' famous Carson House in Eureka.

14 City Hall

15 **Fowler Building,** 1874
Adams Street near Washington Street
One of the earliest stone buildings in town, and for many years the largest. It houses the *Leader*, the oldest continuously published newspaper in the state.

16 **Miller and Burkett Block,** 1889
Whiteway & Schroeder
SW corner Washington and Taylor Streets

17 **Haller Fountain,** 1906
Washington and Taylor Streets
Cast by the Mott Iron Works of New York, the statue of Venus, locally called *Galatea*, rising from the sea is the fragile-looking centerpiece of a fountain ironically dedicated to

the early pioneers and to the builder and commander of Fort Townsend, Granville Haller.

Behind this appropriate Victorian image a flight of steps leads to the upper town past the tallest single-mast flagpole still in use. At the top of the steps, at the intersection of Jefferson and Adams streets, stands the D. C. H. Rothschild house of 1868 **(18)** designed by the local "carpetect" A. H. Tucker and restored and refurnished by the State Parks and Recreation Commission. It is a public museum and an excellent example of the type of Greek or Classical Revival house that is found up and down the Pacific coast in settlements of this time. Houses like this were prefabricated in New England and brought around the Horn to the Mother Lode country in California following the gold rush. House plans were also brought by carpenter-builders.

18 Rothschild house

19 **St. Paul's Episcopal Church,** 1865
A. Horace Tucker
Jefferson and Tyler Streets
Tucker was an important pioneer type, a "carpetect" who built both coffins and buildings from the plans he brought with him, presumably from New England. In addition to this church, which was moved to its pres-

ent site in 1883, he built the Marine Hospital (now destroyed), the Rothschild house, and several other houses whose precise locations are unclear at present. The church is picture-postcard Carpenter Gothic, diminutive in scale with a lovely interior. Happily it is still in use.

20 Bell Tower, 1890
End of Tyler Street

A basic, utilitarian structure used in times past to summon the town's firemen.

21 Frank A. Bartlett House, 1883
End of Polk Street near Jefferson Street

Italianate merging into the fashionable Second Empire Style through use of the Mansard roof. The house reputedly cost $6,000 to build. Though less grand, the house next door is also a good example of the style.

21 Frank A. Bartlett house

22 E. S. Fowler House, c. 1860
NE corner Jefferson and Polk Streets

One of the oldest existing pioneer homes, it is designed in a New England Classic Revival Style that suggests the hand of A. Horace Tucker, builder of the Rothschild house.

23 First United Presbyterian Church, 1890
Whiteway & Schroeder
SE corner Franklin and Polk Streets

Carpenter Gothic with an admixture of the shingled Queen Anne Style.

24 F. W. James House, 1891
1238 Washington Street

Although the ground floor has been resurfaced with untypical, modern shingles, this Queen Anne Style mansion has an interior well worth seeing. It is now a guest house.

25 Post Office (formerly Customs House), 1893
NW corner Washington and Harrison Streets

A fine Richardsonian-Romanesque Style edifice originally planned with a six-story entrance tower that was cut down to three to save money. The heads carved on the column capitals are portraits of local Indians.

26 Four Fuge Houses, 1879
1517, 1529, 1541, 1609 Washington Street

The large corner house of 1879 was the main family house of the group built by John Fuge, a Welsh ship's carpenter. The three cottages were built on speculation or for other members of the family. The style of all four is Italianate with a generous amount of ornamental trim.

27 Frank W. Hastings House, 1890
NW corner Walker and Washington Streets

An excellent example of the turreted Queen Anne, shingled villa. Its interior is in a later style as a consequence of remaining unfinished for about fifteen years because of the depression.

28 Jefferson County Courthouse, 1892
W. A. Ritchie
NE corner Walker and Jefferson Streets

Courthouse buildings were some of the finest vehicles for expressing the confidence of the High Victorian era as confirmed by the exuberant ornament of this variation on a medieval chateau. Here as elsewhere, public interiors rarely lived up to the exteriors. In this building the main stair is curiously out of line with the entrance. Richie also designed the Spokane County Courthouse, which looks even more like a chateau on the Loire.

29 Captain James House, c. 1871
SE corner Van Buren and Lawrence Streets

An early Classic Revival house remodeled in the more ornate Italianate Style in the 1880s.

30 Captain Thomas Grant House, 1887
NW corner Lincoln and Pierce Streets

A two-story, slanted bay, Italianate house of a type fairly common elsewhere, particularly in San Francisco and Portland at this time.

28 Jefferson County Courthouse (courtesy of Jefferson County Historical Society)

31 **Pettygrove House,** 1880
1000 G Street

Built by a son of pioneer Francis W. Petty-grove, this Queen Anne Style house was grand enough to have a third-floor ballroom.

32 **Carnegie Library,** 1913
Lawrence Street near Fillmore

Libraries built with Carnegie grants are typical of small city development in the first decades of the twentieth century. A standard plan usually accompanied the grant.

33 **Jefferson Medical Clinic,** c. 1960
Paul Hayden Kirk
SE corner Lawrence and Harrison Streets

A good example of the 1950s wooden, post-and-beam pavilion by a Seattle architect whose many medical clinics are well known.

The blocks of Lawrence Street between Fillmore and Taylor comprise the up-town district, a shopping area that, according to one account, developed because downtown was too wicked for decent folks. A few late Victorian commercial structures still remain, notably the Odd Fellows Hall (34) at Lawrence and Polk and the Rutz Building (35) at Lawrence and Tyler.

36 **William F. Pfeiffer House,** 1889
NW corner Taylor and Lawrence Streets
Bracketed Italianate Style.

37 **Peter Mutty House,** 1891
SE corner Taylor and Lawrence Streets

A fine example of the Queen Anne Cottage complete, for a change, with its iron roof cresting.

37 Peter Mutty house

38 **United Methodist Church,** 1871–85
NE corner Clay and Taylor Streets

The year 1871 seems an early date for this Carpenter Gothic mixture of the Stick and Shingle styles. The design is close to that of (23) and may be the second church on this site.

39 **Starrett House,** 1889
744 Clay Street at Adams Street

The Starretts were leading mill owners and builders in Port Townsend; this house must have been a showcase for their work. A Queen Anne/Stick Style design, it is worth visiting for the unusual way the rooms open off the great tower. At the top of the spiral stair, on the tower ceiling, are frescoes of the seasons painted by Otto Chapman. They are said to have shocked the respectable, but that was a long time ago.

40 **Elias Devoe House,** 1888
538 Lincoln Street

A red brick Queen Anne with Classical quoins built by a contractor who did a lot of the local masonry work during the boom. Port Townsend has a number of late Victorian houses with L-shaped plans, a high rectangular form, similar shingling, and ornamental

detail. Another of this style is at 514 Franklin, built for Lucinda Hastings, with a covered balcony in front for ship watching.

41 **Chetzemoka Park,** 1905

Initially developed by the Civic Improvement
Club, this park exemplifies the "delight in
the rustic," to repeat David Streatfield's
phrase, and, like Wright Park in Tacoma, is
representative of the earliest intentional landscape design in the state.

Fort Worden State Park and Historic
District adjoins town to the northeast on
the shores of Admiralty Inlet. According
to the "Washington State Parks and
Recreation Commission Bicentennial
Report on Preserving Washington's
History": "Fort Worden was the headquarters of the Harbor Defenses of Puget
Sound, and, as such, it was the most
important segment of the three-cornered
fortified zone at the entrance to Puget
Sound." The system of fortifications, essentially complete by 1912, is representative of that recommended by the
Endicott Board in 1885.

Most of Fort Worden's finest buildings
were erected in the 1904–5 period. The
structures were built according to army
specified plans. Those that remain, the
barracks and officers' quarters which line

Commandant's house, Fort Worden

the parade ground and the other barracks
and service structures to the north on the
hillside, now form a state-managed conference center. Since 1976 a restoration
program has been going on which has so
far refurbished the commandant's house,
restored by Ralph Anderson & Partners,
and officers' quarters on the south side of
the parade ground in a medley of handsome color schemes faithful to the Victorian fashions. The buildings are in the
Georgian Colonial Style, generously
proportioned and well built: the whole
presents an orderly and satisfying scene.
Up on the hill is the Alexander Tower,
built after 1882 by a minister of St.
Paul's in town. A castellated structure
with fancy brickwork, it must have been
even more romantic when it stood alone
on the grassy hillside slope by the sea.
Another interesting structure is the
metal-sided balloon hangar rusting in
the evergreens near the chapel.

Point Wilson Lighthouse (1914) lies beyond town on the point terminating the
Quimper Peninsula. Captain Vancouver
gave this and every other landmark he
came upon in 1792 an English name.
The fog signal and beacon have been
modernized but the rest is as it was—
very picturesque.

39 Starrett house

Everett

The history of Everett is a casebook study of the destruction of an environment by rampant free enterprise. The first step in this process was the removal of the Snohomish Indians to the Tulalip reservation from their centuries-old home on the peninsula enclosed by the Sound and the Snohomish River. In their stead came loggers and trappers whose exploitation of the natural resources opened the area to extractive industry. Mechanization of lumbering, mining, and fishing began in the 1880s. Land grabbing began in 1889 when Bethel J. and Wyatt J. Rucker acquired large tracts on Port Gardner. But it was not until 1891 when John D. Rockefeller put his money in the hands of a set of local and eastern capitalists that real development began.

Planned as an industrial community by the Everett Land Company the town soon produced commercial centers at both ends of Hewitt Avenue. Along with this development came the Great Northern Railroad, heavy industry, and the beginning of a harbor facility. Following the Panic of 1893, a severe financial depression slowed development until the phenomenal boom following the 1906 San Francisco earthquake and fire. The mills of the Northwest furnished timber to rebuild that city. During these years the great influx of foreign immigrants, mostly from Canada, Scandinavia, and Germany, left an imprint on Everett still visible in the many churches which served different national groups. Most of the city's inner suburbs, populated by working class families, developed at this time. Methodically laid out on twenty-five-foot street front lots, the houses address the general grid of streets and sidewalks rather than the city's spectacular site and waterside loca-

Port Gardner Bay, 1908 (courtesy of Everett Community College Library)

tion. The only two precincts that show a deference to site are the Grand Avenue district and the Rucker Hill district where the wealthy and powerful resided.

A 1920s boom, sparked by the demand for building materials following the 1923 Japanese earthquake, witnessed a great surge in the local construction of all building types as well as whole new residential districts. Since World War II, Everett has certainly experienced its share of contemporary building, most of it outside the center city. The historic preservation movement of the mid-1970s has produced concern for the older buildings and will undoubtedly continue to spark restoration and rehabilitation in the central business district and older suburbs.

Students of Washington's history know Everett, not as an architectural center, but as a historic shrine for one of the state's most dramatic and tragic political events, the Everett Massacre. Norman H. Clark's *Mill Town* movingly recounts the historical context and details of this tragedy. Those who are intrigued by the possible relationship between buildings and events will find ample food for thought in this slim volume, an exemplary social history of Everett's first decades.

Downtown

1 **Swalwell Building,** 1892
   Charles Hove and A. F. Heide
   2900 block of Hewitt Avenue at Pine Street
   Designed by the Everett Land Company architects for William Swalwell, the major developer of Everett's east side, the building is a good example of the midwestern commercial style which came west from Chicago with the railroads. The somewhat fortified, medieval look surely symbolized permanence and respectability on the frontier. Adjoining this structure to the east are the Glassberg, Weber, Diefenbacher, and Wuerch buildings which together make a harmonious block. Two blocks north at 2730 and 2712 Pine Street are the Swalwell house and a cottage, both apparently designed by a local architect, F. A. Sexton. The house has been altered, but even in its original state it was not in the "mansion" class. The cottage is a simple design sheathed in patterned shingles. There is also a Swalwell dock site at the foot of Hewitt Avenue on the Snohomish River which served as a principal landing point during the Rockefeller boom.

2 **B. F. Masson House,** c. 1898
   SW corner Pacific Avenue at Broadway
   Built by the coproprietor of one of the city's first brick factories which prospered during the Rockefeller boom. The style and plan are not unusual, but the use of brick in a residence of this period was.

3 **Carnegie Library,** 1905
   A. F. Heide
   3001 Oakes Avenue
   The first library designed as such in Everett and funded by a Carnegie grant. The architect is said to have used a Pomona, California, library as a model which may account for its Mediterranean-Renaissance character.

The blocks from Rockefeller to Hoyt between Pacific and Wall Street contain Everett's civic center. The buildings span over half a century and present a clear picture of the changes in architectural style and physical scale of government over the decades.

4   **Snohomish County Courthouse,** 1910
Siebrand & Heide
Wetmore Avenue between Wall Street and
Pacific Avenue

A. F. Heide designed the first courthouse in
1897 in the then fashionable Romanesque-
Chateauesque Style. When it burned in
1909, changing fashions made the California
Mission Revival Style the current choice. A
comparison between photos of the old building and the new one shows that the format
and composition of the main facade are really
the same. The fire-damaged core of the structure was simply given a new, more stylish
dress. The rest of the block is occupied by the
new Courthouse and County Administrative
buildings, designed in 1967 and 1972 by
Harmon, Pray & Dietrich. They are well sited
to frame the older building and form inner
landscaped courtyards. Stylistically they
evoke the work of Minoru Yamasaki, who
fashioned a contemporary corporate style
based on Neo-Gothic delicacy and ornamental detail.

4 Snohomish County Courthouse

5   **City Hall,** 1930
A. H. Albertson
Wetmore Avenue and Wall Street

A good example of the P.W.A. Moderne
Style that was commonly used for government buildings from the late 1920s to the
early 1940s. Continuing the hierarchical
massing and symmetry of Beaux Arts
Classicism, the building is stripped of Classical detail and given the then popular
geometric and foliate ornament to make it
modern.

5 City Hall

6   **Federal Building and U.S. Post Office**
(now Bureau of Indian Affairs), 1915–17
Oscar Wenderoth
3006 Colby Avenue

As supervising architect for the U.S. Treasury
Department, Wenderoth created the design
prototype for scores of federal buildings built
across the country during his tenure in office.
The favored style of the time was Beaux Arts
Classicism, which gradually evolved into a
more modern version as shown in the City
Hall (5).

7   **Monte Cristo Hotel,** 1925
Henry Bittman
NE corner Hoyt Avenue and Wall Street

Everett's grand old hotel built at the beginning of the automobile age to replace a car-

*7 Monte Cristo Hotel. Photo: Lee Juleen, 1936 (courtesy
of Everett Public Library)*

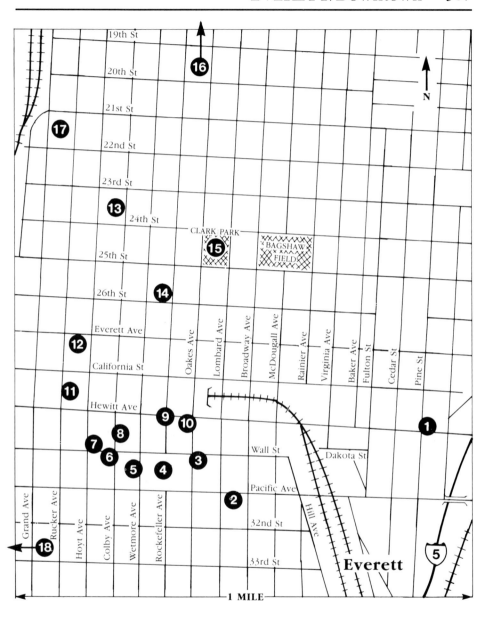

riage era version of itself built by the Everett Land Company at Pacific and Kromer overlooking Port Gardner Bay. Outmoded by freeway travel and the strip, the Monte Cristo no longer enlivens this end of downtown as it did. It would be nice if it were rehabilitated for suitable current use.

8   **Everett Theater,** 1901
Bebb & Mendel
2911 Colby Avenue

The present marquee dates from the reconstruction after a 1923 fire. Enough decor remains to testify to the building's earlier status as the major theater in town.

9   **Central Lutheran Church, and the Central Building,** 1925
Morrison & Stimson
NW and SW corners Hewitt and Rockefeller Avenues

An important downtown corner marked by three business blocks of roughly the same period (the Commerce Block of 1919 and the Hodges Building of 1923 are on the northeast and southeast corners), and a distinguished church design whose substantial character holds its own against the larger scale of the other buildings. The Neo-Gothic Central Building went up at the height of the 1920s boom as did the sadly remodeled Medical-Dental Building of the same year by the same Seattle architects, at the northwest corner of Hewitt and California.

10 **McCrossen Building,** 1894
1814–20 Hewitt Avenue

A significant architectural relic of the Rockefeller boom era.

11 **Marion Building,** 1893–94
A. F. Heide
NE corner Hewitt and Rucker Avenues

Another fairly intact design by the Everett Land Company architect.

12 **Everett Public Library,** 1934, addition 1963
Bebb & Gould; addition by Bryant, Butterfield & Frets
SW corner Hoyt and Everett Avenues

Designed by a famous Seattle firm, the library reflects early Modern European currents such as the Dutch Secessionist school in its massing, ornament, and use of corner windows. A bequest by Leonard Howarth made it possible to enrich the interior with murals by J. T. Jacobsen and sculptured reliefs in a metal alloy called butannia by Dudley Pratt. The 1963 additions merely expand the space and make an unfortunate cleavage in the facade for the covered walk.

13 **Everett High School,** 1910; altered 1959, 1964, and 1969
James Stephen; alterations by Bryant, Butterfield & Frets
2416 Colby Avenue

An impressive example of Beaux Arts academic Classicism by a Seattle architect who designed the city's finest early school buildings during his tenure as official school district architect.

13 Everett High School

12 Everett Public Library. Photo: John Juleen, 1934 (courtesy of Everett Public Library)

14 **Calvary Lutheran Church** (formerly Zion's
Norwegian Evangelical Lutheran Church),
1902
1711 26th Street
An early Lutheran Church erected by a then
new immigrant community in a Gothic Revival vernacular style.

15 **Clark Park and the Stump House**
Block between 24th and 25th Streets, Lombard and Oakes Avenues
The city's first park boasts a bandstand built
in the first decades of the twentieth century,
and a genuine architectural curiosity, a stump
house which was originally part of
Washington State's exhibit at the St. Louis
Fair of 1904. Across the street on the northwest corner of 24th Street and Lombard Avenue is another of Everett's many and various
Lutheran churches erected by the city's important Scandinavian community.

The peninsula north of the central business district was intensively developed
during Everett's boom years with mills
on the periphery at the water's edge,
workers' housing in the central area and
on the eastern slope, and the richer folk
atop the bluff on the west edge. A few
notable public buildings served the
peninsula.

16 **Washington School**, 1907
James Stephen
17th Street between Rockefeller and Oakes
Avenues
Another distinguished Beaux Arts Classic de-
sign by the same architect as the Everett High
School (13).

Grand Avenue

The narrow, 1½-mile strip of blocks
from about 24th to 8th Street and from
Grand to Hoyt Avenue just north of
downtown comprises the so-called
Grand Avenue district. Here in a zone of
better residence the affluent and prominent citizens lived. The site follows the
long ridge above Port Gardner Bay; it
features a fine park-like promenade on
the water side of Grand. Although the
houses date from 1890 to 1925, most
were built during the lumber industry's
peak years following the 1906 San Fran-

cisco earthquake and fire, and before the
opening of the Panama Canal and World
War I. Despite their ownership by
Everett's baronage, the houses are
neither pretentious nor idiosyncratic.
Nor does their appearance suggest authorship by high-style designers. More
importantly, the size, scale, stylistic
range, and landscaping of the lots and
streets combine to create one of the best
examples in the state of the substantial
middle to upper-middle class suburban
American taste of the period.

The following houses are notable; the visitor may find others equally interesting.

Roland H. Hartley House, 1911
2320 Rucker Avenue

Home of a leading Everett industrialist and former governor of Washington, this huge Colonial Revival house has been altered, but still conveys a sense of its original owner's position.

House, c. 1910
2212 Rucker Avenue

One of the finest variations of the theme of the Colonial Revival Classic Box anywhere.

C. A. Blackman House, 1910
2208 Rucker Avenue

The owner of the Rockefeller boom's first shingle mill resided here; the house was built for $6,000.

A. D. Austin House, c. 1905
2201 Rucker Avenue

A. D. Austin house

A. F. Heide House, 1893
2107 Rucker Avenue

Home of one of the Everett Land Company's official architects, who designed many of the city's significant buildings.

David Clough House, c. 1905
2026 Rucker Avenue

The owner, an ex-governor of Minnesota, had already made and lost a fortune in timber in that state before moving to Everett where he became the patriarch of the new timber aristocracy.

Herbert Clough House, c. 1901
2031 Grand Avenue

A Colonial Revival bungalow inflated under a contorted and brooding roof, the most eccentric house in the district.

William C. Butler House, 1910
1703 Grand Avenue

Home of the most powerful single figure in Everett's history, this enormous, but restrained and dignified Georgian Revival house suited the owner's reserved and private nature.

William C. Butler house

Environs

The area south of downtown developed later, and, because of its topography, it followed a more scattered pattern. Though this area has fewer architectural highlights than the older district, a few merit note. The following places can be reached by going south from the central business district on Rucker Avenue. All lie west of Rucker.

Rucker Mansion, 1904–15
412 Laurel Drive

Dramatically sited on a hill overlooking the bay, this house was built by the pioneer family who amassed a fortune in real estate by developing the city's bayside community and other properties. Although the building is mansion-scale, it retains the format of a Colonial Revival bungalow, built of rich materials with particularly handsome beveled glass in windows and doors.

The neighboring blocks are worth exploring for the number of substantial homes with well-landscaped settings in a variety of revival styles. Two fine Colonial Revival examples are the Emerie Bishop house (c. 1912) at 615 Laurel Drive and the Joseph Ebert house (c. 1930) at 619 Laurel Drive. South of the Rucker Hill district lies Everett's most ambitious park.

Forest Park
Federal Street between 41st Street and about 46th Street, accessible from 41st and Mukilteo Boulevard

The nucleus of the park was a forty-acre tract given to the city in 1900 by William G. Swalwell. The rest of the land was purchased in 1909 and developed later as a W.P.A. project. It is a multipurpose park with the traditional programs of forest, floral display, zoo, playfields—everything.

On the extreme southern edge of Everett, Route 526 to Mukilteo slices through Paine Field airport and Boeing's Everett plant. Should the doors be open the road affords dramatic views into the innards of the Boeing 747 assembly shed, the world's largest building in terms of volume. Plant tours are available. In the other direction well north of Everett, the Tulalip Indian Reservation established in 1859 on Tulalip Bay lies about five miles west of Marysville on the Tulalip Road. At the administrative heart of the reservation is the Tulalip Community Center (1974), designed by The Bumgardner Partnership. The mammoth, shed-roofed wooden building houses offices, a library, kitchen facilities, meeting rooms, and a gymnasium. Despite its size the structure does not overwhelm its natural setting, but rather complements the nearby longhouses. The anonymous, barn-like exteriors of these older structures conceal dramatic, interior, heavy timber framing that follows ancient ritual-based patterns.

Tulalip Community Center

A mile or so further along the road is the rustic and simple St. Anne's Roman Catholic Church of 1903. Also in the vicinity, on North Meridian Avenue, is a 1924 Indian Shaker Church built in conformity to a doctrinal tradition peculiar to the Northwest and among the best preserved examples of this type of vernacular architecture.

Further north from Everett the Pilchuck School deserves note from both those interested in recent regional vernacular style building and those concerned with the decorative arts. Pilchuck School is a unique international center of glass art, flat and blown. It can be reached from Interstate 5 by taking the Freeborn Road exit (no. 215) about twenty miles north of Everett. Turn east off the freeway and go one mile on 316th Street Northwest to English Grade Road, then north one mile to 316th Northwest again, and east one mile to Pilchuck. The main glassblowing pavilion, an appropriately heavy, log framed, central-space struc-ture, initially built in 1973, was the first of a series of facilities designed by Thomas Bosworth. Some resident artists have hidden their fine idiosyncratic cab-ins in the nearby woods.

Pilchuck School

Whidbey Island

A long landform so deeply indented by coves that it appears segmented into three parts, Whidbey was judged to be the shore of the mainland until Joseph Whidbey, master of Captain Vancouver's H.M.S. *Discovery*, found Deception Pass in 1792 and sailed down the narrow passages to Puget Sound. The Deception Pass Bridge, constructed by the Public Works Administration in 1935, links Whidbey to Fidalgo Island, in turn connected to the mainland of Skagit County. The island has a rich soil that has promoted diversified farming. Towns are few and small, but history endows the area with considerable interest.

The southern part of Whidbey is reached by a ferry from Mukilteo near Everett. Useless Bay at the very southernmost end has some striking and well-designed contemporary vacation houses along Eastshore Drive:

Paulsell House, 1970
Hobbs/Fukui

Paulsell house. Photo: Art Hupy

House, 1970
The Hastings Group

Thieme House, 1975
Al Bumgardner & Associates
1500 Eastshore Drive

Thieme house. Photo: Art Hupy

To the north on the east side is Langley, a quiet waterside town where those interested in social housing may discover at 300 Anthes Avenue the Brookhaven housing project (c. 1970) by architects Bell & Greve. About the most felicitous public housing project anyone could imagine, the site has a crescent of contemporary bungalows set in a mini-meadow graced by a little stream.

Further north on the west side of the island is Fort Casey constructed around the turn of the century as part of the coastal defense system directly across the pass from Fort Worden. The concrete fortifications ring a broad meadow. They present a somewhat surreal image in their unused state, but military buffs will be impressed by their completeness and particularly by the turn-of-the-century vintage disappearing guns mounted in two of the emplacements. They are of the same type originally installed, though these particular pieces were moved here recently from the Philippines, where they had once been part of Manila's defenses. Over the hill behind are the remains of the base buildings, most of which were erected in 1906. The building complex is similar to, if not as complete as, Fort Worden.

Also nearby is a beautifully shipshape early twentieth century lighthouse containing an interpretive center. The exhibit offers a thorough exposition of the coastal forts and their equipment.

Lighthouse

A few miles north on the Fort Casey road to Coupeville is the Crockett Blockhouse, one of two built on this site in 1855. The other was sold to Ezra Meeker for his restaurant entrance in Seattle's 1909 Alaska-Yukon-Pacific Exposition. Later it was moved to Point Defiance Park in Tacoma. In such bucolic surroundings, it is difficult to take seriously the military implications of this picturesque structure.

As one nears Coupeville, the island's early history presaged by the Crockett Blockhouse takes on more substance. The first land claim, near Coupeville, was taken by Thomas Glasgow in 1848. Frightened off by hostile Indians, Glasgow abandoned the land which was taken over two years later by Isaac Ebey. Ebey's Landing on the coast southwest of Coupeville commemorates the claim site. In 1852, Captain Thomas Coupe took up the 320-acre claim on Penn Cove which was to become the town. Coupe's 1854 board and batten house still stands hidden by trees near the water's edge. The town grew stubbornly despite Indian troubles and the usual frontier privations. By 1856 there were seven blockhouses and a collection of farms. In 1857 the Haida Indians took revenge for the killing of one of their chiefs in the battle of Port Gamble by beheading Ebey, a gruesome episode described in detail in Jimmie Cook's *A Particular Friend, Penn's Cove*, a detailed history of the settlers, their claims, and the buildings of central Whidbey Island, published in 1973 by the Island County Historical Society.

Having prospered as a farming community and fishing port, Coupeville was finally incorporated in 1900. Today

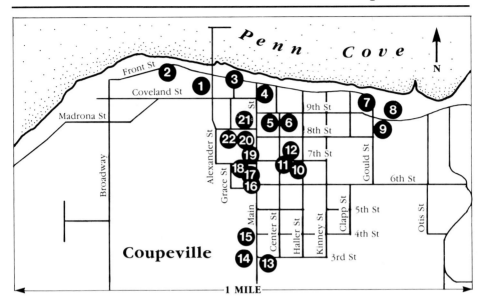

twenty-two square miles including the town and farmland surrounding Penn Cove have been declared the Central Whidbey Historical Preservation District. Although most of the buildings were built in the 1880s and 1890s, the simple wooden building technology provides a continuity from much earlier days. Bits and pieces of high style appear, proving that no outpost was immune to fashion. The urban ambitions of Main Street satisfy the tourist's nostalgia for pioneer townscape while providing the usual spate of shops and eateries. The following tour is easily accomplished on foot.

1   **Alexander's Blockhouse,** 1855
    Alexander Street near Front Street

    One of several blockhouses built on the island; now a museum of local artifacts.

2   **Fairhaven,** 1852
    Front Street west of Alexander Street

    Originally built on the Smith claim across Penn Cove for Captain James Swift, this log house was moved here in 1928 and somewhat modernized.

3   **Commercial Buildings**
    Front Street between Main and Alexander Streets

    A quintessential frontier town street with a variety of shops and eateries. Plaques on the important buildings give dates and other information.

3 Commercial buildings

4   **Colonel Granville Haller House,** 1886
    SE corner Front and Main Streets

    Built around an existing cabin, this house has
    an appropriate frontier simplicity.

5   **Methodist Church,** 1883
    SW corner Ninth and Center Streets

5 Methodist Church

6   **Thomas Griffith House,** 1869
    SE corner Ninth and Center Streets

    A New England saltbox with some alterations
    and a recent rear addition.

7   **Captain Clapp House,** 1886
    SW corner Front and Gould Streets

    A High Victorian cottage with a stylish
    high-peaked roof and a modest amount of
    jigsaw fancywork on the porch.

8   **Captain Coupe House,** 1854
    East end of Front Street

    The oldest Coupeville house on the original
    land claim, built of redwood with board and
    batten and clapboard siding on a saltbox
    form.

9   **John Gould House,** 1894
    SW corner Ninth and Gould Streets

10 **The Parker House,** c. 1886
    H. B. Lovejoy
    SW corner Seventh and Haller Streets

    Originally built for his mother-in-law by
    H. B. Lovejoy, Coupeville's masterbuilder.
    The front porch has been enclosed.

11 **James Zylstra House,** 1889
    H. B. Lovejoy
    SE corner Center and Seventh Streets

    Built by Lovejoy for his own residence.

12 **Albert Kineth House,** 1885
    North side of Seventh Street between Haller
    and Center Streets

13 **St. Mary's Catholic Church** (formerly
    First Congregational Church), 1889
    SE corner Third and Main Streets

    The tower was altered.

13 St. Mary's Catholic Church

14 **Rev. George Lindsey House,** 1889
    Main Street opposite St. Mary's Church

    Re-sided with oversized modern shingles,
    but still quite recognizable as a High Victo-
    rian cottage.

15 Joseph B. Libbey House, 1870
West side of Main Street at Fourth Street

A Downingesque Gothic Revival cottage missing some of the decorative detail but identifiable by the high-peaked, cross-gabled roof and central pointed door over the porch.

15 Joseph B. Libbey house

16 Jacob Jenne House, 1889
NW corner Sixth and Main Streets

A handsome Italianate house recalling the urban-suburban townhouses built at this time up and down the Pacific coast.

17 Joshua Highwarden House, 1888
Main Street between Sixth and Seventh Streets

18 Coupeville Methodist Church, 1894
H. B. Lovejoy
SW corner Seventh and Main Streets

Built by Coupeville's masterbuilder in an appropriate Carpenter-Gothic idiom, the design is enlivened with repeated elements. The interior is remodeled.

19 John and Jane Kineth House, 1887
NW corner Seventh and Main Streets

20 A. D. Blowers House, 1874
SW corner Eighth and Main Streets

21 Masonic Hall, 1874
NW corner Eighth and Main Streets

A large, wood-frame building in a simple Greek Revival style resembling many such buildings erected by the Masons in western hinterlands.

22 Ernest E. Watson House, 1886
H. B. Lovejoy
South side of Eighth Street near Grace Street

Similar to Lovejoy's house for himself (11).

North of Penn Cove is Oak Harbor, center of the island's Dutch community. Hollanders began arriving toward the end of the nineteenth century to take advantage of the rich farmland. At the junction of Zylstra and Swantown roads is an arresting house with an onion domed tower allegedly built by Benjamin Loers in 1911 and designed by W. D. Rotechafer, who had built the same house in Holland, Michigan, on the campus of Northwestern Theological Seminary.

Benjamin Loers house (courtesy of State Office of Archaeology and Historic Preservation)

Anacortes

A ferry terminus and fishing and lumbering center on the northwest point of Fidalgo Island, Anacortes is connected with the mainland over bridged sloughs. Laid out on the flats in the typical grid plan, the town was settled about 1860 and named for Anna Curtis, wife of pioneer Amos Bowman. Downtown has remnants of the late nineteenth century development in a scattering of brick business blocks.

The gem of the town is:

Causland Memorial Park, 1920
Louis LePage
N Street between Seventh and Eighth Streets

Antonio Guadi and the Guell Park in Barcelona, Spain, loom in the background somewhere behind this intriguingly original design. Serpentine walls mosaicked with colored pebbles and rocks surround the perimeter of the block, which is mounded in the middle and planted with a variety of trees and shrubs. The grotto-like bandstand is likewise a work of creative vision and loving care. In all, this is one of the most remarkable small parks on the whole Pacific coast.

The residential area to the northwest on the way to the ferry terminus has some late nineteenth century to early twentieth century houses and bungalows that are worth seeking out.

House, c. 1890
1201 Fifth Street

Captain Hogan House, 1891
1613 Seventh Street

House, c. 1890
1819 Eighth Street

House, 1819 Eighth Street

Causland Memorial Park

La Conner and the Skagit Valley

Barns

The lower Skagit River valley and delta present one of the most serene and lovely rural landscapes in the Northwest. Those who delight in such environments should take the back roads through the area around La Conner to experience the superb barns, variegated fields, and views to the hills and water. La Conner on the Swinomish Slough had a trading post in 1867 and was first called Swinomish until John S. Conner, first permanent settler, renamed the place for his wife, Louise A. Conner. The town streets, lined with simple vernacular buildings in wood and brick, run parallel to the slough along the hillside. There is an agreeable assortment of wharfside activities. One of the nicest examples of small-scale industrial vernacular building is the San Juan Canneries where the fascinating inner workings spill out, Rube Goldberg fashion, onto the backside truck dock.

Now a historic district, La Conner has as its principal monument the Gaches

house on the hill above the main street. Built in 1883, the house is a wooden version of the idealistic Victorian fusion of the castle and the medieval half-timbered house, Americanized by the addition of a front porch. Nearly destroyed by a fire a few years ago the house has been restored with a National Park Service grant by L. A. Bailey & Associates. It is open to the public.

Gaches house (courtesy of State Office of Archaeology and Historic Preservation)

Bellingham

Bellingham's strategic location on a bay in the northwesternmost corner of the state has maintained it as a distinctive regional center since its first settlement. At present Pugetopolis stretches toward it from the south while Vancouver, British Columbia, drifts down from the north. A pattern of continuous urbanization is foreseeable in the not too distant future. Meanwhile the old inner city of Bellingham belies the fast-changing scene.

Before white settlers came here the Lummi Indians were at home in the area. Now their reservation is northwest of Bellingham. In 1792, Captain George Vancouver named the bay from his roster of deserving Englishmen. Whatcom, the name of the county of which Bellingham is the seat, is an Indian name meaning "noisy waters." The name gets its significance from the three creeks that formerly rushed through the site to the bay: Padden in the south; Squalicum in the north; and Whatcom, which has two

falls, one east of town in present Whatcom Falls Park, the other on the bluff downtown two blocks from the Old City Hall. These noisy waters prompted Henry Roeder to settle here in 1852 and the next year locate his sawmill on the creek below the bluff. This first industry, typical of Puget Sound's early settlements, coupled with fur trading and salmon fishing brought more white men to the area the following year. Coal mining followed in 1854. The growing promise of these industries produced no less than four contiguous boom towns: Whatcom in late 1852, Bellingham and Fairhaven in 1853, and Sehome in 1854. The fortunes of these towns rose and fell with such events as the Fraser River Gold Rush of 1858. Sehome changed its name to New Whatcom and consolidated with Whatcom in 1891; Bellingham and Fairhaven had consolidated as Fairhaven in 1890, and together all four formed the city of Bellingham in 1903. Each settlement had its share of intrepid

Holly Street, New Whatcom, 1893 (courtesy of Whatcom Museum of History and Art)

entrepreneurs who combined intuition, physical stamina, and experience to promote their fortunes in the extractive industries of the times. Though gold mining left no mark on the settlement, coal mining was a significant early industry. Sehome Hill, site of Western Washington University, contains one of the principal mines. Other mines were dug east of town in the vicinity of Lake Whatcom.

Because the northern towns of Whatcom and Sehome and the southern towns of Bellingham and Fairhaven were separate for much of their early formative periods, the nineteenth century commercial and residential areas are still distinguishable in the overall urban pattern. This separation also explains the disjointed street layout that leaves such a vivid impression on the Bellingham visitor. Whatcom, platted and largely owned by Henry Roeder, had its first business district along Holly Street extending east from J to C Street, bordered by the early residential area extending

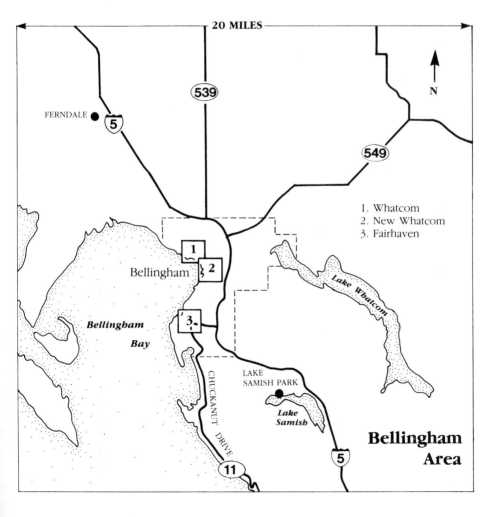

1. Whatcom
2. New Whatcom
3. Fairhaven

Bellingham Area

northwest to the natural boundary of Squalicum Creek. Gradually Whatcom's center moved southeast along Holly to join that of Sehome. Consolidation of the two towns accelerated this trend and led to the erection in 1892–93 of the monumental New Whatcom City Hall on four lots purchased from Henry Roeder. State action in 1893 chose Sehome for a western normal school. The railroads' coming further homogenized New Whatcom and later Bellingham. The Fairhaven and Southern, later absorbed into the Great Northern, had run its track on a long trestle across the tide flats between Squalicum Creek and Sehome Wharf. In 1902 the Great Northern built its present line paralleling the earlier one on fill along Roeder Avenue, across Whatcom Creek, and on the shore to Fairhaven. Also in 1902 the Northern Pacific purchased the Bellingham Bay and Eastern Railroad, originally built by J. H. Bloedel and J. J. Donovan to bring coal from Lake Whatcom to the waterfront, and thereby completed its line through the town. The third line, the Chicago, Milwaukee and St. Paul, also picked up a local railroad, the Bellingham Bay and British Columbia, and joined the other two to create a major rail corridor in front of the central business district and Sehome Hill.

During the 1890s, the street railway system, ultimately called the Whatcom County Railway and Light Company, expanded from the first lines on Holly and State streets to a more comprehensive system that also ran a line out Lakeway Drive and Electric Avenue to Lake Whatcom past the cemetery and the park, major attractions of the day. The streetcar service ended in 1938 leaving

linear commercial districts such as North State Street as reminders of its early heyday.

Following the hardtimes after the 1893 depression, business picked up, creating an increasingly solid central business district. Considerable growth came from 1910 to 1914 as witnessed by substantial buildings such as the Bellingham National Bank Building and the Federal Building, both erected in 1912–13. Social institutions like the Elks Club and the Y.W.C.A. erected buildings (in 1912 and 1915, respectively) as did many churches that had outgrown earlier quarters. The twenties further strengthened the central business district, but the increasing use of the automobile promoted suburban expansion north, east, and south of town. This proceeded at a modest pace; the depression tended to slow development, and even post–World War II growth was not spectacular. The railroad era had made Bellingham a wholesale distribution center for the northwest corner of the state; the shift to trucking came easily. Salmon fishing and canning, logging, and farming are still important to the economic base of the area along with some manufacturing and commerce. During the last quarter century, though, the real growth industry has been higher education as the old normal school by stages became Western Washington University.

Although the counter-culture movement of the 1970s found Bellingham a suitable ecotopian outpost, the results of this movement are yet to be assessed. Preservation forces have reclaimed a number of threatened landmarks, nota-

Bellingham in the late 1920s (courtesy of Whatcom Museum of History and Art)

bly the Old City Hall and early business district of Fairhaven. As elsewhere Bellingham reacted to the bicentennial in 1976 by showing renewed interest in its heritage. The Municipal Arts Commission with the support of the City Council commissioned Daniel Turbeville to produce a fine catalogue of historic buildings. It has been invaluable in editing this guide. There is hope that future development pressures will be met with sensible actions to insure that the city retains its present historic precincts as well as its environmental qualities.

The guide begins in the northern and oldest part of town, Whatcom, takes in Sehome–New Whatcom next, then the campus, and finally Fairhaven.

Whatcom

Oldest of the four Bellingham progenitors, Whatcom lies between the two northern creeks. Here Henry Roeder platted the first town parallel to the shoreline from present Broadway to Whatcom Creek. Later, as the map clearly shows, the plat extending the town northwestward followed the compass points, making one of Bellingham's numerous confusing street-grid junctions.

1   **Bolster House,** 1891
    James F. Bolster
    2820 Eldridge Street

    The first and for many years the only brick house in town, built by a Whatcom building contractor and brick factory owner to advertise the advantages of brick construction for residential use, a hard campaign to win in this land of big timber.

2   **Schramm House,** 1895
    Bernhard Schramm
    2601 West Street

    The home of another Whatcom carpenter and building contractor, this miniaturized Queene Anne villa in transition to the Colonial Revival Style is remarkably intact.

2 Schramm house

3   **Keyes House,** 1892
    2230 Henry Street

    The original owner/builder, Philip M. Isensee, may have used a pattern book for this elegant house in a transitional style. The design has elements of both the earlier, more formal Italianate Style visible in the polygonal bays, bracketed cornice, and doubled, round-headed gable windows and the Queen Anne Style suggested by the use of shingles and arched gable braces that were considered more rustic.

3 Keyes house

4   **George Bacon House,** 1906
    Henry Bacon
    2001 Eldridge Street

    Improbable as it may seem, the architect of this modest Classical Revival house also designed the monumental Lincoln Memorial in Washington, D.C. Owner and architect were brothers; Henry doubtless sent out the plans, which were then carried out by a local builder. The house is well proportioned and authoritative in its detail.

One is tempted to say that Utter Street is utterly charming, an appropriate comment if a poor joke. The scale of planting

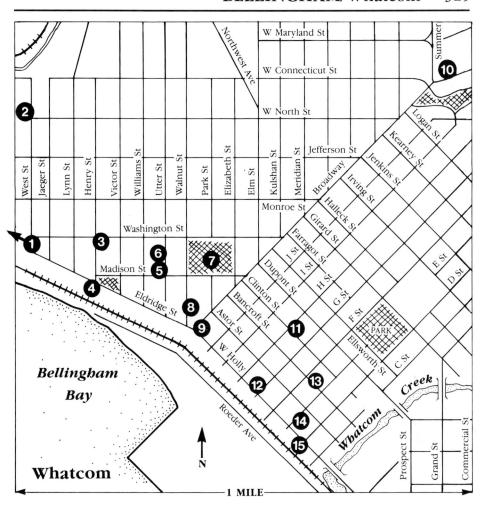

and platting in this and neighboring streets is matched by the scale of the houses. Many are late nineteenth century designs recently rejuvenated. The visitor is urged to walk the blocks in order to discover more treasures like those listed.

5   **Loggie House**, 1885
2203 Utter Street

A rustic villa with Eastlike detail and wrought iron fence.

6   **Robert Shields House**, 1900
2215 Utter Street

Another wealthy lumberman's house showing the endurance of devotion to the Queen Anne Style in its general format and particularly the composition of the left bay, with the ground floor polygonal form set under the rectangular upper floor and the decorative spool work and brackets. The two-story entrance porch embraces what was then the new Colonial Revival Style.

7   **Elizabeth Park** (originally Walnut Street
Park), 1883
Elizabeth and Madison Streets

Henry Roeder gave these two blocks to
Whatcom as a public park. But the land was
not improved until after 1900 when its use as
a baseball diamond was challenged by the
Ladies Cooperative Society, which took in
funds for landscaping and a bandstand.
Roland Gamwell, Bellingham's first park
commissioner, actually completed the improvements in the early twentieth century
and renamed the park for Henry Roeder's
wife. Together with the surrounding buildings this is a small gem of the urban park
movement that produced similar works
for early suburban developments throughout
the country.

8   **St. Paul's Episcopal Church,** 1885
2116 Walnut Street

Used now as a parish hall, old St. Paul's is
largely intact except for the 1913 transept
and a 1920s kitchen on the north side, and a
new bell tower and entrance porch. The design is Gothic Revival by virtue of the steeply
pitched roof decoration. There was no money
for frills; William Todd and Henry Richardson
built the board and batten structure from the
finest lumber with the help of six other men
for $1,300. The scale of the building and its
setting help to preserve the general character
of the edges of the park.

9   **Aftermath Club,** 1904
1412 W Holly Street

A literary and social club, reputedly the first
women's clubhouse in the state, reflecting the
national Women's Club movement of the
time that produced institutional counterparts
throughout the country. The building is
similar in scale and architectural format to
those designed by Julia Morgan about this
time in California. Here the Craftsman idiom
combines with the Mediterranean influence
in the arcaded upper balcony and entrance
porch.

9 Aftermath Club

10   **Victor A. Roeder House,** 1903–8
2600 Sunset Drive

Similar to the Rucker family house in Everett
in siting and use of the Craftsman Style out of
California. The two houses invite comparison. Both the owners were prominent and
successful citizens—Victor, son of founding
father Henry Roeder, managed the family
business and the affairs of the Bellingham
National Bank. It seems logical that they
commissioned prominent architects for their
mansions, but in the absence of evidence that
they did so we may conjecture that their
associations with the lumber industry may
have given them access to plans as well as the
experience to function as their own architect.
Like the Rucker house, the Roeder house was
constructed with the finest and most luxurious materials inside and out. Now owned by
the Whatcom County Park Department, the
house functions as a community cultural center and is open to the public.

10 Victor A. Roeder house. Photo: Michael Sullivan

11 First Congregational Church (now Bellingham Theater Guild), 1902–3
1600 H Street

A good example, more intact than other contemporary local churches, of the small, wooden Gothic Revival mode.

12 Lottie Roth Block, 1890
1100–6 W Holly Street

Built to be a showcase for Chuckanut sandstone by the co-owner of the Bellingham Bay Quarry, also Henry Roeder's son-in-law, the Richardsonian Romanesque Revival Style building was inspired by Elmer Fisher's post-fire work in Seattle using the same material. The eastward-moving business district soon left the building behind; by 1918 it had become the Roth Apartment House with a new floor inserted in the former banking space to maximize apartment rentals.

13 George E. Pickett House, 1856
10 Bancroft Street

The shingled siding and glazed front porch mask the dressed plank exterior of this oldest Bellingham building. Originally the simple, two-story pioneer house, fifteen feet wide and twenty-five feet deep, had a ladder to the second floor. The lean-to was for the kitchen-dining space. Captain George E. Pickett, later a Confederate Civil War hero at

Gettysburg, built the house after putting up a stockade called Fort Bellingham, to protect against Indian raiding parties from British Columbia. Only this house remains from the early settlement on the bluff above Roeder's sawmill.

14 Richards Building, 1858
1308 E Street

Only remnant of the Fraser River gold boom and reputed to be Washington's oldest brick building, this simplified mercantile structure with a brick dentil course and high, pedimented parapet was constructed from Philadelphia-made bricks used as ballast on a ship bringing miners to the gold rush. Its solidity encouraged later use for governmental purposes such as courthouse, county offices, and jail. Abandoned for the new courthouse in 1889, the building has since had a variety of easy-come–easy-go tenants.

15 Great Northern Passenger Depot (now Amtrak Station), 1927
F. Stanley Piper
End of D Street

Bellingham's last depot and the most elaborate of the city's stations. Immediately northwest of the station is the Great Northern, now Burlington Northern, freight depot of 1905.

New Whatcom

Actually the center of New Whatcom, and later the consolidated city of Bellingham, lies in the original town of Sehome. The mines that created the town were entered at the base of the bluff in the present railroad yards near Laurel Street. Curiously, while most of Sehome was platted to the same skewed grid as old Whatcom, the few straight north-south blocks around the New City Hall were part of Whatcom not Sehome.

1 Whatcom Museum of History and Art (formerly New Whatcom City Hall), 1892–93, restored 1965–74
Alfred Lee; George Bartholick
121 Prospect Street

One of the state's finest late nineteenth century institutional structures built in an austere Second Empire Style with overtones of Romanesque Revival. The massive brick structure which builds up from four corner towers to a high central cupola is still the city's major landmark and symbol of authority despite its use since 1940 as the Museum

1 Whatcom Museum of History and Art

of History and Art. When the structure was damaged in a 1962 fire that destroyed the roof and central tower, a masterful campaign by the Whatcom Museum Society raised funds to restore the building and refurbish the interior. Since the existing plan had been well suited to museum use, the original and significant elements were retained; the main gallery spaces were remodeled as simple background spaces; the exterior was faithfully restored. George Bartholick, then practicing in Bellingham and a member of the original preservation group formed in 1939–40, oversaw the five-phase restoration program. Now a major, multipurpose cultural center, the museum has received national recognition for its community-sponsored restoration.

Holly Street forms the axis where the business districts of Whatcom and Sehome meet at Whatcom Creek. After the towns were joined in 1891, the major office and commercial structures were erected here just before the 1893 depression and after the turn of the century. A number of these business blocks remain, usually shorn of their ornate metal and wooden cornices and remod-

eled on the ground floor. Their presence, even with alterations, still makes this historic district legible.

2   **Oakland Block,** 1890
     310–18 W Holly Street

3   **Flatiron Building,** 1907–8
     1311–19 Bay Street

4   **Holly-Bay-Prospect Building,** 1912
     1302–4 Bay Street

5   **Northwest Hardware Company,** 1907
     1220–22 Bay Street

6   **Clover Block,** 1899
     201–7 W Holly Street

7   **Red Front Block,** 1900
     200 W Holly Street

8   **Douglas Block,** 1908–9
     1401–15 Commercial Street

9   **Mount Baker Theater,** c. 1925
     R. C. Reamer
     NW corner Commercial and Champion Streets
     Important downtown landmark.

10   **Bellingham High School,** 1937
     Naramore & Young
     East side Cornwall between Kentucky and Ohio Streets

     A prominent proto-Modern design in poured concrete. Next door is the 1913 Assumption School in a format closely associated with this type of secondary school building of the teens. The two schools make an interesting comparison.

10 Bellingham High School

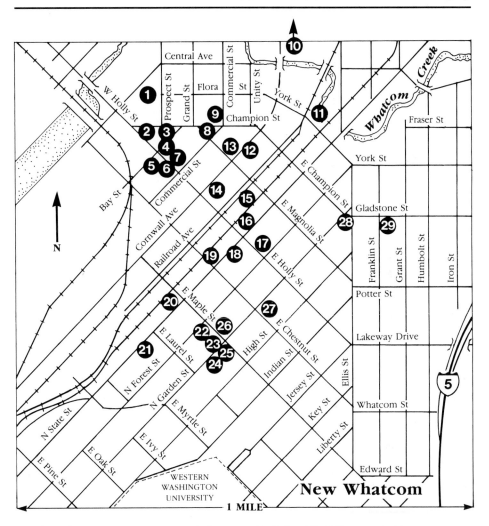

New Whatcom

11 **Three former Whatcom County Railway and Light Power Stations,** 1908–12
201–5 York Street

As architecture these recycled brick structures merit little attention; as urban design they offer an object lesson in the good streetscape manners of much turn-of-the-century industrial building.

12 **Elks Club,** 1912
1412–14 Cornwall Avenue

Another standard component of downtown. Social institutions such as the Elks Club were typically located downtown before the modern trend toward decentralization took hold.

13 **Federal Building,** 1912–13
James Knox Taylor
100–6 W Magnolia Street

The combination Federal Building and Post Office was a typical government institution of the first half of the twentieth century. Frequently the most imposing structure in smaller cities, the eclectic Classic Style of the Beaux Arts was used to create the appropriate monumentality for this important civic structure. Erected under the supervision of Taylor, the design is a handsome variation on the typical theme.

13 Federal Building

14 Bellingham National Bank Building,
1912–13
F. Stanley Piper
101–11 E Holly Street

One of the major buildings of the boom period before World War I, it shows a jump in height from the older structures.

Downtown Bellingham contains many interesting buildings not separately noted here; for instance, in the block to the southeast across Railroad Avenue are the 1902 Spokane Block (**15**) and the 1905 Dahlquist Building (**16**). Visitors interested in pursuing the genealogy of most of these older structures should consult the inventory of historic buildings by Daniel Turbeville cited in the Selected Bibliography.

17 Y. M. C. A. Building, 1905–6
313–15 E Holly Street

18 Hotel Laube, 1900
1226–30 N State

Typical brick and sandstone commercial design of its era.

The Hotel Laube is a remnant, like the 1904 Daylight Block at 1201–13 (**19**), the 1903 Maple Block at 1051–55 (**20**), and the 1891 B. B. Jones Block at 932–36 (**21**).

22 Y. W. C. A. Building, 1915
408 E Maple Street

A substantial building donated by Mrs. Charles X. Larrabee and her daughter. It uses the eclectic Classic vocabulary considered appropriate for such social institutions built at this time up and down the west coast. The design recalls the many Y's from the office of Julia Morgan, the organization's official southwestern regional architect at this time.

23 First Presbyterian Church, 1910–12
1031 N Garden Street

A curious combination of Gothic and Mission Revival styles. Comparison with the 1889 First Presbyterian Church at 519 Maple Street shows a transition from the earlier rustic parish church to a more sophisticated urban format.

24 Robert I. Morse House, 1895–96
Alfred Lee
1014 N Garden Street

Built for the owner of an important hardware company located at 1025–31 North State Street, just down the hill. This most imposing of the area's Queen Anne–Elizabethan Style houses is prominently sited to show off its castle-like quality. The second-story sleeping porch was added in 1914.

25 Montague House, 1902
1030 N Garden Street

26 Axtel House, 1902
413 E Maple Street

Two houses of the same year, probably by the same architect, showing the variations possible within the Colonial Revival–Craftsman mode.

27 Louis White House, 1890
1200 N Garden Street

A prominent banker's Queen Anne villa reminiscent of the work of Longstaff & Black, who designed similar elegant towered houses in Fairhaven.

27 Louis White house

28 **Bellingham Bay Lutheran Church,** 1902
1430 N Garden Street

29 **Bellingham Unitarian Fellowship,** 1910
E. E. Ziegler
1474 Franklin Street

Two wooden Gothic Revival churches that
testify to the important Scandinavian and
German community, employed mainly in the
lumber industry.

Western Washington University

Sehome Hill, like the town below it, was
named for the father of the Bellingham
Bay Coal Company superintendent's Indian mistress. The coal mine that
prompted E. C. Fitzhugh to have
Sehome platted in 1858 closed in
January 1878, bringing depression to
the former boom town. Among the continuing residents with businesses in
Sehome was a druggist from New York
whose wife, Ella Higginson, enthusiastically promoted a teacher training
school near their home high on Sehome
Hill. In 1893, Governor McGraw rewarded her efforts and those of local
politicians by approving the move of the
Northwest Normal School from Lynden
to a ten-acre tract on the hill. From such
an unpretentious beginning has grown
the largest of the three state universities
which started as normal schools (see
Cheney and Ellensburg).

Seattle landscape architect M. J. Car-
keek had suggested the site. The first
building, completed in 1896, was, simply, the Old Main Building. The
number of submissions for its design
testifies to a growing resident population of architects in the state. Skillings &
Corner, a prominent Seattle firm, won
the commission with a restrained design

Old Main Building (courtesy of WWU)

based on the popular Italian Palazzo image and referenced to McKim, Mead & White's much published Boston Public Library. Local architect Alfred Lee helped supervise the construction and himself designed the flanking additions in 1903 and 1907. At the behest of Roland Gamwell a landscape plan was commissioned from S. G. Harris of Tarrytown, New York. The present layout of the walkways and perhaps some of the planting in front of Old Main remains from this plan. Classes did not begin until 1899. The modest growth of the first two decades added a few wooden building plus fourteen acres of level land and twenty of hillside in 1917. The highest enrollment between 1900 and 1930 was reached in 1924–25 with 1,424 students.

The year 1924 initiated the first campus plan by Seattle architects Bebb & Gould. This plan defined and established the old campus space by siting the 1928 Romanesque Revival Library by Bebb & Gould across from Edens Hall, the 1921 women's dormitory by T. F. Doan. This space is essentially undisturbed today. The Bebb & Gould plan was put aside for economic reasons after the 1935 Physical Education Building though the firm continued to design campus buildings.

From 1935 to 1957, eight buildings were added creating a larger, loosely defined campus southwest of the original group. These buildings exhibit a range of Eclectic and Modern styles and a scale compatible with the old campus. In 1937 the Normal School became Western Washington College of Education.

In 1959, the Board of Trustees commissioned a plan for an enrollment of 6,000

from Seattle architect Paul Thiry. This plan, in force until 1963, saw the greatest expansion the college had known with eleven major building projects completed, as many as in the first fifty-seven years. The Thiry plan reinforced and enlarged the north campus residential complex and established the Ridgeway residential area. To serve these areas the Viking Commons and Book Store were built west of High Street. In general, the new buildings reflected current modes of the Modern movement, by now thoroughly assimilated by U.S. architects. Particularly in evidence was a version of the so-called Italian Neo-Liberty Style used by the Seattle firms of Bassetti & Morse and Nelsen, Sabin & Varey to successfully create concrete frame and brick buildings with ground floor arcades, dominant roof forms, and sculptural window hoods and bays. The compatibility of these buildings with the older pre-Modern ones along with intelligent siting continued the campus' generally harmonious character.

At the end of this planning period and overlapping with the next, the 1961–65 Ridgeway Dormitory complex by Bassetti & Morse on the hillside to the

Ridgeway Dormitory Complex (courtesy of WWU)

southwest gave the college, now Western Washington University, one of the most environmentally sensitive living accommodations on any campus in the country. The dormitories were built in three phases. The first group, completed in 1961, were white, concrete frame, three- and four-story structures with brick walls, wooden outside balcony corridors, and broad, overhanging, low-pitched roofs. The buildings were notched and stepped on the steep slope to form an inner court. The more compact Phase II complex (1963) has a similar vocabulary of forms and materials with an irregular L plan. The long side continues the line of the dining commons, also 1963. Phase III (1965) has smaller cube-like units, strung together by covered walks that jog up and down on the slope. Pine trees embower the last group of buildings, which compose and recompose themselves in a well-orchestrated sequence as the observer walks through and around them.

In 1964, architect-planner George Bartholick completed the Central Campus Development Plan. This plan achieved the creation of the Central Campus Quadrangle by squaring off the corner of the old Campus School Building with the new Educational Psychology Building (Miller Hall) and siting the Physics-Math Building (Bond Hall) to close the square. Both buildings are by Nelsen, Sabin & Varey and were completed in 1967–68. The brick-paved square has a fountain and sculpture, *Skyview*, by Isamu Noguchi. The plan also proposed the Arts Addition (1968) by Al Bumgardner & Partners and other additions to older buildings. The Northwest Residence Hall complex with Mathes and Nash halls, built in 1966–67 by Henry Klein, has brick walls rounded to follow the hill. Its design reflects the influence of Alvar Aalto on the project designer, Folke Nyberg.

Mathes Hall (courtesy of WWU)

Central Campus Quadrangle and Bond Hall (courtesy of WWU)

In addition to the judicious filling in of the existing campus with new buildings, perhaps the most praiseworthy element of Bartholick's plan was the subtly worked out circulation system. The pattern of brick walkways flowing in and out of a continuous ground fabric of brick connects up the spaces and contributes enormously to the fine urban village ambiance. Once more urban de-

Miller Hall (courtesy of WWU)

sign proves to be a more powerful tool for creating a meaningful environment than brilliant but isolated architectural form making.

To meet student housing needs on campus, the concept for cluster colleges as modules of future growth was adopted. The first of these was Fairhaven College, designed by Kirk/Wallace/McKinley with landscape plan by Richard Haag Associates, completed in 1970.

In 1968 Bartholick completed the South Campus Academic Area Plan in response to predictions of ever greater enrollments. Lying midway between the North Campus and Fairhaven College the area is a natural corridor for expansion. So far only two of the projected

Fairhaven College (courtesy of WWU)

buildings have been built: the 1972 Environmental Studies Center and the 1974 Social Sciences Building by Ibsen Nelsen & Associates. These two

Social Sciences Building

massive concrete buildings set up contrapuntal structural rhythms. The lecture halls, labs, and other secondary forms grow out of the main building volumes. A galleria between the buildings and those to be built to the west will provide a crystalline enclosure to protect students from the proverbial Northwest drizzle.

The current campus plans drawn by George Bartholick are coordinated by campus planning director H. A. Goltz. The Landscape Master Plan is by Seattle landscape architects Jongejan/Gerrard.

Fairhaven

Of the two southern boom towns, Fairhaven is the most legible as a self-contained nineteenth century community. Ballast bricks accumulated over several decades of quiet service as a miners' lumber port provided a ready resource when the boom finally hit. A furor of optimism caused by the news that the Great Northern might terminate here put the brick pile to use in constructing a business district. The name of the Terminal Building, put up in 1889 at the beginning of the boom, commemorates this promise. The same brand of deflation followed the railroad's choice of Everett as had left the business blocks on Port Townsend's main street unfinished when the Northern Pacific

Nineteenth century business district

chose Tacoma more than a decade earlier. The national depression of 1893 dealt Fairhaven the coup de grace. Preserved by economic stagnation until the early 1970s, Fairhaven's nineteenth century business district was rescued by a far-sighted developer, Ken Imus, who bought up almost all the buildings and rehabilitated them for contemporary uses.

Architecturally, these business blocks recapitulate the Romanesque and Classic stylistic vocabulary ubiquitous in late nineteenth century U.S. cities. Predominantly brick with some Chuckanut sandstone, the group has a strong coherence of style, scale, and use of materials.

1   **Bellingham Bay Hotel,** 1901
    909–11 Harris Avenue

2   **Jenkins-Boys Building,** 1903
    913–15 Harris Avenue

3   **Morgan Block,** 1890
    1000–2 Harris Avenue

4   **Knights of Pythias Building,** 1891
    1208–10 11th Street

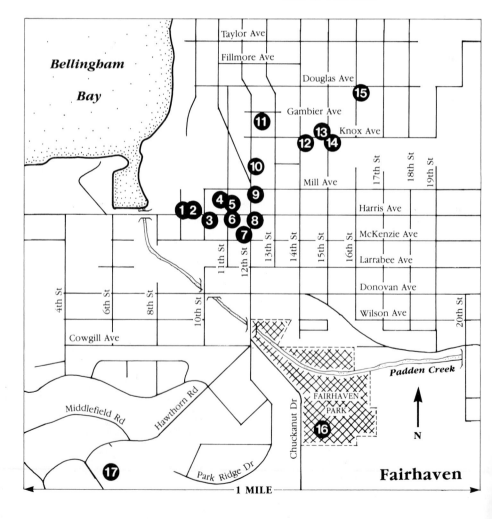

Fairhaven

5 **Terminal Building,** 1889–90
1101–3 Harris Avenue

6 **Nelson Block,** 1900
1100–2 Harris Avenue

7 **Waldron Block,** 1890–91
1308–14 12th Street

8 **Mason Block** (now The Marketplace), 1890,
restored 1973
1200–6 Harris Avenue

9 **Monahan Building,** 1890
1209 12th Street

10 **Fairhaven Public Library,** 1904
Eliot & West
1117 12th Street

A simplified version of the California Mission Revival Style.

11 **House,** 1890
Longstaff & Black
1210 Gambier Avenue

Built for themselves by Bellingham Bay's most prominent nineteenth century architects, this house though altered echoes the eastern architectural fashion called by Vincent Scully, the Shingle Style. Longstaff and Black were from Boston, center of the region where the shingled Queen Anne Style began. They came to Bellingham to build a hotel and stayed to design many important local buildings including Fairhaven's premier house, the Gamwell house (15).

12 **Sacred Heart Roman Catholic Church,**
1912–13
1105 14th Street

Late Gothic Revival showing the persistence of this style for suburban parishes.

13 **Henry Bateman House,** 1891
1034 15th Street

A pleasantly rambling Queen Anne villa embellished with spool work and other wooden filigree.

14 **James F. Wardner House,** 1890
Longstaff & Black
1103 15th Street

15 **Roland G. Gamwell House,** 1890–92
Longstaff & Black
1001 16th Street

Nelson Bennett, the same Fairhaven booster who persuaded James Wardner to come to Fairhaven, also convinced Roland Gamwell to try his fortunes in real estate here. Gamwell, a graduate of M.I.T. and a Bostonian, then was instrumental in having Longstaff and Black hired away from Boston to build the Fairhaven Hotel. Logically, he also hired them to design his house, clearly intended to be the showplace of Bellingham Bay. In contrast to the simpler shingled Queen Anne villas the architects designed for Wardner and themselves, the Gamwell house exhibits all the complication and opulence the style was capable of. With the destruction of most of the mansions of this period in Seattle, the Gamwell house is now the state's best reminder of this extravagant age.

15 Roland G. Gamwell house

The south slope of Sehome Hill fulfills all the requirements of the early affluent suburban development at the edge of downtown but aloof from it. A range of period houses dots the hill including some contemporary designs near the university campus. Mill Street, at the edge of the hillside development, has a cluster of nineteenth century speculative houses at the intersection of 15th Street.

At the south edge of Fairhaven, 12th Street, the main north-south thoroughfare, bends and becomes Chuckanut Drive. Just at this point it passes Fairhaven Park (16), given to the city in 1909 by one of Charles Larrabee's land companies. During the twenties and thirties the park served as a camping ground for automobile tourists. Chuckanut Drive was in those years the local route for the Pacific Highway that ran from the Canadian to the Oregon border, and this park use was but one more precocious bit of the early car-oriented strip development in Washington. Cornwall Park on the northern outskirts of Bellingham had a similar campground equally accessible from Meridan Street which carried the Pacific Highway north toward Canada.

West of Fairhaven Park and Chuckanut Drive, south of Cowgill Avenue, is a modern development identifiable by curving streets covering the former estate of Charles X. Larrabee (17), co-founder with Nelson Bennett of the Fairhaven Land Company in 1888. The family home, Lairmont, at 405 Fieldstone Road, was designed by Seattle's Carl Gould of Bebb & Gould and built in 1914–15; it is comparable to their eclectic residential work in Seattle.

Environs

Chuckanut Drive—formerly U.S. 99, the Pacific Highway, now Route 11—winds south from Bellingham and along the shoreline clinging much of the way precariously to rock cliffs between Bellingham and the Skagit County line. The design, variously attributed to Bellingham engineer J. J. Donovan, first surveyor for a North Cascades highway, and George Cotterill, Seattle mayor and engineer who sluiced down Denny Hill in Seattle and laid out the bike trails that presaged the city's parkways, is one of the state's loveliest motor routes.

The other route south, Interstate 5, also has some scenic delights, particularly Lake Samish Park. To reach this Whatcom County park, take the North Lake Samish exit and then follow Lake Samish Road south to the park. Here George Bartholick designed the park facility in 1968, a nicely scaled building continuing the Northwest timber tradition distilled out of North American, Scandinavian, and Japanese influences. The site plan and landscaping are by Jongejan/Gerrard.

North from Bellingham on Interstate 5 is Ferndale, where in 1903 a retired Swedish architect, Holan Hovander, built his family home and a farm on the Nooksack River. The house is a fine example of a turn-of-the-century, conservative, wood frame structure with a brooding, high-peaked roof of many gables accentuated with white scalloped trim. Now a Whatcom County park, the Hovander homestead is located at 5299 Neilson Road, south of Ferndale off Hovander Road. The Nooksack River valley itself has been the subject of an exhaustive, but imaginative regional planning study by landscape architects Jones & Jones. The possibility that such environmentally sensitive concepts as this may be achieved argues well for the district's future.

Hovander house (courtesy of Whatcom County Parks)

Lake Samish Park facility

San Juan Islands

The San Juan Islands, the peaks of a submerged mountain chain, are clustered in the northern waters of Puget Sound at the southern end of the Strait of Georgia. The U.S.-Canadian boundary line weaves through some 172 islands and hundreds of tide-washed rocks leaving a hundred or so islands to Canada and the rest to the United States. The San Juans' history began early with the international quest for the Northwest Passage to China and the subsequent fur trade established by the Hudson's Bay and other companies. The Spanish and the English, long at odds over the northwest coast, explored and mapped the coastal area. Francisco Eliza charted the islands and named them in 1790 while Captain George Vancouver, working closely with Juan Francisco de la Bodega y Quadra to settle conflicting land claims of the two countries, explored Puget Sound and must have used up his entire address book and the roster of his crew in naming geographic areas and points of interest.

So pastoral and peaceful is the islands' appearance that it is difficult to picture them as the international tinderbox they were in 1859. By this time the Oregon Treaty of 1846 had established the boundary between Canada and the United States at the 49th parallel, but difficulty arose over the interpretation of the channel boundary between Vancouver Island and the mainland. Both countries wanted San Juan Island. The British insisted on Rosario Strait as the boundary; the Americans on Haro Strait. On San Juan Island was the Hudson's Bay Company sheep farm which the Americans considered to belong to them. The British, on the other hand, considered that the twenty-five or so American farmers were squatting on their land. On June 15, an American, Lyman Cutler, shot one of the sheep farm manager's pigs as it rooted up his potato patch. For a few months it appeared likely that the incident would precipitate war. Finally cooler heads prevailed and joint military occupation of the island lasted for the next twelve years with all parties celebrating major holidays together. In 1872, Kaiser Wilhelm I of Germany, to whom the question had been referred for arbitration, awarded the islands to the United States. In later years commercial fishing, shipbuilding, and tourism contributed to the islands' economies in addition to farming and sheep raising. Today the San Juans have mostly resort homes and a tourist economy.

The San Juans are served by the Washington State Ferries. The green and white boats are as integral a part of the scene as the gulls and the low-lying green-backed forms of the islands themselves. From Anacortes the ferry passes across the Rosario Strait between Decatur and Blakely islands to dock first at Lopez and Shaw islands, favored vacation home communities privately owned for the most part and not very receptive to sightseers. From Shaw the boat proceeds to Orcas Island, the largest island and the most topographically interesting. From the dock the principal road, ideal for biking as are most of the island roads, leads around the East Sound to the town with the same name. Here are a few

Ferry and San Juan Islands (courtesy of Washington State Ferries)

frame business buildings, stores and inns, and the W. R. Griffin house, a late nineteenth century frame structure which houses a museum of local artifacts. The East Sound Historical Museum is an assemblage of cabins of original homesteaders moved here from other sites.

Continuing on the main road for a few miles the visitor comes to the turn off for the Rosario Estates Resort, the 1320-acre private estate of Robert Moran, a successful shipbuilder and former mayor of Seattle who came to the island for his health and became its principal benefactor. The large stone house he built for

himself after 1910 is now the heart of a resort that includes other more recent buildings. Of no particular architectural distinction, the house is chiefly interesting for the marine hardware used throughout on windows, doors, cabinets, etc. The main room has a mezzanine with a full pipe organ.

Next on the itinerary is the Moran State Park deeded to the state in 1921. Moran built the arched entranceway and roads through the park, but the park buildings are the products of a Washington State Parks' Civilian Conservation Corps project of 1934 to 1940. The principal architect was Ellsworth Storey, who designed two groups of public buildings and the Mount Constitution Observation Tower, which were built by the Corps workers.

As Storey's work in Seattle makes manifest he had totally mastered the Craftsman Style and developed a sure vocabulary of vernacular carpentry building elements. His Moran Park work exhibits this mastery in a particularly appropriate situation and setting. The lower park buildings, lying to the left and right of the main road near Cascade Lake, consist of an 18′ × 30′ picnic shelter with two nearby facilities for men and women and, on the beach side, two connecting bathhouses near a 20′ × 40′ shelter. These monumentally conceived structures have stone bases and log superstructures with members as large as thirty inches in diameter. Yet they are so perfectly scaled as to provide a sheltered, intimate atmosphere. In common with all the best park architecture, these sensitively sited, utilitarian buildings convey something of the nature of shrines in the wilderness. The Mount Constitution Tower provides, on a clear day, an unforgettable view of the mainland with Mount Baker as the most dramatic landmark. The cyclopean masonry tower has an interior stair leading to an open upper terrace and the top, covered deck. Though reminiscent of medieval stone towers guarding mountain passes, the structure makes no particular reference to style or period. In its economy of means and perfection of scale, the slightly tapering stone form seems to grow out of the heart of the mountain and sum up its spirit. Note the ceilings in the stair tower where the concrete is imprinted with cedar needles and bark which were laid on the forms.

Cascade Lake bathhouses

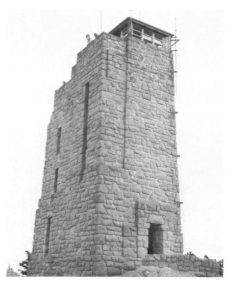

Mount Constitution Tower

Camp Orkila, 1976
TRA
Northwest coast, south of Point Doughty

Camp Orkila began its operation in 1906 as the first organized resident camp of the Seattle Y.M.C.A. A recent master plan developed by the architects and camp planning consultants has resulted in a major modernization of the facilities. These include a new marine trip base, the first winterized housing cluster, called Wally Fisher Lodge, and other remodeled buildings such as that for arts and crafts. The vocabulary of materials and forms fits well with the rustic, woodsy character of the older buildings and the site.

Camp Orkila

After leaving Orcas, the ferry docks at Friday Harbor on San Juan Island. On the north shore of the harbor the University of Washington's Institute of Oceanography is visible from the water. The labs, founded in 1904 by Professors Foster, Kincaid, and Frye for the field study of the marine sciences, were built on 484 acres of a former military preserve now a marine biological preserve. New buildings, designed by Ralph Anderson, were built over the period from 1962 to 1967. They exemplify the architect's characteristic design approach within the Japanese-influenced Northwest wood tradition. The whole installation is well worth a visit.

Institute of Oceanography. Photo: Mary Randlett

From Friday Harbor roads circle the island passing the historic sites of the American and English camps, scenes of the "Pig War." There are no buildings left at American Camp but at English Camp a blockhouse and several other restored wooden buildings evoke the life led here by the English between 1860 and 1872. Both sites have interpretive centers and idyllic settings.

Near English Camp is Roche Harbor, the most picturesque waterside settlement on the northwest coast. The sharply indented harbor is framed by other islands and is usually lively with sailboats. The road passes by the lime pits of the former Roche Harbor Lime Company founded in the 1880s by John S. McMillan. The Hotel de Haro (1886), originally the company hotel, contributes through its verandas and cupola a Victorian spa image on a diminutive scale. The flower garden that sweeps down to the harbor completes the picture postcard effect. A walk through the nearby woods leads to The Mausoleum, a memorial to the McMillan family. The mysterious monument, consisting of a seven-columned, open rotunda, is full of Masonic symbols described in a pamphlet available at the hotel.

Hotel de Haro

Although the future of the Arcadian environment of the San Juan Islands is unpredictable, there is one development that offers hope for its survival. The project, near Friday Harbor, is a cooperatively owned tract called Three Meadows. It includes 210 acres of common land with bird sanctuaries and wildlife preserves, meadows, ponds and pastures, a large cedar-pole barn, and farming equipment; and 150 privately owned, five-acre parcels for each of the thirty families involved. The enlightened logic behind the development is that relatively high density areas like Friday Harbor must be balanced by low density development if the island's water supply is to remain adequate. So far regulations are minimal: no commercial use of private or common land, one building site per owner, and limited cutting of trees. Because the project is still in the early stages of development, the future strains placed, for example, on the common land are hard to foresee, but the present situation is to be praised.

Olympic Peninsula

The thick arm of land that separates Puget Sound from the Pacific contains some of the most spectacular landscape in a state given to awe-inspiring and memorable scenery. From the desolate, driftwood-strewn ocean beaches, up the coastal rivers embowered in remarkable temperate rain forest, to the high alpine world of the Olympic Mountains, nature reigns and humans have providently not interfered too much. A highway rings the base of the central massif and provides access to the scenery. Just east of Port Angeles the National Park Service has a smoothly graded scenic parkway that takes the visitor to the other world above the tree line in the mountains at Hurricane Ridge. Over on the west side a long spur runs up the Hoh River to the interior of the rain forest where a Park Service interpretive center and instructional foot trail try to explain the mysteries of this place.

Two resort lodges nestled on foothill lakes are perhaps the most attractive and scenic of the man-made works on the peninsula. In the drier northern foothills Crescent Lake Lodge, and on the southwest of the mountains, in the heart of the rain forest, Lake Quinault Lodge, hew to the park vernacular tradition of simple timber building. The principal city of the region, Port Angeles, holds little to draw an architectural eye except the Clallam County Courthouse at Fourth and Lincoln streets. In the wet but captivating world of the Olympic Peninsula, nature remains preeminent.

Clallam County Courthouse

Aberdeen and Hoquiam

Originally four miles apart, the lumber towns of Aberdeen and Hoquiam have now grown together. Once they were separated by such dense stands of timber that only a water approach from Grays Harbor, which both face, was possible. Twelve miles west across a broad bay lies the harbor mouth, which admits both lumber ships and the nearly constant drizzle and fog that characterize the region. In 1792 Captain Robert Gray of Rhode Island first visited the harbor which today bears his name, but no settlers came till 1859. Then the James Karr family settled on the banks of one of the rivers flowing into the harbor and named the place Hoquiam, meaning "hungry for wood." Aberdeen was first settled in 1867, and eleven years later a Scot named George R. Hume established a small fish cannery he called the Aberdeen Packing Plant for Aberdeen, Scotland. In the early 1880s George H. Simpson built the first sawmill. Aberdeen was platted in 1884 and Hoquiam in 1885. Over the next decade and a half the two cities matured and developed businesses, schools, newspapers, hotels, and churches. During the early decades of the twentieth century, the Grays Harbor district experienced a growing demand for timber as the lumbering industry shifted from the Midwest to the Northwest. And like Everett, the Grays Harbor district has a long history of labor problems and disputes aggravated by the alternate booms and busts of the timber trade. Yet the wood products industry still reigns, followed distantly by fishing, canning, and seafood production.

Approaching from the south or east, the motorist reaches Aberdeen first. Industry occupies the waterside area; downtown has one moment of architectural interest, the Weir Theater at 204 East Heron Street. But the residential section on the heights to the north has some fine early twentieth century houses in the area from Broadway to North M Street and 8th to 12th Street.

John B. Elston House, 1908
217 N Broadway

Allegedly a copy of the 1903–4 Boke house in Berkeley, California, by Bernard Maybeck. The owner of the Aberdeen house so admired Maybeck's design that he obtained the plans and built one of his own. Though the detailing is not as sophisticated as in the original, the plan and brace-frame cedar construction are quite at home in this heavy timber country.

John B. Elston house

House, c. 1910
1005 N Broadway

House, c. 1910
1119 N Broadway

Two handsome Colonial Revival houses.

House, 1965
Gene Zema
500 W Eighth Street
Contemporary Northwest woodsy design by a Seattle architect who did many similar houses in that city.

500 W Eighth Street

House, c. 1906
807 N M Street
A sweeping veranda and generously scaled detail make an outstanding house somewhere between the Queen Anne and the Colonial Revival styles.

807 N M Street

Hoquiam begins on the other side of Myrtle Street.

Carnegie Library, c. 1910
Cland & Stark
621 K Street
Clearly influenced by Frank Lloyd Wright, this work by a pair of Madison, Wisconsin, architects has distinguished exterior ornament and a warm, wood paneled, many fireplaced interior. A fine monument.

On Hoquiam heights is the older residential area. The main monuments of interest are the two houses of the Lytle brothers, prominent lumbermen, at 509 and 515 Chenault Avenue. Now called Hoquiam's Castle, number 515 is a towered Queen Anne house of 1897 with a stone base, a clapboarded first floor, and upper floors sheathed in clapboard and fish scale shingles.

Hoquiam's Castle (courtesy of State Office of Archaeology and Historic Preservation)

Polson Park and Museum House, 1923
Arthur B. Loveless
1611 Riverside Avenue
The big, shingled, Colonial Revival mansion of Arnold Polson, son of pioneer lumbering capitalist Alex Polson. The grounds, both the level landscaped area east of the house and the hillside above full of rhododendrons and azaleas, remain from Alex's estate, but only the foundation remains of his house.

Montesano

Montesano dates from 1870 when it was established here following an earlier settlement across the Chehalis River known first as Scammon's, later as Wynooche, before receiving the present name meaning "healthy mountain" in Spanish. The location at the head of navigation on the river explains its choice as county seat first of Chehalis, later Grays Harbor County. Montesano prospered during the 1870s and 80s from lumber, agriculture, and after 1889 as terminal for a railroad spur. The town plan is the ordinary grid, but felicitously enlivened by a jog in First Street so that the traveler approaches on axis with the town's chief monument.

Grays Harbor County Courthouse, 1910, expansion 1970
Watson Vernon; Bennett, Johnson, Stevens & Smith
Broadway between Main and First Streets

An appropriately monumental Beaux Arts Roman Revival public building constructed of curious yellowish-greenish-brownish sandstone. A set of fine murals on themes such as power, justice, truth, science, thought, and art along with local historical themes embellishes the period interior. An old jail building remains in a major expansion for new county facilities thoughtfully integrated with the original landmark.

City Hall and Fire Station, 1914
Watson Vernon
104 N Main Street immediately east of Courthouse

A good example of the Mission Revival Style, a dry country image unaccountably popular in wet, gray Washington during the early years of the century. Somewhat altered to accommodate more and larger fire engines, and to fit new square-topped aluminum windows into the former arched openings.

To the west a fine big Craftsman Style wood villa completes this brief essay on architectural tastes of the years that hatched the City Hall and Courthouse.

Grays Harbor County Courthouse

Chehalis and Centralia

According to the Writer's Program guide to Washington (*The New Washington: A Guide to the Evergreen State*), Chehalis began in 1873 as a settlement around a warehouse beside a railroad track, the line built by the Northern Pacific from Kalama to Tacoma. The importance of the railroad's coming was sufficient to move the Lewis County seat here from Claquato in 1874. The town was first named Saundersville after the donation land claimant, S. S. Saunders, but was changed in 1879 to Chehalis. Typically, lumbering provided the economic base for growth along with dairying and farming. Today the town is still prosperous and has a few sights for the tourist interested in architecture and history.

The principal historical monument is the O. B. McFadden house at 1639 Chehalis Avenue, built in 1859 for Judge Obadian McFadden by Shuyler S. Saunders on the southern half of the Saunders donation land claim. McFadden was the first associate justice in the Washington Territory and later chief justice, state legislator, and congressional delegate. Extensively altered, this is, at heart, a log house.

At Division and St. Helens Avenue is the 1884 Episcopal Church of the Epiphany recalling the early churches of New England with an intricate ceiling truss and handmade furniture of local red cedar.

A logical monument to Chehalis' founding is the Northern Pacific Railroad depot.

About three miles east of Chehalis on State Route 6 is the first county seat, Claquato, condemned to oblivion by its location off the course of the Northern Pacific. Preserved here unaltered is the Methodist Church of 1858, one of the state's oldest, with a steeple designed to symbolize Christ's crown of thorns.

Claquato Methodist Church (courtesy of Lewis County Historical Society)

O. B. McFadden house (courtesy of State Office of Archaeology and Historic Preservation)

John R. Jackson's log house (1845) can be found in Marys Corner on the Jackson Highway about three miles east of Interstate 5 at the Marys Corner exit ten miles south of Chehalis. A peeled log cabin, it was the home of pioneer settler John R. Jackson, central figure in the early development of the Washington Territory and representative in the first territorial legislature. In this simple building Jackson entertained mighty military men like Grant, McClellan, and Sheridan. In 1850 the house was converted into the first U.S. district court north of the Columbia River.

Centralia, sister city of Chehalis and four miles to the north, was called the "Hub City" of southwestern Washington by the 1950 edition of the Writers' Program guide because of its strategic position midway between Puget Sound and Portland. The town is most famous for the 1919 Armistice Day riot, often called the Centralia Massacre, which furnished one of the bloodier confrontations between the I.W.W. and anti-radical elements in Washington's troubled labor movement history.

Another monument of hostile times is the 1855 Borst Blockhouse built for defense during the Indian Uprisings and now at peace in an inviting lakeside park ideal for picnicking.

The older residential areas of Centralia have a number of turn-of-the-century houses of simple but engaging appearance set on beautiful, tree-lined streets.

South Bend

Pacific County seat, South Bend has a long history of lumbering and oyster canning. With the arrival of the Northern Pacific Railroad in 1895, these industries accelerated. The town's buildings are picturesquely crowded together on a narrow shelf between the hills and the river; the most dramatic is the County Courthouse (1910–11), a Classic Revival structure set in a landscaped park overlooking the city. It was designed by C. Lewis Wilson. Nearby, E. J. Roberts Park (1977) designed by Talley & Associates exemplifies recent concepts in the landscape architecture of playground parks.

Pacific County Courthouse (courtesy of State Office of Archaeology and Historic Preservation)

Columbia River Forts

Cape Disappointment commands the entrance to the Columbia River from the Pacific. First reserved for military purposes in 1852 this site functioned as a key element in the coast defenses of the Northwest from the Civil War through World War II. In the late nineteenth century, Fort Canby here became a part of an elaborate system of defenses that included Fort Columbia upstream on the Washington side and Fort Stevens in Oregon across the river's mouth on a long sandspit. The considerable remains of the two Washington forts are now State Heritage Park sites. An interpretation center at Fort Columbia explains the system. From the standpoint of military architecture and fortification design these installations parallel those at Forts Worden, Casey, and Flagler that guarded Puget Sound at Port Townsend and on Whidbey and Marrowstone islands. Forts Columbia and Canby may be reached off Route 401 near Ilwaco west of the bridge to Astoria, Oregon.

Oysterville

Oysterville is the northernmost settlement on the Long Beach Peninsula, a finger-like appendage of the mainland lying parallel to it and enclosing Willapa Bay. The tidelands historically provided an ideal breeding ground for shellfish, a situation well known to the Chinook Indians, one of whom guided Robert H. Espy and Isaac A. Clark to the area. Both men filed donation land claims and in 1854 Clark laid out the townsite. From 1855 to 1893 it was the Pacific County seat. Until the transcontinental railroad arrived in the San Francisco Bay area in 1869 and subsequently brought shipments of eastern seed oysters to create a local industry, the bountiful harvest of Willapa Bay had a lucrative market. But competition from California took its toll, and added to this adversity were winter freezes and disease. Though periodically revived in the 1930s and 1940s, commercial operations have largely ceased at this time. The consequences of economic decline were not all bad. Today Oysterville is a Historic District that preserves a remarkable stand of wooden vernacular buildings dating mostly from the 1870s, a period rarely represented architecturally in the state as a whole. Several houses are pattern-book examples of the Gothic Revival Style. The town grid has lost Front Street to the tidewater, but, with the exception of the 1878 Captain Stream house on the west side of Main Street north of Pacific, the primary historic structures line Fourth Street. The 1940 Oyster Cannery at the north end of First Street on the water is certainly one of the town's most picturesque remnants. Along Fourth from Pacific south are the following structures:

D. C. Stoner House, 1905
SE corner Fourth and Pacific Streets

Greenman House with Swan Restaurant, c. 1869
SW corner Fourth and Pacific Streets

Robert H. Espy House, 1871
NE corner Fourth and Division Streets

John Crellin House, c. 1869
NE corner Fourth and Merchant Streets

Oysterville Public School, 1907
School Street

Tom Crellin House, 1869
NE corner Fourth and Clay Streets

Tom Crellin house (courtesy of State Office of Archaeology and Historic Preservation)

Oysterville Baptist Church, 1892
Fourth Street at foot of Clay Street

W. D. Taylor House, c. 1870
West side of Fourth Street, south of Clay Street

Old Pacific County Courthouse, c. 1865
West side of Fourth Street, south of Clay Street

Ned Osborne House, 1873
West side of Fourth Street, second from south end

Charles Nelson House, 1873
South end of Fourth Street, west side

Longview and Kelso

These twin cities at the confluence of the Cowlitz River with the Columbia have sharply contrasting histories and together offer an intriguing case study in environmental design. Longview, the larger and newer of the two, has the practically unique distinction of being a totally planned but privately developed city in the early twentieth century City Beautiful mode. Kelso, older and smaller, has a completely unexceptionable genesis, piecemeal, relatively unplanned, the result of the usual mixture of private speculation, husbandry, and fragmented public initiative. Neither abound in architectural riches, but they are worth experiencing for the environmental gestalt they provide.

Kelso lies immediately adjacent to Interstate 5, mostly on the east of the Cowlitz but with a smaller part originally called Freeport on the west side contiguous to Longview. Peter Crawford, a Scot, first settled here in 1847, platted the townsite in 1884, and named it for his hometown in Scotland. Today Kelso is home to the Cowlitz County government. At 110 Grant Street is the Captain Nat Smith house built about 1885 by a sawmill owner and steamboat captain. Later the house, a conventional design of the time, was owned by Tom P. Fisk, a lawyer who purchased options on the land on the other side of Cowlitz for his client R. A. Long.

Longview memorializes R. A. Long, Kansas City capitalist and board chair of the Long-Bell Company. Steven Dotterer in *Space, Style and Structure* describes the beginning succinctly:

Longview resulted from the Long-Bell Lumber Company's decision to move operations from their depleted lands in the South to the Pacific Northwest. This decision was implemented in 1918 through the purchase of 70,000 acres of timber and several thousand acres for a mill site near the mouth of the Cowlitz River. Originally no town was planned, but the need to provide housing for workers (and hopefully attract a stable non-I. W. W. work force) led to the purchase of more land and the development of a model city. R. A. Long, the head of Long-Bell, asked his Kansas City friend J. C. Nichols to act as developer. Nichols, who developed Kansas City's country club district, refused, but did agree to help get the project going. He selected Hare & Hare, Kansas City (landscape) architect-planners, and George Kessler, the man responsible for Kansas City's parks and boulevards, to design the town. [Vol. 2, p. 463]

Kessler, Hare father and son, and Nichols had a long record of accomplishment in Kansas City, where their work, principally the famous Country Club district, elaborated a picturesque and modest version of City Beautiful movement ideas. These ideas, drawn originally from European royal cities and landscape parks, conceived of cities as designable in one piece like Versailles or the public buildings and boulevards of post-medieval Paris. The Chicago World's Columbia Exhibition in the crash year of 1893 gave Americans their first glimpse of how such cities might look. A few fragments of City Beautiful new towns had been laid out by pioneer city planners such as John Nolan and Charles Robinson, professional contemporaries of the Hares. World War I had given the movement a real boost, and an interesting shift in focus to modest villages rather than civic centers, through the construction of workers' communities mainly at the emergency shipyards. The immediate progenitors of Longview are probably the World War I settlements in Bridgeport, Connecticut, and in Camden, New Jersey.

Entering Longview the most direct way from Kelso via the Route 4–Allen Avenue–Ocean Beach Highway bridge, turn left on Washington Way at the edge of West Kelso. This is one of the major diagonal avenues that slice through Longview's central residential gridiron district to the civic center plaza, R. A. Long Square. Here the idea of the plan visibly unfolds. Due east the original commercial district lines Broadway and terminates at the railroad depot. On the west side of the square the Monticello Hotel (1923) rises, an original brick and terra cotta landmark. At each corner a diagonal boulevard directs traffic to outlying residential areas, Cascade Hills, Sunset, Olympic, and the most modest St. Helens to the southwest. These neighborhoods sit beyond the amenable crescent of Sacajawea Park, formerly a swampy slough now a linear urban park. On the west beyond the neighborhoods, a natural area park, Mount Solo, defines the town.

The generous industrial district, the reason for Longview's existence, lies along the Columbia south of the central residential area. Weyerhaeuser's plant here, the company's largest operation, integrates three sawmills and other units including plywood, pulp, kraft and paperboard, a chemical plant, and a research lab. Other industry abounds, but the characteristic pulp mill perfume permeates the air and never lets the vis-

Monticello Hotel, c. 1928 (courtesy of Photo Collection, UW Library)

itor forget this is wood products country. Plant tours are available.

Longview occupies ground occupied several times before. The Cowlitz River delta was a strategically located, fertile site first chosen by the Hudson's Bay Company in 1846–47 for farming and warehousing. In 1849 settlers came, followed by loggers; they named their settlement Monticello. In 1852, the Monticello Convention met here preliminary to the creation of the Washington Territory and the designation of Monticello as the Cowlitz County seat in 1854. But in 1866–67 a series of floods swept the town away and discouraged rebuilding. The area was abandoned until R. A. Long appeared.

Given that the site was a hazardous flood plain, the first step in building the town was to construct fourteen miles of dikes, designed by Long-Bell engineer Wesley Vandercook and built at an enormous cost. Twenty-five years later in the disastrous floods of 1948 when the whole river plain was inundated including much of the Portland-Vancouver area, and fourteen Columbia Valley residents were drowned, the Longview dikes finally paid for themselves—they held.

Steven Dotterer sums up other aspects of this landmark in town planning:

The planners of Longview declared that their model city would not grow "from the inside out" like the typical American City. By "inside out" growth they meant the process of business and industrial districts expanding outward and destroying residential areas. To avoid this the planners placed each land use in its own nucleus. These nuclei were separated by expansion space and linked by broad boulevards . . . there were separate areas for millworkers, executives, apartment dwellers and home gardners. . . .

Longview represents also an early effort to accommodate the automobile. Bypass roads were provided so that not all traffic had to drive through the center of town. The boulevards and streets were made very wide to accommodate autos, though Nichols said after a 1940s visit that he wished they were wider. No streetcars were used because of the rough surface usually associated with their rails. Instead, a Long-Bell subsidiary provided bus service.

Though planned in 1922 for a 1930 population of 50,000 people, by the 1940s there were only half this number. The Long-Bell construction had been completed by 1927 when Geddes Smith of *The Survey* magazine visited Longview. Smith commented that Longview was the "gaping skeleton of a city" where nothing was next to anything and everyone had to travel over vacant areas to reach work or shopping. Things were too far apart to walk to. He suggested that the old "inside out" way might not be good, but it was "organic" and kept things together. The weakness of the planning at Longview was that the city had to reach its planned size to work properly. As it was, only changing space requirements for each land use filled out the plan. Though the planners of Longview were able to provide the parks, boulevards, and other amenities lacking in the plans of most earlier towns, their lack of control over (or understanding of) social and economic forces kept the city from developing as they proposed. [*Space, Style and Structure*, vol. 2, pp. 464–66]

Vancouver

The original settlement of Vancouver, insignificant in size by today's standards, was known throughout the international commercial world of the nineteenth century. Founded during the winter of 1824–25, the camp functioned as a Hudson's Bay Company fur-trading post and supply depot. Under the direction of Chief Factor John McLoughlin, Fort Vancouver became the headquarters of the company's Columbia Department, a trading empire which embraced the present-day states of Washington, Oregon, and Idaho as well as British Columbia. After the Treaty of 1846 drew the boundary between the United States and Canada at the 49th parallel, the fort's dominion over the area declined. In 1860, Fort Vancouver closed its gates; by 1866 most of the buildings had succumbed to fire and neglect.

One hundred years later, the National Park Service began restoration of the fort's stockade and major buildings. Today, the effort to re-create its 1846 form gives a creditable idea of the fort's physical appearance if not its once intense activity. This activity and the life lived here are recalled in brochures available at the park information center. Visitors during the summer may be lucky enough to get a piece of fresh-baked hardtack from the reconstructed bakery. Once a year the staff harvests wheat from the fort garden and bakes bread, also given out to the visitors.

Within the palisade, the chief factor's house, in Canadian rather than U.S. vernacular, probably designed by McLoughlin himself, is totally restored and well furnished. An unusual and striking wood-frame structure—the

Fort Vancouver with Mt. Hood in background. Photo: Hermine Duthie

only one painted white—the house has a Colonial appeal reinforced by a generous veranda with ceremonial branching stair.

With the American settlement of the Willamette Valley in Oregon, Vancouver lost its position as the region's leading commercial center. Portland quickly rose and by the 1870s Vancouver functioned as its satellite. In 1879 the Northern Pacific tracks were extended to Vancouver from Kalama, the downstream terminal of the Tacoma line, and a car ferry established across the Columbia. A few years later, it was connected along the north shore of the Columbia River to the transcontinental main line near the confluence with the Snake. As a minor transportation hub and as port of entry from Oregon into Washington, Vancouver participated in the good years of the late nineteenth and early twentieth centuries as well as the slow years thereafter.

During World War II a sudden boom hit as the river's tidal flats, the same ones that attracted the fur traders, proved ideal as emergency shipways. In the area east and toward the river from the old Hudson's Bay Company post a great shipyard rose, while on the bluff farther east a temporary new town of war housing appeared almost overnight. It was in this settlement that famed Portland architect Pietro Belluschi built two prototypical, car-oriented shopping centers that received international publicity. They became models to be followed across the country in the postwar suburban building binge. The centers themselves long ago disappeared.

In the last generation Vancouver has become further integrated as a part of the Portland metropolitan economy. Suburban sprawl, a declining central business district, and the other typical environmental issues of the period afflicted it. Now, despite the urban renewal bulldozer and creeping suburban tracts, some environmental treasures remain, and adaptive reuse is under way. On the river bank above the reconstructed Hudson's Bay Company stockade is the first United States Army base in the Northwest, Vancouver Barracks, built as Columbia Barracks in 1848. Originally the base comprised four square miles, but in 1948 it was deactivated and all but one square mile was sold. The remaining part includes the historic area with a number of turn-of-the-century, white-painted, wooden and brick buildings of a substantial and utilitarian character typical of this era of military architecture in the Northwest. (For comparison see Fort Worden, Fort Casey, and Fort Simcoe.)

1   **Officers' Row**
    E Evergreen Boulevard

    Ten houses and eleven duplexes that line the blocks along Evergreen Boulevard facing the old parade ground. The stately trees and careful landscaping were typical of all nineteenth century military bases. Most of the houses date from 1867 to 1906. The earlier log houses, built just after the base was established, no longer stand, except for the Ulysses S. Grant House and Museum. A log building of 1849, the house was sheathed with clapboards and somewhat remodeled about 1885. With its hip roof and double wrap-around veranda, the house recalls southern plantation architecture. Grant was associated with the building when he was quartermaster at the Vancouver Barracks in 1852–53. The appropriately furnished museum is operated by the Vancouver Soroptimist Club and features military memorabilia.

1 Ulysses S. Grant house

At 310 East Evergreen Boulevard is the so-called Marshall house, built in 1886 as the commanding officer's residence at a cost of about $15,000. George C. Marshall, supreme allied commander in World War II, secretary of state and author of the Marshall Plan, lived here from 1936 to 1939. Generous scale and modest ornamentation plus an open polygonal cupola lift the building above its   plainer neighbors.

1 Marshall house

2   U.S. Army Post Hospital (now U.S. Army Reserve School Building), 1903–4
McClelland Road

A large, brick building with screened wooden porches visible from the freeway. A drive or walk around the working part of the military base reveals a number of similar substantial brick buildings apparently flexible enough to still be functional.

3   House of Providence (now Providence Academy), 1873, wing added 1891
Mother Joseph
400 E Evergreen Boulevard

A substantial if somewhat severe academic Georgian Revival building following a format typical of most Northwest institutional architecture of this period. What is untypical about the building is its designer, a Canadian nun of the Sisters of Charity of Providence, whose father was an architect. Vacated some years ago, the academy is now an office, restaurant, and shop complex as a result of a promising two-year rehabilitation program. Very little about it has changed. The second-floor chapel is a quite correct exercise in Gothic Revival design and is well worth restoring.

3 House of Providence

The present-day town of Vancouver, platted in 1850 and incorporated in 1857, lies across the great divide created by the freeway and has Main Street as the thoroughfare of the central business district. At the lower end of Main around Sixth Street is a collection of early twentieth century business blocks which preserve the scale of the older development. At Main and Eighth streets (4) is a bank building of the 1930s essentially Neo-Classic, but overlaid with delicate foliate and patterned geometric ornament. The

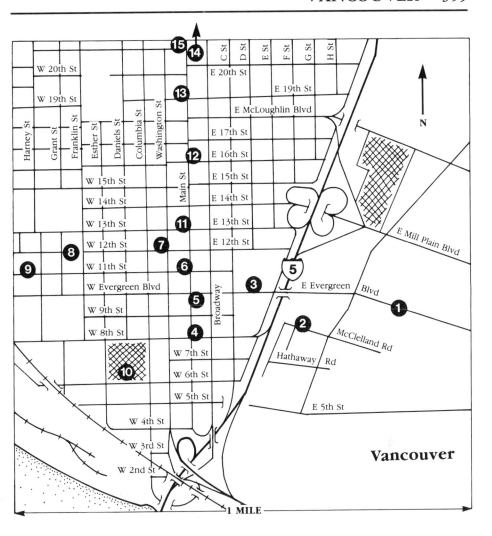

Vancouver

rounded, fluted forms of the main entrance and openings along the Eighth Street facade recall the Classical Revival temples built for banks in earlier decades. Other manifestations of early Modern design can be seen in the vicinity, notably across the street in a much altered department store.

5   **Commercial Building**
Main Street and W Evergreen Boulevard
An Italianate Palazzo complete with brick and tile polychromy and a wood-bracketed, tile roof.

6   Pacific Northwest Bell Telephone Build-
    ing, c. 1925
    112 W 11th Street

A gem of commercial Art Deco designed with
typical cast terra cotta ornament and varieties
of fancy brickwork.

6 Pacific Northwest Bell Telephone Building

7   **St. James Catholic Church,** 1884
    Donald MacKay
    204 W 12th Street

A Neo-Gothic church with an academic correctness that imprinted much of the church
architecture of the West, where it was a
common practice to have the plans sent out
from the East. The commanding site on a
rise, also occupied by the parish house and
garden, is also typical of the authority
churches formerly had in determining the
character of cities and towns. St. James was
the first masonry cathedral in Washington.

8   **Clark County Courthouse,** 1940
    Day W. Hillborn
    1500 Franklin Street

Another institutional building which bears
the fashion stamp of its day, this time early
Modern in concrete which in its symmetry
and massing reveals its stylistic origins in
Beaux Arts Classicism.

9   **Pepsi Bottling Company,** c. 1935
    812 W 11th Street

A nice small-scale example of the Streamline
Moderne favored by pop bottling plants built
in the thirties.

7 St. James Catholic Church

9 Pepsi Bottling Company

10 Slocum House (now the Old Slocum House Theatre Company), 1867
Esther Short Park

A relic of Vancouver's original residential section down by the river. In 1966 this Italianate villa was moved a block from its site in the urban renewal area. Apparently the house was modeled after Charles and Laura Slocum's house in Rhode Island. With a widow's walk, central cupola, elaborate jigsaw work, porch brackets, and a rich interior, the house is judged to have been the city's first elegant mansion. Esther Short Park is named for the wife of Amos Short, who donated this land when he replatted the townsite in 1850.

10 Slocum house

In the blocks north and east of Main are several nineteenth century houses, among them:

11 L. M. Hidden House, 1885
Oliver M. Hidden
13th and Main Streets

The residence of an important family who owned a long-lived brick factory which between the 1870s and recent times produced material for Portland and the lower Columbia as well as most of Vancouver's brick buildings. The house design is in the stylish American Eastlake Style of the 1880s with a good interior and notable fireplaces. The stable still exists, as does a stone and wrought iron fence. Currently a restaurant.

12 Clark County Historical Museum, 1901
Dennis Nicholas and William Kaufman
16th and Main Streets

The former Carnegie Library, now a museum which features a pioneer doctor's drug display, an early printing press, an 1890 country store, and other exhibits. It is operated by the Fort Vancouver Historical Society and the county, and is open Tuesday through Sunday.

13 First Christian Church, 1925
19th and Main Streets

A domed building with a Byzantine flavor sustained by lots of fancy brickwork.

14 Covington House, 1848
Leverich Park

A hewn log cabin moved from its original site five miles northeast of Vancouver. Its owners, the Richard Covington family, came from London to teach the children of the Hudson's Bay Company employees at Fort Vancouver. Moved and restored in 1926 the house now rests in a corner of Leverich Park and is maintained by the Vancouver Women's Club. It is open June through August; check times.

15 First Presbyterian Church, 1956
Steward & Richardson
4300 Main Street

A simple A-frame structure with an elegant wood interior that reveals architect Kenneth Richardson's early association with Pietro Belluschi.

11 L. M. Hidden house

East of Vancouver is Vancouver Lake with a recent park on its shore designed by Robert Perron.

North along Interstate 5, near the banks of the Columbia, is an area of early settlement. At Ridgefield, Judge Columbia Lancaster built his Greek Revival mansion about 1850 on what is now called Lancaster Road. The judge was an important figure in the state's early political history and first delegate to Congress from the Washington Territory.

La Center and Woodland are old and quaint towns worth visiting as is the Cedar Creek Grist Mill, ten miles east of Woodland on County Road 16, built in 1876 by the George W. Woodland family. One of the few braced frame structures left in the state, it was important to early local agricultural history.

Lancaster house (courtesy of State Office of Archaeology and Historic Preservation)

Columbia Gorge/Maryhill

Between Vancouver and Maryhill on the dry eastern slopes of the Cascades lies one of the most poetic passages in Northwest scenery, the great Columbia Gorge. Rich historic associations are deposited on this enormous notch through the mountains below Mount Hood's snow capped form. Native Americans clustered here, drawn by the enormous salmon runs on the river. Their myths and legends invest nearly every natural feature with meaning. Yet today few signs of their presence remain save for petroglyphs such as those at Horsethief Lake State Park about twelve miles west of Maryhill.

From the time of Lewis and Clark to the present, the gorge has served as the main transportation link across the Cascades. However, just as today Interstate 80N with all of its associated development follows the Oregon side, throughout the period covered in this guide, settlement and environmental design work have concentrated on the south bank of the Columbia. For the scenery-loving traveler in Washington this is all to the good. Little two-lane State Route 14 on the Washington shore offers a splendid alternative to the bulldozed speedway of Interstate 80N. Route 14 passes through only a few small towns including tiny Stevenson, principal town and county seat of mountainous Skamania County, and North Bonneville, a recent

New Town planned by Royston, Hanamoto, Beck & Abey, San Francisco landscape architects. The fact that North Bonneville exists at all is a testament to 1970s small-town citizen activism, in this case triggered by U.S. Army Corps of Engineers expansion plans for Bonneville Dam hydro power which promised to flood out the old town site.

At the eastern end of the gorge, well out into the barren, wind and sun swept hillscape of the interior, lies a genuine architectural curiosity, Maryhill (1914–26). This small European palace stands high above the river like a Rhinecastle in the wilderness, an effect that necessarily is mysterious and romantic. It exists because of Sam Hill, railroad planner, son-in-law of Jim Hill, and public-spirited promoter of the Good Roads movement. He commissioned the design from the noted Washington, D.C., Beaux Arts firm Hornblower & Marshall, which also designed Hill's townhouse in Seattle (Capitol Hill, 17). Both houses use the same stylistic vocabulary drawn straight from the eighteenth century English Renaissance Palladian mode associated with Inigo Jones, and use the same materials and detailing, primarily poured concrete. Maryhill, however, given its improbable setting, intensified by the lush green ring of formal gardens that surrounds it, is much the more memorable of the two.

Maryhill is named for Hill's wife. It was intended as a dramatic, remote coun-

Maryhill (courtesy of State Office of Archaeology and Historic Preservation)

try residence for entertaining friends among the cosmopolitan elite of Europe and America. Hill never occupied it, dedicating it instead to the public as a museum. Nearby, on the east side of the intersection with Route 97 before it crosses the bridge into Oregon, Hill built an even more curious monument, a crude plaster replica of Stonehenge intended to memorialize Klickitat County's fallen in World War I. Some enthusiasts for pop eccentricities find this a particular high point of design in Washington. To do so takes concentration, however. Columbia River landscape is so powerfully affecting that most of man's works look either ridiculous or destructive.

Trans-Cascade Routes and Landmarks

Five highways and three railroads cross the Cascades between the Columbia River Gorge and the Canadian boundary. Nature not man dominates the mountain environment except where clear-cutting has stripped the once dense blanket of timber from the western slopes. One rail route, the original Northern Pacific line through Stampede Pass used today by Amtrak passenger trains, travels a relatively untouched course without highways. Two automobile routes, the Mt. Rainier–White Pass road, and the newest and northernmost, the North Cascades Highway, are sufficiently carefully laid out that they rank as works of environmental design. The others tend toward dull strip development.

The Mt. Rainier route, designated U.S. 12 where it crosses the divide, connects with State Route 706 on the west slope through the National Park. Interesting, early efforts to exploit the region's recreational potential include Mineral Lake

Mineral Lake Lodge (courtesy of State Office of Archaeology and Historic Preservation)

Lodge fifteen miles southeast of Mt. Rainier on Mineral Lake. Built by Scandinavians in 1906 for the Tacoma vacation trade, it is perhaps the first such resort in the area.

At Paradise Valley high on Mt. Rainier within the National Park, the Paradise Inn (1917, additions 1922 and 1926) offers a compelling example of the National Park style. Architects Heath & Gove of Tacoma designed it. Several rows of dormers against the steep gables dominate the exterior of the inn's multiple intersecting wings. The interior reveals a cathedral-like lobby and dining hall of unsawn log framing and trusswork. This structure ranks with the later Timberline Lodge in Oregon as one of the two major works in this mode in the Northwest. Below, nearer the Nisqually entrance at the Longmire Park Headquarters, an earlier, similar lodge burned in 1926. Also at Paradise is the new Visitors Center (1965), a contemporary expression in mountain-like form by Wimberly, Whisenand, Allison & Tong with McGuire and Muri. On the north slope at Sunrise the complex of log structures, lodge, blockhouses, and visitor center dates from 1930–32 and 1943. Park engineer for many of the scenic roads was Eugene Ricksecker.

The other worthy environmental design passage in the Cascades occurs along State Route 20, the northernmost crossing. It is the composite result of Seattle City Light power resource development in the Skagit River Valley, and the North Cascades Highway across the crest and down the east slope completed in 1968 by the U.S. Park Service and

Forest Service. Approaching from the west on State Route 20, Newhalem comes first. Here where for so long the road ended, City Light built its outpost village and base camp. The reason for this was twofold: difficult access that included being totally cut off in winter, and the technological need to keep a substantial operating force on site. From Newhalem and the first major power-house, development expanded upstream to include Diablo Dam (1927–30) with its own support village, and Ross Dam (1950). Rather sadly the snowplow, the four-wheel-drive vehicle, and automated power generation technology have radically eliminated the need for a live-in work force. Diablo Village, the most perfect of the settlement designs, has probably vanished or is about to at this writing.

The whole installation is well set up for visitors. It exudes serious environmental concern. The architecture of villages and power installations measures up to the brightest standards of New Deal social design. City Light engineer J. D. Ross conceived of and directed the development from 1911 to 1939. He is buried at Newhalem beneath a stone on which appears an obituary written by President Franklin D. Roosevelt:

J. D. Ross one of the great Americans of our generation was an outstanding mathematician and an equally great engineer. He had also the practical ability to make things work in the sphere of public opinion and successful business. More than that he was a philosopher and a lover of trees and flowers. His successful career and especially long service in behalf of the public interest are worthy of study by every American boy.

What a period piece those words seem in our present world of shrinking environmental expectations.

Ross Dam and Powerhouse (courtesy of Seattle City Light)

Above Newhalem the spectacular North Cascades Highway provides the most scenic automobile crossing of the range. Especially fine is the view going up the east slope below Liberty Bell Peak. Here the Cascades are the most mountainous-looking mountains west of the Tetons. The highway design is especially felicitous, a rare example of sensitive landscape architecture triumphing over brute engineering. Winthrop, a rather silly commercial stage-set western town, lies at the bottom of the grade.

The little town of Chelan at the foot of fiord-like, glacier-fed Lake Chelan has but its location to cause its inclusion here. An engaging, rustic Episcopal church would not otherwise merit notice. The day-long boat ride up Lake Chelan to Stehekin—the only other access is by seaplane—takes one back to a remote and pioneer settlement of log cabins, with a one-room school and a general store. Perhaps the most eye-catching design around appears in the two passenger ferries, the work of the crew during off-season when, welding torches in hand, they whip up these angular essays in naval architecture from raw steel plate.

Route 2 which crosses the Cascades between Everett and Wenatchee goes through Leavenworth. Platted in 1892 and made a railroad division point in 1898, the city of Leavenworth fell to worrying about its image in the 1960s. Rejecting western American models, those in charge of such things were totally captivated by Solvang, a Danish community in Southern California. The result is that today, with still another shift in geographic reference, the town has all but recycled itself into an alpine village, or at least a movie set version of one.

Four miles north of Wenatchee is the Rock Island Railroad Bridge where the Great Northern spanned the Columbia in 1893. Forged 3,000 miles away in the Edge Moore Bridge Works of Wilmington, Delaware, it is still standing safely today.

St. Andrews Episcopal Church (courtesy of State Office of Archaeology and Historic Preservation)

Wenatchee

Seat of Chelan County and apple capital of the world, Wenatchee owes its prosperity to the success of irrigated orchard lands. Although fur traders visited here as early as 1811, and missionaries set up shop in the 1860s, real settlement awaited the railroad boom marked by the arrival of Jim Hill's Great Northern in 1892. Early small-scale irrigation proved the fertility of the valley's volcanic soil and the suitability of the climate, in the process preparing the ground for the major engineering work, the Highline Canal, that would transform the valley after 1903. Engineer W. Chase, who had developed major canals in the Yakima Valley, helped local rancher William T. Clark build the system. Part of the complicated inverted syphon that transports water across the valley is visible just west of the Wenatchee Avenue bridge. This major ditch and other later ones have helped to create the present Wenatchee landscape of orchard-carpeted river terraces, alternatively pink, green, and bare with the seasons, spread out below the surrounding high, treeless, yellow-brown hills. With the forested, snowcapped Cascades still farther in the distance the ensemble is a memorable one and almost overshadows the commercial sprawl that is common in modern Wenatchee.

The city holds little to draw the architectural observer. For those who stray off the main drag far enough, there is at the intersection of Miller and Millerdale-Russell streets a pair of modern school campuses that would be notable anywhere in the Northwest. The earlier of the two, Pioneer Junior High (c. 1955)

by Naramore, Bain, Brady & Johanson of Seattle, occupies the northeast quadrant of the intersection of Miller and Russell. It sports a concrete-shell roof structure that follows a sinesoidal curve. Diagonally across the intersection rises the formidable, abstractly cubistic, brown brick bulk of the Wenatchee Senior High School (1970). Done by local architects Fraley, Layton & Associates, it testifies to design's coming of age in Washington's smaller urban centers.

The pre-1950 city of Wenatchee lies inscribed within the right triangle outlined by Wenatchee Avenue at the riverside hypotenuse and the right angle intersection where the schools are located. Newer houses and roadside development sprawl beyond these limits and have begun to chew at the base of the hills. In town some of the older blocks near the center have an attractive look created by embowered bungalows interspersed with some triangular park blocks. Downtown many buildings remain from the two decades after the disastrous fire of 1909. Several are interesting, including the high-rise Cascadian Hotel, now apartments, with decent circa 1930 modern ornamentation, and a much earlier, stone, trackside warehouse on Columbia Street at the foot of First Street. The civic center a couple of blocks above downtown has two ambitious monuments: a 1924 Georgianesque County Courthouse by Morrison, Stimson & Solker, and an assertively tasteless new white marble Post Office and Federal Building. Perhaps the town's one most interesting historic structure is the turn-of-the-century, multistory brick millhouse that together with adjoining wooden and concrete elevator silos forms the Centennial Flouring Mill complex. Especially notable is the fact that as of this writing the period milling machinery inside is still complete. With luck the preservation movement may reach Wenatchee in time to save this industrial relic.

Out on the northeast outskirts of town at the 1300 block of Fifth Avenue, Wenatchee Valley College preserves an idiosyncratic, Craftsman Style dwelling. Originally the William T. Clark house, though called Wells house for its donor and long-time occupant, it is embellished with fine pyramidal river-boulder porch supports and an improbable castellated round corner tower of the same material.

In the same direction but miles upstream on the eastern outskirts of Cashmere, a satellite apple town, a *volksmuseum* called Pioneer Village preserves a number of mid nineteenth century log cabins moved here from various parts of Chelan County. Most of them have a

Wells house

highly restored look though one, dated 1872 and a part of the Miller trading post, seems totally authentic. The collection along with an early irrigation waterwheel lies in the backyard of the Willis Carey Museum on East Cottage Avenue, a half block from the intersection with Route 12/97.

In or near Wenatchee three Columbia River crossings merit historical note. The 1908 bridge in town now recycled to carry water and gas pipe across the river has a characteristic spidery look to its trussed cantilever span. Downstream four miles is the Great Northern's Rock Island Bridge fabricated in Wilmington, Delaware, and erected in 1893 as the last physical link in that transcontinental rail system. Still another four miles downstream is the Rock Island dam, a late 1920s private utility effort, now swallowed by the public power system, but notable as the first of the main stem Columbia hydro projects.

Chelan County Courthouse (courtesy of State Office of Archaeology and Historic Preservation)

Cle Elum, Roslyn, and Vicinity

For ten miles along the north side of the Cle Elum River and the Yakima after their confluence, an important coal-mining district flourished off and on from the early railroad days up to World War II. The major mining towns Ronald and Roslyn lie just north of modern Interstate 90, just west of the railroad division point at Cle Elum, and about twenty-five miles northwest of Ellensburg. Roslyn, the larger of the two Northern Pacific company towns, was platted in 1886 by the Northern Pacific Coal Company; it flourished from about 1880 to the turn of the century, and again during World War I. Certainly no ghost town, Roslyn is nonetheless much quieter than it used to be, its picturesque setting much cleaner. The hills around downtown are studded with a variety of unpainted wood houses and shanties. However, the real estate boom has hit and a modest gentrification is under way. Most of the town is still roofed with corrugated metal and one hopes some shanty vestiges will remain. The important monument is the Northwestern Improvement Company Store, constructed with local brick in 1889 by the Northern Pacific Railroad

Northwestern Improvement Company

and remodeled in 1916. Once this store provisioned everyone in the area; today it is largely a museum. The mixed population of the miners is evident in the number of churches, among which the Roman Catholic Church of Immaculate Conception and the Presbyterian Church are notable.

Upstream of Roslyn the hamlet of Ronald provides more of the same as well as bigger piles of mine tailings and a still working lumber mill.

Nearby Cle Elum, four blocks wide and one mile long, parallels the Northern Pacific tracks. First Street, an enormously wide main drag, and Front Street, facing the tracks, sport a few simple, little, two-story brick business buildings of 1900 to 1920. One of these houses the Cle Elum State Bank (1906). Two stories high, 25 feet wide by 80 deep, this brick box has been cleaned up on the outside and sports a shiny night deposit apparatus, an inauthentic-looking hanging sign, and trim painted an improbable black. Inside, the antique oak counterwork complete with pink marble deal plates and bronze wire grilles joins a couple of original-looking ceiling lamps and the vault door to give a period flavor to an otherwise plastic interior.

Twelve or fifteen miles north just off Route 97 lies the silver and lead mining town called Liberty, now almost a ghost town. The collection of minimal cabins and shacks here, mostly still lived in and remarkably neat, forms a historic district which shanty buffs will find delightful looking.

Ellensburg

The seat of Kittitas County, Ellensburg was first called Robber's Roost after the name of a trading post established by Jack Splawn and Ben Burch near the confluence of Wilson Creek and the Yakima River. Wilson Creek took its name from Wilson the Renegade, a horse thief who had a cabin nearby. The trading post itself was a 14×18 foot hewn log structure located near what is now the corner of Third and Main streets. In 1871 John Shoudy and William Dennis bought the trading post along with 160 acres; in 1873 Shoudy commissioned a civil engineer to survey 80 acres for a townsite named Ellensburgh for Mrs. Shoudy. The post office found the "h" superfluous and it was deleted in 1894. By 1880 the town had hotels, saloons, blacksmiths, a washhouse, wheelwrights, carpenters, a barber, and a nursery. Outside town were four sawmills, a brickyard, and a brewery. Civilization had come.

After the Northern Pacific chose Ellensburg as a terminal and distribution center for the Kittitas Valley in 1884, the boom was on. In 1886 the railroad reached Ellensburg; the following year it reached Puget Sound putting the town on the transcontinental route. The boom accelerated. A lot of Ellensburg burned up in 1889, the year of several such fires in Washington. However, redevelopment was swift, producing an impressive stand of fireproof brick structures by the following year. Another significant development of 1890 was the establishment of the Washington State Normal School, successfully upgraded over the years until in 1977 it became Central Washington University. The depression of the mid-1890s was succeeded by another boom period that coincided with the arrival of the Chicago, Milwaukee and St. Paul Railroad in 1907. In the long period between then and now, Ellensburg has grown moderately with farming, dairying, and education the main industries.

In a pattern recognizable throughout the country, the campus of the normal school evolved as a major regional architectural site. Here is located the most ambitious collection of serious building design on the east slope of the Cascades, a testament to both administration and their architects. The current campus development plan was drawn up by Bassetti & Morse and landscape architect Richard Haag. A campus map, available at the information center near D and Eighth streets, will facilitate seeing the following selection of the more interesting structures. The numbers are keyed to the 1977 edition of this campus map.

1   **Barge Hall,** 1894
    E. C. Price
    A high Victorian design drawing on medieval architecture and recalling many Old Mains across the country.

2   **Smyser Hall,** 1925
    John W. Maloney

3   **McConnell Auditorium,** 1935
    John W. Maloney
    Flanking Barge Hall, these two well-scaled Classical Revival buildings complete the old nucleus of the campus.

1 Barge Hall

3 McConnell Auditorium. Photo: Corrine Loomis (courtesy of CWU)

2 Smyser Hall. Photo: Corrine Loomis (courtesy of CWU)

30 Lind Hall. Photo: Corrine Loomis (courtesy of CWU)

The rest of the buildings continue to reflect the architectural styles in good currency when they were built. Some date from the late 1920s and 1930s, others range from 1950 to the 1970s. Among the more interesting are:

5 **Bouillon Building,** 1961
Bassetti & Morse

30 **Lind Hall,** 1947
John W. Maloney

34 **Randall Hall,** 1969
Kirk/Wallace/McKinley; Richard Haag Associates, landscape architects

39 **Library,** 1960–61
Bassetti & Morse; Richard Haag Associates, landscape architects

40 Nicholson Pavilion. Photo: Corrine Loomis (courtesy of CWU)

40 **Nicholson Pavilion,** 1959
Ralph H. Burkhard

47 **Psychology Building,** 1972
Grant, Copeland, Chervenak

49 **Michaelson Hall,** 1969
Kirk/Wallace/McKinley; Richard Haag
Associates, landscape architects

This building together with (34) comprises
the fine and applied arts complex.

**Meisner, Sparks, Hitchcock, Quigley,
and Beck Halls,** 1965–66
Fred Bassetti & Company; Richard Haag
Associates, landscape architects

Listed as numbers 3, 23, 33, 48, and 54 on
campus map.

The first of two dormitory groups by this
Seattle architect; the second is the Student
Village off Adler Street, a winning, wood-
shingled, gabled and shed-roofed complex
built in 1968–70.

47 Psychology Building

Like the campus, downtown Ellensburg
packs a good number of architectural
styles into a compact area of the central
business district. Most buildings are
post-1889, when a disastrous fire consumed downtown.

Land Title Building (originally National Bank
of Commerce), 1910
F. R. Spangler
Pearl Street and Fifth Avenue

A fine example of the Beaux Arts Classicism.

Student Village. Photo: Corrine Loomis (courtesy of CWU)

Land Title Building

City Hall (originally National Bank of Ellensburg), 1930
F. R. Spangler
Pearl Street and Fifth Avenue
Diagonally opposite the Land Title Building, recycled from the former bank into an elegant Moderne city hall. Directly across the street is a good nineteenth century brick commercial block completing this impressive intersection which is necked to assist pedestrian use.

County Courthouse, 1955
John W. Maloney and John H. Whitney
Fifth and Main Streets

Davidson Block, 1889
Pearl and Fourth Streets
Another fine nineteenth century commercial relic of which Pearl Street has a generous share.

Kittitas County Museum (formerly Cadwell Building), 1889
Attributed to Cadwell
114 E Third Avenue

At 107 and 114 East, and 109 West, Third are the Kreidel, the Cadwell, and the S. R. Geddis blocks, three fine 1889 structures. More vintage buildings from 1889 occupy the block of Main Street between Third and Fourth avenues. The 1923 Elks Lodge occupies the northwest corner of Main Street and Fifth Avenue, while on the outer edge of the historic district at 111 West Sixth Avenue is the 1890 Masonic Temple. Altogether this stand of turn-of-the-century commercial buildings is one of the finest in the state.

Davidson Block

Four miles east of Ellensburg is the Olmstead Place State Park, homesteaded in 1875 by Samuel Olmstead as a beef and dairy ranch. The original cottonwood log cabin with many family furnishings and memorabilia is open to the public. The family house and some outbuildings, including a handsome gambrel-roofed barn, are nearby.

Olmstead Place

Yakima

Cattlemen drove their herds into the Yakima Valley in 1858 on the heels of the Yakima Indians, whom the U.S. Army had forcibly relocated on reservation lands. Though beef production for the goldfields prospered through the 1860s, population growth was slow indeed until irrigation demonstrated the great productiveness of the volcanic soil. Early in the 1850s, Roman Catholic priests at St. Joseph's Mission near the present city had worked with Kamiakin, a chief of the Yakimas, to irrigate a small area of the desert, but the first significant irrigation system came only in 1872 with the construction of a canal from the river to the town. From then on, expanding waterworks gradually ended cattle ranching and brought diversified farming and fruit growing to the valley.

The city lies at the eastern end of what was once the most used trans-Cascade route. Originally an Indian trail, in 1852 the military road from Fort Steilacoom to Fort Simcoe crossed over the Naches Pass and the Yakima Valley. Governor Stevens selected it as the preferred railroad route across the mountains. Because of this, the enormous Northern Pacific land grant included much of the valley. To dispose of this wealth in real estate the firm established a Yakima land office in 1880 though the tracks only reached Union Gap and Yakima four years later.

In 1883, anticipating the imminent arrival of the railroad, a town of four hundred souls was incorporated as Yakima City. A year later, much to the consternation of the citizens, the Northern Pacific in a typical grab for land value profits sited its station four miles to the northwest, calling it North Yakima. After some controversy Yakima City

Yakima Valley, 1930s. Photo: A. Curtis (courtesy of Photo Collection, UW Library)

gave in, put its nearly one hundred buildings on rollers and skids and moved north to the new location. In 1886 the new city was chartered and made the county seat. Over the next couple of decades both the Chicago, Milwaukee and St. Paul and the Union Pacific added lines that reached the valley, although the former entered farther north at Ellensburg.

Around the century's turning the federal government became seriously interested in irrigation. With the beginning of the Sunnyside Project in 1905, the whole valley was affected. Since then, big public investments in a series of canals and reservoirs have transformed the valley and in turn have brought new settlers, more orchards, and cultivated fields somewhat like a miniature of California's Central Valley. Before Grand Coulee's completion the Yakima Valley irrigation district was the largest and most prosperous in the state. Its success laced the valley with a dense infrastructure of railroads, roads, and lesser towns from Selah to Union Gap (old Yakima), Moxee City, Zillah, Granger, Sunnyside, Toppenish, and Prosser. All are accessible and most are visible along Interstate 82, or will be if this apparently never-to-be-completed freeway finally reaches the Columbia.

Yakima City, or since 1918 simply Yakima, grew with valley agriculture into a proper regional capital. Originally laid out in classic railroad town style, it occupied a plot of small square blocks put down by the Northern Pacific surveyors to square with the tracks, though skewed to the compass points. These blocks occupied a terrace between the right-of-way and the river. Early on, development leaped the tracks, bypassed the industry and warehouses stretched along them, and moved west. Eventually the street orientation was squared with the compass, creating that crank in alignment so characteristic of railroad towns from Ohio and Indiana all the way out here. After the Second World War a newer pattern took over as the city sprawled endlessly westward toward the mountains. This design, with its spaghetti-like appearance on a street map, features curvilinear streets and culs-de-sac and is widely attributed to Federal Housing Administration influence.

In May 1980, Yakima had the unenviable distinction of being one of the cities hardest hit by ashfall from the May 18 eruption of Mount St. Helens. A total of 600,000 tons of volcanic material was estimated to have fallen on the city. Although clean-up efforts soon disposed of most of the ash, Yakima residents continue to cast a wary eye to the west, in the direction of the volcano.

Downtown

Over the first half of the twentieth century a respectable set of buildings grew up to embellish downtown and give it a distinct image. Among them Maloney's Larson Building serves as the exemplary regional counterpart of Albertson's magnificent Seattle Tower, the masterpiece of Moderne architecture in the state. The main buildings are laid out along the spine formed by East Yakima Avenue. In a fortunate reversal of what has happened in all too many small American cities, the inevitable 1960s urban renewal project did not bulldoze out all the landmarks, but instead actually helped save a number of them while at the same time strengthening the commercial life of the city center. Yakima deserves applause for this enlightened civic consciousness. Perhaps

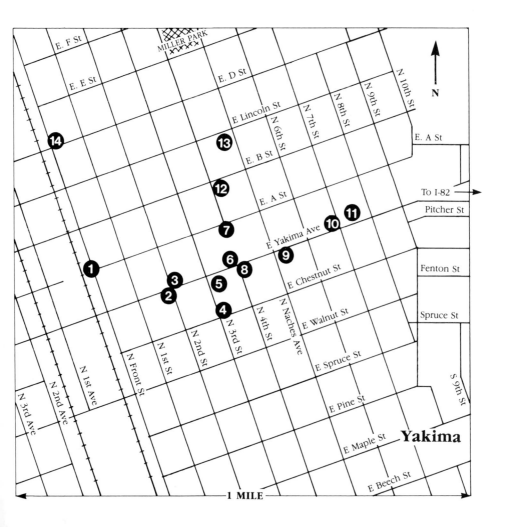

the only sour note in this is the paucity of contemporary design on a par with the several distinguished earlier works.

1   **Northern Pacific Depot** (now Amtrak/ Burlington Northern Station), c. 1910
    N Front and A Streets
    California Mission Revival Style in buff brick with Classical overtones.

1 Northern Pacific Depot

2   **A. E. Larson Building,** 1931
    John W. Maloney
    6 S Second Street
    An eleven-story mini-skyscraper in a remarkably pure Zigzag Moderne Style. It is both Yakima's principal landmark and its most interesting architectural jewel. On the exterior, setbacks in the then most fashionable mode give it a characteristic profile; and a rich materials palette of salmon-colored brick, black granite, travertine, bronze, terra cotta, and copper enlivens the surfaces. The crowning moment of the design, however, occurs in the entrance vestibule and elevator lobby. Patterned terrazzo floors, marble walls, polychromed and sculpted plaster ceilings, and exuberant Zigzag ornamental metalwork create an extraordinary totality focused on the intricate cast bronze elevator doors. One of the original elevator cabs remains with its flashy chrome and enamel interior. Overall the building is intact save only the corner storefronts that were butchered in a mindless bank remodeling job.

3   **Miller Building,** c. 1915
    E Yakima Avenue and N Second Street
    This substantial business block diagonally across from the Larson Building helps demarcate the principal downtown corner, which has been further dressed up by half-block-long park-like extensions of the sidewalks called "semi-malls" in the technical jargon of city planners.

4   **Post Office,** 1911
    James Taylor, supervising architect
    S Third Street and E Chestnut Street
    A fine Beaux Arts Style palace facade in limestone, organized around an engaged Ionic colossal order.

5   **Capitol Theater,** 1920, restored 1978
    Frederick Mercy, Sr.; William Paddock, restoration
    19 S Third Street
    A restored Renaissance Revival palazzo movie theater, now a public performing arts center. Outside, the new marquee and entrance treatment do not quite fit; but inside, A. H.

2 A. E. Larson Building (courtesy of State Office of Archaeology and Historic Preservation)

5 Capitol Theater (courtesy of State Office of Archaeology and Historic Preservation)

Heinsbergen, eighty-three-year-old theater interior designer and executor of the original murals and ceiling paintings, consulted on the admirable restoration.

6 **Masonic Temple** (now Great Western Federal Savings and Loan Building), c. 1915
321 E Yakima Avenue

Mansard-roofed, small high-rise in a style favored for this purpose; for example, Salem, Oregon, boasts a near twin presumably done by the same architect.

7 **Yakima Mall**, c. 1970
N Third Street to Naches Avenue, between E Yakima Avenue and A Street

An enclosed mall megastructure that ties a new parking deck and shopping center into an existing Bon Marche department store and thereby creates a modern retail center downtown. Not interesting aesthetically as architecture, but sound planning well fitted into the urban fabric and decently embellished with a little decorative plaza on the axis of Fourth Street.

8 **Chinook Hotel**, 1950
E Yakima Avenue and S Fourth Street

A curiosity, this small high-rise was framed out but not completed during the 1930s, and finally finished in 1950 as a hotel sheathed in one of the nation's first all aluminum curtain walls. Now it has been stripped again to a frame to be reconstructed as a modern commercial center of offices and stores.

9 **St. Michael's Episcopal Church**, 1889, portico 1923
Edward T. Potter; Whitehouse & Price
E Yakima and S Naches Avenues

A picturesque church of native lava rock with a lovely carved wood "Gothicky" portico by a Spokane firm locally famous for church design.

9 St. Michael's Episcopal Church

10 **First Baptist Church**, c. 1915
E Yakima Avenue and N Seventh Street

A mighty fortress of faith in rough ashlar stonework.

11 **Yakima Center**
E Yakima Avenue and N Seventh Street

A small-scale public convention facility with adjoining motel done in vernacular roadside contemporary architectural style.

12 **Row Houses**, c. 1910
113–19 N Fourth Street, 401–8 E B Street

An early twentieth century, two-story, brick, row house group with unifying common front veranda. With a similar group at 317–31 East A Street nearly in the shadow of the Yakima Mall parking structure, these houses constitute a rare passage in Northwest vernacular residential design.

13 **St. Joseph's Catholic Church**, 1903
N Fourth Street and Naches Avenue

A fine simplified Romanesque design in black lava rock set off on its site with harmonizing rectory and school structures.

14 **Fire Station No. 1**, c. 1970
    N Front and D Streets

A decorated brutalist concrete structure, the sort of serious and knowing contemporary architecture that is too rare in these parts. This firehouse contrasts with its now recycled Italianate predecessor at Fourth and Walnut.

Across the tracks running west from downtown, West Yakima Avenue extends out several miles along a ridge once known as Nob Hill. From 12th Avenue out to 36th (avenues are on the west side of town, streets on the east), Yakima Avenue becomes the spine of a modest zone of better residence. Somewhat later than similar districts in other Washington cities, and more varied perhaps in style terms, this area provides a veritable botanical garden of residential designs including Bungalow, Prairie, Spanish Colonial Revival, Tudor, and even a few early, simplified Queen Anne cottages. Among the more interesting are a Classic Box with Bungalow or Craftsman verandah, now the Boy Scout headquarters at 2 North 16th Avenue; a Mission Revival house at 1716 West Yakima; a large Colonial Revival with coursed ashlar walls at 1811 West Yakima; a Streamline Moderne residence at 5 Park Avenue; a Prairie Style house at 1908 West Yakima; and a rambling Queen Anne farmhouse at 2109 West Yakima. The district is punctuated with some decent eclectic church designs, among them two somewhat overscaled but imposing examples are First Presbyterian on South Eighth Avenue at West Yakima and St. Paul's Catholic at the corner of North Chestnut and South 17th. Beyond this residential area where the modern sprawl has engulfed the older agricultural patterns lies the Carbonneau house (c. 1910) at 670 South 48th Avenue, a big, blocky stone farmhouse with corner towers, one round, the other octagonal. Interesting mainly by virtue of its colorful builders, a former Yukon goldrush queen named Belinda Murlrooney and the reputed French count and champagne merchant whom she married, the house hints at the former character of this landscape of drive-ins, shopping malls, warehouses, and condominiums.

Environs

North of town about eight miles, Interstate 82 crosses Selah Creek at a pair of handsome, spindly concrete arch bridges which suggest the high aesthetic quality that is attainable but too often not attempted in civil engineering works.

To the south, Fort Simcoe (1856–c. 1910), an instructive, visually attractive, well-restored relic, terminates Route 220 about twenty-five miles west of Toppenish, in turn about twenty miles downriver from Yakima. Originally established in response to the Indian Uprisings of 1855–58, Fort Simcoe was transferred to the Bureau of Indian Affairs, which it served until 1923. Notable among the remaining buildings in this picturesque military compound around a tree-lined parade ground are the commanding officer's quarters, in the Gothic Revival Style. They were designed by U.S. Army draftsman-architect Louis Scholl from The Dalles using A. J. Downing's pattern book of Gothic country house designs. Even though most of three sides of the original quadrangle is gone, Fort Simcoe is the only remaining site that offers a reasonably unaltered image of the mid-nineteenth century military outpost in the Northwest. The surroundings of Fort Dalles in Oregon, Fort Steilacoom, and Fort Walla Walla have experienced massive changes over the years. The reason Fort Simcoe remains as it does is, of course, its location buried in the remote part of the Yakima Indian Reservation. A side benefit of the trip from Toppenish to the fort comes in the miles of hops plantations set out on their high networks of poles and wires over the level irrigated valley floor, surrounded in the distance by picturesque, bare, purplish-tan foothills and mountains, and capped on the west by Mount Adams' snowy pinnacle.

Commanding officer's quarters, Fort Simcoe (courtesy of State Office of Archaeology and Historic Preservation)

Columbia Plateau

About a hundred and fifty miles of impressive, sometimes lunar, landscape called "channeled scablands" interspersed with the rich, dryland farming country of the plateau above lie east of the riverside park at Vantage where Interstate 90 crosses the Columbia. This landscape extends to Spokane near the eastern boundary of the state. At the crossing, the river though placid seems scarcely diminished by the many dams of the Columbia River project. Beyond the Vantage crossing the freeway climbs out of the valley in one of the minor scabland channels. It is part of an enormous system resulting from the catastrophic failure eons ago of a glacial dam in the northern panhandle of Idaho. The failure explosively released the waters of immense prehistoric Lake Missoula on the west slope of the Rockies. Untold cubic miles of water scoured great passages through the deep volcanic soil of the Palouse formation, even swept out canyons in the underlying basalt. The forbidding traces of these channels give rise to the name "scablands." Interstate 90 crosses Moses Lake which fills part of one of the largest of these channels, locally called "coulees."

To the north of this lake lies Grand Coulee, terminating at Dry Falls where the Interpretive Center Building (1974) is by Brooks/Hensley/Creager. Exhibits here explain the remarkable local geology which some scientists find analogous to surface features of Mars as revealed in recent satellite probes. Below Dry Falls is Sun Lakes State Park, an early thirties, auto travelers' park modernized with pleasant though ordinary facilities including the ubiquitous fields of recreational vehicle hookups. The park is situated in the characteristically bewitching scablands combination of desert-like canyon bottom and lush wet oasis.

Between Interstate 90 and Dry Falls, the town of Ephrata, originally a creature of the Great Northern railway and later revived by the Columbia Basin Project irrigation boom, vividly demonstrates a typical succession of planning influences. These include the railroad surveyors who laid out the original plat to parallel the tracks, the U.S. Geodetic Survey which later enforced the north-south grid system, the Federal Housing Administration planners who favored long curvilinear streets, and the car-oriented strip commercial development which produced attenuated town patterns along main highways.

About forty miles west of Dry Falls is Waterville, Douglas County seat. Here a fine-looking addition to the roster of Washington courthouses caps a generally Richardsonian two stories and basement with a Queen Anne cupola. It was built in 1905.

On the Columbia River at the north end of Grand Coulee lies America's largest single hydroelectric engineering work. The main dam and first turbo-generating units were completed in 1941 in time to power the atomic bomb fuel plant at Hanford. The 1976 extension of the dam along the north wall of the canyon and the new turbine house were designed with the consulting advice of the late Marcel Breuer, Bauhaustrained architect, exponent of the International Style, and master of faceted concrete work. The decorative but heroically scaled result is unique among such engineering works.

Among the most environmentally impressive aspects of the Grand Coulee Dam project is the pumped storage facility which reverses its turbines to pump Columbia River water into the formerly dry coulee, converting its forty-mile length into a storage reservoir for irrigation water. Visitor facilities at the dam provide a complete explanation of the project's many dimensions. The nearby villages of Electric City and Grand Coulee retain faint vestiges of construction camp days, and the plan of the latter reveals the curious blend of City Beautiful and Social Housing motives which characterized New Deal settlements.

Fifty miles to the west downstream from the Grand Coulee installations is Chief

Douglas County Courthouse (courtesy of State Office of Archaeology and Historic Preservation)

Joseph Dam where there is a fort-like, brutalist concrete Administration

Grand Coulee Dam (courtesy of Washington State Historical Society)

Building (1977) by Adkison, Leigh, Sims, Cuppage. Just north of this, also on the river, is the site of the 1811 Astor fur traders' outpost, Fort Okanogan. As a state historical site it merits a fancy interpretive center building devoted to explaining this early settlement.

Prime areas of fertile volcanic soil in this great bend of the Columbia are irrigated with Grand Coulee project water. Two main canals lead southeast and southwest from the reservoir in a broad fan containing a million acres more or less of arable, now watered land. The landscape transformation wrought by the project is everywhere visible. Hay, grain, and other crops have replaced sagebrush and scattered bunch grass. Most memorable are the monster irrigation machines, spidery assemblies of wire and aluminum pipe that wander by themselves across the now green acres. At one time the great American environmental historian-philosopher, Lewis Mumford, imagined a green landscape here peopled by earnest husbandmen who lived in nearby agricultural villages embowered in new verdure. How perverse is the actual outcome of the country's most ambitious agricultural reclamation. A green landscape, yes, but one peopled by machines not yeomen-farmers, the devices tended by workers who arrive in pickup trucks from remote railroad towns like Coulee City, Ephrata, Othello, and Quincy.

South of Moses Lake the network of scabland channels connects back to the Columbia. Here the Hanford Atomic Energy Works covers hundreds of square miles. North of the Hanford Works and below Priest Rapids Dam lies the only remnant of the free-flowing Columbia. Treasure it! From the back route, State Highway 240, between the Vernita Bridge over this free section of river and the Tri-Cities area, some of the Hanford's gargantuan and mysterious concrete bunkers can be seen in the distance.

N reactor, Hanford (courtesy of UNC Nuclear Industries)

Tri-Cities

Richland, a tiny agricultural settlement became an instant city for atomic bomb workers during the middle of World War II. At the height of construction in the forties more than 50,000 people camped here making it the fourth largest city in the state. It sprawls along the river terrace just south of the Hanford Works. The original emergency settlements were planned in great secrecy with the aid of the Army Corps of Engineers. After 1948 Richland was transformed into the present planned garden suburb under a master plan by Gordon Trumbull, Inc., with architects Graham, Anderson, Probst & White of Chicago. The curious leaf-vein street pattern and angled building lots in the older area just south of the town center preserve the flavor of the New Deal vintage greenbelt planning which must have motivated the wartime design. In the same area, the original, stock plan, government-issue house modules have been so creatively reworked over time by their owners that it requires an architectural detective to spot the original fabric.

Richland, Pasco, and Kennewick constitute the Tri-Cities. Pasco came first in time, Kennewick soon after as a westside terminal for the Northern Pacific Railroad ferry across the Columbia. Later a railroad-sponsored irrigation scheme created Richland. In 1940 Richland was by far the smallest of the future Tri-Cities. Now the largest, it has replaced Pasco as the region's most populous center.

Across the river from Richland and Kennewick, Pasco as the oldest appears the most substantial of the Tri-Cities. The railroad established it in 1884 when Villard's empire collapsed and the Northern Pacific could no longer use the Columbia River tracks of the Oregon Railroad & Navigation Company. Within months, a town was founded, the division point railroad shops and operations offices moved here from Wallula and Ainsworth, and a ferry put in service across the Columbia. Though Pasco quickly developed into a farm market center it never became the regional capital some had hoped for. It did become the Franklin County seat with a grand Neo-Classic Courthouse (1907) sporting a fine marble interior. C. Lewis Wilson & Company, architects from Seattle, designed it.

Franklin County Courthouse

Pasco boasts the Columbia Basin Community College which has an Arts, Music, and Drama Complex (1977) by Brooks/Hensley/Creager, an exemplary work in the Brutalist tradition. Surrounded with berms and nearly windowless to conserve energy, it is a concrete block, cut into and pulled apart to create a complex interior circulation pattern with small courts at the ground level and open bridges connecting upper floors. By night, from projection turrets set in the berms, movies, slides, and advertisements are shown on the exterior wall.

Arts, Music, and Drama Complex. Photo: Gordon Peery

The Columbia River bridge (1978) on Interstate 82 between Kennewick and Pasco was designed by Arvid Grant & Associates of Olympia with Dr. Fritz Leonhardt of Stuttgart as a design consultant. A distinguished engineering work, the bridge has a stayed cable structure, meaning that the cables radiating like spokes from the towers hold the narrow roadway in compression to create a rigid system. On the Kennewick side a plaza with a concrete fountain, designed by David Williams, is slated for construction in the near future.

On Interstate 90, the route from Vantage to Spokane is predictably uneventful from an architectural point of view. The landscape becomes more scabland, along with grassland and wheatfields where the deep soil remains, finally becoming pine woods close to Spokane.

Ritzville and Sprague

Situated just off Interstate 90, Ritzville, Adams County seat, has a pleasant residential neighborhood on a hill. At 408 Main Street, Dr. Frank R. Burroughs built an eclectic house in 1889 which he remodeled in 1902 with the help of a California architect, J. Flood Walker. As Ritzville's only physician for many years, Dr. Burroughs summed up in his house and its artifacts what it meant to be a family doctor in the early days of rural eastern Washington. The Adams County Courthouse (1940–42) was designed by Whitehouse & Price.

From Ritzville to Spokane, Interstate 5 follows the bottom edge of one of the mightiest scabland channels. About twenty-five miles northeast of Ritzville, the white Gothic Revival spire of the Church of Mary Queen of Heaven (1902) signals to those speeding by on the freeway to visit Sprague. Here in a small railroad town built for division point

Church of Mary Queen of Heaven

shops of the Northern Pacific, a fragment of a typical turn-of-the-century main street and a pleasant central park may serve as distractions from the freeway monotony.

Medical Lake

Off Interstate 90 on Route 902 to the northwest is Medical Lake, the first real spa of the Northwest interior. The curative powers of the lake water, a sodium bicarbonate solution, were well known to the Indians. White settlers began to discover them in the 1870s and by 1889

the town had a full complement of facilities. The peak years followed the institution of regular service to Medical Lake from Spokane about 1905 by the Washington Water Power electric line. The line was built on the old Seattle, Lake Shore & Eastern Railroad bed after this historic effort by residents on the east and west sides of the state to build their own railroad had failed. Until 1922 when the automobile so diminished the line's ridership that service was discontinued, the cars were crowded with health- and pleasure-seekers who patronized the Coney Island Pavilion and Boathouse, Camp Comfort, and Stanley Park. The latter was developed by Lord Stanley Hallett, an Englishman whose 1877 homestead later became most of the town. Hallett's idiosyncratic baronial house, called "the Castle," still stands at East 623 Lake Street. Local opinion had it that from opposite the southeast corner of the house the high parapet with its elaborate brick frieze and crenellation resembled a crown. Mostly it resembles nothing else in the whole state. Started in 1900, the house, though not large, took three years to build. Much of this time was spent by a family named Cook chipping the bricks to round them, one doesn't know quite why. The trees on Lake Street were planted by Hallett, who also named the adjacent streets of Stanley, Hallett, and Legg.

Hallett house (courtesy of State Office of Archaeology and Historic Preservation)

At the northwest corner of Ladd and Washington streets is the Community Church, formerly Congregational, a simple, white, wooden, Gothic Revival building erected by the prominent religious leader Cushing Eells in 1889. The rest of the town is pleasant to explore and has some interesting late nineteenth century houses.

Nearby, to the west, on the lakeshore is the Eastern Washington State Hospital, of no particular architectural interest. However, a little further on the hospital road is Lakeland Village, a facility for the handicapped, opened in 1915, with buildings designed by Whitehouse & Price. The Administration Building, a handsome and solidly built Georgian Revival structure, is well sited on a rise of land in a park-like setting studded with specimen trees that complete a period piece of environmental design. The rest of the complex has more Georgian Revival buildings around a quad and other later buildings up to the present.

On Route 2 a mile or so north of Medical Lake is Deep Creek, now a ghost town, where the fine gambrel-roofed Colonial Revival schoolhouse of circa 1905 testifies to the strength of the erstwhile agricultural community.

Lakeland Village Administration Building

Cheney

South off Interstate 90 on the road to Cheney is the Cheney Junior High School (1979) by Brooks/Hensley/Creager. This arresting complex of mastaba-like buildings with precast insulated concrete panel walls involves several innovative ideas in education as well as energy-conserving design. The plan expresses the idea of a shopping mall with a variety of educational activities spaced along its length. The classroom buildings of four sections or pods have movable interior partitions to allow for flexibility of use and size. The free-standing sculpture, *Gate III*, at the main entrance is by Lee Kelly; the bas reliefs sandblasted into the walls are by Kay Slucarenko.

Cheney Junior High School

In its early days Cheney vied with Spokane for regional dominance. While it did not win the struggle, in 1890 the state made it the home of a normal school that has since evolved into Eastern Washington University. (Campus maps are available in the library.) The original, early twentieth century buildings, notably Showalter Hall (Administration) and Martin Hall are of buff brick with ivory terra cotta trim, the then fashionable combination of colors and materials. Showalter has eclectic Classic styling and a quiet dignity reinforced by its generous and mature landscaped setting. Martin shows the stylistic evolution to Moderne with decorative detail derived from the vocabulary of Art Deco. Most of the campus buildings date from the educational boom times of the post-World War II period. A notable grouping around a central campus quad with contemporary landscaping by the architects for the Landscape Master Plan, Richard Haag Associates, includes: the John F. Kennedy Memorial Library (1966) by Barnard & Holloway; Patterson Hall (1970) by Barnard & Holloway; and the Pence Union (1971)

Showalter Hall (courtesy of Archives and Special Collections, EWU Library)

by Brooks/Hensley/Creager. To the east of this central campus area on Cedar Street between Tenth and Eleventh streets are Streeter and Morrison halls (1968 and 1970) by Kirk/Wallace/McKinley. On Seventh Street near Washington Street is a complex devoted to the Fine and Performing Arts (1977) by Barnard & Holloway. A most ambitious recent addition to the campus lies off Washington Street, the main approach to the campus. It is a multi-phase complex completed in 1977 and designed by Adkison, Leigh, Sims, Cuppage, for the departments of Health, Physical Education, Recreation, and Athletics. Organized along a two-level mall is a procession of monumental concrete buildings with expressed frames and textured board-form walls. Intricate sculptural wood lanterns on the buildings are complemented by free-standing pieces along the way. At the open end of the mall is a vista of hills rolling away

Pence Union. Photo: Gordon Peery

to the horizon where an occasional farm machine can be seen working the soil. The whole scene provokes circumspection about man's designs on the land.

Across from Showalter Hall on Fifth Street are the Philena Apartments, built around 1915 in the image of an Italian palazzo by Governor Martin for members of the faculty. At F and Third streets is the Lowe house of 1904, a late Queen Anne Style house with exuberant wooden decorative detail. Further downhill is the main street of Cheney which preserves touches of the town's turn-of-the-century character including the Interurban Depot for the Washington Water Power Company electric lines that ran until the mid-thirties. One-half mile southwest of Cheney on a rise overlooking the town is the Sutton Barn, a mortise and tenon, braced-frame structure that was hand built by master craftsman William Bingham in 1884. It is now owned by the university. At the south end of Chapman Lake on Rock Creek near Cheney the Dydball Grist Mill, built in 1897 by a Norwegian immigrant, Ole C. Dydball, and in operation until

Lowe house

1955, still preserves its original equipment in place. Industrial architecture buffs take note.

North of Sprague on State Highway 2, about thirty miles west of Spokane, the Lincoln County seat, Davenport, has an 1897 Courthouse of buff brick and limestone in the predictable Classic Revival Style. It occupies a commanding site above the Main Street. There is an older residential area that features the circa 1886 Hoople house with elaborate jigsawed brackets on the front porch, and the 1899 McInnis house, 1001 Morgan Street, a Queen Anne towered villa. A walk around the area will reveal other interesting buildings.

Health, Physical Education, Recreation, and Athletics facility. Photo: Ritch D. Fenrich

Spokane

Downtown Spokane, as seen from Sunset Hill to the west (drawing from Spokane Sketchbook)

Spokane occupies a dramatic inland site on a series of river terraces centered on the main falls of the Spokane River. Old Spokane House, established in 1810 by the English North West Company as the present state of Washington's first European fur trading post, lay but ten miles downstream. Native Americans as well as fur traders knew and used the valley. By mid-century the Spokane area took on new significance as a station on the historic Mullan Road constructed in 1859–60 by the army to connect Walla Walla, Wallula, and the Columbia River with Fort Benton, the head of navigation on the Missouri River.

Spokane began as Spokane Falls in typical Northwest fashion with a sawmill purchased from two squatters by founding father James N. Glover in 1873.

Besides running the mill and general store, Glover and others platted the town in 1878 on its extraordinary site by the upper Spokane Falls. Incorporated in 1881 when the transcontinental railroad connection became a certainty, Spokane Falls became just plain Spokane ten years later.

A great deal happened in the 1880s. The Northern Pacific arrived in 1881; it was followed in a few years by the Union Pacific, the Great Northern, the Milwaukee, and the Canadian Pacific. Spokane became the major railroad center in the West. In addition to transcontinental lines, a number of rail lines such as the Seattle, Lake Shore & Eastern and the Washington Central took up land in the city's center. Until it was cleared away for the 1974 Expo, a great plate of steel spaghetti along with trestles and support structures for the railroads occupied the river banks in the geographic center of the city.

The railroad boom and Spokane's position as the only city in the region with direct main-line connections to the east brought about its emergence as the regional capital during the gold rush of the 1880s. This gold boom differed fundamentally from the one a generation earlier in Walla Walla: it was based on lode mining not placer mining. Instead of small caches of gold dust collected over the eons by stream action, Spokane's economy derived from mines that exploited hard rock mineral veins. Soon

significant silver, copper, lead, and zinc production joined gold in contributing to the city's wealth. Spokane prospered from mining through the nineties and on until the First World War, by which time eastern and San Francisco investors had captured the mining profits, and ore processing had become localized at mine sites in Idaho and Montana. The names of the mining districts serviced by Spokane during its meteoric boom years include many of the country's most famous hard-rock veins: Coeur D'Alene, Pend Oreille, Kootenay, Metaline. Actually it all began in Colville, Washington, with the discovery of the Old Dominion mine in 1885.

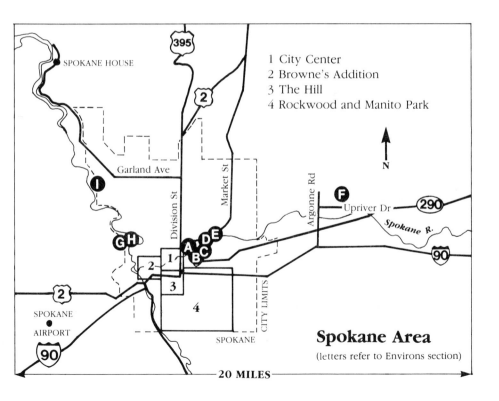

1 City Center
2 Browne's Addition
3 The Hill
4 Rockwood and Manito Park

Spokane Area
(letters refer to Environs section)

20 MILES

Riverside Avenue, looking east, c. 1905 (courtesy of Eastern Washington State Historical Society)

Railroads and minerals made Spokane the nascent capital of the Inland Empire, the local name for a district including eastern Washington, the Idaho panhandle, and pieces of eastern Oregon, southern Idaho, western Montana, and southern British Columbia. By the 1890s Spokane had eclipsed all rivals. Ranching and the growing importance of wheat-raising on the rich Palouse soil simply added impetus to growth.

In August of 1889, a four-hour fire consumed thirty-two blocks of downtown, but, like Seattle, the city recovered dramatically and organized the Northwestern Industrial Exposition in 1890 to prove it. The 1890 *Souvenir Book* was reprinted for the 1974 Expo; it is worth perusing for images of the city and its prominent citizens, along with expressions of high optimism about the future.

Spokane grew phenomenally following the fire. The city went from a negligible population in 1880 to 36,000 people in 1890, then trebled in the next decade. In the last eighty years, the metropolitan area has trebled again.

A major factor in this growth was the development of electric power. Spokane built the first hydroelectric plant west of the Mississippi in 1885. This facility sparked the growth of a network of electric lines that gradually laced the Spokane area. In 1889 the Ross Park

Electric Street Railroad Company ran the first line out to the new residential area of the same name north of the river. About the same time the Spokane Street Railway began to serve Browne's Addition immediately west of downtown. Shortly thereafter the Spokane and Montrose Motor Transit and later the Cook Steam Motor Line ran up the hill to the south to Cook's Addition. The most popular lines ran out to the parks, the Traction Line to Manito and another line to Twickenham Park (later called Natatorium Park), the predictable amusement park, in the bend of the river where Spokane Falls Community College is now. These small lines were then acquired by the Spokane and Inland Empire Railroad System Company, which was in turn subsumed by the Washington Water Power Company. The latter developed orchard lands and recreational facilities, such as those at Medical Lake. Though development was reasonably spread out, it was patchy. Overall, the physical remains of Spokane's boom years occupy a small rectangle about two miles square centered on the river terrace where the business district is located.

A somewhat indirect product of the city's early prosperity is the park system, which until the post-World War II period provided the city with well over the national average of per capita public park area. The first park, called Coeur d'Alene, comprised four city blocks donated in 1891 by A. M. Cannon and J. J. Browne. For several years thereafter parks were increased in an unplanned way by public donations. In 1904 public demand for systematic direction led to the organization of a City Beautiful Committee. Aubrey L.

White, a prominent citizen who had profited from mining along with his neighbors in Browne's Addition, headed the committee. Later that year an amendment to the proposed city charter established a Board of Parks Commission of ten members chaired by White, who then proceeded to commission a park plan from the Olmsted Brothers. Since there were no funds until a bond issue was passed in 1911 after the adoption of the City Charter in 1910, it was difficult to implement the plan. Still, White managed to cajole tax-free land from his friends who owned substantial tracts up and down the Spokane River. With money from the first two bond issues he continued to acquire the land that comprises the Up River Tract, Down River Park, and Audubon, Cliff, Hays, Cannon Hill, Sterling Heights, and High Bridge parks, increasing the

Coeur d'Alene Park (courtesy of Eastern Washington State Historical Society)

acreage from 173 to 1,934. So faithful was the commission to the Olmsted Plan and its City Beautiful ideals that today the park system has a strong and coherent character. The lead paragraphs on the "Need for Parks" from the Olmsted Plan reveal the durability of their message. A sample passage runs:

. . . city life involves a continual strain of the nerves, through the need of avoiding dangers of the factory and street, owing to the multitudinous harsh noises and the vivid and eye-tiring sights and through having to give attention to so many things and to talk to so many people. Even to the well this is tiring to the nerves . . . it is to those whose nerves are tired—and they are a large proportion of the dwellers in a city—that the parks are most immediately beneficial.

A final introductory note concerns the approach to Spokane. From the west on Interstate 90 the downtown matrix appears to rise suddenly from the riverbanks. From Sunset Hill, the Burlington Northern Railroad Bridge designed by Howard, Needles, Tammen & Bergendoff, winner of the AISC Bridge Award in 1974, and the Latah Creek Bridge of 1916, designed by Ben Garnett, make a dramatic city gateway. Going west from town this highway leads to the Spokane International Airport with space-age terminal rotunda designed in 1965 by William H. Trogdon and Warren Cummings Heylman, who also designed the adjacent terminal, built a year later.

Spokane International Airport Terminal (courtesy of Eastern Washington State Historical Society)

City Center

An architectural appraisal of downtown shows vigorous development in the 1890s with many fine brick and stone business blocks reflecting the railroad-borne midwestern influence from Chicago and St. Paul. In the twentieth century's first decades, taller terra-cotta-faced Neo-Classic office buildings followed. The recent surge of downtown activity, sparked in part by Expo '74 and the railroad clearance project, produced Brutalist concrete banks and parking structures, contemporary commercial glass boxes, and an urban design scheme of skyways linking the major department stores to parking garages and to each other.

The authors of *Spokane Sketchbook* observed, "Early in its development, Spokane had given up its view of the river for the privilege of running rail-roads through the center of town. Be-sides keeping the river a secret, however, the railroads had a more beneficial effect. In combination with the natural terrain, they effectively contained the sprawl of the downtown area—an uncontested blessing" (p. 83). The city's key posi-tion in the regional economy, combined with its relative stagnation during the early automobile years, has contained the downtown and produced a satisfying look of urbanity. Until recently the ten-block sequence along Riverside Avenue manifested this with scarcely a gap-tooth parking lot from Adams on the west to Bernard on the east side.

The Olmsted Brothers first bemoaned the loss of the riverside and falls beneath the tangle of railroads and commercial development. Today Spokane has re-gained that great amenity. Expo '74, dedicated officially to "the harmony of man and his natural environment," pro-vided the vehicle for dismantling the tracks along with associated warehouses, terminal, and service structures. It re-placed them with a verdant River Front Park (29) extending across Havermale Island to the north bank, very like the Gorge Park advocated by the Olmsted Brothers. Present-day beliefs that lean toward rehabilitation rather than radical surgery may question the demolition of the 1902 Great Northern Station. Its historic presence must be conjured up from the Clock Tower (31) which has been saved, but the main point is that the city gained from Expo '74 a great central park. When surplus water and hydro-generating conditions permit, the falls which first attracted the notice of early settlers return to amaze the citizens and tourists of today. In fact, the man-made features of the fair scarcely compete with this great natural attraction—when the water is turned on. It is best viewed from the Monroe Street Bridge. The bridge itself is a work of architectural importance built in 1911 from a design by engineer J. C. Ralston and architect Kirtland K. Cut-ter. When completed, this was the world's longest bridge spanned by con-crete arches; Cutter's part was designing the superstructure, which he embel-lished with buffalo skulls on the sidewalk arches. On the river bank below stands the Washington Power Company's 1889 generating plant, a benchmark in the development of hy-droelectric technology.

Aerial view of Spokane in 1938, with Monroe Street Bridge in foreground (courtesy of Eastern Washington State Historical Society)

Starting just southwest of the Monroe Street Bridge on the west side of the city center's most densely built-up area, the Riverside Avenue historic district embraces the boulevarded section of the street with traffic islands, commemorative statuary, and a median strip planted with linden trees. Its design follows a scheme prepared by the Olmsted Brothers. The S-curved avenue—the only break in the downtown grid—with its harmoniously scaled and detailed buildings of Beaux Arts, eclectic Classic persuasion marks a high moment in the west coast City Beautiful movement. The vista west from the intersection of Monroe and Riverside, both soothing and dignified, caused the section to be called the Civic Center in the early twentieth century. From further east at the intersection of Post and Riverside, the curving south side of the street, climaxed by the Review Building, commemorates the city's phoenix-like rise from the ashes of the 1889 fire. The imposing Chateau Style edifice visible across the river is the Spokane County Courthouse (34), built in 1895.

1   **Smith Funeral Home**, 1912
    Jones & Levesque
    W 1124 Riverside Avenue

2   **The Elks Club**, 1919
    Baume & Cutter
    W 1116 Riverside Avenue

3   **Masonic Temple**, 1905, addition 1925
    Rand & Dow; Rigg & Vantyne
    W 1108 Riverside Avenue

    A rhythmic colonnade which reinforces the perspective of the street. The addition respectfully carries on the original concept of fine textbook Roman Revival design.

3 Masonic Temple

4   **Chamber of Commerce**, 1933
Whitehouse & Price
W 1020 Riverside Avenue

A fragment of a Florentine Renaissance cloister in harmony with its neighbor.

5   **The Spokane Club**, 1910
Cutter & Malmgren
W 1002 Riverside Avenue

Spokane's oldest club, founded in 1890 and housed, like similar institutions across the land, in the grand eclectic manner.

5 The Spokane Club

6   **Our Lady of Lourdes**, 1902–8, interior remodeled 1971
Preusse & Zittel
W 1115 Riverside Avenue

7   **Catholic Diocese Chancery** (formerly Great Northwest Life Insurance Company), 1924
G. A. Pehrson
W 1023 Riverside Avenue

8   **Spokesman-Review Building**, 1891
C. B. Seaton & C. Ferris White
W 927 Riverside Avenue

Romanesque Revival in red brick and gray Montana granite culminating in a five-story tower. The building was projected in the 1890 Expo Souvenir Book as a sign of civic progress. Today it is the perfect exclamation mark for the west end of downtown.

9   **Chronicle Building**, 1923
Cutter & Pehrson
W 926 Sprague Avenue

A Gothicized terra-cotta-faced building allegedly Cutter's last work in Spokane. The largely glazed ground floor is a showcase for the presses.

10 **Fox Theater Building**, 1931
R. C. Reamer
W Sprague Avenue at Monroe Street

A well-preserved Moderne movie palace. The lobby has fortunately not been remodeled and is worth seeing.

11 **Federal Building—U.S. Courthouse**, 1967
Culler, Gale, Martell, Ericson; McClure & Adkison; Walker & McGough
NE corner W Riverside Avenue and Monroe Street

A blockbuster that mostly negates the urban design potential of its site in the Riverside historical district.

12 **Crescent Building**, 1880
W 919–25 Riverside Avenue

The only building to survive the great fire, it originally housed the Crescent Store, now moved a few blocks east.

13 **Post Office Building,** 1909
Taylor (Treasury Department architect)
NW corner W Riverside Avenue and Lincoln Street

A handsome Classic Revival building in Bedford limestone which dignifies the vista down Lincoln Street to the river's edge. Too bad the new Federal Building did not achieve the grace of this one.

14 **Public Library** (formerly Sears-Comstock Building), 1929
W Main Avenue and Lincoln Street

A pleasantly scaled Moderne design with fancy brickwork.

14 Public Library

15 **Montgomery Ward Building,** 1929
W 808 Spokane Falls Boulevard and Post Street

A smaller and more ornamented version of this company's stock design built all over the West; present plans are to rehabilitate the structure as the new city hall.

16 **Washington Water Power Company, Post Street Substation,** 1909
Cutter & Malmgren
Post Street, block north of Spokane Falls Boulevard

A fine industrial design in a modified fortress form that shows off the decorative potential of

brick. The substation's administrative counterpart, the WWP Office Building, designed in a more Classic mode by the same architects, formerly stood a block away, but was destroyed by fire in 1978.

17 **Lincoln Building,** 1964–65
Whitehouse, Price & De Neff
NE corner Lincoln Street and W Riverside Avenue

The first downtown building to provide a public, street-level plaza.

18 **Great Western Building** (formerly Empire State Building), 1898
J. K. Dow
W Riverside Avenue at Lincoln Street

Spokane's first fireproof building, with central elevators too.

18 Great Western Building

19 **Pacific National Bank of Washington,** 1974
Trogdon/Smith/Grossman
SW corner W Riverside Avenue and Post Street

A Brutalist building that makes a reasonable use of its context, relating to its neighbors through its color, materials, and a well-designed plaza on Sprague Avenue sensitively tied to the 1890s Sullivanesque building next door. The sculpture is by Harold Balazs.

Mallon Ave

Broadway **34**

College Ave

Ide Ave

N

Spokane Falls

Spokane River

Spokane Falls

33

32

FOOTBRIDGE

35

RIVER FRONT PARK

31

16

15

29 **30**

14

24

Spokane Falls Blvd

W Main Ave

1 2 3 4 5

6 7

11

13

23 **25**

26 **27**

W Riverside Ave

17

8 12

9 18

19

28

W Sprague Ave

10

20

W 1st Ave **36**

21 22

Adams St

Jefferson St

Madison St

Monroe St

39

Lincoln St

Post St

Wall St

Howard St

Stevens St

Washington St

Bernard St

W 2nd Ave

Browne St

Division St

W 3rd Ave

37

38

90 **City Center**

W 4th Ave

W 5th Ave

◀──────── **1 MILE** ────────▶

20 **Davenport Hotel,** 1914
The Matador Restaurant, 1908
Kirtland K. Cutter
W 808 Sprague Avenue

Spokane's grand old hotel with the kind of spacious, lavishly appointed lobby that to-day's equivalent seems unable to provide. An enormous stuffed polar bear in a glass case and singing birds add the right exotic notes. Louis M. Davenport was a famous hotel man and restaurateur; the Matador, next door, was his contribution to Spokane's culinary fame in the boom days following the fire. Cutter exhibited his architectural aplomb by contrasting the flamboyant California Mission Style of the Matador with the florid Beaux Arts eclecticism of the Davenport.

20 Davenport Hotel

22 Office of Brooks/Hensley/Creager, Architects, 1967 rehabilitation
S 121 Wall Street

A praiseworthy and conscientious remodeling of an older building.

23 Washington Mutual Savings Bank Building, 1973
Kirk/Wallace/McKinley
W 601 Main Avenue

24 City Hall, 1912
Zittel
N 221 Wall Street
A substantial brick building reflecting midwestern influence.

25 Parkade Building, 1967
Warren Cummings Heylman & Associates
W Main Avenue and Howard Street

26 Sherwood Building, c. 1910
Cutter & Malmgren
W 510 Riverside Avenue
Neo-Gothic in white terra cotta embellished with nice grotesques which may divert the viewer from seeing the purity of the structural expression of this steel-frame office building.

21 Farm Credit Building, 1970
Walker, McGough, Foltz, Lyerla
SW corner W First Avenue and Wall Street
Granite-faced concrete and dark glass help to create an exercise in monumentality typical of today's banking image.

26 Sherwood Building

21 Farm Credit Building. Photo: Morley Baer

27 Old National Bank Building, 1910
D. H. Burnham & Company
W 422 Riverside Avenue
A rare west coast design in gleaming terra
cotta from this famous Chicago firm chosen
for this commission by a design competition.
The U-shaped plan and Florentine Renaissance styling are typical of the building type
at this time.

28 Paulsen Center, 1928
G. A. Pehrson
407 W Riverside Avenue

August Paulsen Building, 1906
Dow & Hubbel
417 Riverside Avenue
Two buildings that commemorate the name
of an important Spokane citizen. The latter
was once the tallest building in the city; the
former is a well-scaled office building with
elegant decorative detail on the upper stories.

Moving north on Stevens Street toward
the river and then along Main, the visitor can experience Spokane's skywalk
system, an ambitious attempt to hold
downtown together through related
parking and shopping. It seems to have
worked. On the Howard Street side of
the 1967 Parkade Building (25) by Warren Cummings Heylman & Associates, a
small plaza provides a convincing inter-
ruption of the built-up urban fabric.
From the Parkade Building, canopied
skywalks spin off to the remodeled 1890
Bennett Block, the Bon Marche, and the
Washington Mutual Savings Bank
Building (23) by Kirk/Wallace/
McKinley. Further west, skywalks connect the Washington Mutual Bank with
the Crescent Store, Nordstrom's, Penney's, and Woolworth's. These skywalks provide contemporary evidence
of Spokane's continuing cultural link to
the East. The idea was hatched in Minneapolis and St. Paul, and, while considerably developed there, Spokane has
for its size a more completely realized
system.

29 River Front Park (formerly Expo '74 site),
1972
Robert Perron & Associates; original Expo
Plan by Thomas R. Adkison
North side Spokane Falls Boulevard between
Post and Division Streets

The park owes its existence to the small
world's fair of 1974 that produced the political consensus and capital necessary to clear the
site of its former tangle of railroad structures
and related facilities. Perron, a Portland
landscape architect, developed a design
which places manicured greensward and
formal, still-water elements closest to the
business district. To the north it gets rougher
and more naturalistic until at the falls the attempt is to reconstruct the predevelopment
appearance. Fragments of the fair remain in
the park, notably the Opera House (30), the
railroad Clock Tower (31), and a carefully restored early twentieth century carrousel that
operated in the demolished Natatorium Park
from 1909 to 1968. The carrousel was carved
by Charles I. D. Looff for his daughter and her
husband, Louis Vogel, who owned the park.
When the park closed in 1968, the carrousel
was dismantled and stored until popular
opinion was mobilized, principally by Constance Huneke, to have it restored and run on
the fairgrounds. C. William Oliver, final
owner of the park, supervised the reinstalla-
tion. An ephemeral feature of the fair was the
U.S. Pavilion by Naramore, Bain, Brady &
Johanson, remodeled by Trogdon/Smith/
Grossman, a great tent sheathed in plastic
that weathered poorly and had to be removed.
The intricate structural system of cables and
tubular steel masts, now revealed, is a spec-
tral sight that is both aesthetically pleasing
and a suitable memorial—if it can be preserved.

30 Spokane Riverpark Center, 1974
Walker, McGough, Foltz, Lyerla
Spokane Falls Boulevard between
Washington and Browne Streets

Built as the Washington State Pavilion for
Expo '74, now a multi-purpose auditorium,
opera house, and convention center, it has an
almost scaleless, monumental exterior that
testifies to the difficulties of contemporary
architecture as urban design. The auditorium
interior is a more successful environment.

30 Spokane Riverpark Center. Photo: Photography Unlimited

31 Clock Tower from Great Northern De-
    pot, 1902
    Havermale Island in River Front Park
    The old tower, stylistically an eclectic Italian
    campanile, marks the key role of this place in
    Spokane's history. Hindsight suggests that
    we might be richer if the whole terminal
    building had been saved.

North of the river and close in to
downtown relatively little of enduring
architectural or landscape quality
attracts the visitor's attention. A pair of
monuments—one modest, the other
monumental—do merit a visit.

32 Flour Mill, 1895, renovated 1974
    Environmental Concern, Inc.
    621 Mallon Avenue
    A recycled 1890s mill housing shops, restau-
    rants, and offices that occupies a wonderful
    site right on top of the falls.

*31 Clock Tower in River Front Park (courtesy of Eastern
Washington State Historical Society)*

33 **Spokane Civic Theatre**, 1966 and 1970
Moritz Kundig
Howard Street and Dean Avenue (off map)
A 350-seat community theater with ancillary
facilities, built in two phases entirely with
private contributions.

34 **Spokane County Courthouse**, 1895, altera-
tions and additions 1953, restoration 1976
Willis A. Ritchie; Whitehouse & Price;
Heylman & Associates

Public Safety Building, 1974
Walker/McGough/Foltz/Lyerla
W 1116 Broadway

The most splendid and picturesque of the
group of Washington county courthouses designed by Ritchie, whose architectural training apparently consisted of a correspondence
course from the superintendent of architecture in the U.S. Treasury Department. The
Jefferson County Courthouse in Port
Townsend, also by Ritchie, and the Stadium
High School in Tacoma complete the roster of
monumental Chateauesque Style buildings in
the state. Subsequent modernizations of the
interior have obliterated its nineteenth century character. In 1976 a long-range plan
under architects Warren Cummings Heylman & Associates began to restore the
original character while accommodating new
courtrooms and equipment. The complex
program proceeds without changing the
building's exterior or structural system of
masonry bearing walls. The connecting Spokane Public Safety Building by Walker/Mc-
Gough/Foltz/Lyerla uses the quiet contemporary formal academic style to avoid
competing with Richie's wondrous chateau.
This much cannot be said for the mistaken effort in the nearby Human Services Building
(1976) to pick up on the rounded turret
forms of the courthouse in a minimum-
budget office structure. If it were not so big it
would be funny.

34 Spokane County Courthouse

East of River Front Park some of the
original Expo site has been developed by
private business. At Cavanaugh Landing
(Division Street at North River Drive),
an amenable riverside hotel demonstrates possibilities for the further development of the area and contrasts with
the unfortunate high-rise hotel of the
same vintage next door to the Riverpark
Center.

35 **Central Pre-Mix Concrete Company**, 1979
Walker, McGough, Foltz, Lyerla
N 805 Division Street
An energy-efficient office building with an
earth berm on three sides. The design is a
good advertisement for the product and
creates a welcome man-made yet natural form
in the cluttered landscape.

On the south, the central business district has long been walled off by the
Northern Pacific tracks. Years ago these
were reworked to provide grade-
separated street crossings and the result-

ing solid viaduct in the middle of the block between First and Second avenues. The viaduct was part of the Northern Pacific Station development described below.

36 **Northern Pacific Station** (now Amtrak depot), 1914
    W 221 First Avenue at Bernard Street

    This station represents an entrepreneurial rather than an architectural achievement. It was designed to unsnarl conflicts between main line railroads and city street traffic. At about the same time, Robert Strahorn, the Union Pacific's Spokane promoter, successfully engineered a passenger terminal on a similar grade-separated downtown site to serve his railroad, the Chicago, Milwaukee, St. Paul and Pacific, and the Canadian Pacific. This terminal and the other Strahorn landmark in Spokane, a thousand-foot-long viaduct that spanned diagonally across the falls and *over* the Monroe Street Bridge, are both gone, to no one's dismay.

The Chinese wall of the railroad viaduct tended to concentrate the prime central business area and to arrest development beyond it. The blocks immediately south of the railroad structure, between it and the freeway, contain but a few consequential buildings and no civic spaces.

37 **First Covenant Church**, c. 1945
    Whitehouse & Price
    W Second Avenue and Division Street

38 **St. John's Lutheran Church**, 1950
    Whitehouse & Price
    W Third Avenue and Division Street

    Two of many parish churches designed by the architects of the Episcopal Cathedral of St. John. The care and craftsmanship of these churches, which recall the work of Eliel Saarinen and the Swedish modernists, make their interiors a generally rewarding experience. Whitehouse was an accomplished wood carver and designer of ecclesiastical furniture. Most of his churches have a finely carved and polychromed reredos. See also the nearby Central Lutheran Church (The Hill, 1).

39 **Garage**, c. 1930
    W Second Avenue between Lincoln and Monroe Streets

    A whimsical work of early pop architecture, it uses a building-scaled car radiator to frame the entrance.

Browne's Addition

Dramatically situated on a bluff rising above the river, the very geography contributed to the exclusive nature of this early residential area. Now a historic district, it was named for J. J. Browne, one of the self-made first citizens written up with particular pride in the 1890 exposition *Souvenir Book*. Browne arrived in Spokane Falls in 1878 and homesteaded 160 acres near the falls, later the heart of the city. According to the *Souvenir Book*, "he did not content himself with the possession of that land alone but has been purchasing property most extensively." Presumably his banking and law practice assisted this enterprise.

Although there is no house bearing his name in the addition, mansions of other prominent early citizens remain, mostly

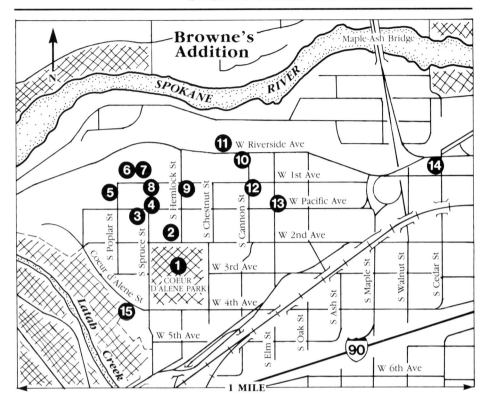

Browne's Addition

W Riverside Ave
W 1st Ave
W Pacific Ave
W 2nd Ave
W 3rd Ave
W 4th Ave
W 5th Ave
W 6th Ave

SPOKANE RIVER
Maple-Ash Bridge

COEUR D'ALENE PARK

S Poplar St
S Spruce St
Coeur d'Alene St
Latah Creek
S Hemlock St
S Chestnut St
S Cannon St
S Elm St
S Oak St
S Ash St
S Maple St
S Walnut St
S Cedar St

90

1 MILE

designed by the indefatigable Kirtland Kelsey Cutter. Arriving in Spokane in 1886 after an east coast education which included study at the New York Art Students League and subsequent travel in Europe, Cutter worked briefly for his uncle, Horace Cutter, a prominent banker. Rarely has an architect been so blessed by catastrophe as Cutter was by the 1889 fire. It provided him with $568,000 worth of business that same year. Alas, many of his great houses are gone, including some in Browne's Addition. Those that remain testify to a high level of competence and a general mastery of the then fashionable range of styles. Besides Cutter works, Browne's Addition has an example of just about every architectural style favored in the Northwest between 1880 and 1930.

At the center of the addition is the lovely Coeur d'Alene Park (1) with a facility designed, according to the Craftsman aesthetic, to resemble a natural rock pile. It is similar to other structures throughout the city park system. The fine open planting of mature trees includes both native and exotic species.

2   **Patrick F. Clark House**, 1898
    Cutter & Malmgren
    W 2208 Second Avenue

    Spokane's most opulent remaining turn-of-the-century mansion. Clark, a Coeur d'Alene mining magnate, spared no expense for his house. Cutter was sent to Europe to acquire furnishings and ideas; New York's Tiffany &

Company executed much of the interior including a pair of dazzling stair hall windows with a peacock motif. The house is an interesting amalgam of California Mission Revival and Chicago Prairie School with a touch of the old Florentine palazzo. The interior is well worth a visit.

6 W. C. Wakefield house

2 Patrick F. Clark house (courtesy of Eastern Washington State Historical Society)

3   The Westminster Apartments, 1905
Sweatt & Stritesky
W 2301 Pacific Avenue

An unusually bold half-timbered apartment house, among the first luxury apartments in Browne's Addition compatible with the neighborhood.

4   Luhn House, c. 1889
Cutter & Malmgren
W 2236 Pacific Avenue

5   John A. Finch House (now the Virginia Apartments), 1898
Cutter & Malmgren
W 2340 First Avenue

Colonial-Georgian Revival built for one of the leaders of the Inland Empire who was also a partner of Amasa Campbell (see 7).

6   W. C. Wakefield House, 1898–1900
Cutter & Malmgren
W 2328 First Avenue

A fine example of the California Mission Revival Style.

7   Amasa B. Campbell House (now Eastern Washington State Historical Society Museum), 1898
Cutter & Malmgren
W 2316 First Avenue

A beautifully maintained interior makes this half-timbered Old English Style house, now owned by the adjacent museum, particularly memorable. Its design recalls the Stimson-Green house, also by Cutter, in Seattle.

8   Houses
W 2325, 2315, 2303, 2231, 2225, 2221 First Avenue

A remarkably intact group of houses, representative of turn-of-the-century styles.

9   Jay P. Graves House, 1900
Cutter & Malmgren
W 2123 First Avenue

Another variation of the Colonial-Georgian Revival theme.

10   Warren Hussey House, c. 1890
W 2003 Riverside Avenue and Cannon Street

A notable Queen Anne Style house that preserves its carriage house.

11   Colonial Apartments, 1890
W 2020–30 Riverside Avenue

A most unusual Queen Anne townhouse row.

12   E. J. Roberts House, 1890
W. J. Carpenter
W 1923 First Avenue

Am impressive villa in the Old English phase of the Queen Anne Style built for a railway and mining tycoon who engineered the Canadian Pacific Railroad from Winnipeg to Vancouver, B.C., in the 1880s.

12 E. J. Roberts house

13 **Isaac Baum House,** 1889
    Herman Preusse
    W 1830 Pacific Avenue

14 **Carnegie Library,** 1904
    Preusse & Zittel
    S 10 Cedar

    One of the most ubiquitous of urban institutions from this period.

15 **House,** c. 1890
    364 Coeur d'Alene Street

    A Queen Anne shingled villa. This pleasant curving street also has a modest example of the Streamline Moderne Style at no. 358.

The Hill

Spokane's other early fashionable neighborhood was "the Hill," which rises sharply a few blocks south of downtown. The city's highest viewpoint is Review Rock in Cliff Park. Institutional and commuter traffic needs have eroded the ridge on the edge of town, but a line of mansions, now mostly institutions themselves, remains. As usual, Kirtland K. Cutter designed most of them. Unfortunately, his own house, a Swiss Chalet Style structure he remodeled after his marriage, is gone. Residential styles from later periods and apartment houses have filled in the areas not occupied by institutions.

1 **Central Lutheran Church,** 1945
   Whitehouse & Price
   W Fifth Avenue and S Bernard Street

   See St. John's Lutheran Church (City Center, 38) for a discussion of the type.

1 Central Lutheran Church

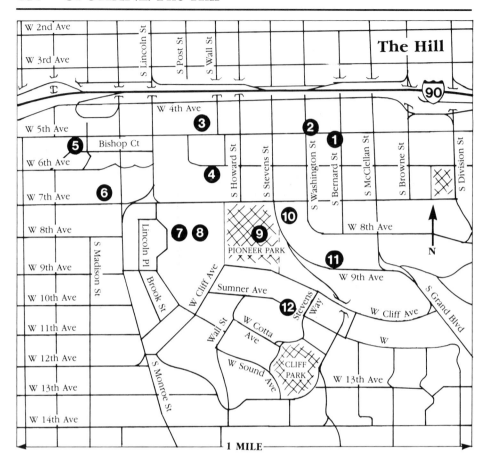

2   **Westminster Congregational Church,**
    1890
    W. Niver; J. K. Dow
    S 407 Washington Street

    Allegedly the first stone church in the state
    and the oldest congregation in Spokane.

3   **Lewis and Clark High School,** 1912
    L. L. Rand
    W 515 Fourth Avenue

    A major city landmark representing the best
    of this period of early public school design.

4   **F. T. Post House,** 1900
    Cutter & Malmgren
    W 727 Sixth Avenue

5   **Studio Apartments,** 1949
    McClure & Adkison
    S 1102–4 Madison Street

    A fine example of the Americanized Interna-
    tional Style of the post–World War II period,
    a modular box of post-and-beam construction
    with proper forties touches like the pipe and
    canvas-paneled railing on the balcony.

6   **House,** c. 1920
    W 1023 Seventh Avenue

    A boldly scaled Swiss Chalet with Jerkin-
    head, or clipped-gable, roof and some of
    the finest sculpted hedge and stone wall land-
    scaping in town.

5 Studio Apartments

6 House

7   **Austin Corbin II House,** 1898
Kirtland K. Cutter
W 815 Seventh Avenue

A seventeen-room Colonial Revival mansion
in buff brick with white, wood porticoes and
generous Georgian detail. Southern decor was
apparently emphasized in its early days.

8   **F. Lewis Clark House** (now Marycliff
School), 1896
Kirtland K. Cutter
W 701 Seventh Avenue

A baronial half-timbered Old English Style
residence surrounded by great stone walls. A
notable beehive water tower near the house is
a shingled extension of a round rock pile. The
gatehouse (1889–90) by Cutter & Poetz is
also a notable example of rockery architecture.

9   **Daniel C. Corbin House** (now Park De-
partment Arts and Crafts Center), 1898
Kirtland K. Cutter
W 507 Seventh Avenue

A quiet Georgian-Colonial house on a fine
site.

10   **Unitarian Church,** 1960
McClure & Adkison; Moritz Kundig, as-
sociate
James N. Glover House, 1888
Kirtland K. Cutter
W 321 Eighth Avenue

A well-sited and well-detailed wooden
church with patterned concrete walls and
light fixtures designed by Harold Balazs. The
congregation owns the James N. Glover
house, a half-timbered Teutonic manse which
broods over the city as did its original master.
Glover was an archetypal entrepreneurial
pioneer. After coming to Oregon with his
family as a child, Glover grew up to range the
Northwest territory, taking Oregon apples to
sell in California, going to Lewiston to try
mining, and dreaming of having a city of his
own. Elected mayor of Spokane in 1884, he
also founded the First National Bank of Spokane and prospered with the city during the
boom decade of the 1880s. Financially ruined
by the 1893 depression, Glover lived on in
this house from which he could survey the
city whose birth he had so ably assisted.

11   **I.B.M. Office Building,** 1965
Kirk/Wallace/McKinley
S 800 Stevens Street

A post-and-beam structure with curving end
walls of rubble lava masonry, carefully
worked out and nicely sited. Diagonally
across the intersection are the Comstock
Arms Apartments (1928) by Whitehouse &
Price.

12 Houses
W Sumner Avenue

West Sumner Avenue offers a fine streetscape with a striking parade of substantial houses in the residential styles favored from 1910 to 1970. The following architects contributed: Whitehouse & Price, nos. 234 (1936), 315 (1920), 503 (1936), 506 (1925), and 726 (1926); Kenneth Brooks, no. 723 (1956, with 1970 addition); Don Murray, no. 611 (1966). Number 612, the Gaiser house (c. 1900), is by Cutter & Malmgren.

12 W 506 Sumner Avenue

Rockwood and Manito Park

South and east of the Hill area two somewhat later residential districts complete the roster of close-in neighborhoods in which the more well-to-do built architect-designed dwellings. Even so, modest builder houses dominate both the Rockwood area, which peels off on the same contour-dictated diagonal as Stevens Street and Grand Boulevard, and the more regularly platted zone around Manito Park. Rockwood and the winding streets around it preserve a fine piece of the Olmsted Brothers' City Beautiful boulevard and parkway planning. Breaking the grid was an Olmstedian principle that was rarely accomplished. When it was, the effect is most convincing although here not only curves but also luxurious and mature landscaping contributes to the fine streetscapes and vistas. Rockwood Boulevard (1) is bordered by a raised strip, now grassy, where the electric tramway ran, discreetly separated by a greenway from the road. Rock-faced masonry pillars at Highland Boulevard, 21st Avenue, and 11th Avenue mark the entrance to this exclusive zone of better residence.

2 **St. John's Episcopal Cathedral,** 1926–54
Whitehouse & Price
E 127 12th Avenue

A distinguished English Gothic Revival building begun in sandstone from Tacoma and Boise and finished in limestone from Indiana. One of the city's major landmarks, the design is remarkable for the high quality of craftsmanship in both interior and exterior detail, an achievement of Harold Whitehouse, who designed the furnishings as well as the building.

3   **August Paulsen House,** 1912
J. K. Dow
E 245 13th Avenue

Another rendition of the very fashionable half-timbered house on a superb site. The building is now owned by the Episcopal Diocese of Spokane.

4   **House,** 1954
Walker & McGough
E 431 16th Avenue

A handsome post-and-beam pavilion in the Harvard tradition.

5   **Joel Ferris House,** 1908
C. Ferris White
E 515 16th Avenue

6   **Eric A. Johnson House,** 1908
C. Ferris White
E 615 16th Avenue

A pair of houses by a prominent early architect; the Ferris house has a strong Prairie School character.

7   **Walker House,** 1956
Walker & McGough
1624 Crest Road

A modular, boxy house, typical of the 1950s.

8   **Trogdon House,** 1964
William H. Trogden
S 1918 Syringa Road

A quiet design expressive of the contemporary Northwest timber tradition.

9   **Three Houses,** c. 1925
Whitehouse & Price
1121, 913, 835 Overbluff Road

10 **Three Houses,** c. 1940
Whitehouse & Price
711, 730, 733 Plateau Road

Three later designs than the ones on Overbluff; no. 730 was designed by Whitehouse for himself and his family.

11 **House,** 1954
Warren Cummings Heylman
E 2020 18th Avenue

A three-level house on a wooded, sloped site with a formal, modular boxy design that uses wood most expressively.

12 **Altamont Boulevard,** c. 1890
Substantial late nineteenth houses, notably at nos. 2314 and 2334, line this loop road, apparently a trolley circuit at one time. Number 1138, a large Colonial Revival house, is by Whitehouse & Price.

13 **J. E. Ferris High School,** 1963
McClure & Adkison
E 3020 37th Street

An extensive educational plant typical in style and plan of those built to accommodate the boom population following World War II.

14 **Temple Beth Shalom,** 1968
Walker, McGough, Foltz & Lyerla
E 1322 30th Street

Sculptural massing in concrete.

2 St. John's Episcopal Cathedral

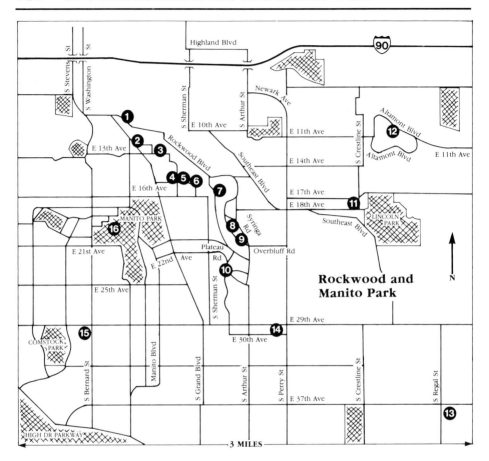

Rockwood and
Manito Park

15 Unity Church, c. 1965
    Barnard & Holloway
    E 29th and S Bernard Streets
    A set of shingled, hip-roofed pavilions.

16 Manito Park
    A fine example of the urban-suburban parks
    built, in this case in the 1920s, near streetcar
    lines to serve the town population for whom
    this was still the country. Playfields, informal
    landscaping, the Japanese Garden, and a con-
    servatory and duck pond vary the park-goer's
    fare. The formal Duncan Gardens by the con-
    servatory feature a fountain designed by
    Harold C. Whitehouse as a memorial to Louis
    M. Davenport, the hotel owner.

Those who have an interest in the 1920s
period revival houses and their suburban
settings will be rewarded by an exploration of the area around Manito Park.
Many of the notable houses were
designed by the grand old firm of
Whitehouse & Price. Harold Whitehouse's first house after coming to
Spokane in 1907 is at East 242 Manito
Place. Others of later dates are mentioned in entries (9) and (10) above. Also
worth seeing are houses at 740 Plateau
Road, and, on the way to Lincoln Park,
at 1830 and 1930 Southeast Boulevard.

E 242 Manito Place

13 J. E. Ferris High School. Photo: Ritch D. Fenrich

Environs

Relatively little development of architectural distinction happened on the north side of the Spokane River. Going east from downtown, a number of significant institutional buildings and campuses achieve notable levels of design. The locations of these are shown on the map of the Spokane region (page 393).

A   **James Monaghan House**, 1902
Preusse & Zittel
E 217 Boone Avenue

A forbidding but perhaps appropriate mansion for one of the city's prominent mining and business magnates.

B   **St. Aloysius Catholic Church**, 1909
Preusse & Zittel
E 402 Boone Avenue

Now part of the Gonzaga campus.

C   **Gonzaga University Administration Building**, 1903–05
Preusse & Zittel
E 502 Boone Avenue

A Romanesque Revival design in granite and brick.

D   **Washington State Community College Adult Education Center** (formerly Holy Names Academy), 1890, 1900
Patrick Donohoe; Preusse & Zittel
N 1114–216 Superior Street at Boone Avenue

A dignified turn-of-the-century institutional design which reflects the work of Richard Norman Shaw and others in the English Queen Anne Style.

E   Washington Water Power Company,
    Central Service Facility, 1959
    Kenneth W. Brooks and Bruce M. Walker;
    Lawrence Halprin, landscape architect
    E 1411 Mission Avenue

A National A.I.A. Award–winning design
and a perfect example of the 1950s aluminum
curtain-wall office building. Even the color
scheme is a superbly typical combination of
blue spandrels and blue-green glass set between end walls of buff brick. Sited in a
twenty-eight-acre park, the building has a
lovely garden and water element in front designed by a famous San Francisco landscape
architect who first received national and international fame about this time.

E Washington Water Power Company, Central Service
Facility

F   Hutton Settlement, 1971
    Whitehouse & Price
    E 9907 Wellesley Avenue

A children's home established as a memorial
to one of Washington's great ladies, May
Arkwright Hutton. Those who wish to learn
more about her colorful political career may
do so in Norman Clark's *Washington*, a bicentennial history. Designed in the popular
Tudor Revival Style of which Whitehouse
was a master, the well-scaled complex sited in
a meadow has a refinement of detail and careful use of materials that indicate a substantial
budget well spent.

On the west side of the central area, the
Spokane River valley, the Latah Creek
valley that joins from the south, and the
pine-forested river terraces that articu-
late these valleys give the district a very
distinctive topography. Except on the
wider, more favorably situated terraces
the landform has severely restricted development. High Drive along the east
bluff over Latah Creek offers spectacular
view sites for both large contemporary
houses and public parks. Much of the
bottom terrace along the Spokane River
is park too. On the west side one of the
largest terraces provided the site for Fort
George Wright (**G**). Golf courses and
cemeteries occupy other terraces. At various places outcrops of volcanic basalt
have cooled into fascinating formations
of large, vertically oriented, hexagonal
crystals. The old Spokane House site of
1810 and a modern interpretative center
lie downstream at the confluence with
the Little Spokane.

F Hutton Settlement

G **Fort George Wright Historic District,** 1897
Randolph Road

This military reservation replaced Fort
Spokane and was in use from 1897 to 1958.
One of the best preserved posts in the Inland
Empire, its tree-lined streets and red brick
buildings typify the well-ordered suburban
residential quality that these turn-of-the-
century military installations convey today.
On the site is St. Michael's Mission, a miniature, shorthand version in wood of a monumental Georgian church, moved here from
another site.

H **Convent of the Holy Names,** 1967
Walker & McGough
Fort George Wright

Hidden in the pines on a lower terrace by the
river bank below the main fort is this rather
surprising cloister in the contemporary
academic style widely used for government
and institutional structures.

I **Fairmont Cemetery Chapel,** c. 1900
Kirtland K. Cutter
Fairmont Cemetery

An exceptionally fine example of the Arts &
Crafts or Craftsman movement aesthetic
which combines natural materials with complete faithfulness to the ideal. The product
is an intimately scaled structure with rubble
lava masonry walls heavily buttressed at the
corners to make it appear that the rocks were
simply piled up in between. The broadly
overhanging roof is topped with three small
cupolas. The gable of the apse end, also shingled, features a great round art glass window
with an intricate design. In its setting this is
surely one of the high moments of the
Craftsman Style in the Northwest.

I Fairmont Cemetery Chapel

H Convent of the Holy Names. Photo: Morley Baer

The Palouse

South from Spokane on State Highway 195, the traveler is immersed in the great rolling wheatland which is the Palouse. Extending to the Snake River and beyond through the Walla Walla district, this extraordinarily fertile region results from layers of windblown, glacial dust deposited over the landscape eons ago. Among the world's richest wheatland, by the 1880s the Palouse and the previously settled Walla Walla area shared with central California the distinction of having the most mechanized farm industry in the nation. Today, modern combines with air-conditioned, self-leveling cabs for the driver's comfort have replaced the ones drawn by thirty-three or more mules or horses. Even so, the harvest is a dramatic scene. The undulating golden landscape, ribboned with brown where freshly plowed, is sporadically animated by monstrous machines careening over the hills.

On the Belmont Road south of Interstate 90 is Mica with an interesting collection of late nineteenth century buildings. By the roadside, on the Heathdale Ranch, sit a pair of very impressive barns built by ex-packers and/or gold miners from California.

Just north of the town center of Rosalia, the moving eye is caught by a presumptuous towered house in a free-wheeling style that is hard to pin down except for placing it in the early twentieth century.

On Route 23 east from Steptoe, a singular and fitting landmark is a great polygonal, domed barn precariously leaning, perhaps not too much longer.

Four miles west of Garfield is the agricultural ghost town of Elberton, developed in the 1870s. It was abandoned about the century's turning, and much of the town burned in 1905. What remains is a flour mill, church, post office, a few commercial buildings, and the largest prune dryer, allegedly, in the world.

Colfax, Whitman County seat and the oldest town in the Palouse, is the improbable home of the Whitman County Port District from which wheat moves to foreign buyers via the Snake and Columbia rivers. At North 623 Perkins is the 1880s house of the first settler, James A. Perkins, on a tree-shaded lot which also has the original homestead cabin. The main street has some nice stretches of nineteenth century commercial buildings presided over by the substantial form of the Whitman County Courthouse.

The dramatic topography created over eons by the tortuous Snake River marks the entrance to Lewiston, Idaho, created by early mining interests as a supply

Steptoe barn

James A. Perkins house

station. The work of man has proved to be an anticlimax here. State Highway 12 from Lewiston to Walla Walla passes through wheatlands again. Pomeroy, platted in 1877, comes next with a row of nineteenth century, false-front, brick commercial buildings on Main Street. Here the 1901 Garfield County Courthouse is a distinctive brick and stone building designed in a somewhat hesitant way, combining elements of a large Queen Anne Style house with those of a modest public institution. A notable statue of Justice weights the building's monumental side.

Further down the road is Dayton, platted in 1871, a fine example of an original wheatlands market town with both the state's oldest existing county courthouse and oldest extant railroad station. Located on the Touchet River, whose waters helped nourish the tree-lined streets, Dayton is a distribution point for the surrounding dryland farming area. Both the trees and the town's grid, parallel to the old Walla Walla and Columbia, now Union Pacific Railroad, testify to the hand of man.

The Columbia County Courthouse (1886) at 341 East Main Street is unhappily stripped of its Italianate cupola and detail as well as the statues of Justice and the American Eagle which used to dignify the roof gables.

The Depot (1881) at Second and Commercial streets has been restored. Its residential scale and character illustrate the compatibility of early small-town public buildings with their general context. The older residential areas of Dayton on the north side around Fourth and Richmond are pleasant to explore.

Waitsburg, platted in 1869 on a miniature delta formed by the Touchet River and Copper Creek, has a pleasant setting. The main sight is the 1883 home of William Perry Bruce, at Fourth and Main, in simplified Italianate Style.

Garfield County Courthouse

Dayton Depot

Pullman and Washington State University

Pullman was platted in 1882 as Three Forks and renamed two years later, in general celebration of the railroad era, for the inventor of the sleeping car, George Pullman. In 1885 the Oregon Railroad & Navigation Company's railroad came as far as the town, and in 1888 the Northern Pacific also arrived with a branch line from Spokane.

As an important center for eastern Washington's agricultural industry, Pullman has prospered and changed over the years. The present, largely modern city holds little of interest for the architectural sightseer; the main attraction is the campus of Washington State University.

Following the achievement of statehood in 1889, a commission from the legislature was established to select a site for a college of agriculture and the mechanic arts, a type of educational institution encouraged by the federal government

and subsidized in part by the 1862 Morrill Act, which placed large land grants at the disposal of the states to create funds for planning and building the colleges. Since the University of Washington was near the western edge of the state, eastern Washington was a logical place to establish the college. When the residents of Pullman heard of the commission's impending tour of the area, they developed a strategy to secure the college for their town. On the day of the visit everyone left home to crowd the streets with as many humans, animals, and vehicles as could be mustered. Convinced that Pullman was a veritable boom town, the commission granted it the college. In 1891 the town put up a 160-acre section of land and $12,000 cash to get the campus going. The first courses were offered in 1892 by a faculty of five to a student body of sixty; the first class graduated in 1897.

Early photo of Washington State University, looking west (courtesy of Eastern Washington State Historical Society)

Pullman's remoteness from real boom towns like Spokane created grave difficulties as far as the design and construction of buildings were concerned. Both architects and materials had to be brought from far away. At first, the Board of Regents failed to create a realistic budget. Then a strong president, Enoch A. Bryan, arrived in 1893. He gave firm direction to campus planning. By 1900 the Board of Regents could report to the legislature that it had "pursued the policy of building moderate sized, plain, substantial department buildings rather than the putting of large amounts of money into imposing structures."

The problem of obtaining suitable materials was solved by using sandstone from a nearby quarry instead of granite as was originally proposed, and by manufacturing brick from a clay deposit on the campus grounds. No buildings survive from the hand of the first architect, H. Preusse, from Spokane, but Thompson and Stevens halls by the Seattle firm of Stephen & Josenhans still exist.

12 Stevens Hall (courtesy of WSU)

By 1905 when the Agriculture College, Experiment Station, and School of Science became simply the State College of Washington, the still recognizable campus core was solidly built. By 1959 when the name was again changed to Washington State University, the campus had dramatically increased its size and would continue to do so. Continuous federal funding for programs in agriculture, engineering, and the sciences is manifest in the number of buildings devoted to these departments. But expansion of all departments has taken place in the modern era with general education becoming an important goal of the university.

Architects for the campus buildings have continued to come from all over the state. The visitor will recognize firm names and design formats that are represented on most of the state's higher education campuses. For years the college architect gave general direction to campus development. The post was occupied by Stanley A. Smith, architect for Waller (2) and Wilmer-Davis (14) halls, who was succeeded in 1955 by Philip Keene and after 1972 by Earl L. Muir—now called facilities planning director. Among the campus buildings, the following have been selected for their architectural interest; the visitor may well find others equally interesting. A very complete campus map is available at the information kiosk, and in the following sequence the numbers in brackets are keyed to the 1979 edition of this map. We begin at the Stadium Way entrance.

1   Stephenson Residence Complex, 1969
    (174)
    Walker & McGough

1 Stephenson Residence Complex. Photo: Gordon Peery

2   **Waller Hall,** 1935 (200)
     Stanley A. Smith

3   **Stimson Hall,** 1922 (177)
     Rudolph Weaver
     Waller and Stimson are two of the few re-
     maining older campus buildings in the Col-
     legiate Georgian mode.

4 Physical Sciences Building (courtesy of WSU)

3 Stimson Hall (courtesy of WSU)

5 Fine Arts Center. Photo: Morley Baer

6   **French Administration Building,** 1967 (3)
     Kirk/Wallace/McKinley

4   **Physical Sciences Building,** 1973 (142)
     Naramore, Bain, Brady & Johanson
     A very urban looking importation in the
     Brutalist-Formalist mode.

5   **Fine Arts Center,** 1973 (68)
     Naramore, Bain, Brady & Johanson
     A notable late Brutalist design.

At this juncture the great echelon of
building volumes along Stadium Way
demands recognition. The range of
rather banal-looking dormitory blocks
to the northwest connected across the
highway by spindly pedestrian bridges
has a powerful automobile-age gateway

effect which is picked up across the way by two bold new structures, Physical Sciences (4) and Fine Arts (5).

7   **Coliseum,** 1973 (35)
     John Graham & Co.

8   **Regents Hill Dormitory,** 1952 (152)
     Paul Thiry

8 Regents Hill Dormitory (courtesy of WSU)

11 Avery Hall (courtesy of WSU)

9   **Holland Library,** 1950 (106)
     John Maloney

10   **Bryan Hall,** 1909 (24)

11   **Avery Hall,** 1971 (17)
     Fred Bassetti

     An interesting understated application of the architect's favorite Neo-Liberty Style, designed to harmonize with the old quad.

12   **Stevens Hall,** 1896 (176)
     Stephen & Josenhans

13   **Thompson Hall,** 1895, 1968 (189)
     Stephen & Josenhans; remodeled by DeNeff, Deeble, Barton

     Thompson and Stevens are the two oldest buildings on campus; their setting gives an idea of the old campus core located on the ridge above town.

13 Thompson Hall (courtesy of WSU)

14   **Wilmer-Davis Halls,** 1936 (204)
     Stanley A. Smith

15   **President's House,** 1912, 1967 (146)
     Rudolph Weaver; remodeled by Trogdon & Smith

Walla Walla

The history of Walla Walla is closely tied to that of early white settlement in the Washington Territory and Indian-white relations during that period. The area lay on the pioneer route west first trekked by Lewis and Clark. Beginning with Fort Nez Percé, established in 1818 by the North West Company as its principal fur trading post on the Columbia, various military outposts were located on the Walla Walla River at or near its confluence with the Columbia. The Whitman Mission at Waiilatpu was nearby. In the aftermath of the Whitman Massacre, the so-called Indian Uprisings beginning in 1855 sparked the establishment the next year of Fort Walla Walla on the present site, the third to bear that name. The buildings were constructed between 1858 and 1906. About seven of them are still in use by the Veterans Administration Hospital which now occupies part of the original site. Nearby in Fort Walla Walla Park is the Pioneer Village, a collection of log and frame buildings moved here from other sites and furnished with local heirlooms and artifacts by the Walla Walla Valley Pioneer and Historical Society. Though all buildings share the same primitive technology, there are interesting variations in construction which give a good idea of the types of pioneer vernacular dwellings in the Northwest. Above the village, the agricultural museum features a spectacular 1920s combine, harnessed to thirty-three fiberglass mules by means of the famous Shenandoah hitch by which one man could control the entire team.

Following the discovery in 1860 of the Clearwater River goldfields in Idaho, Walla Walla reached a population of 3,500 to become the largest city in the Washington Territory. This initial growth was due largely to its position near the end of the Oregon Trail. Once the city had begun to grow, a series of gold rushes during the sixties kept it

Pioneer Village

Walla Walla in the 1870s (courtesy of Eastern Washington State Historical Society)

booming. Like Spokane later, Walla Walla was a major supply depot for the mining district and was also the winter resort of miners. As gold petered out, the city began to prosper as a center of Washington's agricultural industry because of its favorable location in the state's fabulous wheat-growing region. In addition to the usual market-center functions, considerable manufacturing developed, particularly of farm machinery. In 1875, Dr. D. S. Baker constructed a steam railway linking Walla Walla to Wallula on the Columbia River. The combination of railroad, river barge, and schooner made it possible to ship Walla Walla wheat to the world.

In the 1890s the arrival of the transcontinental railroad ushered in an era of great prosperity for eastern Washing-

ton, but Walla Walla began to lose its regional leadership position. The railroads chose to cross the Rockies well to the north thus triggering the growth of Spokane at the expense of the older center. Not until years later did a mainline connection tie Walla Walla into the national transportation network. Slower growth and relative age had advantages. By 1910, as a city of 20,000, it boasted a major educational institution, Whitman College, and such cultural amenities as a symphony orchestra and an opera house. The next decade brought substantial population decline. Subsequent ups and downs have left Walla Walla a notably pleasant and comfortable small city with an architectural heritage which its inhabitants have come to value.

Whitman Mission in 1843 (courtesy of Eastern Washington State Historical Society)

Whitman Mission, 1836–47
Seven miles west of Walla Walla, south off U.S. 12

The Whitman Mission visitor center contains a museum with exhibits about the history of missionary activity in the Northwest. Self-guiding foot trails lead to the mission site where the reconstructed foundation walls bear witness to the 1836 mission, one of the earliest in the Northwest. Here the visitor can reconstruct the brief eleven-year existence of the mission, and the Whitman family's life and work there, both terminated by the massacre. This tragedy spurred Congress to establish the Oregon Territory in 1848. Though the site has no architectural significance, a knowledge of its history contributes to an understanding of local history.

In Walla Walla proper, considerable worthy architecture remains.

1 **Andrews Livery Stable,** c. 1880
927 W Alder Street

A plain, rectangular wooden barn made very important by the addition of a Mission Revival Style false front.

2 **St. Patrick's Roman Catholic Church,** 1881
South side of W Alder between Sixth and Seventh Avenues

A Gothic Revival church in brick; next door is the Central Catholic High School, an interesting eclectic work. The school's older part on Seventh Avenue is an Art Deco block with industrial steel-sash windows.

3 **Walla Walla County Courthouse,** 1915–16
Osterman & Siebert
W Main Street between Fifth and Sixth Avenues

A fine expression of the eclectic Classic design that testifies yet again to the broadly influential training of the Ecole des Beaux Arts. The limestone exterior complements an interior of black-veined white marble and a handsome stairway of golden oak. Next to the courthouse is the notable, if not very believable, Neo-Classic jail.

4 **Dacres Hotel**
Fourth Avenue and W Main Street

When completed, the Dacres was considered as fine as any hotel in the country. Somewhat altered in the early 1900s, it has remained virtually the same since then and was in operation till 1963.

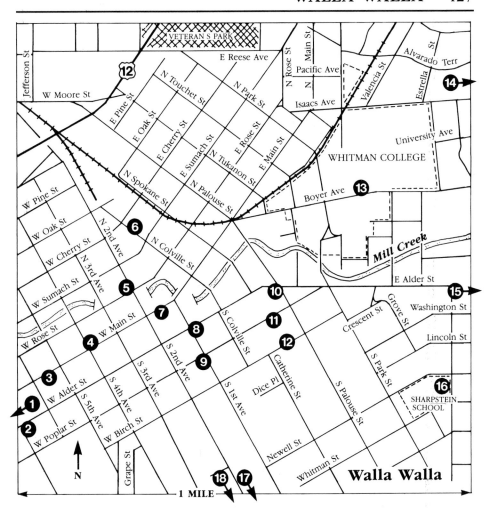

Walla Walla

5   **Marcus Whitman Hotel,** 1928
    Sherwood D. Ford
    107 N Second Avenue
    A Moderne Style hotel by a prominent Seattle
    firm.

6   **William Kirkman House,** c. 1876
    214 N Colville Street
    A bracketed, Italianate villa with ornamental
    quoins and a porch that curves around two
    ground-floor bays. The house was built for
    one of the first families in Walla Walla,
    whose fortune came from cattle-raising and
    meat-packing.

7   **Nineteenth Century Commercial Blocks**
    E Main Street, First to Second Avenues
    The old central business district along Main
    Street has retained a remarkable number of its
    nineteenth century business buildings. At
    present some of them stand sadly vacant, but
    a lot of practical and well-designed rehabilita-
    tion has taken place. Noteworthy at this writ-
    ing are: the present Ellis Hotel on the south-
    east corner of Second and Main; 9 to 25 East
    Main, a fine block with a backside that has
    been muralized in a festive and appropriately
    architectural way; 10 to 16 East Main, the
    Seil Building; and across the street past the

6 William Kirkman house

12 Houses, 1896–c. 1910
W Birch Street between Catherine and S
Palouse Streets

The prime turn-of-the-century residential
district in this area with some of the finest
Colonial Revival houses to be seen in the
state. They are enhanced by broad avenues
lined with vintage trees. Along the north side
of East Birch Street and clustered at the intersection with South Palouse are a variety of
Colonial Revival houses. The most gracious
and lavishly detailed are on the southwest and
northwest corners of West Birch and South
Palouse. At 208 South Palouse is an equally
fine example of the Queen Anne villa, from
1896.

216 S Palouse Street

intersection of Second Avenue the Die Brucke
Building, with the Liberty Theater in Neo-
Chinese next door.

8   Baumeister Block, 1889
SE corner E Alder and S First Avenue
Another rehabilitated commercial building.

9   Pacific Northwest Bell Co., c. 1930
SW corner E Poplar and S First Avenue
Zigzag Moderne, the bona fide local example.

10 Public Library, 1905
S Palouse and E Alder Streets

A stock Carnegie Library design, well sited
from an urban design standpoint. Across East
Alder is the First Congregational Church in a
Georgian Revival mode, and on the opposite
corner the Central Lutheran Church in the
Romanesque Revival mode. Together, the
three early twentieth century buildings create
a dignified civic complex, disparate in style
but harmonious in scale.

11 Michael B. Ward House, c. 1876
224 E Poplar Street

A late bracketed Italianate house with a central hall plan and overtones of the Colonial
Revival.

208 S Palouse Street

13 Whitman College, 1899-present

Chartered in 1859 as the Whitman Seminary and named by the Reverend Cushing Eells in memory of his missionary colleagues, Marcus and Narcissa Whitman, it became Whitman College in 1882, and is the oldest institution of higher learning in the state. The Memorial Building at 345 Boyer Avenue, designed by G. W. Babcock, is an 1899 Romanesque Revival structure of cream-colored brick and sandstone. With its clock tower, rusticated round-arched entrance, bold dormers, and generally monumental scale, the design exhibits those features of Henry H. Richardson's complex and rich vocabulary of forms which were most commonly borrowed for export to faraway places. The elm-bordered stretch of Boyer on which the Memorial Building faces is laced on the opposite side by a meandering creek punctuated by pools inhabited by ducks.

13 Cordiner Hall. Photo: Roberge Studio

In 1909 a Greater Whitman Master Plan for 1,100 students was executed by the Portland firm of Raymond & Lawrence. Conceived by Dean Archer Hendrick, the plan laid out a quad system which has been loosely followed. The main quad behind the Memorial Building is the traditional academic common. Other buildings to seek out are the Harper Joy Theater (1958), a pleasantly informal, wood-topped, concrete structure by Harold Crawford; Cordiner Hall (1969), a very formalistic design by Seattle's Naramore, Bain, Brady & Johanson; and Sherwood Center (1968), a Brutalist concrete palisade by Thomas Adkison of Spokane which serves as the Physical Education and Recreation Building.

13 Sherwood Center. Photo: Roland C. Colliander

14 Walla Walla Community College, 1974, 1976

Environmental Concern, Inc.; Gessel/Smith/Mosman; Brooks/Hensley/Creager
500 Tausick Way

The first phase of this campus, the academic core facility, was designed to make expansion possible by the removal of perimeter walls; the interior design also featured a movable wall system. Phase two, a vocational facility, is composed of relocatable, precast concrete exhibition modules moved here from Spokane's Expo '74, chiefly the Republic of China Pavilion, originally designed by

14 Walla Walla Community College

Brooks/Hensley/Creager. The latter was moved almost in its entirety; the other five were acquired as structural shells. What catches the motorist's eye is the gleaming geodesic dome in the campus foreground, the most visible bit of Bucky Fuller influence in the Northwest.

15 **Pioneer Park**
Bounded by E Alder, S Roosevelt, Whitman, and Division Streets

A place of green, green grass and dappled shade, this park square is planted with exotic and native trees and flowers in the best turn-of-the-century urban park tradition. A Craftsman Style building serves the Walla Walla Garden Club.

16 **Sharpstein School,** 1898
410 Howard Street

Walla Walla's oldest school is a handsome double Italianate block with a central tower on one end.

17 **Max Baumeister House,** 1900
Stone Street and Edwards Drive

A transitional design combining the Colonial Revival with a Craftsman top.

18 **Ben Stone House,** 1909
1415 Modoc Street

Based on a "$5,000 Fireproof House" by Frank Lloyd Wright published in *Ladies' Home Journal* in 1908. Stone had a Portland firm, possibly Bennes, Hendricks & Tobbey, adapt the plans for his use.

Glossary of Architectural Styles

Architectural sightseers, like birdwatchers, generally delight in classifying the species of building they are looking at. Unfortunately buildings have a way of not conforming as precisely to their style as do products designed by nature. There are more sports in architecture than in nature and there is consequently more confusion about what style to call them. This means that the whole business should not be taken too seriously. Still, it is possible to categorize major stylistic trends and through the process to date buildings and consequently understand how a given piece of the environment was developed. There are by now many published style guides that deal broadly with architectural development for the United States in general. The following list attempts to deal with the sequence of architecture in the Northwest and particularly in the state of Washington. The user is welcome to disagree with the categories and descriptions below. Over the years the authors have found that such disagreements provide some of the liveliest entertainment that architecture offers.

Nineteenth Century Styles

Pioneer, 1850s to 1870s

During the period of early settlement before the railroad era, virtually all buildings were made of logs. The cabins that housed the early pioneer homesteaders, and frequently served commercial and other needs as well, represent not so much a style as a building type resulting from primitive technology. The most familiar structure was that in which round or hewn logs notched at the ends—Lincoln logs—were stacked horizontally and made weathertight with clay or reinforced mud. Log structures were built throughout the state during this whole period.

Granary, Fort Nisqually (courtesy of City of Tacoma)

O. B. McFadden house, Chehalis (courtesy of State Office of Archaeology and Historic Preservation)

Classic and Gothic Revival, 1850s to 1880s

By the time Washington had areas of sufficient population density to achieve the kind of architectural sophistication provided by pattern books and more advanced technology, the mid-century Classic Revival phase, Greek and Roman influenced, had run its course in the rest of the country except in provincial areas. The picturesque phase of the Gothic Revival was being widely disseminated, also by pattern books. One of the most influential, Alexander Jackson Downing's *The Architecture of Country Residences* (1850), spawned similar works that collectively had a major impact on western building. Still, the sawmills and skilled carpenters who could produce these stylish buildings tended to be found in urbanized areas such as those around Puget Sound. Although there are few pure versions of either style, the Downingesque cottage was more often faithfully reproduced. Unfortunately its distinctive jigsawn ornament was too fragile to last unless well maintained. The most common survivor from this period is a simple wood-frame structure, also built of brick in some areas, combining both Classic and Gothic elements. Even if nonresidential these buildings have a residential scale. They vary greatly in amount of detail and are often so simplified as to have little stylistic identity. As a basic vernacular this eclectic style continued well into the 1870s, but today is a rare type in the state.

Characteristics:

Rectangular, gable-roofed volumes of one or two stories, with horizontal emphasis.

Roof with a low or a high pitch depending on whether the emphasis is Classic or Gothic.

Symmetrical with a balanced disposition of openings. Even side hall plans tend to be regular as though they were half of a symmetrical composition.

Broad entablatures, occasionally with moldings and/or dentils.

Gable ends form a Classic triangular pediment sometimes with a full cornice molding and sometimes with the horizontal cornice broken in the central section, leaving only short returns at the eaves.

Engaged piers or pilasters at the corners or broad corner boards to suggest same.

Windows and doors sometimes have classically detailed frames or surrounds, but more often are plain.

Entrances sometimes have side and transom lights.

Decorative detail and general format is often Classic in the broad sense, including American Georgian and Federal elements.

Rothschild house, Port Townsend

Commanding officer's quarters, Fort Simcoe (courtesy of State Office of Archaeology and Historic Preservation)

Ecclesiastical Gothic Revival, 1850s to 1920s

Whereas the Gothic Revival Style went in and out of fashion in residential architecture, it was an enduring style for church architecture from the pioneer to the modern period. The early churches of brick or wood were usually built from pattern books often furnished by the established parishes back east. These were gable-roofed structures with an emphasis on high vertical volumes and a bell tower either over a side entrance or atop the roof over the entrance. The churches varied in their degree of architectural sophistication and complexity depending on the location and the wealth of the parish. In the early twentieth century, designs often incorporated other stylistic elements from a variety of other styles such as the California Mission Revival, the Georgian Colonial Revival, which appeared also in the 1920s and 1930s, and the Craftsman Style. Academic standards of correctness also affected ecclesiastical architecture around the turn of the century and later when Gothic was differentiated into such styles as French, English, Perpendicular, and so forth. Churches were then often copied from specific European prototypes in France, England, Germany, and other countries. Although the style ranges over a variety of forms and decorative motifs, certain identifying characteristics persist.

Characteristics:

Volumes covered by high-pitched, gable roofs.

Use of the pointed arch for openings and in interior structural and decorative forms; more academically correct buildings have buttresses.

Use of the Gothic decorative vocabulary: pinnacles, crockets, finials, stylized animal and foliate forms, crenellated roof parapets.

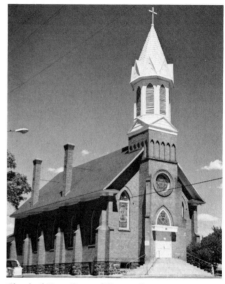

Church of Mary Queen of Heaven, Sprague

St. James Catholic Church, Vancouver

Italianate, late 1870s to 1880s

A style derived originally from early nineteenth century romantic paintings of the north Italian landscape that depicted a towered farmhouse or villa. The building's irregular profile supposedly reflected the informality of nature. This picturesque image and its building form were enthusiastically appropriated by A. J. Downing and others for the American landscape. Called an Italianate villa, this type was quite popular all over the East in the 1860s; it is not well represented in the Northwest. In fact, the style has not survived in any developed form in Washington, although there are certainly buildings identifiable as Italianate through certain signature details such as bracketed roof eaves.

William Kirkman house, Walla Walla

Characteristics:

Emphasis on the vertical in volumes and openings.

Broadly projected roofs supported by ornamental brackets, sometimes paired.

Frequent use of polygonal bays.

Occasional use of quoins on corners and colonnettes between bay windows.

Occasional towers or cupolas with hipped roofs.

French Second Empire, or Mansard, 1870s to 1880s

A rare style in Washington that has mostly survived in rather small houses with Classic detail that incorporate a Mansard roof. The style was briefly in vogue for institutional buildings but none have survived in any well-developed form. The addition of a Mansard roof was a convenient way of modernizing a house without changing its basic form.

Frank A. Bartlett house, Port Townsend

Eastlake–Queen Anne, 1880s to 1900

Charles Eastlake was an English architect whose American influence was broad indeed if we count the extensive use of his name in connection with home building and furnishing. His book, *Hints on Household Taste*, first published in London in 1868 and in New York in 1872, went through many American editions and spawned a school of design that was the height of fashion around 1880. In the West the style mutated into a decorative vocabulary elaborated by the lumber industry's advanced tool technology. This vocabulary consisted largely of flat-sawn, often incised, stylized motifs with a linear, two-dimensional character that bespoke the use of mechanical equipment. Since Eastlake advocated a return to the preindustrial hand-crafted furniture and interiors of the Middle Ages, he was properly outraged when the editors of a San Francisco architectural periodical wrote him of the identification of his name with the much decorated houses of that city. His rejection of the authorship of the style was to no avail since his name continued to be used. Eastlake ornament was applied to furniture as well as houses of different forms. One of its most consistent uses was in the surface treatment of a house design called Elizabethan. This was a wooden imitation of the medieval half-timbered house with decorative terra cotta tiling that served as a historic prototype for the architects of the English Domestic Revival movement. In the United States the most admired and published work of this movement was by Richard Norman Shaw. On the east coast, Shaw's manor houses for the English industrial barons were a source of inspiration for such architects as Henry Hobson Richardson. The vernacular flowering of the Shavian influence on the west coast produced not only a nineteenth century sub-style, but also an enduring design format that surfaced again and again, as we shall see.

Characteristics:

Vertical emphasis with high-peaked, gable roofs that often have turned-wood cross braces in the gable and decorated barge boards.

An overall decorative surface treatment that uses structural members to frame decorative panels and to mimic half-timbering.

A variety of flat-sawn, linear motifs both incised and cut out like stencils, used singly or in layers; turned knobs applied singly or in series. Heavily decorated porches with turned posts, open-work railings, and roof brackets or braces. In modest versions of the style, ornament is usually confined to the gable end of the roofs and the porches.

E. J. Roberts house, Spokane

L. M. Hidden house, Vancouver

Queen Anne Revival, mid-1880s to early 1900s

An eclectic style that originated in England taking its name from the architecture of a transitional period in which Classical ornament was applied to buildings still medieval in form. The most famous English designer in this style, Richard Norman Shaw, worked increasingly in the public sphere during his long career, producing buildings that abandoned medieval imagery. In the United States the style followed that of Shaw's early manor houses but acquired a life of its own as the climactic flowering of the picturesque. Built in a spreading, gracious, and informal style, the towered villas with wrap-around living porches also evoked the old adage, "A man's home is his castle." These exuberant castles were mostly fortified against pernicious city influences. Their anti-urban stance indicated that they were a refuge from the rigors of business in the city. Although at their best in a pastoral setting, they were also compressed with or without a vestigial tower and porch into a town house form and set on narrow suburban lots. Under the influence of the Colonial Revival, with its horizontal emphasis and lavish use of shingles as decorative sheathing, a new style developed known as the Shingle Style with a mimimal use of Classical detail and a more embellished Georgian Revival mode. Interior plans were much more open with a great central living and circulation space—called a living hall, because it contained both a fireplace and a grand staircase—flowing freely into other ground floor rooms. Even the compressed Queen Anne often has a reduced version of the living hall with a stairway if not a fireplace.

Characteristics:

Irregular plans, elevations, and roof silhouettes.

Vertical emphasis at first, later horizontal.

Textured surface usually differentiated on each floor, with channeled siding on the raised basement and varieties of cut shingles on the upper floors. The popular fish-scale shingles are an imitation of the terra cotta tiling used on the English houses. Porches and balconies are embellished with a lavish use of spindle, spool, and lattice work. There is also considerable use of Classical detail, columns, pilasters, dentil courses, and moldings; the late Queen Anne–Colonial Revival type uses only Classical detail.

Stained glass and leaded, beveled glass windows.

Towers with various roof forms.

208 S Palouse Street, Walla Walla

Bucklin house, Seattle

Romanesque Revival, late 1880s to 1900

The style often bears the name of Henry Hobson Richardson, who created a personal version of it for his Trinity Church in Boston (1872). Richardson's work in the idiom also included influential homes, libraries, railroad stations, the famous Allegheny County Courthouse (1884–88), and the renowned Marshall Field Warehouse in Chicago (1885). The style came west with the railroads from Chicago and other midwestern cities such as Minneapolis and St. Paul. Never a rigid formula, it fused with other picturesque styles such as the Queen Anne and found wide use in ecclesiastical, governmental, and other types of institutional structures.

Smith Tower Annex, Seattle

Characteristics:

Irregular plans, elevations, and silhouettes, with a horizontal emphasis. Low, round towers; hip or gable roofs; sometimes parapeted, round bays.

Broad, round arches with deeply recessed, cavernous entranceways; arcades; windows often banded with deep reveals and stone mullions; squat, round columns and bands of colonnettes.

Rock-face masonry walls sometimes with a pattern of colored stone.

A heavy and massive character.

Peter Kirk Building, Kirkland

Chicago School Commercial, 1885 to 1910

Named for Chicago because the enormous demand for commercial buildings in the constricted downtown area at the end of the nineteenth century brought the style to its full development in the hands of such architects as William Le Baron Jenney, Louis Sullivan, William Holabird and Martin Roche, and Daniel Burnham and John Wellborn Root. Called skyscrapers, these tall commercial buildings were usually between six and twenty stories, an achievement made possible by the invention of the elevator and other technological developments such as the fireproof skeletal steel frame with wind bracing and foundation improvements. Ornament was usually minimized, the structural frame was expressed, and more glass was used. A standard feature was the so-called Chicago window, with a fixed central pane of glass and casement windows on either side for ventilation. In the Northwest, though few buildings even approached fifteen stories, the taller office buildings reflected the Chicago innovations. Ornamental detail, if any, was concentrated around the entrance and at the roof line. Romanesque geometric and foliate forms and the related but more refined Sullivanesque ornament were the typical surface decorations. Cast panels of ornament were available by mail order catalogues from the Midwest. Early twentieth century buildings are more stark and stripped of historic ornament.

Characteristics:

Strong modular character through expression of the structural frame. Masonry cladding.

Ornament restricted to ground floor entrance "belt cornices" and roof cornice; spandrels sometimes have decorative panels.

Geometric and foliate ornament often with grotesques of animal or human form. Architectural enrichment often only on the main or street facade.

Old City Hall, Tacoma

Maynard Building, Seattle

Twentieth Century Styles

Colonial Revival, 1900 to 1920

Interest in the country's colonial past whetted by the centennial gradually produced a vernacular house type that was more Georgian or late Federal than Classic. This type was the mainstay of streetcar suburbs all over the country. In the Northwest, it is best represented in Seattle, where it has been nicknamed the "Classic Box." Although the type has a great range of enrichment, its boxy form and hip roof, typically with a central attic dormer and broadly overhanging, bracketed eaves, are its chief identifying elements. Another colonial type, more faithful to the New England or Dutch farmhouse, has a gambrel roof.

Characteristics:

Simple, rectangular volumes giving a strong boxlike form.

Symmetrical, balanced facades.

Hip or gambrel roofs usually with brackets; the eaves of the hip roofs often have elaborate scroll brackets or modillions.

Shingles or horizontal drop siding, often with wide boards milled to imitate the narrow clapboards of colonial times.

Classical detail: columns, pilasters, cornices, door and window frames with moldings, entablatures, dentil courses; sometimes a use of decorative plaster cartouches on walls and enriched consoles to support a stepped-out upper story.

Windows with upper sections of leaded, diamond-paned sash; also foliate patterns in beveled glass, and sometimes Moorish keyhole windows.

Isaac Stevens School, Seattle

A. D. Austin house, Everett

Prairie School, 1905 to 1920

A style originating in the work of Frank Lloyd Wright around 1900 in the Chicago area that was publicized by the *Ladies' Home Journal* and broadcast across the country by builders and contractors using house plans or pattern books. In Washington it was an easy variation on the Classic Box since it used the same form. The Seattle practice of Andrew Willatsen, who worked in Wright's Chicago office, produced Prairie School houses that rose above the level of the vernacular and helped popularize the style. Although equally in vogue as a commercial and institutional style in other parts of the country, its use in the Northwest was primarily residential.

Characteristics:

A strong, blocky form with a low-pitched hip or gable roof with boxed eaves.

Exterior surface of stucco, horizontal siding, or shingles.

Strong horizontal emphasis with openings set in bands sometimes tied together by continuous moldings; bands of windows placed directly under the roof soffit.

E. E. Vogue house, Seattle

Symmetrical, balanced facades sometimes with ground-floor wings or porches on either side.

Windows with geometric patterns achieved by arrangement of the muntins or by use of leaded glass.

Projecting sections of walls which rise above the second-floor level to form closed-in balconies.

Thin wood strips set in geometric patterns on wooden panels.

Black house, Seattle

Craftsman, or Arts & Crafts, 1900 to 1920

Kin to both the Colonial Revival and the Prairie School styles, the Craftsman aesthetic was best expressed by the *Craftsman* magazine, published in New York from 1901 to 1917 under the direction of Gustav Stickley. The finest flowering of the style occurred in California in the work of the Greene brothers and the development of the California bungalow by such practitioners as the Heineman brothers. In general the Craftsman house or bungalow strived for an informal, hand-crafted look through the use of natural materials and asymmetrical elevations. Interiors had inglenooks, over-scaled fireplaces, alcoves, built-in furniture, and an extensive use of wood paneling and wainscoting—all features intended to promote intimacy or coziness and a feeling of living in touch with nature.

Characteristics:

Boxy forms with low-pitched gable roofs usually braced with exposed roof rafters that are often false and not real projections of structural members.

Asymmetrical elevations and informal plans.

Exterior sheathed in stucco, wood shingles, or board and batten; decorative half-timbering or expressed structural members; and combinations of these with clinker brick or river boulders.

Massive front porches with tapered porch posts and over-scaled trusses in gable roofs.

Shed-roofed dormers with exposed rafter ends.

Lower wall sections and porch bases often battered to suggest the house rising out of the earth; low stone walls sometimes continue the porch base along the entrance walk.

Exaggerated chimneys of clinker brick, rock-face stone, or river boulders.

1622 40th Avenue, Seattle

Wells house, Wenatchee

Tudor Revival,
or English Arts & Crafts,
1900 to 1920

The English Arts & Crafts movement came to the Northwest via Canada, where it made a great impression. Architects such as Samuel Maclure, who practiced in British Columbia, designed houses that are closely related to the work of Washington architect Kirtland Kelsey Cutter and the firm of Bebb & Mendel. Visually these predominantly half-timbered houses also derive from the work of Richard Norman Shaw and the English Domestic Revival movement in the 1860s and 1870s. Although in Canada and British Columbia the picturesque medievalizing influence stamped a variety of building types, in Washington its use was chiefly residential for an affluent clientele.

St. Patrick's Rectory and Office, Seattle

Characteristics:

Long rectangular forms more horizontal than vertical with gable roofs.

Rock-faced ashlar masonry on the lower floor and half-timbering on the upper floor; the latter serves both as a romantic, historic reference and as a decorative wall surface.

Massive stone or brick chimneys.

Casement windows with diamond-paned sash; a use of stained glass in the more opulent houses, emulating or actually using Tiffany designs.

Interiors with living halls, inglenooks, alcoves, and bays all sheathed in rich wood paneling with occasional use of decorative plasterwork imitating Tudor ceilings.

Park-like, gardenesque settings.

John Leary house, Seattle

California Mission and Spanish Colonial Revival, 1910 to 1930

Moving directly up from California, this style was readily adopted in Washington even though no Spanish missions had ever figured in the area's past. The usually light-colored stuccoed buildings with arches or arcades, a curved false gable, tile roofs, and occasional towers served a variety of functions from railroad stations to governmental buildings and apartment houses. Essentially a romantic, picturesque style with few identifying elements, the mission influence gradually gave way to a general Mediterranean image using the same materials but incorporating Spanish or Italian villa detail. In the 1920s Mediterranean and Renaissance Revival styles fused to create a general period revival type called a "California house." The earlier phase was often asymmetrically composed; the later more balanced and symmetrical.

University Heights Elementary School, Seattle

Snohomish County Courthouse, Everett

Characteristics:

Two-story, rectangular buildings with the ground floor often extended as an arcaded porch or as wings with round arched openings.

Stuccoed surfaces, light colored.

Decorative wood elements in the form of false projecting beam ends or brackets.

Wooden balconies.

Tile roofs. The Mission Revival always uses a curved false gable; the Mediterranean style generally has a gabled or hipped roof. Tiled pent roofs often project from walls over windows or doors. The real Mission Revival nearly always uses a star-shaped or pointed quatrefoil window in the gable end.

General use of the broad, round arch.

Later decorative motifs taken from Moorish architecture.

Beaux Arts,
Eclectic Classicism, 1900 to 1930

The Ecole des Beaux Arts was established in the Napoleonic period in Paris. Following the Civil War it became increasingly fashionable for American architects to seek training there. The aesthetic doctrine and teaching techniques of the Ecole were then introduced into U.S. schools of architecture with the result that American architecture became as dominated by the French academy as that of France. Characterized by the use of the Classical vocabulary of forms, the general design approach was eclectic, using Greek, Roman, and Renaissance architecture as references. Beaux Arts principles of design held sway into the 1930s. However, the style evolved from a ponderous, bombastic phase around the turn of the century to a quieter, simpler mode. Although no examples of the earlier phase exist in Washington, the later mode became the almost universal style for governmental institutions, libraries, and banks. Other kinds of commercial buildings such as the tall office buildings of the teens and twenties, hotels, and department stores were also dressed in a variety of Neo-Classic forms that might all be loosely labeled Beaux Arts.

Characteristics:

Colonnaded temple-form buildings sometimes with pavilion ends and central domed rotundas resulting in a formal, symmetrical, and hierarchical composition for the building mass.

Symmetrically composed facade with a triple horizontal division: a base (usually rusticated), a middle zone, and an attic zone. This division applies equally to low, horizontal buildings such as small libraries and to tall office buildings.

Use of the Classical orders—Doric, Ionic, Corinthian—and composite columns singly and in pairs with a predilection for colonnades and porticoes reached by broad flights of steps.

Round arched openings set in recessed areas with columns to either side either singly or in a series to form columned arcades.

Full entablatures sometimes enriched with anthemions, urns, balustrades, and a variety of Classical surface ornament such as decorative swags and cartouches.

Lavish interiors with colonnades, rotundas, branching stairs, and monumental spaces; even modest buildings have a more or less grand central lobby.

Land Title Building, Ellensburg

Everett High School

Classical, or P.W.A. Moderne, 1930 to 1941

Beaux Arts design stripped of its Classical ornament but maintaining the composition and massing of the Beaux Arts–inspired buildings. The style was the hallmark of the Public Works Administration which attempted to ease unemployment during the depression through large and small construction projects.

Characteristics:

Basic Classical composition.

Piers used instead of columns, occasionally fluted but with no capitals or bases.

Fenestration in vertical, recessed panels.

Smooth surfaces in stone, terra cotta, marble, or concrete.

Use of low relief, cast sculpture, and ornamental friezes around openings and on spandrels.

Non-Classic decorative vocabulary using Art-Deco motifs.

City Hall, Everett

Armory, Olympia (courtesy of State Office of Archaeology and Historic Preservation)

Art Deco, or Zigzag, and Streamline Moderne, 1920 to 1941

The French spelling of the word was taken over, like the term Art Deco, from the 1925 Exposition Internationale des Arts Décoratifs et Industriels Modernes held in Paris. The thrust of the exposition was toward the future and an artistic expression to complement the machine age. The past was definitely spurned. Essentially a system of decoration, Art Deco motifs were applied to all designed objects including clothing, jewelry, and furniture as well as the interiors and exteriors of buildings. The essential motifs—zigzags, chevrons, parallel lines, and stylized vegetation—came from all kinds of cultural sources, some of them filtered through Cubist painting and some, for example, taken straight from North American Indian art. The ornament could be rich and bold or quite abbreviated, depending on space and budget. By the 1930s the style had turned to aerodynamic forms in an attempt to reflect the new transportation technology. Curved forms loosely adapted from ocean liners and airplanes changed the angular look of the earlier Art Deco. Also called Modernistic and just plain Modern, the forms characterized mainstream American architecture until World War II.

Characteristics: Art Deco

Smooth volumes squared off at the top or parapeted with fenestration in recessed vertical strips.

Stepped, pyramidal towers sometimes rising out of blocky horizontal bases and sometimes soaring straight up from the ground.

Multiple references to the forms of mountains, ziggurats, and Mayan temples.

Use of smooth-faced stone, terra cotta, and metal for exterior cladding with accents in terra cotta and glass.

Polychromy often an integral part of the design.

Medical Arts Building, Tacoma

Exchange Building, Seattle

Characteristics: Streamline Moderne

Smooth, light-toned, stuccoed forms often with rounded corners.

Strong horizontal emphasis with banded surfaces and windows.

Entranceways with curved walls.

Considerable use of glass brick, round windows to suggest portholes, and metal pipe railings—another nautical reference.

Metallic or glassy surfaces, usually vitrolight, a patented glass material.

KOMO Broadcasting Studio, Seattle. Photo: Jim Ball

Boeing Company Administration Building, Seattle (courtesy of Office of Urban Conservation)

International Style, late 1930s to early 1940s

This style was also represented at the Art Deco Exposition in Le Corbusier's Pavilion de l'Esprit Nouveau. It was christened by Henry Russell-Hitchcock and Philip Johnson in their book derived from the exhibit of European architecture held at the New York Museum of Modern Art in 1932 and titled *The International Style: Architecture since 1922.* Perhaps the major difference between the Moderne and the International Style lay in the latter's rejection of all ornament and heightened use of the Cubist aesthetic of intersecting and overlapping planes to achieve a sense of weightlessness.

Characteristics:

Light, horizontal volumes often cantilevered over the ground plane.

Horizontal, nonmassive character achieved through use of ribbon windows and glazed corners; walls and glazed surfaces kept in the same plane.

White stuccoed walls and flat roofs.

Thin vertical supports for upper floor decks with solid railings.

Nichols house, Seattle

Americanized International Style, the Modern Ranch House, late 1940s to 1970

The post-World War II, single family house was a fusion of several influences including the bungalow, Frank Lloyd Wright's Usonian houses of the 1930s, and the International Style houses of Le Corbusier and Mies van der Rohe. The form was also strongly influenced by the houses designed in this country by the European émigrés Walter Gropius and Marcel Breuer. Developed during an unprecedented demand for housing caused by the lack of building during the depression and World War II, this house at first reflected the still straitened budgets of the early postwar period. Thus in the late forties and early fifties, the house was a modest one-story pavilion of 1,500 to 2,500 square feet, usually set on a large lot in the rural-suburban fringe of the city. Generous use was made of glass to increase the sense of interior space, while outdoor decks and patios doubled as additional living rooms. This Modern house was most typically a post-and-beam structure with a flat or broad low-pitched gable or shed roof. Exposed structure, an expressive use of modern materials, and the incorporation of landscaped areas sometimes inside the house were the main contributing elements to the architectural character. As affluence increased, the house expanded over the

Surrey Downs, Bellevue

landscape, incorporating more courts and patios but usually preserving a one-floor plan, although multi-leveled houses were frequently built on hillside lots. Many architects practicing in the early postwar period designed houses for small tract developments. These were in turn copied and proliferated during the great suburbanization period. Often they were called ranch houses and even California ranch houses, revealing in these names a continuing nostalgia for a lost rural past.

Characteristics:

Wood frame, typically post-and-beam structure, expressed on exterior and interior.

Extensive use of glass in window walls and horizontal bands; glass sliding doors opening directly onto decks and patios.

Use of exterior and interior plywood; also exotic wood like teak.

Low-pitched, broadly spreading gable roofs and flat or shed roofs with wide overhangs.

Informal arrangement of intersecting volumes resulting in the so-called open plan that puts living, dining, and kitchen space together in one room. A typical plan has an H form with living and sleeping spaces divided by a corridor containing the entrance.

Separation between indoor and outdoor spaces minimized through use of glass and occasionally planted areas that appear to continue through glazed walls. House organized around a mechanical core with kitchen, laundry, and bath plumbing centralized.

Studio Apartments, Spokane

Americanized International Style, Corporate Structures, 1950s to 1960s

The curtain-walled office tower that originated in the 1920s designs of Mies van der Rohe was first achieved by the 1951–52 Lever House in New York, designed by Skidmore, Owings & Merrill. It became the most characteristic commercial structure of the postwar decades. This modular, thin-skinned structure with alternating metallic and glass panels enclosing a smooth horizontal or vertical rectangular volume expressed both the industrial age and the anonymity of the corporate world. By now there are innumerable variations on this structural theme.

Characteristics: General

A rectangular spatial volume often with a portion raised off the ground on slender steel stilts, creating a ground-level plaza. In the 1960s, metal curtain walls were frequently replaced by precast panel wall systems with decorative surface treatments that promoted a greater visual unity between the structural frame and the wall surface.

Characteristics: Early Phase

Vertical or horizontal rectangular volumes frequently with the front section on steel stilts to create a ground-level plaza.

Metal and glass curtain walls used to create a thin, fragile, planar surface and a cage-like effect through an emphasis on modularity.

Frequent use of blank masonry end walls; careful separation of the materials used for wall surfaces.

A strong, anonymous, industrial character.

Characteristics: Late Phase

Structural frame externalized.

Greater use of masonry frames.

Infill panels of concrete cast with decorative aggregate, textures, and patterns.

IBM Building, Tacoma

Faculty Center, University of Washington. Photo: Richard S. Heyza

Brutalism, 1960s to 1970s

A style that originated in monumental, sculptural buildings by Le Corbusier such as the apartment house in Marseilles, the Unité d'Habitation (1947–52), of "brut" or untreated concrete. As a stylistic term, Brutalism was first used to describe the work of the English architects Peter and Alison Smithson. Their goal was an honesty in structural, spatial, organizational, and material concepts that resulted in buildings judged elsewhere to be rude and ruthless. The original puritanical extremism of the early Brutalist buildings as represented by the Smithsons' Hunstanton School (1954), or Louis Kahn's Yale University Art Gallery (1952–52), merged with an international movement only superficially comparable. In the vernacular the style became an alternative to the thin-skinned curtain-wall style that preceded it. Like much of what is labeled Brutalist, the Northwest work that comes under this stylistic umbrella reflects more a Le Corbusier–inspired interest in plasticity of form and the expressive qualities of concrete than the tough-minded moral imperatives of the English school. That it has become style rather than ideology is witnessed by the fact that exposed mechanical systems, ducts, and pipes are now polychromed as decorative elements. Perhaps the late

Psychology Building, Central Washington University

phases of Brutalism are better described as Formalism, implying an expression of sculptural form for its own sake.

Characteristics:

Buildings with a high degree of plasticity and a variety of forms projected horizontally and vertically.

Emphasis on the raw expression of materials, particularly concrete.

Exposed mechanical system, pipes, vents, ducts, etc.

Openings as holes or voids, not part of the wall plane.

In late Brutalist or Formalist designs, brick often used as surface material.

Highways Administration Building, Olympia. Photo: Tom Upper

Residential styles,
late 1960s to present

Houses of the last fifteen or so years in Washington reveal a continuing interest in the traditional Northwest timber tradition, itself a reflection of northern European and Oriental timber traditions. The modular, post-and-beam pavilion type with a sweeping gable roof, broadly overhanging eaves, and an expressive use of joinery gave way in the early 1970s to a more volumetric composition either of multiple stacked boxy forms or of one box cut into and faceted in a cubistic way. The shed roof without overhangs replaced the sweeping gable form, and shingles were increasingly used as siding. Spatial flow changed from horizontal to vertical as houses acquired upper floor spaces often along diagonal axes. Heavily influenced by the contemporary work of Charles Moore, William Turnbull, Robert Venturi, and the New York 5, today's Northwest house is the product of a new eclecticism that makes it possible once more to rifle the past for forms and imagery. Recent issues such as energy conservation and a growing scarcity of timber constrain residential design in new ways.

House, Bellevue (see Bellevue, 12)

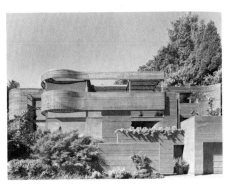

Gerald Williams house, Seattle

Builder's styles, circa 1920 to 1960s

Vernacular styles in Washington as elsewhere have followed mainstream developments, simplifying aspects of custom design for economy's sake, but preserving enough appropriate detail to be up to date. In general, the styles of the 1920s were period revival ranging from Georgian to a northeastern Colonial Revival type to Tudor Revival. Much of the stylistic identity was carried by the pitch of the roof, the plan type, and the choice of materials. Although the post–World War II house discarded its historicist detail, its form varied in similar ways. Two types stand out: one was a modified version of Frank Lloyd Wright's Usonian house, a kind of midwestern ranch type; the other reflected the California ranch type which had an almost parallel development in the Northwest. The current builder's residential styles exhibit the same trends toward eclectic forms that the custom designed house does. Current condominium vernacular styles reflect the shed-roofed, boxy forms that originated in the 1960s work of Moore/ Lyndon/Turnbull/Whitaker, notably the Sea Ranch Condominium on the northern California coast.

Characteristics:

1920s:

Georgian Revival: two-story boxy form; hip roof; central hall plan; wood clapboard or shingle siding; Classical detail.

English Cottage, or Tudor Revival: one and one-half story, central or side hall plan; high pitched gable roof, often with cross-gables; decorative half-timbering with wood or brick. This style continued into the 1930s.

1930s:

Colonial Revival: two-story rectangular form; gable or gambrel roof; central hall plan; Classical millwork elements; wood clapboard or shingle siding. There is also a *Colonial Bungalow* type of one story with horizontal siding and very little detail.

1950s:

Midwest Ranch House: one story, with off-center entrance in an L plan; hip roof; aluminum sash and corner windows; Roman brick veneer and stone base; prominent chimney; wrought iron detail.

California Ranch House: one-story rectangular L plan; low-pitched or gable roof; carport at one end; vertical wood siding; front porch at ground level; no steps; both large glass and ribbon glass windows.

Georgian Revival

Tudor Revival

Colonial Revival

Colonial Bungalow

California Ranch House

Midwest Ranch House

Sketches by Victor Steinbrueck

Selected Bibliography

American Institute of Architects. *Contemporary Architecture in Spokane, Washington.* Spokane: A.I.A. Spokane Chapter, 1967.

American Institute of Architects. *Spokane's Historic Architecture.* Spokane: Eastern Washington State Historical Society, 1978.

√ Andersen, Dennis A. "A John Parkinson Album." *Pacific Northwest Quarterly* 69 (April 1978): 71–74.

————. "Carl August Darmer: Architect for the City of Destiny." *Pacific Northwest Quarterly* 71 (January 1980): 24–30.

Anglin, Rob. "Report on Bungalows in Seattle." Submitted to the Office of Urban Conservation, City of Seattle, 1979.

Bal, Peggy. *Fairchild, Heritage of the Spokane Plains.* Spokane: privately printed, 1979.

Bean, Margaret. *Age of Elegance.* Spokane: Eastern Washington State Historical Society, 1968.

————. *Campbell House.* Spokane: Eastern Washington State Historical Society, 1965.

Board of Park Commissioners, Seattle. *Parks, Playgrounds, and Boulevards of Seattle, Washington.* Seattle: Pacific Press, 1909.

Brewster, David, and Rebecca Earnest. *The Seattle Book:* the Weekly's *Guide to Seattle.* Seattle: Madrona Publishers, 1978.

Calvert, Frank, ed. *Homes and Gardens of the Pacific Coast.* Vol. 1. Beaux Arts Society, 1913. Reprinted in 1974 by Christopher Laughlin, Historic Preservation Committee of Allied Arts of Seattle.

Clark, Norman H. *Mill Town: A Social History of Everett, Washington, from Its Earliest Beginnings on the Shores of Puget Sound to the Tragic and Infamous Event Known as the Everett Massacre.* Seattle: University of Washington Press, 1970.

————. *Washington: A History.* New York: W. W. Norton & Co., 1976.

Colliander, Roland, and others. *Spokane Sketchbook.* Seattle: University of Washington Press, 1974.

Cook, Jimmie Jean. *A Particular Friend, Penn's Cove.* Coupeville: Island County Historical Society, 1973.

Croly, Herbert. "The Building of Seattle: A City of Great Promise." *Architectural Record* 32 (1912): 1–21.

Cunningham, Michael. "A Photographic Comparison of Selected Northwest Residential Architecture of the 1940s and 1950s." Master's thesis, University of Washington, 1976.

Denison, Allen T., and Wallace K. Huntington. *Victorian Architecture of Port Townsend, Washington.* Seattle: Hancock House, 1978.

Dilgard, David, and Margaret Riddle. *A Survey of Everett's Historical Properties.* Everett: City of Everett Bicentennial Committee, 1976.

"Downtown Seattle Buildings." *The Quarterly* (U. of Washington College of Architecture and Urban Planning), Winter 1980.

Grey, Elmer. "The New Suburb of the Pacific Coast." *Scribner's Magazine* 52 (1912): 36–51.

"Houses of the Northwest." *Architectural Record* 113 (April 1953): 159–78.

Johnston, Norman J. "A Far Western Arts and Crafts Village." *Journal of the Society of Architectural Historians* 35 (March 1976): 51–54.

———. "The Frederick Law Olmsted Plan for Tacoma." *Pacific Northwest Quarterly* 66 (July 1975): 97–104.

Jones, John Paul. *The History and Development of the Present Campus Plan for the University of Washington*. Seattle, 1940.

Kirk, Ruth, and Richard D. Daugherty. *Exploring Washington Archaeology*. Seattle: University of Washington Press, 1978.

Knuth, Priscilla. "Picturesque Frontier: The Army's Fort Dalles." *Oregon Historical Quarterly* 67 (1966): 293–346, and 68 (1967): 5–52.

Kreisman, Lawrence. *Apartments by Anhalt*. Seattle: Office of Urban Conservation, 1978.

———. *Art Deco Seattle*. Seattle: Allied Arts, 1979.

LeWarne, Charles Pierce. *Utopias on Puget Sound, 1885–1915*. Seattle: University of Washington Press, 1975.

Lyndon, Donlyn. "Seattle: Metamorphosis from Fair into Center." *Progressive Architecture* 46 (July 1965): 196–202.

McKenzie, Roderick D. *On Human Ecology*. Chicago: University of Chicago Press, 1968.

Meinig, Donald M. *The Great Columbia Plain: A Historical Geography, 1805–1910*. Seattle: University of Washington Press, 1968.

Morgan, Murray. *Puget's Sound: A Narrative of Early Tacoma and the Southern Sound*. Seattle: University of Washington Press, 1979.

———. *Skid Road*. Rev. ed. New York: Viking Press, 1960. Comstock paperback edition, 1971.

Municipal Plans Committee. *Plan of Seattle: Report of the Municipal Plans Committee Submitting Report of Virgil G. Bogue, Engineer*. Seattle: Loman and Hanford Co., 1911.

Neil, J. Meredith. "Administrators, Architects, and Campus Development, 1890–1905." *Journal of the Society of Architectural Historians* 29 (May 1970): 144–55.

Nyberg, Folke G. *Seattle Urban Design Report*. Seattle: Department of Community Development, 1971.

———, and Victor Steinbrueck. *A Visual Inventory of Buildings and Urban Design Resources for Seattle, Washington*. Seattle: Historic Seattle Preservation and Development Authority, 1975–77.

Pomeroy, Earl. *The Pacific Slope*. Seattle: University of Washington Press, 1965.

Rogers, John L. "The Work of William J. Bain." *Architect and Engineer* 146 (August 1941): 16–37.

Sale, Roger. *Seattle, Past to Present*. Seattle: University of Washington Press, 1976.

Seattle, City of, Office of Urban Conservation (Earl Layman, Historic Preservation Officer). *Seattle's Landmarks I*. Seattle, 1978.

Sherwood, Don. "Description and History of Seattle Parks." Unpublished manuscript in the Museum of History and Industry, Seattle.

Tacoma, City of, Office of Historic Preservation (Patricia Sias, Historic Preservation Officer). *Historic Preservation in Tacoma*. Tacoma, 1978.

Steinbrueck, Victor. *Market Sketchbook*. Seattle: University of Washington Press, 1968.

————. *Seattle Architecture, 1850–1953*. New York: Reinhold Publishing Co., 1953.

————. *Seattle Cityscape*. Seattle: University of Washington Press, 1962.

————. *Seattle Cityscape #2*. Seattle: University of Washington Press, 1962.

Streatfield, David. "Parks from Seattle's Past." *Puget Soundings*, October 1979, pp. 26–31.

Thiry, Paul, and others. "Have We an Indigenous Architecture?" *Architectural Record* 113 (April 1953): 140–46.

Turbeville, Daniel E., III. *An Illustrated Inventory of Historic Bellingham Buildings, 1852–1915*. Bellingham: Municipal Arts Commission, 1977.

Vaughan, Thomas, ed. *Space, Style, and Structure: Building in Northwest America*. 2 vols. Portland: Oregon Historical Society, 1974.

Voorhees, V. W. *Western Home Builder*. Seattle: privately printed, 1911.

Writer's Program, Works Progress Administration. *The New Washington: A Guide to the Evergreen State*. Rev. ed. Sponsored by the Washington State Historical Society. Portland: Binfords & Mort, 1950.

Woodin, Larry Alan. "Wendell H. Lovett, Architect." Master's thesis, University of Washington, 1979.

Index